MICHAEL KEENE

Examining Four Religions

Collins Educational
An imprint of HarperCollins*Publishers*

Reprinted 1998

ISBN 0 00 322135 0

Designed by Carla Turchini
Commissioning Editor Domenica de Rosa
Project Editor Thomas Allain Chapman
Editor Paula Hammond
Production Sue Cashin
Cover design XAB Design
Printed and bound by Printing Express Ltd., Hong Kong.

Contents

2

JUDAISM

3

CHRISTIANITY

4

ISLAM

Unit 20 Then and Now

Unit 21 The Mosque and the Five Pillars

Unit 22 Celebrations and Feasts

Unit 23 From Birth to Death

Unit 24 Muslim Beliefs

Introduction

This book does not ask you to be committed to any particular religion or, even, to be religiously inclined. It does ask, however, that you be alive to the truth of what 'being religious' involves. The important thing to remember – as you follow what it means to be a Hindu, a Jew, a Christian or a Muslim – is that these things really matter to those who are committed. It may turn out that all of the religions dealt with in this book have ultimately the same goal, but that assumption does not lie behind this book. Nor is any attempt made to compare one religion with another since that would be an insult to millions of believers. Each religion and each belief will be dealt with individually, and seriously, since it is taken that way by those who believe.

There are three reasons why the study of religion is as important as the study of any other subject. First, religion is concerned with the most important questions in life. Not only does it ask the question 'Where did I come from?' but also 'What will happen to me after I die?' as well as many questions in between. Religion wonders whether a Supreme Being, God, exists in the same breath as asking what that God might require of humankind.

Secondly, the study of religion allows humanity to face up honestly to the fact that religion has often damaged the health of humankind with untold 'holy' wars and tortures carried out in the name of God. Religion has been responsible for the persecution of minorities, outcasts and slaves, and the subjugation of women over the centuries. Yet, if we are to build a safe and peaceful world in the future, then everyone must take time to study and understand religion, since religious passions are the strongest of all.

Thirdly, just as religion has destroyed much, so it has created much of beauty. Many of the world's most priceless paintings, buildings, poetry and music have come into being because men and women have wanted to express their feelings about God.

In this book four religions – Hinduism, Judaism, Christianity and Islam – have been chosen to introduce you to something that involves, in some way, about three out of every four people on the Earth. In each double-page spread you will be given questions, information and extracts from the different holy books designed to make you think. You may find that many common themes run across the different religions. At the same time, by studying two or more of the religions covered, you will also find that each religion has its own distinctive beliefs and ways of approaching God. Religions may have much in common but, to believers, one of them is unique. By working your way through the many questions and discussion points, you will discover what it is that makes each of them worthy of the commitment of millions of followers.

What is Hinduism?

What is distinctive about Hinduism?

FOCUSING QUESTIONS

Which is more important in Hinduism – belief or actions? Why?

What is the ultimate aim of every Hindu?

How does a Hindu hope to reach moksha?

The religion of Hinduism does not speculate on whether God exists or not – nor if there is one God or many. It leaves worshippers free to believe in one God (monotheism), many gods (polytheism) or even no God at all (atheism). Worshippers may or may not follow the strict moral code of Hinduism, perform religious rituals and ceremonies, or regularly attend a temple to worship. Hindus do not believe that the truth about God can be put into precise words.

Dharma

When Hinduism began, 5,000 years ago, in the area around the River Indus in India there were no other known religions. The Hindu holy books simply refer to the religious beliefs of this time as 'dharma' – the eternal law. Dharma was the only moral order, and through this mankind learnt how to be humane and just in its behaviour. The law of dharma allows people the greatest possible freedom in faith and worship. It does not tell them what they must believe about God, the human soul or the creation of the world. It simply allows them to pray to their personal God in any form that they wish. This is why almost every Hindu family has its own god through which it prays to the one God – Brahman.

DISCUSS

Hindus speak about dharma – moral laws which were in the universe since time began. Do you think there are 'moral laws' on which everyone would agree? If so, what do you think they are?

A. This man is worshipping his family god at home. What does the law of dharma have to say about this form of worship?

From the scriptures

These are the words of God found in the Hindu holy book, The Bhagavad Gita:
'Whenever there is a decline of dharma [righteousness] *and a rise of adharma* [unrighteousness] *I incarnate* [take on human form] *myself. For the protection of the good, for the destruction of the wicked and for the establishment of righteousness, I come into being from age to age.'*

1 What word is used to describe those occasions when God takes on human form, and what does it mean?
2 Why might it be necessary for God to become a human being?
3 What do you think the attitude of Hinduism might be to other major world religions?

Understanding Hinduism

There are four main elements which are central to Hinduism:

1 The ultimate aim of every Hindu is to obtain liberation ('moksha') which is union with Brahman. In order to reach this stage a person must free themselves from the cycle of births and deaths into which every human soul is locked. The way that a person lives determines the number of rebirths that they have, and the form in which they return to Earth in their next life.

2 To help a person control the way they live Hinduism provides them with certain 'disciplines'. A life-span is divided into four stages called ashramas:
i) The period of training and education.
ii) The life of the householder.
iii) The life of retirement.
iv) The life of the holy man.
Each of these stages makes its own demands and carries its own responsibilities. The disciplines, or yogas, appropriate to each ashrama can help a person to build up good karma.

3 In order to reach moksha a person must live a righteous life, work hard and prosper, and enjoy the good things. All of these should be reached by the end of the second ashrama. Time can then be set aside to reach the final objective – moksha.

4 Each person has a 'spark of God' in them, but it shines more brightly in some than in others. Those who possess this quality most noticeably are avatars. Avatars are sent by God to restore righteousness. Some avatars are the gods in human form; others are prophets and leaders from other religions like Muhammad and Jesus, whilst some are Hindu holy men or women.

B. Above, an eighteenth-century carving showing an image of Krishna holding up Mount Govardhana. Krishna, the popular Hindu god, has visited Earth nine times and is expected once more. As in this carving, he is usually pictured in the company of pretty maidens. Why do you think that Hindus find this behaviour acceptable in a god?

FOR YOUR FOLDER

1 Some people find the many different approaches to God allowed in Hinduism confusing. This is because Hinduism is interested in the way a person behaves rather than what they believe. This comment comes from a past President of India: *'While it* [Hinduism] *gives absolute liberty in the world of thought, it encourages a strict code of practice. The theist* [a person who believes in God] *and the atheist* [a person who does not believe in God] *may both be Hindus if they accept the Hindu system of culture and life...what counts is conduct, not belief.'*

This quotation sums up the basic difference between Hinduism and other religions. Put that difference in your own words.

2 Explain, in your own words, the meaning of: moksha; dharma; karma; ashramas.

In the glossary: Ashrama; Avatar; Bhagavad Gita; Brahman; Dharma; Karma; Moksha; Yoga.

Beginnings

Where *are the roots of Hinduism to be found?*

FOCUSING QUESTIONS

What are the links between the Indus civilisation and Hinduism?

Where do the ancient holy books of Hinduism came from?

What makes Hinduism distinctive among the major world religions?

Over the centuries many cultures and peoples have added their contribution to Hinduism – the religious faith of 550 million people. Although new ideas, beliefs and practices have been absorbed, however, the faith of Hinduism has remained essentially thc same.

The Indus Civilisation

Hinduism dates back to around 1800 BCE in India, but it has no single founder. The word 'Hindu' comes from the Sanskrit word for the River Indus, which is 'Siddhu'. The ancient Persians pronounced this as 'Hindu' and so all the people in that area were called Hindus. Soon, the name came to be applied to all the people of India. Today it only refers to members of the Hindu religion.

Traces of writing from this early civilisation have been found but, as yet, no-one has been able to de-code it, and so our entire knowledge of this period comes from excavated remains. From these, a picture emerges of a group of people who were at least as advanced as the much better known Egyptian and Mesopotamian civilisations of the same period.

A. This map shows the area in which Hinduism was born. From reading the text on these pages, what do you know about the people who lived 'across the river'?

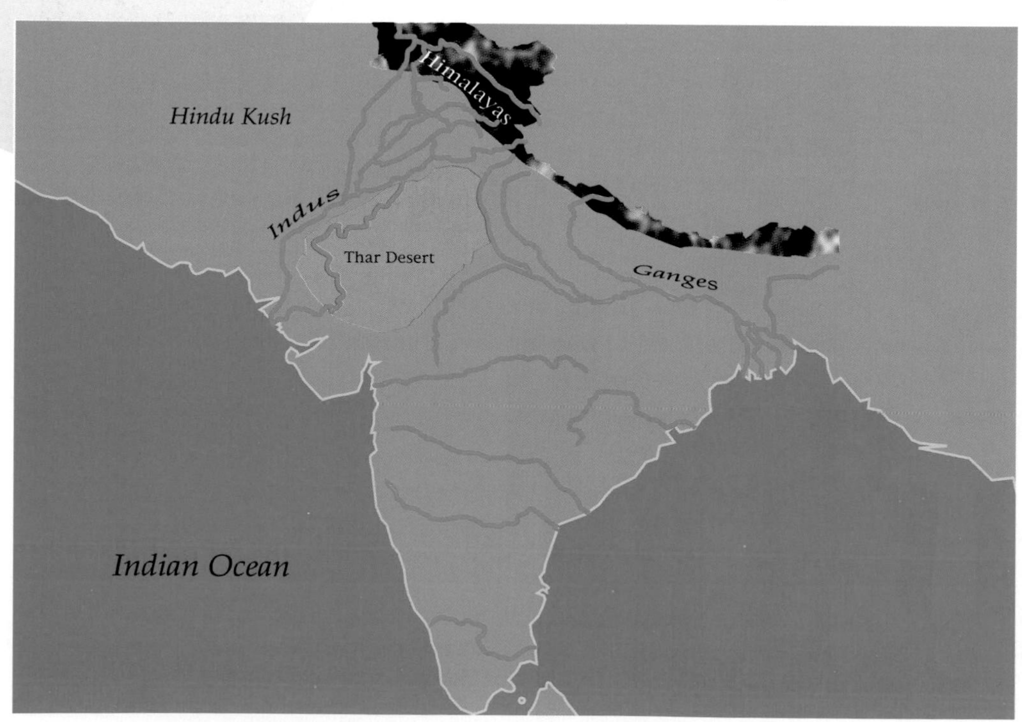

We know little about the religious beliefs of this time, but statues have been found which provide us with some clues. Many statues of goddesses suggest that a heavy emphasis was placed upon fertility, and it seems likely that some of their gods and goddesses formed the basis of the deities of the Hindu religion. A male god, for instance, which sat cross-legged and was surrounded by animals probably became the important Hindu god, Shiva.

B. These worshippers are gathered inside a Hindu temple. If it is not their common beliefs that draw these people together what is it?

The Aryans

In about 1500 BCE a powerful army of invaders, the Aryans, overwhelmed the Indus people. They came to India from the great plains of central Asia through the mountain passes of the Himalayas. For the next 1,000 years they extended their influence over the whole of India.

The Aryans brought the Sanskrit language with them and developed the caste system. This placed people in different groups (called castes or varnas) in which they remained for their whole lives. To begin with the Aryans sacrificed animals to their gods, but they soon intermarried with the Indus people and dropped this practice. In about 1600 BCE the first collection of hymns and writings were put together in a group of books called The Vedas (meaning knowledge). The earliest and most important of these books is the Rig Veda which contains hymns about nature. Praise is given to many gods in the Vedas and amongst them are: Indra, the god of Heaven, Aditi, the mother goddess, Agni, the god of fire. The Aryans also developed forms of worship and spiritual practices which remain, in some shape or form, in Hinduism today.

The development of Hinduism

Hinduism clearly owes a lot to the Indus civilisation and to the Aryans. From the Indus people it inherited its emphasis on the goddess which is one of the distinctive features of Hinduism. From the Aryans it took the caste system and a respect for nature.

As Hinduism spread further into southern India, it incorporated more new ideas. The religious teachers there preferred to speak of a loving rather than an abstract God. Hymns were written about the warm love that existed between God and each worshipper. This movement became known as the Bhakti movement, and from it came the much-loved Hindu holy book – The Bhagavad Gita.

FOR YOUR FOLDER

1

a) Who were the people 'who lived across the river' and what do we know about them?

b) How did the religion of north India combine with that of the Aryans – and what was the result?

2 Mahatma Gandhi, a Hindu holy man and political leader, had this to say about his religion:

'Hinduism is a living organism liable to growth and decay and subject to the laws of nature. One and indivisible at the root, it has grown into a vast tree with innumerable branches.'

This quotation makes seven important points about Hinduism. Work out what they are and note them down in your folder.

In the glossary: Agni; Bhagavad Gita; Bhakti; Caste; Indra; Rig Veda; Shiva; Varna; Vedas.

Varnas and Castes

What is the caste system and what part does it play in Hinduism?

FOCUSING QUESTIONS

What are the four different varnas and how are they different from castes?

Who are the 'children of God' and why were they so called?

How does the caste system still affect modern Indian society?

According to the traditions of Hinduism the four classes (or varnas, meaning 'colours') were established in India by Brahma (the creative power of God) at the creation of the world. As time passed, though, many different tribes came under the influence of the Hindu religion and the more elaborate caste system grew out of this. Castes are divisions in society based solely on a person's occupation. There are many hundreds of castes and subcastes in India.

Divisions

The four different varnas came from a story in the Rig Veda in which Brahma makes the first (primal) man, Perusha. Perusha was later sacrificed and from his body the four different varnas were taken:

1 The highest (white) varna – the brahmins – came from the mouth of Perusha. The brahmins are priests whose task is to perform religious ceremonies and teach the Scriptures. Brahmins must keep themselves pure as they handle holy objects and approach the different gods in worship.

2 The second (red) varna – kshatriyas – came from the arms of Perusha. This varna supplies the warriors and rulers of India who must govern and defend the different communities against enemies from outside.

3 The third (yellow) varna – vaishyas – came from the thighs of Perusha. These are people in the community who have a talent for farming or commerce.

4 The fourth (black) varna – the shudras – came from the feet. The workers in the community belong to this caste and they provide services for those in the other castes.

Each varna, over time, divided itself into numerous levels called castes and sub-castes. Close relationships between the different castes have always been frowned on, since it is believed that those in the higher castes can be 'polluted' by those beneath them. Such 'pollution' can take place through touching, eating prohibited foods or intermarriage.

1 In many parts of India the caste system seems to matter little – until it comes to marriage. The vast majority of Hindus still marry members of the same caste. Why do you think this is?

2
a) Imagine that you are a brahmin. How would you set about defending the caste system and your own place in it?
b) Imagine that you are an 'untouchable'. How might you (i) support the position given to the brahmin in your society? (ii) oppose the system?

FOR YOUR FOLDER

A. This photograph shows a Hindu brahmin (priest). What must this priest do to preserve the purity of his brahmin status?

The 'untouchables'
The 'Untouchables' do not belong to any varna. In every Indian village there are tasks which are regarded as 'unclean', including tanning leather, disposing of the corpses of animals, butchering, and brewing alcohol. The Untouchables, who performed these jobs, were compelled to live outside the village, and excluded from any public activity, especially worship. The great Indian reformer, Mahatma Gandhi, tried to change the status of this group by calling them 'Harijans', meaning 'children of God'.

The features of caste

There are three main features of caste in India. They are:

- Membership of a caste is by heredity. Someone is born into a particular caste and they cannot change it.
- Each member of a caste must marry someone else from the same caste. In India, some young people do now marry outside their caste since it became legal in in 1950.
- There are regulations about accepting food and drink from members of other castes, e.g. a brahmin may not accept food from, or eat with, a carpenter. When members of different castes are invited to the same celebration, such as a wedding, they eat in different areas. The cooks for such occasions have to be brahmins since they cannot pollute members of lower castes.

The caste system today
In the cities of India the caste system is slowly breaking down. The different castes are now free to mix socially and to eat together. Since 1950 it has been illegal for anyone to be treated as an 'untouchable'. Hindu temples are now open to everyone and opportunities in education and employment are extended to all castes. However, in some country areas of India, the caste system still operates, and some religious rituals are only celebrated with members from the same caste.

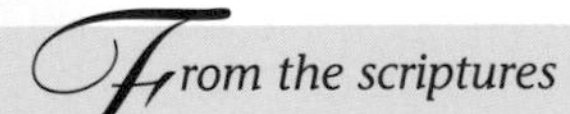

From the scriptures

This passage comes from the tenth Book of the Rig Veda:
'When they divided primal Man how many divisions did they make? What was his mouth? What his arms? The brahmin was his mouth. The kshatriya his arms. His thighs the vaishya. The shudra from his feet.'

1. Who was the *'primal Man'* and why is he so called?
2. Why was the primal man divided up into different parts?
3. What is the link between this myth and the caste system?

In the glossary: BRAHMA; BRAHMIN; CASTE; HARIJANS; KSHATRIYA; RIG VEDA; SHUDRA; VAISHYA; VARNA; VEDAS.

Hinduism in Britain

How *did the Hindu community arrive in this country and how does it maintain its traditions and way of life?*

FOCUSING QUESTIONS

How did the majority of Hindus came to be living in Britain?

How important are temples in the religious life of Hindus?

How has the Hindu community adapted itself to life in Britain ?

Although the homeland of Hinduism is India many Hindus have made their homes elsewhere – including Fiji, Sri Lanka, the West Indies, Africa and Great Britain. 400,000 Hindus now live in England. Most of them arrived as immigrants from the west coast of India, especially the state of Gujurat, or from the Punjab, in the north-west. Others have come from east Africa – mostly from Kenya and Uganda. Although a few Hindus came to Britain before the First World War the great influx took place in the 1950s when the Government of this country encouraged immigration to solve a shortage of labour. This policy was reversed in the 1960s and 1970s and immigration to Britain was virtually stopped.

The Hindu community in Britain

When Hindus came to Britain in the 1950s they settled mainly in the largest industrial cities – London, Coventry, Birmingham, Bristol, Leicester and Leeds – because that was where the available work was. The first generation of Hindus have shown themselves to be staunch in their religious beliefs, since this has been an important means of keeping their identity as Hindus in a foreign country. Many second generation Hindus, though, have come under the influence of Western society and have moved away from traditional religious beliefs and practices.

A. This Hindu temple has been converted from a redundant church. Many Christians are upset when this happens. Why do you think this is?

Hindus do not need to attend a temple to worship God, although more than 150 temples have now been opened in Great Britain. Many are converted churches or houses (see Photograph A), although a few have been purpose-built. The most notable new building was opened in Neasden, north London, on August 20th, 1995. This temple (called a mandir), with its carved domes, pinnacles and towers was built according to instructions taken from the ancient Hindu Scriptures.

B. Left, an 'extended' Hindu family. Why might the temple play an important part in the life of this family?

Many Hindus only travel to their nearest place of worship when a special festival is being celebrated. In Britain temples are as much community centres as they are places of worship. Here, children are taught the mother-tongue of their parents whether it is Gujarati, Hindi or Punjabi, as well as traditions like singing and dancing. The learning of the language is very important, as Hindus believe that religion, language and culture are inseparably bound up with each other. Neglect one of them and the others will be affected.

Hindu life in Britain

To a certain extent Hindus have adapted and changed their customs to fit in with the British way of life. Hindu communities in Britain do not apply the caste system as rigidly as many societies in India do. For most Hindus in this country caste only matters when it comes to choosing a marriage partner. In Britain also young Hindus are less likely to support the 'extended family' arrangement (see Photograph B) by which many generations of the same family live under the same roof or very close to each other. As children leave home in search of work or go to university so the extended family breaks down.

Hinduism is not really concerned to make new converts. Attempts to convert are limited to the 'reconversion' of former Hindus who were 'tricked' into accepting another religion. There has been, nevertheless, a steady stream of Western people who have become interested in the teachings of this ancient religion. Often they are attracted by the teachings of the faith after they have studied under a 'guru' (spiritual teacher).

FOR YOUR FOLDER

Answer each of these questions in your own words:

1 In which areas of the country are the main Hindu communities – and why?
2 How has the Hindu community in Britain adapted itself to life in this country?
3 Do you think that Hindus should have to change to fit in with life in countries which are not predominantly Hindu, or not? What are the dangers if they let go of too much of their traditional way of life and religious faith?

In the glossary: CASTE; GURU; MANDIR.

The Temple

How *do Hindus worship?*

FOCUSING QUESTIONS

What is bhakti?
What is havan?
What is arti?

The Hindu temple is called a mandir, meaning place of worship. Temples in India are built within a walled enclosure and face the rising Sun. The main part of the temple is called the mandapa and is where Hindus assemble for worship. A temple is dedicated to a particular god, often Krishna, and a statue of this god is kept in a room called the garbhagriha at one end of the mandapa. It is separated from the mandapa by a covered space often closed off by curtains. The priest enters the garbhagriha to wash and dress the image of the god and present it with flowers, incense, fruit and other offerings. During worship the curtains may be opened so that worshippers can offer gifts to the god. The garbhagriha usually has a roof shaped like a tower. This represents a mountain – considered a sacred part of nature in Hinduism. The ceiling of the garbhagriha is usually beautifully carved or decorated with tinsel or small lights (See Photograp A).

A. Above, Hindus worshipping in a temple. Why do you think that mountains are a sacred part of nature for every Hindu and how is this represented in many temples?

Worship in the temple

Although the main focus of Hindu worship is the home, many Hindus also visit the temple regularly. In the temple, worship starts at dawn when the priests greet, wash and dress the image of the god. The worshippers then come to offer their 'bhakti' (devotion). They do this by lighting a candle and saying their prayers. 'Anjali', the putting of their hands together and raising them to their chest, is carried out. Then, as they leave, they are given 'prashad' (sacred food) which has been offered to the god earlier in the day. In the evening a retiring-to-bed ceremony is carried out by the priests to the accompaniment of bells and drums during which the statue is again washed and then put to rest for the night.

B. Offerings presented to the god at a home shrine. What do you think is the point of offering food to an image of a god?

From the scriptures

These words of the god Krishna are recorded in The Bhagavad Gita:

'Whatever a zealous soul may offer,
Be it a leaf, fruit or water,
That I willingly accept
For it was given in love.'

1 What do you understand by the phrase *'a zealous soul'*?
2 What do you notice about the nature of the gifts mentioned here?
3 What is it that makes a gift acceptable to the god?

Group acts of worship

Group worship, called puja, can take place in three ways:

1 Havan, the offering of fire. Using wood, camphor and ghee (melted butter) the priest kindles a sacred fire on a portable fire-altar. During this, sections of the Hindu sacred texts, the Vedas, are recited. The fire represents the mouth of the god devouring the offerings in front of him. Prayers for purity follow, with the priest ceremonially washing each part of his body before the worshippers copy his actions (see Question 2 in FOR YOUR FOLDER for this prayer).

2 Arti, the welcoming ceremony. This involves the use of a flat tray with five candles on it. The candles represent the five elements (fire, earth, air, ether, and water) and are waved in front of the shrine. Incense and flowers representing the earth are presented, a fan is waved to represent the air, and a conch shell is sounded to represent ether. The other element, water, is found in the shell. A spot of red paste is put on the forehead of the image of the god before the dish is passed round so that the worshippers can pass their hands over the flames and then over the heads. By doing this they receive God's power and blessing.

3 Bhajan, the singing of hymns. Bells, tambourines and triangles are played and some people dance. There are readings from The Bhagavad Gita before the prayer for peace – *'O God let there be peace, peace, peace'* – ends the service.

FOR YOUR FOLDER

1
a) What name is given to a Hindu temple?
b) What does this word mean?
c) What is the name of the room which is often separated from the mandapa by curtains?
d) What would you expect to find in this room?
e) How is special attention given to the image of the god in this room?
f) Imagine that you are entering a Hindu temple for the first time. What do you think might be the first thing to catch your eye? Can you explain why?

2 As the priest ceremonially washes himself he says:
'Let my tongue have speaking power, ears have the power of hearing, the nose inhaling power and the eyes seeing power. May the arms and the thighs have strength and all the limbs be full of energy.'
What do you think the priest is praying for here? Does he simply want renewed physical strength or could he be asking for something more? If so, what?

In the glossary: Bhagavad Gita; Bhakti; Garbhagriha; Havan; Mandir; Puja; Vedas.

Worship in the Home

What part does the home play in the spiritual life of the Hindu man or woman?

FOCUSING QUESTIONS

Which god is often adopted by Hindu families – and why?

What is the Gayatri Mantra?

What happens during an act of worship in a Hindu home?

Most Hindu worship takes place at home and not in the mandir (temple). Many Hindu homes have niches in the wall or a small shrine in which the image of the god is placed so that offerings can be made by members of the household (see Photograph A). The main reason for the home being used in this way is that the family is the basic unit in Hindu religious society and is given the responsibility of safeguarding Hindu traditions and customs.

Within the Hindu family children are brought up to observe the five daily duties of every Hindu:

1. To carry out some yoga and meditation.
2. To show reverence and to offer worship frequently to the family's god.
3. To show an unquestioning respect for the elders and ancestors of the family.
4. To extend the hospitality of the family to all those who are needy, and to holy men and women.
5. To display a respect and kindness to all living creatures.

A. Hindus worshipping at a home shrine. Why do you think that worship in the home is so important for the 'health' of Hindu society generally?

B. Left, a child praying at home. How do you think having a family shrine helps each Hindu – young and old?

Acts of worship

Every Hindu home usually has a shrine containing a picture of the family god. Often this god is Krishna who is known particularly for his love and kindness during his nine visits to Earth. Worship will only be offered to one god and it begins by lighting a lamp which has had its wick dipped in ghee (melted butter). Incense sticks are lit and the names of God are repeated along with the daily prayer – the Gayatri Mantra. This prayer says.

'Let us meditate on the glorious light of the creator.
May he guide our minds and inspire us with understanding.'

Brahmins say this prayer three times a day – at dawn, at midday and at sunset. It is also used during public celebrations such as for a birth or a marriage.

A reading from one of the holy books may then take place in front of a mandala – a mystical design intended to help the mind concentrate on God or the self. During this time the worshipper sits upright and cross-legged on the floor breathing deeply to aid concentration. The sacred syllable, AUM, is chanted over and over again. Every person takes part in the 'puja' (worship) by passing a flame from one to the other as a symbol of the god.

Woman and worship

Women carry a very heavy spiritual responsibility in Hindu homes. They must make sure that all of the religious rituals are carried out properly and that special festivals are celebrated in the appropriate way. Hinduism is a religion with a very rich tradition of story-telling and women make sure that these stories are passed on to their children. Before carrying out the daily puja the woman of the house rises early in the morning, has a quick shower or bath, while chanting God's name, and puts on some clean clothes. Cleanliness of the body is very important in Hinduism. She may worship God in many ways, such as by washing, dressing or decorating the statue, offering it flowers, incense, light or food. This makes way for other members of the family to offer their acts of puja.

FOR YOUR FOLDER

1
a) Name two places in which Hindu worship takes place.
b) Describe two main features of Hindu worship.
c) In your opinion, how important is strict religious observance to a Hindu?
d) Describe the special religious responsibilities which a Hindu mother carries within her family.

2 Using Photographs A and B as a guide, describe what happens in a Hindu act of worship in the home.

3 Photograph A, on Page 18 shows a Hindu shrine in the home.
a) What is a Hindu act of worship, whether at home or in the temple, called?
b) What are the five daily religious duties of every Hindu?
c) Who do you think may have set this shrine up and whose duty is it to maintain it?
d) What happens in a Hindu family before an act of worship in front of the shrine is carried out?
e) What is the Gayatri Mantra?

4 Vinoba Bhave, a modern Hindu and a disciple of Mahatma Gandhi, said:
'The worship of an image is the art of embracing the whole universe in a little object.'
What do you think he meant by this?

In the glossary: AUM; BRAHMIN; GAYATRI MANTRA; GHEE; KRISHNA; MANDALA; MANDIR; MEDITATION; PUJA; YOGA.

Helping People to Worship

How does Hinduism help people in their worship of God?

FOCUSING QUESTIONS

What does the sacred syllable symbolise to the Hindu worshipper?

How does the sacred syllable play an important part in the everyday life of a Hindu?

Why are Hindus told not to disclose their mantras to anyone else?

Like every other religion, Hinduism tries to help men and women in their worship of God. In this section, we will look at three ways in which this happens – through the sacred syllable, through the singing of mantras, and through mandalas.

The sacred syllable

The sacred syllable of Hinduism, AUM, first occurred in the holy books, The Upanishads, and is made up of three sounds – a, u and m – together with a humming nasal sound. Hindus believe that, when spoken, this three-fold sound represents:

- The first three Vedas, the ancient Hindu holy books.
- The three worlds – Earth, Atmosphere and Heaven.
- The three main gods in Hinduism – Brahma, Vishnu and Shiva.

For many Hindus, however, AUM represents much more than this. They take it to refer to the whole universe and its oneness with God. It is understood as meaning 'Yes', in the sense of 'Yes, there is an Eternal Being behind the everchanging world'.

AUM (see Photograph A) is also a symbol of spiritual good. Hindus like to have it somewhere in their homes, on a poster or a plaque which is part of the family shrine. It is also found on practical objects such as paper-weights. Many Hindus wear it around their necks rather like some Christians wear crucifixes. It is placed at the beginning and end of all Hindu books. It is muttered before any Hindu act of worship, before all prayers and readings from the holy books, and at times of meditation.

Mantras

Mantras play a very important part in Hindu worship. They are a formula of words which, repeated over and over again in meditation, raise a person's level of consciousness and their awareness of God. Hindus believe that they act to free the mind from the everyday concerns which clutter it up. Often Hindus do not have the time to set aside for the saying of a mantra and so they chant it quietly on their way to or from work. The Gayatri Mantra is taken from the Rig Veda and says:
'Let us meditate on the most excellent light of the Creator. May He guide our minds and inspire us with understanding.'

A. A photograph of the sacred syllable AUM written in Sanskrit. If you were to visit a Hindu home where would you be likely to see the sacred syllable?

There is a form of yoga called mantra yoga. In this, the spiritual 'guru' (teacher) gives each person a mantra of their own. This secret mantra is for their use only, and must not be disclosed to anyone else. When the words of a mantra are spoken during yoga, some Hindus believe that the yogi (person doing the yoga) is given power over physical objects to move them at will. Others believe that, through yoga, the soul is released from the body and united with God.

Mandala

A mandala is a symbolic diagram. The diagram is usually surrounded by a circle in which patterns can be made in stone, paper, sand or metal. The spaces in the mandala represent the gods, with Vishnu in the centre. In religious services mandalas are used to call down the gods.

FOR YOUR FOLDER

1
a) Which name is given to the sacred syllable by Hindus?
b) What are the three sounds which go to make up the sacred syllable?
c) How might you recognise the sacred syllable if you heard it?
d) Altogether there are ten things that a Hindu is reminded of each time he or she utters the sacred syllable. What are they?
e) Name five ways in which a Hindu might be made aware of the sacred syllable in their everyday life.

2 If you live anywhere near to a Hindu temple or community centre, try to arrange a visit. Look carefully at the outside of the building. Would visitors be able to tell that it was a Hindu temple? With permission, take photographs or make your own drawings of the building. Look at the images of the gods and the offerings made to them. Try to find out the answers to these questions:
a) What use do Hindus make of the sacred syllable in their private and public worship? Is the sacred syllable anywhere in the temple?
b) How do Hindus use mantras when they visit the temple to worship? Do they always sing them in the temple? What spiritual benefits do they believe come to them when they sing a mantra?
c) Is there a mandala in the temple? How is it used? What meaning is attached to it by the worshippers?

In the glossary. AUM; BRAHMA; GURU; MANDALA; MANTRA; MEDITATION; RIG VEDA; SANSKRIT; SHIVA; UPANISHADS; VEDAS; VISHNU; YOGA.

Food

Why do the vast majority of Hindus find a close link between their eating habits and their religious beliefs?

FOCUSING QUESTIONS

What is vegetarianism?

What is ahimsa?

What part do cows play in Hindu religious life – and why?

There are few hard and fast rules in Hinduism about the diet of worshippers, but most Hindus do see a close link between what they eat and their religious beliefs. There are a number of ways in which these beliefs have a strong influence on what they eat – and when.

Vegetarianism

Many Hindus are vegetarians and this stems from their deeply-held belief that all life is sacred. Therefore they feel that it is wrong to kill animals for food. Many Hindus who are vegetarians also avoid eggs as well as meat, and some do not eat strong foods like onions and garlic. Others do not eat red foods – such as beetroot, carrots or red wine – since red is the colour of blood and it reminds them of killing animals.

Hindus who are not vegetarians may also rarely eat meat for purely practical reasons. Meat in India is extremely expensive. It is also difficult to keep, as the climate is very hot, and refrigerators are rarely found outside of the large cities. As a consequence, high-protein vegetables, such as lentils, are common in a Hindu diet, together with lots of milk and cheese.

The sacred cow

Whilst some Hindus eat meat occasionally, very few eat beef. The Hindu belief in ahimsa – a respect for the sacredness of all life – is extended to all creatures, but cows occupy a unique place in Indian society. They are not worshipped, but they are treated with the greatest possible respect, and are not killed by Hindus for meat. Cows are seen as a symbol of the earth – giving so much yet taking so little in return. On a practical level, few things are more important in village life than the products of the cow, such as milk and cheese. It makes sense, therefore, to keep it alive and healthy for as long as possible.

This concern for the cow's welfare is expressed in many different ways in Hindu communities. Sometimes garlands are placed around the necks of the cows to honour them, water is poured at their feet and oil rubbed over their foreheads. Cow dung is never thrown away but is used as a disinfectant, fuel or medicine. The urine of the sacred animal is believed to be 'holy water' which purifies everything it touches. When a cow dies, its body is treated with great respect and buried with as much dignity as possible.

DISCUSS

1. What reasons are there which might persuade a person to become a vegetarian? Do you find them persuasive or not?
2. Why do some people believe that their religious principles compel them to be vegetarians, while others do not? Explain your answer.
3. If you were to adopt a vegetarian life-style which arguments in favour of it would you find compelling?

Fasting

Fasting is an important spiritual discipline in most of the world's religions, and Hinduism is no exception. Fasting is not compulsory, but many Hindus fast on festival days, although this often means simply avoiding certain foods such as rice and wheat. During Ramnavami (Rama's birthday), for instance, Hindus abstain from eating everyday vegetables, cereals and salt, and instead eat unusual delicacies. In the course of the festival of Navaratri people only eat one meal a day consisting of fruit and sweetmeats made from milk. Some Hindus actually fast one day a week – or more. Women in Hindu families are much more likely to fast than men.

FOR YOUR FOLDER

1 Mahatma Gandhi, the great Indian leader of the 1930s and 1940s, taught the principle of non-violence (ahimsa). He said this about the cow: *'The cow is the mother to millions of Indian mankind. Protection of the cow means protection of the whole dumb creation of God.'*

a) What is the basic Hindu attitude to all forms of life?
b) What contribution does the cow make to life on earth?
c) How do Hindus show the respect that they have for the cow?
d) What do you think Gandhi meant when he said that the cow was *'the mother to millions of Indian mankind'*?
e) How would you explain Gandhi's comment that in protecting the cow humankind is *'protecting the whole dumb creation of God'*?

2 Imagine that a discussion is taking place between someone who is not a vegetarian and a Hindu who is. How do you think the Hindu might attempt to explain the spiritual and practical benefits that he or she finds in being a vegetarian? How do you think that the other person might argue that vegetarianism is unnecessary – or unnatural?

A. An Indian vegetarian meal. Why are many Hindus vegetarians?

In the glossary: AHIMSA; FASTING; NAVARATRI; RAMA; VEGETARIAN.

Festivals

How many different kinds of festivals are there in Hinduism?

FOCUSING QUESTIONS

How do some Hindu festivals reflect India's dependence on agriculture for its survival?

What are melas?

What are the seasons upon which the Indian year is based?

There are an almost unlimited number of festivals in Hinduism and, almost without exception, they are all very colourful and happy occasions. Hindus consider celebrations to be important because they guarantee the continuation of Hindu religious traditions and help children to learn about the gods. The vast majority of these festivals are small local events, and are therefore only celebrated in certain parts of India, or by certain groups within the Hindu community. Some involve fasting and private worship in the home. Others are public festivals in which the whole community takes part.

It is possible to divide these many festivals into three broad categories:

1 Festivals which are based around specific seasons or the agricultural year. In a country like India, with its heavy dependence on agriculture, the seasons are very important. Sowing and reaping times are always a cause of great celebration. One such festival, Navaratri, is held in honour of the Hindu goddess, Durga (see Photograph B), and lasts for nine days. In northern India this is the time when the Winter crops are sown (September/October). To symbolise this event, barley is sown on a small dish at the start of the festival so that by the end it has begun to sprout.

Holi is held in Spring and centres around the activities of the god Krishna on his visits to Earth. By now the Spring harvest has been safely gathered in and so the farming communities enter into very lively celebrations. Before the midday meal, puja (worship) is offered to a small bonfire, and a portion of special food is thrown into the flames as an act of thanksgiving.

2 Festivals which celebrate important events in Hindu legend and mythology. These are called 'melas'.

A. This photograph shows Hindus enjoying the festival of Dassehra in the Indian city of Mysore. Are you surprised that the major world religions place such a heavy emphasis upon celebration? What do you think is the main reason why so many festivals are held?

Kumbha Mela is held once every three years at four different places in northen India. The myth behind the event is of a battle between the gods and the demons over a jug which held the nectar of immortality. The gods won, but during the battle four drops of nectar were spilled on the sites where the melas are held. One of these spots is the place where the rivers Ganges and Jamuna, in India, meet. The point at which these rivers merge is considered to be among the most holy places in Hinduism.

3 Festivals based on the Hindu calendar, which follows a pattern of six seasons (each lasting for two months) and is 354 days long. The six seasons are Spring (March-May); Summer (May-July); the rainy season (July-September); Autumn (September-November); Winter (November-January); and the good season (January-March). Of this type of festival, Divali (the 'Festival of Lights') takes place over five days in October or November and is the most widely celebrated Hindu festival.

Dassehra is also held in October or November and is the climax of the year. This festival celebrates the goodness of the gods and goddesses whilst spreading a feeling of joy and peace through the Hindu community. Dassehra is considered a lucky day by all Hindus.

Saraswati can be held at any time during the year. Saraswati is the popular goddess of learning and knowledge and her festival is important to adults and children alike.

DISCUSS

1 Why are festivals so important in so many societies, and why do they often have a religious basis?

2 Hinduism is full of festivals but what do you think worshippers are trying to achieve through their celebrations?

FOR YOUR FOLDER

1 Answer each of these questions in your own words:

a) What do all Hindu festivals centre around in one way or another?
b) What symbolic action is important during the festival of Navaratri?
c) What takes place at the point where the rivers Ganges and Jamuna meet in India?
d) How do the seasons in India reflect the dependence of the people on the land?

2

a) Why do you think that some festivals are held at the time when the seed is sown? What do the people believe that they might gain by praying at this time?
b) Why do you think that symbolic actions, such as at Navaratri, play such an important role in many festivals?
c) Why do you think that many Hindu festivals bring together the seasons and some 'event' in the life of the gods?

In the glossary: DASSHERA; DIVALI; DURGA; HOLI; KRISHNA; KUMBHA MELA; PUJA; SARASWATI.

B. This photograph shows a thirteenth-century image of the Goddess Durga. Can you guess why she has so many arms?

Divali

How *do Hindus celebrate Divali, and why is it such an important Hindu festival?*

FOCUSING QUESTIONS

What is the link between Vishnu/Lakshmi and Rama/Sita and the festival of Divali?

What are the different ways in which Divali offers a new start to each member of a Hindu family?

Why does dancing play a very important part in Hindu religious and social life?

DISCUSS

1 How do Hindus use myths during festivals to consider aspects of their own lives which may need to be changed?

2 How do Hindus use the festival of Divali to prepare themselves for the challenges of the year ahead?

Divali, the Festival of Lights, occurs during October or November when it is Autumn in India. School children and workers are given a holiday for this five-day new year festival which has two meanings depending on where it is being celebrated.

Welcoming Vishnu and Lakshmi

For many, Divali is celebrated to welcome Vishnu and his bride, Lakshmi, the goddess of prosperity and happiness, into every Hindu home. The god Vishnu is believed to have visited the Earth nine times and on each occasion he brought Lakshmi with him. Vishnu represents everything that is male in life and Lakshmi everything that is female. When Lakshmi is shown as Vishnu's wife she wears a dark colour, but when she is representing fortune she is dressed in yellow.

During Divali, Hindu mothers perform a Lakshmi puja to attract health and wealth to the family in the coming year. Men also perform puja to bring the prosperity of Lakshmi upon their businesses while they close the past year's accounts and open new books for the year ahead. In many homes an attempt to attract good fortune is made by playing cards or other games of chance late into the night. Divas (candles) are lit so that Lakshmi can find her way into the homes of every worshipper (see Photograph A).

A. Right, candles being lit in a Hindu home during Divali. Divali is also known as the Festival of Lights. Can you explain why?

B. Left, Divali lights in front of a home shrine. What is the significance of light during Divali?

The rescue of Sita

For others, Divali marks the return of Rama who rescued Sita, his wife, from the demon, Ravana, who had kidnapped her. To do this Rama had to face incredible danger, and so Divali celebrates the perseverance of love and devotion. Boys in the family are told to be like Rama and girls like Sita. Family vows are renewed whilst husbands and wives remember the marriage promises they made to each other. Everyone in the family considers whether they have faithfully performed their duties to each other.

During Divali houses are cleaned from top to bottom, clay oil lamps are lit and gifts are given. Rooftops and windowsills are lit with earthenware oil lamps, which are regarded as pure lights. When darkness falls, candles in clay dishes are floated down rivers. Firecrackers are used to scare away evil spirits. Everywhere a worshipper looks he or she sees symbols to show that light conquers darkness, and good triumphs over evil.

In Britain, Divali is celebrated by Hindus on just one night when fireworks are let off and the adults enjoy a large meal together. The celebrations are usually arranged by Hindu temples and clubs on the nearest Saturday to the actual date of Divali.

Dancing

Music and dancing play a very important role in the colourful festival of Divali, as in other parts of Hinduism's religious and social life. In Hindu worship dancing is often used to tell stories of the gods. Shiva is sometimes called 'The Lord of the Dance' and it is often claimed that dance was passed down from the gods to human beings. At one time, only Hindu women were allowed to dance in the temple, but now all brahmins can be involved as well. During the dance, every hand movement carries an important message about good or evil. Women representing demons are dressed in black robes, while those representing goddesses wear green dresses with pearls. All brahmins must have their faces whitened. Guitars, cymbals, drums and sitars are played by musicians.

FOR YOUR FOLDER

1
a) How long does the festival of Divali last?
b) What does the festival mark for all Hindus?
c) Which two stories involving the gods are behind the festival of Divali?
d) Why does the mother in each Hindu family perform a Lakshmi puja?
e) How do Hindu businessmen try to make sure that the coming year is a prosperous one?
f) Give three examples of the way that light plays a very important part in the Divali festival.

2 Imagine that you are staying in a Hindu home during the festival of Divali.
a) What preparations would you notice being carried out by the mother as the festival approached?
b) What would you notice the father of the house doing?
c) How would you soon become aware that Divali is known as the 'Festival of Lights'?

3 Write your own description of this festival under the title 'Celebrating Divali'. You can, if you wish, use your imagination and pretend that you are a 'fly on the wall', seeing what is going on, but not being seen by anyone.

In the glossary: BRAHMIN; DIVALI; LAKSHMI; PUJA; RAMA; RAVANA; SHIVA; SITA; VISHNU.

Holi

How *do Hindus celebrate the festival of Holi, and why is it such a popular festival with all members of the family?*

FOCUSING QUESTIONS

Why is the festival of Holi held and what makes it a time of fun and widespread enjoyment?

How do people begin the Holi celebrations and how do they try to make peace with each other?

Why is the lighting of a bonfire in each village a very important part of the Holi celebrations?

Holi, the most popular of all Hindu festivals, is celebrated both publicly and privately on the day of the full moon in the month of Phalgun (March) – the last month of the Hindu year. It is linked with many stories in the Hindu holy books and Hindus in different parts of India emphasise one or other of them. This festival lasts between three and five days.

At one time Holi was a fertility festival and so it often involves a recreation of the god Shiva's marriage procession. The festival is also linked with Krishna, and in particular the story of Krishna as a baby killing the demoness Putana. In many homes 'puja' (worship) is offered in front of a bonfire during a midday meal and a portion of food is thrown on the flames as a form of thanksgiving.

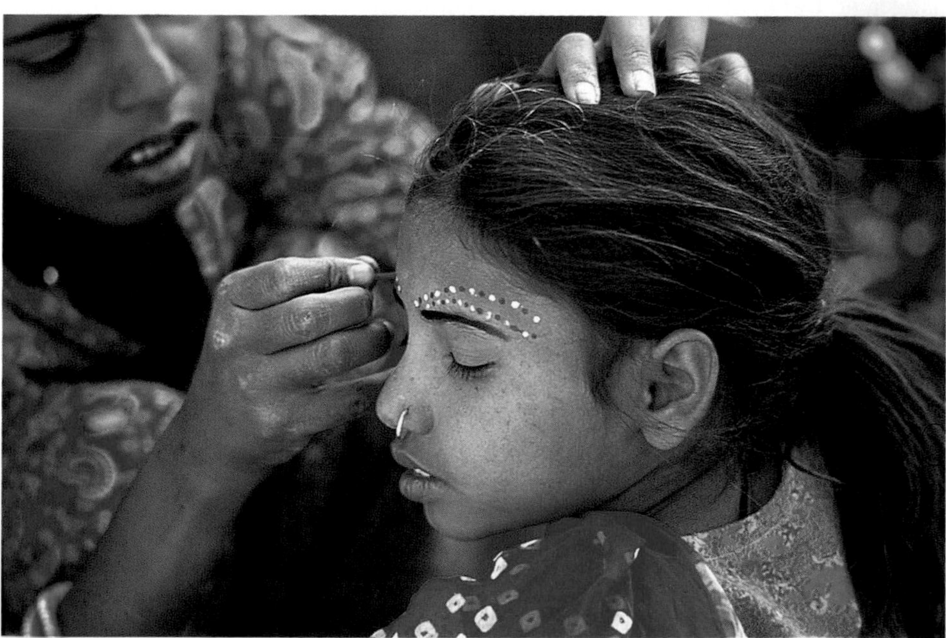

A. This girl is preparing for a festival. How important do you think it is for children to be involved in celebrations such as Holi?

Celebrating Holi

The Holi celebrations in India begin with people throwing coloured water and powder at each other in the street (see Photograph B) – just as the god Krishna used to do to the milkmaids (called gopis) when he was on Earth. A person's position or caste matters nothing on this day since everyone is likely to be covered in coloured dye. Balloons full of red, blue, pink and green powder are thrown and children also use homemade bamboo syringes to fire the dye. Fortunately it all washes out at the end of the day.

At noon, the throwing stops and the people return home to wash and change their clothes. They then set out together to visit their friends to make any necessary amends for misunderstandings that may have occurred between them in the last year. This is very important in maintaining a Hindu community that is at peace with itself. People rub dry, red powder on each other's foreheads and wish each other a 'Happy Holi'. In some parts of India all of this excitement takes place at the end of the festival and not at the beginning.

As darkness falls, bonfires are lit in each village and coconuts are roasted and eaten as 'prashad' (holy food). The people walk around the fire as an act of reverence to the gods and rub their foreheads with cool ash as a sign that they will enjoy good fortune and prosperity in the year ahead. Women also walk their young children around the fire in the hope that they will grow up to be strong and godfearing. This practice is inspired by a legend in which Krishna saved a young prince from being burned alive by his father because of the prince's faith in Krishna. To reinforce the message of strong faith, everyone takes a piece of charred wood from the bonfire home with them to keep illness and disease away from the family.

In Mathura, the traditional birth-place of the Lord Krishna, Holi festivities last for several weeks as pilgrims flock to the town from all over India. There the hot, dry season starts at Holi and this is the time when people sleep in the open-air. As they often sleep on their flat roofs, so the area outside the house needs to be cleaned. To aid this, bonfires are lit and coloured water is squirted throughout the village. Holi is the only Hindu festival at which even the poorest people in the village have a real opportunity to enjoy themselves.

B. These people are enjoying the festival of Holi. Why do you think that it is important that issues such as caste are forgotten on days like this?

DISCUSS

1. What do you think that Hindus, young and old, learn about the divisions and classes in Indian society from celebrating Holi together?
2. What difference do you think that it makes to village life if the people have a set time each year when they can settle any grievances that they have against each other?
3. Do you think that it would be helpful if non-Hindu societies also set such a time aside each year?

1 Try to visit a Hindu temple to join in the celebrations for Holi, or another festival. You will find that they are likely to take place in the evening or over a weekend. You will be made very welcome. Try to talk with one or two Hindus while you are there about the festival and what it means to them. Then write up your own description of your visit in the form of a letter to a friend.

2
a) Explain why you think that Hindus living in Britain tend to celebrate fewer festivals and also why most of the celebrations take place in the home or temple rather than out-of-doors.
b) Why do you think that many festivals have a light-hearted side to them although the underlying meaning may be a serious one? How does this show itself in the Hindu festival of Holi?

3 Do you get the overall impression that religion can be fun as well as having many serious moments? Explain your answer by referring to the religious practices of Hindus and others.

FOR YOUR FOLDER

In the glossary: Caste; HOLI; KRISHNA; PRASHAD; PUJA; SHIVA.

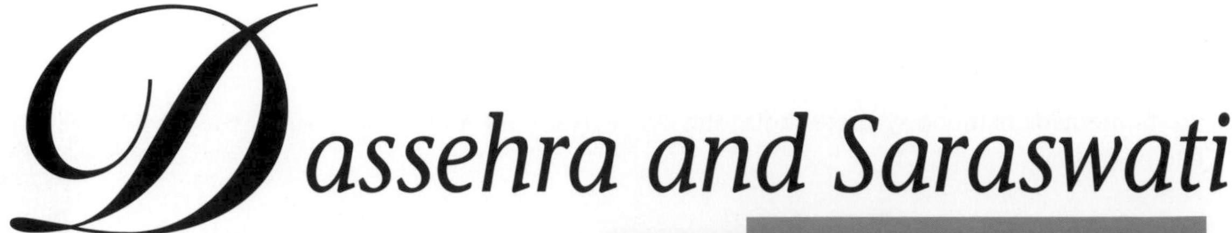

Dassehra and Saraswati

***How** do Hindus celebrate the festivals of Dassehra and Saraswati and why are they important occasions in the Hindu community?*

FOCUSING QUESTIONS

- Which legend is celebrated during the festival of Navaratri?
- What happens at Dassehra?
- What happens at Saraswati?

In one of the Hindu holy books, The Ramayana, the story is told of the god Rama who was the seventh 'avatar' of Vishnu. Rama's stepmother hated him and desperately wanted to replace him as the king's successor by her own son. She managed to get Rama banished to the forest. The demon king, Ravana, then kidnapped Sita, Rama's wife, and carried her off to Sri Lanka. Rama searched for his wife until eventually confronting Ravana and killing him. The couple returned to the forest and were restored to their home with great celebration. When the king died Rama replaced him and reigned for 10,000 years.

Navaratri

In northern India the crops are sown in September, and to celebrate this the festival of Navaratri is held. At Navaratri, Hindus are reminded of Rama's fight against the demon to secure the release of his wife. Rama cut off the demon's ten heads and the festival encourages people to cut out the ten demons that lurk within themselves – passion, pride, anger, greed, infatuation, lust, hatred, jealousy, selfishness and crookedness.

The festival, which lasts for nine days, reminds Hindus that Rama worshipped Durga, the goddess of motherhood, when he needed help to rescue Sita. During the festival, folk-dancing takes place around a Durga shrine and newly-weds return home to see their parents. It is a time, as are many Hindu festivals, to celebrate the triumph of good over evil.

A. Below, an image of the demon king Ravana towers over the other figures in this rock carving from Cambodia. Images of Ravana are usually very large. Can you suggest why?

Dassehra

Navaratri is immediately followed by the festival of Dassehra. Durga, the goddess who helped Rama defeat Ravana, has been worshipped for the nine days up to the festival of Dassehra. On the tenth day her spirit departs from the statue. The statue is put in the river to see whether it floats. If it does it is regarded as a good sign as it will take away all the people's unhappiness.

Originally, Dassehra was a festival of war, but now it celebrates the fight between Rama and the evil demon, Ravana. During the festival pictures of Rama are prominently displayed and his victory over Ravana is celebrated. Giant statues of Ravana are filled with firecrackers and set alight by firing fiery arrows at them.

Dassehra is the climax of the Hindu year. It celebrates the goodness and the protection of the gods which is extended to all in the Hindu community. It is also used as an opportunity to create goodwill and friendship in the community and to deal with any arguments or bad feeling that might exist.

B. A statue of Saraswati. What happens during the festival of Saraswati?

Saraswati

This festival can be held at any time during the year. Saraswati is the goddess of education and learning and her festival involves everyone in the community – especially children. During the festival the priest chants a hymn and a clay jug is placed on a bed of unthreshed rice in front of a statue of Saraswati. The priest rings a cow bell whilst a worshipper rings a conch bell three times chanting the words *'O Saraswati, come to life'*. The priest raises the statue up high and the worshippers stand in front of it in awe and wonder.

The goddess Saraswati is popular in the Hindu community. She has four arms and these represent mind, intellect, conscience and self. Hindus believe she was involved in the creation of the world when she provided the sound from which Krishna created the Vedas, the ancient Hindu Scriptures. No one knows the sound that she made – it could have been music or speech. This is the reason, though, why she is worshipped as the goddess of the arts and learning.

DISCUSS

The myth of Rama and Sita illustrates the belief that good will finally triumph over evil. There are many similar myths in the different world religions. Why do you think these religions have been so taken up with the problem of good and evil, and why do you think they all believe that good will triumph in the end? Do you share their optimism?

FOR YOUR FOLDER

1 Read the story of Rama and Sita again. Carry out some research of your own to add to the information from these pages.

a) What does it mean to describe Rama as the seventh 'avatar' of Vishnu?
b) Why do you think that the demon Ravana had ten heads?
c) Can you think of any other story or event from any religion which also demonstrates the belief that good will always triumph over evil?
d) Why do you think that this is such an important theme in all world religions?

2

a) Who tried to replace Rama as the king's successor by her own son?
b) How did she try to do this?
c) Who helped Rama to defeat the demon Ravana?
d) Describe, in your own words, how the story of Rama and Sita demonstrates that, in the end, good will always triumph over evil.

3 Write notes on:

a) Navaratri.
b) Dassehra.
c) Saraswati.

In the glossary: AVATAR; DASSEHRA; DURGA; NAVARATRI; KRISHNA; RAMA; RAMAYANA; RAVANA; SARASWATI; SITA; VEDAS; VISHNU.

Pilgrimages

***Why** do most Hindus undertake a pilgrimage to a holy place at some time during their lives?*

FOCUSING QUESTIONS

What do Hindus hope to achieve by visiting a holy place on a pilgrimage?

What is special about the pilgrimage site at Varanasi?

Why might a place have been originally set aside as holy and worthy of a pilgrimage?

Whilst pilgrimages to holy places, or teachers, are not compulsory for Hindus, to undertake one is to offer a special kind of worship to God. Although pilgrimages are not mentioned in the Vedas, The Upanishads do praise a pilgrimage as one of the most effective ways of making progress in the spiritual journey. Sometimes, especially at festival times, the pilgrimage may only involve a short journey, but on other occasions journeys of hundreds of kilometres may be undertaken.

Why make a pilgrimage?

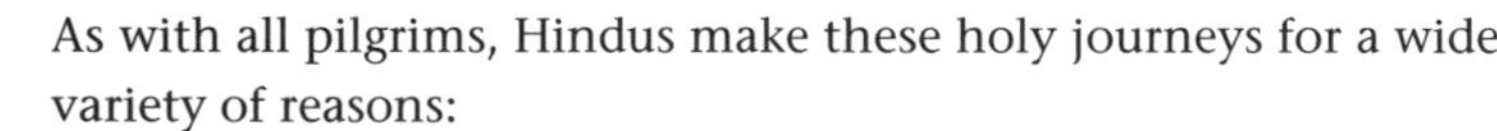

As with all pilgrims, Hindus make these holy journeys for a wide variety of reasons:

- to gain religious merit by visiting one of the holy shrines, as The Upanishads encourage them to do;
- to fulfil a religious promise that they have already made;
- to gain prosperity and good fortune for themselves and their family;
- to purify themselves by bathing in the waters of a holy river;
- to scatter the ashes of a loved one in the waters of one of the holy rivers. Anyone who has their ashes scattered on the waters of the Ganges at Varanasi in India, for instance, is believed to enter straight into Heaven;
- to simply express their devotion to God.

Holy places

Destinations for Hindu pilgrimages can be divided into two main groups:

1 Temples or places associated with important events in Hindu history or myth. The River Ganges, for example, is very important in the Hindu religion and many pilgrims

A. This photograph shows pilgrims washing in the waters of the River Ganges, India. Rivers are amongst the most sacred, and important, of natural features to Hindus. Why do you think that they are given this degree of importance?

B. These pilgrims are rowing out to the place where the rivers Ganges and Jamuna meet. Why do Hindus consider this to be a sacred place?

visit it (see Photograph A). Along its banks many great temples have been built. Huge crowds gather, particularly for the main festivals. Some 500,000 pilgrims travel to the festival held each year in the Jaganatha temple in the city of Puri, in India.

Varanasi is the most famous pilgrimage destination and it is situated at the spot where the rivers Ganges and Jamuna meet, in India. Shiva is believed to have lived there and also two small foot-prints said to belong to Vishnu can be seen there. Rama is worshipped in Varanasi and the annual Dassehra festival re-enacts the love-story of Rama and Sita there every year. As many Hindus as possible hope to visit Varanasi.

2 Places of great natural beauty, such as rivers and mountains. There are seven sacred rivers in India – including the Ganges, the Indus and the Jamuna. There are many places of pilgrimage in the awe-inspiring Himalayan mountain range. Places such as these are chosen either because of their importance to life in India (rivers) or for their breathtaking beauty (mountains).

DISCUSS

Why do you think that so many religious people find pilgrimages to be an important part of their spiritual journey in the twentieth century?

FOR YOUR FOLDER

1 In Photograph A you can see pilgrims bathing in the water at Varanasi, on the banks of the River Ganges, India.

a) What do you think that these pilgrims hope to achieve by washing in these waters?
b) Can you find out what myth explains why the River Ganges has been seen as holy by Hindus for centuries?

2

a) Varanasi is situated at the point where two rivers meet. Why does this make the city particularly holy and important?
b) If someone brings the ashes of a loved one to scatter over the waters at Varanasi what are they hoping for?

3

a) What do you understand by the word 'pilgrimage'?
b) List three different reasons why a Hindu might undertake a pilgrimage.
c) How might a beautiful place inspire thoughts of God and so become a pilgrimage centre?
d) Find out, and make a list of, all seven of the sacred rivers in India.

In the glossary: Ganges; Rama; Shiva; Sita; Upanishads; Varanasi; Vedas; Vishnu.

The Four Stages

***What** are the four stages in life through which a Hindu can pass and what does he or she hope to achieve at the end ?*

FOCUSING QUESTIONS

What are moksha and karma?

What are the ashramas?

What are the characteristics of each ashrama?

The ultimate aim of every Hindu is to obtain liberation ('moksha') which is union with God (Brahman). To achieve this, a person must free himself or herself from the chain of birth and death. The number of times a person is reborn is determined by an individuals actions during their lifetime. These actions determine a person's karma. Positive karma enables a person to move up through the cycle of birth and death towards moksha. Negative karma moves them down the cycle, further away from liberation or freedom. Two things in particular affect a person's karma:

- Religious actions. Hinduism provides a scheme of religious actions which can affect a person's karma – if they are faithfully carried out.
- Social actions, like caring for family. Such actions naturally accompany religious actions.

Hinduism teaches that, by controlling their karma (actions), all souls have the chance to attain moksha. In order to help control actions, Hinduism divides a person's life-span into four categories (ashramas) – each of which carries its own duties and responsibilities.

A. What are the responsibilities of those people who are in the householder phase?

Stage one

The student or immature phase (eight to twenty year olds). This is the time for training, learning, education and personal purity, which involves bathing twice a day. This stage starts when the sacred thread (see Pages 38/39) is placed around the shoulder of a young boy and he comes under the influence and teaching of his personal guru. The age at which this happens depends on which of the first three castes he is in. The fourth caste, the shudras, cannot wear the sacred thread.

Stage two

The householder phase (twenty to fifty year olds). This is when a Hindu follows a career, earns money, marries and has children. During this time he or she carries out their

FOR YOUR FOLDER

1 The Laws of Manu make it clear what is demanded of people in the student phase:
'Let him not injure others in thought and deed; let him not utter speeches which make others afraid of him, since that will prevent him from reaching heaven...Let him abstain from honey, meat, perfumes...substances flavouring food, women...and from doing injury to living creatures...from the use of shoes and an umbrella, from desire, anger, covetousness, dancing, singing...from idle disputes...and lying, from looking at or touching women.'

a) How would you sum up the quality of life which is being expected of someone in the student stage?
b) Look at the different things in this extract that someone in this stage is expected to avoid. Which of them do you think could distract him or her from acquiring learning and education?
c) Do you think these demands are realistic for someone living in the twentieth century?

2 *'When a householder sees his skin wrinkled and his hair white...then he may resort to the forest...Abandoning all food raised by cultivation, and all his belongings, he may depart into the forest, either committing his wife to his sons, or accompanied by her...Let him wear a skin or a tattered garment; let him bathe in the evening and in the morning, and let him always wear his hair in braids; the hair of his body, his beard, and his nails being unclipped... Let him live without a fire, without a house...Let him live wholly silent.'*
(The Laws of Manu)

a) Which of the four stages do you think that The Laws of Manu are speaking about here?
b) What is a someone called who enters this phase?
c) List what this person must give up.
d) What is the person in this stage hoping to achieve?

In the glossary: Ashrama; Brahman; Caste; Guru; Hermit; Karma; Laws of Manu; Meditation; Moksha; Sacred Thread; Sadhu.

B. This Hindu holy woman is a follower of the god Shiva. What is a sadhu and how would you recognise one if you saw him or her?

responsibilities to society and is released from all basic human desire by marrying and having children. Each person should choose a career befitting their caste and eat, speak and behave in a suitable way for their calling.

Stage three

The hermit stage. This stage begins when a Hindu's first grandchild is born. During this time he or she is expected to pray, study and meditate. For the first time a Hindu is released from the need to learn and provide for others. The Laws of Manu, an old Hindu holy book, advise that, during this stage, the man or woman should retire to the forest, but this rarely happens today.

Stage four

The phase of the holy man (sadhu). Few Hindus reach this stage, since the holy man (or, much rarer, holy woman) only possesses a loin cloth, food bowl and water pot. Sadhus shave their heads to show that they no longer belong to this world and do not wear the sacred thread. The Laws of Manu tell the sadhu to: *'Take no thought of the future, and look in indifference on the present.'*

Hinduism, then, sees the whole of life as a search for union with God. The start of the search is the beginning of life itself. The end is moksha – union with God.

Birth

Which samskaras are linked with the birth of a new baby and what symbolic actions are carried out?

FOCUSING QUESTIONS

Why are the different samskaras carried out?

What ceremony is carried out as soon as a baby is born?

How does a Hindu child receive its name?

In Hinduism there are sixteen 'samskaras' (ceremonies) which mark the important stages in life, from pre-birth to death. If the correct actions are undertaken at each stage then the bad effects of karma can be cancelled, and a better rebirth hoped for in the next life.

The first four samskaras

Many Hindus live in extended families which means that children, parents, grandparents, uncles, aunts, and cousins all live together – or very close to one another. They help one another and make decisions together which take into account the needs of all family members. Samskaras are essentially family rituals and all members of the family are involved.

There are three samskaras which are carried out before the child is born. The first of these takes place before a baby is conceived, when prayers are offered up that the couple may be able to have children. The second takes place after conception when prayers are offered up that the mother and child might be kept safe from evil spirits. The third samskara, after about seven months of pregnancy, again seeks protection for the baby and its mother.

The fourth samskara involves washing the baby. As soon as a Hindu baby is born he or she is washed. The sacred syllable, AUM, is written on the baby's tongue using a golden pen dipped in honey. After she has given birth the baby's mother is isolated until she has carried out the ceremonies which are needed to purify her. A symbolic mark (called a turmeric) is made on the forehead of the baby.

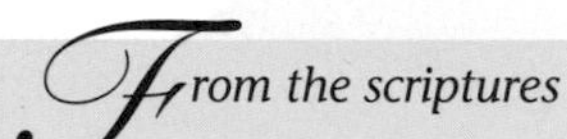

From the scriptures

To a Hindu, religion is very closely related to family life since, as The Bhagavad Gita (1:40) says:
'If the family breaks up, the religion will be lost as well.'

Describe two practical ways in which Hindus try to ensure that the family is the place where most worship takes place.

The name-giving ceremony

The fifth samskara is the name-giving ceremony (see Photograph A). This is carried out on the eleventh or twelfth day after a baby is born. The name of the baby is kept secret until this day in case evil spirits carry the child off before he or she can receive the protection of the fifth samskara. Scarlet threads are tied to the child as a symbol of its protection and it is given a piece of gold to hold as a sign of good fortune ahead. Sometimes a priest is involved in this ceremony, and generally draws up a horoscope for the baby, using its exact date and time of birth. The baby's name must begin with one of two or three letters from its zodiac sign. Most Hindu children are given two names – a public name by which he or she will be

A. During the Hindu naming ceremony, left, why do you think that the sacred syllable is written on the new baby's tongue in honey using a golden pen?

known to relatives and friends, and a secret name which will only be used on special religious occasions.

The baby's name is announced by the oldest woman in the family. All of the women present songs which include the baby's name. Each married women is presented with a handful of cooked pulses along with light refreshments. In India, the village blacksmith then pierces the ear-lobes of the child.

The tonsure

For boys, the sixth samskara is the first haircut – carried out in the fourth, sixth and eighth months after birth. In India, this is carried out in the temple or the home but in England Hindu families tend to visit the barber's shop. The hair is never cut off completely and a small tuft is left at the front. In some areas of India this ceremony is also carried out on baby girls. The baby's hair is then weighed and an equivalent amount in gold is given to the poor of the area.

IN THE GLOSSARY: AUM; KARMA; SAMSKARA.

FOR YOUR FOLDER

1 Can you explain:
a) What a samskara is?
b) Why three samskaras are carried out before a baby is born?
c) Why most of the hair is cut off a Hindu boy soon after he is born?
d) What part a Hindu priest plays in the naming of most babies – and why this is important?

2 The birth and the naming of a child are accompanied by many ceremonies in Hinduism. What value do these ceremonies have for Hindus?

3 Copy this chart and fill in as much information as you can:

Samskara	when	what happens	any prayers
1			
2			
3			
4			
5			

The Sacred Thread

What *happens during the sacred thread ceremony and why does it mark such an important event in the lives of most Hindu boys?*

FOCUSING QUESTIONS

What is the tenth samskara?

Why are boys who have received the sacred thread described as being 'twice-born'?

Why is receiving the sacred thread so important for every Hindu boy?

The sacred thread ceremony is the tenth and most important samskara. It is also called Upanayana (meaning 'drawing near') and is performed upon brahmin boys (those belonging to the priestly caste) between the ages of five and eight; for kshatriyas (the soldier caste) at eleven and for vaishyas (the farmers and merchants caste) at twelve. Those who undergo the ceremony are called 'twice-born' since it marks the beginning of the first of four stages – called brahmacharya.

Upanayana

The ceremony of Upanayana consecrates (makes holy) the body. What happens is like a second, spiritual, birth and marks the true beginning of a child's education. Hindus consider this spiritual birth to be much more important than the child's first birth. They argue that the child's mother only carried her baby for nine months whereas the new teacher, the guru, will carry spiritual responsibility for him for many years. From this moment the responsibility for the child passes from his mother to the senior male members of the family.

A. All important Hindu ceremonies take place in front of a holy fire. Can you think of one reason why fire is such an important religious symbol.

Upanayana can be carried out by the child's grandfather, father, uncle or any male relative. In practice it is invariably performed by the father if he is still alive. The best day for the ceremony is chosen by the priest after consulting the child's horoscope. The boy's head is shaved to indicate the removal of any bad karma (evil from a previous life) and he bathes before putting on a piece of cloth covering the lower half of his body – a 'dhoti'. The boy and his mother eat some food from the same plate after which the mother plays no further part in the ceremony. The boy and his father face each other and a piece of cloth is held up between them as songs are sung. A fire is lit and prayers are said to Agni, the god of Fire.

The sacred thread

The sacred thread has three strands and is made holy after water has been sprinkled on it. The Gayatri Hymn, taken from the Rig Veda, is sung ten times before the thread is put around the boy's head, resting on his left shoulder and hanging below his right hand. His father says: *'May this sacred thread destroy my ignorance, grant me long life and increase my understanding'*, and his son repeats the words after him. The boy asks his father to teach him the Gayatri Hymn and he recites the words: *'Our concentration is on the most radiant light of the Sun God. He sustains the Earth, the Heavens and the space in between. May the Sun keep our thoughts alive.'*

B. A boy wearing the sacred thread. What is this child about to begin now that he has received his sacred thread?

DISCUSS

Brahmin boys receive their sacred thread between the ages of five and eight, the children of kshatriya parents at the age of eleven, and vaishya children at the age of twelve. Why do you think that the higher the caste the younger the children who receive the sacred thread?

The three strands of the thread are a reminder to the boy of the three debts that he owes to God, to his parents and ancestors, and to his wise teachers. Only after he has paid these three debts can he be entitled to moksha. The knot which ties the strings (the brahma granthi) is a reminder that whoever comes to know God has repaid all three debts.

Obligations of wearing the sacred thread

Those Hindus who wear the sacred thread take on five daily obligations:

- To worship God – by offering puja.
- To show reverence for the holy men and women by reciting the Vedas.
- To honour relatives, elders, and to make offerings of rice and water to ancestors.
- To help the poor and holy men and women by offering them food and shelter.
- To feed all animals.

FOR YOUR FOLDER

1 Long ago, Hindu boys would leave home after receiving the sacred thread and spend years studying with their guru far away from home.
a) What do you think was the value of the ceremony then?
b) What do you think is the value of the ceremony now?

2 Do you know of any other initiation ceremonies in other religions which take place when a girl or boy is on the verge of adulthood? Do you think that they are a good idea? What useful purpose might they serve? What do you think is the ideal age for such a ceremony?

3 Describe what is said and done during the sacred thread ceremony. Explain the religious meaning of the ceremony. How is the life of a boy likely to be different after going through the ceremony?

IN THE GLOSSARY: AGNI; BRAHMACHARYA; BRAHMA GRANTHI; BRAHMIN; CSTE; DHOTI; GURU; GAYATRI HYMN; KARMA; KSHATRIYA; MOKSHA; PUJA; RIG VEDA; SACRED THREAD; SAMSKARA; UPANAYANA; VAISHYA; VEDAS.

Marriage

What makes a Hindu wedding distinctive?

FOCUSING QUESTIONS

What objective does a Hindu set himself as he begins the second ashrama?

Why are most Hindu marriages 'arranged'?

What promises do the bride and a groom make to each other during a Hindu wedding?

When a Hindu marries and becomes a 'householder' he reaches the thirteenth samskara. The first ashrama, that of the student, is now completed. During the second ashrama a Hindu sets himself the objective of attaining some religious merit in the hope that, at the end of his life, he might be able to avoid being reborn again.

In the Hindu faith a girl may marry at the age of fifteen and a boy at eighteen, although they must accept the laws of the country in which they are living. A Hindu must marry someone from the same caste and faith – with the marriage being arranged by their parents. Hindus believe that karma destines them to marry a certain person, and it is up to their parents to find that person for them.

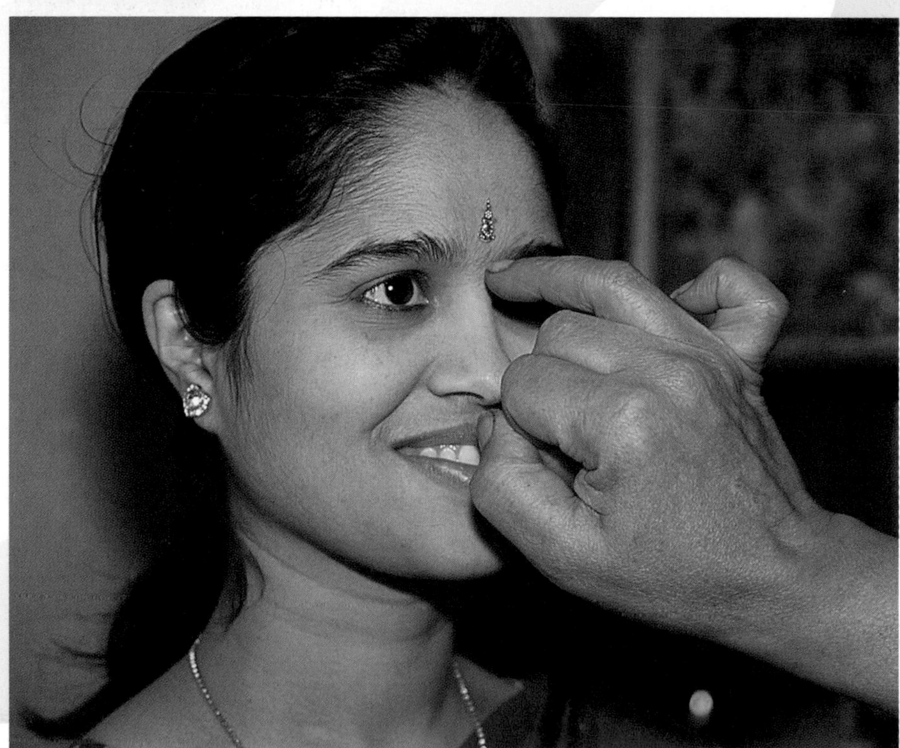

A. Why do you think that all married Hindu women wear this red mark in the middle of their forehead?

Preparing the bride

A Hindu bride prepares herself carefully for her wedding. Friends rub henna over most of her body with special attention being paid to her eye make-up. A new sari is put on with gold and red bangles and jewellery. A red spot of washable powder is placed in the centre of her forehead to show that she is blessed. All married Hindu women wear this spot in public (see Photograph A).

The wedding ceremony

The wedding ceremony takes place around a sacred fire, which is a sign of the pure presence of God. The priest, who conducts the service, keeps the fire going throughout the ceremony by pouring ghee (melted butter) on the flames. He also throws the traditional Indian symbols of rice and spices on the fire to guarantee that the couple will be fertile and have many children. The bride's family 'hand her over' to the groom by placing her hand in his and then her brothers pour fried rice over the clasped hands to show that they agree with the marriage. The couple then take seven steps

around the fire making a promise with each step. For the last circuit of the fire, their clothes are tied together. As they walk the groom says to his bride:
'With utmost love to each other may we walk together...May we make our minds united, of the same vows and the same thoughts. I am the wind and you are the melody. I am the melody and you are the words.'

On the last step they say to each other:
'Into my will I take thy heart
Thy mind shall follow mine,
Let the heart of yours be mine
And the heart of mine be yours.'

A Hindu marriage is not binding on the couple until the last step has been taken. Marriage is then a lifelong commitment. The couple go outside to look at the Pole Star together. As they do so, the wife promises her husband that she will be as constant as the Pole Star towards him and will not stand in the way of any good and righteous actions that he might perform. The Laws of Manu say that the wife must love and respect her husband – even if he has been unfaithful – and Orthodox Hindus do not accept divorce.

B. A Hindu wedding in southern India. What do the Laws of Manu have to say about marriage?

DISCUSS

Many Hindu marriages are 'arranged'. A Hindu woman pointed out recently that in Western countries many couples fall in love, marry and then fall out of love. Hindu couples, meanwhile, are introduced by their parents, marry and grow into love. Do you think that this woman had a good point?

FOR YOUR FOLDER

1 In many Hindu families is usual for the parents to arrange the marriage of their children.

a) What do you think that Hindu parents take into account when they are arranging the marriage of one of their children? Draw up a list of priorities you might have if you were a Hindu parent arranging a marriage.
b) Why do you think that many Hindus still prefer 'arranged' marriages to Western-style marriages?
c) Do you think that many young Hindus living in this country might find it harder to accept an 'arranged' marriage than someone living in a village in India? Why?

2 Read carefully the words that the bride and groom say to each other during the wedding service. How do you understand each of these phrases:

a) *'With utmost love to each other may we walk together...'.*
b) *'May we make our minds united, of the same vows and the same thoughts...'.*
c) *'I am the wind and you are the melody. I am the melody and you are the words...'.*
d) *'Let the heart of yours be mine And the heart of mine be yours.'*

In the glossary: Ashrama; Caste; Karma; Laws of Manu; Samskara;

Death

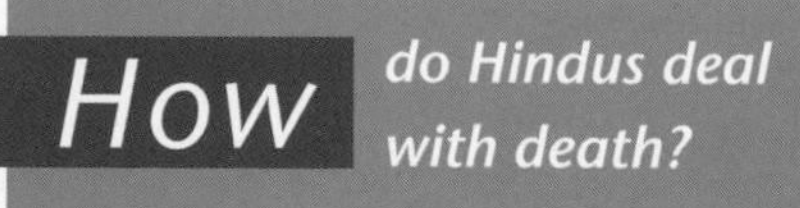

FOCUSING QUESTIONS

What is anyesti?

How is a Hindu person cremated?

What are shraddha?

Anyesti, the sixteenth and last samskara, is the funeral ceremony. The usual Hindu practice is to reduce the dead body to ashes by fire (cremation). The only two exceptions allowed to this rule are sadhus (holy men or women) and young babies who are buried.

Funeral rites

Cremation usually takes place in India on the same day that a person has died. This is necessary because of the hot climate. Soon after death the body is washed and dressed in special clothes, often a red cloth, by members of the family. It is then carried to the cremation ground on a small stretcher. If there is a river nearby then the cremation ground is likely to be sited close to it. Otherwise it will be a special area some distance from the village. By tradition the eldest son leads the funeral party to the cremation ground and the youngest son leads it on its way home.

Hindu funeral rites are carried out by a priest and the pyre of wood is lit by the eldest son or by some other male relative if the dead person did not have a son.

The cremation

If possible a Hindu hopes to die within reach of the River Ganges, in India. Mourners do not weep for relatives, since death is seen as a release from this life of illusion (maya) to a new and better life. The body is sprinkled with sandalwood oil and covered in garlands of flowers. It is dipped once in the river and then placed on a pile of wood (called a pyre) for cremation. 'Untouchables' supervise the cremation and tend the ever-burning sacred fire from which the burning branches are lifted to light the funeral pyre.

The eldest son walks anti-clockwise around the fire – since in death everything is reversed – before setting light to it. Ghee is thrown on the fire to help it burn. When the corpse is almost completely burned the son performs kapalakriya – he cracks the skull with a long bamboo stick to release the dead person's soul. Then he puts out the fire by throwing a pail of water over his left shoulder before walking away.

Within the next day or two, the bones and ashes of the deceased are collected together, placed in a cloth, and lowered into a river – preferably the Ganges. If the river is the Ganges then any further reincarnation is prevented and the person goes straight to Brahman. Hindus in Britain are usually cremated at the local crematorium.

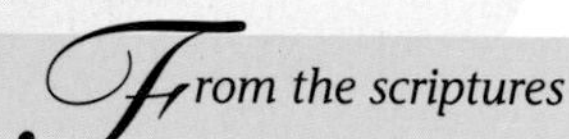

From the scriptures

Words from The Bhagavad Gita are recited at every Hindu cremation. They are:
'Worn out garments are shed by the body,
Worn out bodies are shed by the dweller,
Within the body new bodies are donned by the dweller, like garments.' (2.22)

If you look closely at these words you will see the Hindu attitude to the relationship between body and soul. What is it ?

1 What is suggested by calling each person a *'dweller'*?
2 When are new bodies *'donned by the dweller'*?

A. In this picture the male members of the family can clearly be seen in a prominent position beside the beside the body. Why do men, particularly the eldest son, play such an important role in Hindu funeral rites?

B. What do you think that it means to say that in death for Hindus everything is reversed?

Shraddha

Daily ceremonies (shraddha) are carried out for eleven days after cremation so that the naked soul can find a new body in which to pass on to its next form. Balls of cooked rice and milk are presented as offerings for the welfare of the dead person's spirit. If this does not happen then the soul will remain as a ghost haunting and upsetting relatives. Only sons can perform these ceremonies.

On the fourth day friends visit the dead person's house, comfort the relatives, give presents, and say prayers for the soul of the dead person. A final sympathy meeting, on the twelfth day, marks the time when the soul is free to pass on to a new life.

Suttee
Suttee is the sacrifice that a Hindu widow made voluntarily by being burned to death on top of her husband's body. This was supposed to guarantee the two of them millions of years of bliss together in Heaven. Although the practice was made illegal in the nineteenth century, it still occasionally happens in some remote Indian villages.

FOR YOUR FOLDER

1
a) Explain why you think that Hindus almost welcome death and how this affects the way that they treat it.
b) Do you think that people should welcome death when it comes? Can you imagine a situation in which you might do so?

2 A Hindu family prepares the body for cremation and carries out the most important parts of the service. In Britain these tasks are carried out by undertakers with the family barely involved.
a) Why do you think that there are these two very different approaches to dealing with death?
b) Do you think that the Hindu approach to death helps them to cope with the death of a loved one?
c) Do you think that we deal with death in Britain in the best possible way – or not?

In the glossary: Anyesti; Brahman; Ganges; Maya; Sadhu; Samskara; Shraddha; Suttee; Untouchables.

Shruti and Smriti

What *are the two categories into which the Hindu holy books are divided and what is the essential difference between them?*

FOCUSING QUESTIONS

Why are the different holy books are so important to Hindus?

What is meant by shruti, and which books fall into this category?

What is meant by smriti, and which books fall into this category?

There are many holy books in Hinduism. They are used extensively for personal devotions and acts of worship (puja) carried out both at home in front of the family shrine and in the mandir (temple). The holy books also play a prominent part in Hindu festivals and in ceremonies such as the sacred thread. Hindus teach the holy books to their children from a very early age and scenes from them are often acted out in the temple for their benefit.

Hindus believe that a deep knowledge of the scriptures is very important since this will provide them with:

- An answer to many of the ultimate questions in life. Nothing could be known, for instance, about God or the soul ('atman') unless it was revealed by Him in one of the holy books. This He has done in The Vedas and The Upanishads which directly record the words of God.
- An answer to some of the practical questions about life, such as how other forms of life should be treated.

The holy books

Hindu holy writings fall into two categories – smriti and shruti.

That which is heard

The smriti (meaning 'that which is heard') are believed to have been received by the holy men directly from God. These books, which include the four Vedas and The Upanishads, are eternal and go back into the very distant past. This is what gives these books their unique authority.

The Vedas are made up of four books – the Rig Veda, the Sama Veda, the Yajur Veda and the Atharva Veda. They were recorded in Sanskrit between 1500 and 800 BCE, and the most ancient, and the most sacred, is the Rig Veda. Hymns from this holy book are still used at special events like marriage and cremation.

The Upanishads (meaning 'sitting down near your teacher') are a very valuable part of the smriti. They contain a record of the discussions that gurus (teachers) had with their disciples about such things as God, karma and the soul.

DISCUSS

Hindus believe that The Vedas and The Upanishads, their two most important holy books, contain the 'word of God'. Other religions make a similar claim for their own holy books.

1. Can you name any books which other religions believe to be 'the word of God'?
2. What do you think this phrase means?
3. Why are books such books believed to carry unique authority?

That which is remembered

Shruti (meaning 'that which is remembered') are scriptures which are based on human recollections of God's message. They are later books and are considered less important that the smriti. They do, however, include some of the best-loved books in Hinduism: The Mahabharata, which is the world's longest poem, containing over 3,000,000 words; The Bhagavad Gita ('Song of the Lord') which is the climax of The Mahabharata and much admired by Hindus and non-Hindus alike; and The Ramayana which contains 24,000 couplets.

The Laws of Manu (the 'Manusmriti'), which Hindus believe are based upon the laws that Manu, the father of the human race, received from God is also part of the shruti. The Paranas, which contain myths about gods, wise men and rulers was the most recent of the books which Hindus accepted as being sacred, and was not in its present form until the twelfth century CE.

A. A Hindu holy man reading from the Holy Scriptures. What do the words 'shruti' and 'smriti' mean?

FOR YOUR FOLDER

1
a) Name three ways in which Hindus make use of their holy books.
b) Name two books which fit into the smriti group.
c) Name two books which fit into the shruti group.
d) What is the name of the book which contains the world's longest poem?

2 Someone has said that *'the old holy books have no use for people today'*. What do you think about this point of view? Would religious people such as Hindus, Muslims and Christians agree with this opinion? Give reasons for your answer.

3 In the past, the sacred stories and legends of Hinduism were kept alive and passed around by word-of-mouth long before they were written down. Can you think of two advantages and two disadvantages of keeping material alive in this way for a long period of time?

In the glossary: Atharva Veda, Atman, Bhagavad Gita; Karma; Laws of Manu; Mahabharata; Sama Veda; Puja; Ramayana; Rig Veda; Sacred Thread; Sama Veda; Sanskrit; Shruti; Smriti; Upanishads; Vedas; Yajur Veda.

The Vedas

What is distinctive about The Vedas and The Upanishads?

FOCUSING QUESTIONS

How was the material in The Vedas preserved before it was written down?

What is the nature of the material in the Rig Veda?

What makes The Upanishads an important Hindu book?

The Vedas (meaning 'knowledge') consist of four collections of writings (the Rig Veda, the Sama Veda, the Yajur Veda and the Atharva Veda) which were written down in Sanskrit between 1500 and 800 BCE. The Vedas are the oldest books known. The material contained in The Vedas, though, had been passed down by word-of-mouth for centuries before they were written down. The priests of the Aryan civilization, called rishis (seers), were responsible for preserving them. They are written in poetic form with a deep, inner meaning and magical potency.

A. Hindus meeting together to discuss the scriptures. How important do you think the scriptures are in the daily lives of Hindus?

The Rig Veda

The Rig Veda was in use in its present form by about 900 BCE, though some parts of it may date as far back as 1500 BCE. Many of the hymns in the Rig Veda were recited during Aryan ceremonies and contain a mixture of prose, verse, spells and incantations. The collection, arranged in ten volumes, contains 1,028 hymns altogether. These are made up of many mantras which are dedicated to various nature gods.

The different hymns reflect the nomadic life led by the Aryans whose words cry out to their gods as they charge into battle, rejoice in the Sun rising in the morning, or reflect on the loneliness of a silent evening. Three gods, in particular, were worshipped by those who composed the hymns: Agni, the fire-god, who was essential for all sacrifices; Indra, the warrior-god, who guaranteed success in battle; and Varuna, the god who fixed the paths of the planets and directed the course taken by the rivers.

The Brahmanas
The Brahmanas are commentaries on the different texts in The Vedas which set out to explain much of the symbolism in the books. They were given by priests who received special powers and insights from the gods so that the inner meaning of The Vedas would be open to those who genuinely seek for it. Most of The Brahmanas probably existed by 300 BCE although some material was added later. They are not widely used by Hindus today.

The Upanishads

The Upanishads were composed between 800 and 300 BCE, and arose out of the teachings given by gurus to their pupils (the word itself means 'sitting down near to your teacher'). The teaching concerns itself mainly with Brahman, karma and the soul. The Upanishads seek to explain what it means to be a human being by saying that we are not simply the clothes we wear, the food we eat or the face that we have. These things are only important on the surface – our real self is our 'atman' (soul) which we only fully discover when we reach union with Brahman. The Upanishads also stress that the many gods mentioned in The Vedas are really just one – Brahman, the Supreme Spirit, who is the source of energy behind all things.

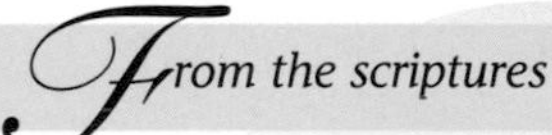

This extract comes from The Vedas:
'What sin we have ever committed against an intimate, O Varuna, against a friend or a companion at any time, a brother, a neighbour, or a stranger, free us from it O Varuna. If, like gamblers at play we have cheated, whether in truth or without knowing, free us from our guilt, O God. So may we be dear to you, O Varuna...For an awakened soul Indra, Agni, Aditya, Candra – all these names represent only one basic power and spiritual reality.'

1 Who is Varuna?
2 Who is Indra?
3 Who is Agni?
4 Someone has said that the basic concern of religion is to free its followers from feeling guilt for their sins. Is there some evidence in this quotation to support this statement?
5 Who do you think is the *'awakened soul'* referred to in this quotation?
6 There is a great deal of debate about whether Hindus believe in many gods or just one. What would The Vedas say in answer to this question?

DISCUSS

The Upanishads grew out of teachings that gurus gave to their disciples. Part of that teaching was about the importance of the soul. Do you agree with Hindus, and most religious people, that the human soul is far more important than the body? If so, what do you think the soul is?

FOR YOUR FOLDER

1
a) What does the word 'Veda' mean?
b) How many books are there in The Vedas, and which of them is the most important?
c) Which gods are the most important in the Rig Veda?
d) What are The Brahmanas?
e) What does the word 'Upanishads' mean, and how does the name explain where the writings came from?
f) 'Who are we?' according to The Upanishads?

In the glossary: Agni; Atharva Veda; Atman; Brahman; Brahmanas; Guru; Indra; Karma; Rig Veda; Sama Veda; Sanskrit; Upanishads; varuna; Yajur Veda.

The Mahabharata

What is The Mahabharata and why does it have a special place in Hinduism?

FOCUSING QUESTIONS

- Who are the Pandavas and the Kauravas, and how does jealousy arise between them?
- How were the Pandavas eventually banished from their kingdom – and what happened in the end?
- What important religious themes emerge from the story told in The Mahabharata?

The Mahabharata and The Ramayana are the two great epic poems in the Hindu Scriptures. The Mahabharata, with about 100,000 verses, was composed in the ninth century BCE, although it was added to, and changed, over the next 700 years. There is a Sanskrit saying: '*What is not in this epic is not in India*' underlining the belief that the poem contains all that is essential in Hinduism. The most sacred part of this immensely long poem is The Bhagavad Gita which occupies just a small part of the sixth book. It is the most loved of all the Hindu holy books.

A. An ancient Hindu manuscript showing the armies of the Kauravas and the Pandavas about to do battle.

The story of The Mahabharata

As with many other Hindu holy books, the story at the heart of The Mahabharata concerns the conflict between the forces of good (the Pandavas) and evil (the Kauravas). The story begins with the death of King Pandu, leaving the throne to his brother, Dhrtarastra. The new king takes his nephews into his own household and treats them like sons. Drona, a great weapons-master and Bhisma, 'grandfather' of the clan, are brought in to educate the boys in the use of weapons. Although Dhrtarastra's own sons (the Kauravas) are highly skilled, the sons of King Pandu (the Pandavas) excel in the use of every weapon. This leads to jealousy between the two sets of boys and the Kauravas try to set fire to the Pandavas home. The five Pandavas flee to the forest where they live for a long time as brahmins.

Believing that their cousins have died, one of the Pandavas, Arjuna, is tempted out of the forest, in disguise, to take part in a special archery contest. To win the contest he has to hit a revolving target five times using the strongest bow that has ever been made. The Kauravas know that only Arjuna is strong enough to pull the bow, and fearing the revenge of the Pandava princes, the Kauravas agree to share the kingdom with them – but gave them the poorest land. However, as a result of much hard work, this land becomes the most productive in the kingdom.

Once again the Kauravas fear for their own safety and plan to rid the kingdom of their cousins by persuading the eldest of the Pandavas, Yudhisthira, to take part in a dice game with the whole kingdom at stake. The dice are loaded, and all of the brothers are sent into exile, but are told that they can return after thirteen years if they remain unrecognised for the whole of this time. After thirteen years, however, the Kauravas resort to war rather than yield up their kingdom. Eventually, the Pandavas are victorious and there is a great rejoicing throughout the kingdom.

The story ends with the Pandavas retiring from the life of action. Their 'dharma' (duty) has been fulfilled and they retire to the Himalayas to look forward to death and, beyond that, the life of bliss promised in so many of the Hindu holy books.

Themes

There are many themes in The Mahabharata which also run through many other Hindu books. The themes of anger and jealousy, of cheating and trickery are to be found elsewhere. So, too, is the final triumph of good over evil. When the Kauravas are defeated and the Pandavas retire from a life of right action (dharma) to one of meditation in the Himalayas the poem has the perfect Hindu ending.

FOR YOUR FOLDER

1 The story told in The Mahabharata is one of the most popular in Hinduism. Imagine that a Hindu parent is telling the story to two of his or her children. What lessons do you think they would want their children to learn from the story?

2 Look at Photograph A, which shows a scene from The Mahabharata?

a) Which two armies are facing each other?
b) Who had spent thirteen years in exile before the scene shown in this painting – and why?
c) Why are the two armies about to go to war?
d) What happened in the end?
e) How did the successful leaders celebrate their victory?
f) What lessons do you think Hindus today are likely to draw from this story?

3

a) Write a speech from one of the Pandava princes to the people claiming back the kingdom.
b) Write a speech to be given by Arjuna to his brothers explaining why he wanted to enter the archery contest and asking for their support.
c) Write a speech by one of the Kauravas explaining why the brothers had decided to go back on their promise to share their kingdom with the Pandavas after their exile.
d) Write a speech by Arjuna explaining why he and his brothers had decided to retire from a life of action to one of meditation after they had regained their kingdom.

In the glossary: BHAGAVAD GITA; BRAHMIN; DHARMA; MAHABHARATA; MEDITATION; RAMAYANA; SANSKRIT.

The Bhagavad Gita

What *is the story behind The Bhagavad Gita and what important themes emerge from the story?*

FOCUSING QUESTIONS

How does Krishna persuade Arjuna that he must return to the battle?

What is bhakti?

What does Hinduism teach about the soul?

The Bhagavad Gita (meaning 'Song of the Lord') consists of just over 700 verses which were written some time between 400 BCE and 100 CE. It did not become a popular Hindu text, however, until the ninth century CE when the philosopher, Shankara, wrote a commentary on it. Today it is one of the most popular of all religious texts.

The story of The Bhagavad Gita

The story told in The Bhagavad Gita concentrates on the final battle that took place between the Pandavas and the Kauravas at Kurukshetra. Arjuna is shocked at the idea of fighting members of his own family and tells his charioteer to withdraw from the battle. The man turns round and starts to argue with him. Arjuna is very surprised by this but gradually he comes to realise that his charioteer is none other than the god, Krishna, who has appeared to teach him a very important truth. Krishna assures him that the world is being threatened by chaos and that only Arjuna can restore order to it. He must face up to the truth and accept God's will as it is now being revealed to him by Krishna. Krishna asks Arjuna for his devotion: *'Just fix your mind upon me, the Supreme Personality of the Godhead, and engage all your intelligence in me. Thus you will live in me always'* (9.34).

A. An illustration from an early edition of the Bhagavad Gita, showing Arjuna with his charioteer, Krishna. What surprised Arjuna when he discovered the identity of his charioteer and how is this crucial to the content of The Bhagavad Gita?

B. A rock carving from the third century CE, showing scenes from The Bhagavad Gita. What did Arjuna's victory in battle teach him about his duty to God?

Krishna tells Arjuna that he should fight because that is his duty as a kshatriya (a member of the warrior caste). Right actions, he is told, must be performed whatever the outcome of that action may prove to be. So Arjuna, helped by Krishna, re-enters the battle and defeats the Kauravas even though they have far superior forces and weapons.

Themes

In The Bhagavad Gita Krishna teaches Arjuna some of the most important truths found in Hinduism – about the true nature of God, and about the human relationship with God. The main teachings which are stressed are:

- The importance of 'bhakti' – devotion to a personal god. Time and time again this is emphasised: *'My devotee who is ever content, constant in meditation, and exercises self-control, who has complete faith in Me and has dedicated his mind and intellect to Me, is dear to me.'*
- In The Bhagavad Gita God is not impersonal. In the form of Krishna he is warm and loving.
- Everyone has a duty to work without expecting any return from their labour.
- The soul (atman) cannot be destroyed. After a life has ended the soul enters a new body in a form which has been determined by the previous life. As Krishna points out, a person should not grieve deeply over the death of someone else since this cannot be avoided. Even if someone dies in battle they should know that their soul, the only part of them that really matters, cannot be destroyed. That is eternal.
- The Supreme Spirit, Brahman, is eternal and everything in the universe is part of Brahman. It is possible to understand part of Brahman as everything that is good in creation.

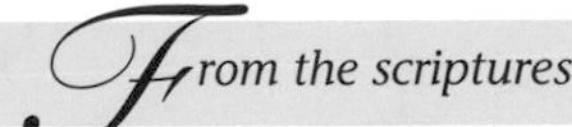

From the scriptures

The belief that the soul is indestructible and eternal lies at the heart of Hindu belief. This extract from The Bhagavad Gita teaches this:

'Atman is not born and never dies. It is eternal, everlasting and ancient. It is not destroyed when the body dies. If a man knows for certain atman is constant and exists eternally, how can that man kill anything or cause anyone's death? As a man throws away used and worn-out clothes after death to enter new ones, so does atman leave worn-out bodies after death to enter new ones.'

(2.21-22)

1 What is atman?
2 How many different statements about atman can you find in this quotation?
3 From reading this what would you guess would be the Hindu attitude towards: abortion, euthanasia (the mercy-killing of those who are dying), and suicide?
4 What happens to the atman after death?
5 Is there anything within your own experience which might lead you to believe in reincarnation?

FOR YOUR FOLDER

1 Answer these questions in your own words:
a) When did The Bhagavad Gita become a popular work – and why?
b) Who was Arjuna and how did he find himself talking with Krishna?
c) What was the outcome of the conversation between Arjuna and Krishna?
d) How did Krishna try to persuade Arjuna that it was right for him to fight?

2 There are five themes that emerge from The Bhagavad Gita. Explain what they are.

In the glossary: Atman; Bhagavad Gita; Bhakti; Brahman; Krishna; Kshatriya.

The Ramayana

What *story forms the basis of The Ramayana and what is its spiritual meaning?*

FOCUSING QUESTIONS

What is the origin of the story told in The Ramayana?

How does The Ramayana show the ideal characteristics of Rama, Sita and Lakshman?

How does the finale to the story of Rama and Sita show a blemish in the king's character?

Along with The Mahabharata, The Ramayana is one of the the great epic poems in Hinduism. The origins of the tale seem to lie in a Buddhist story which went through several revisions before finally reaching its written form around 300 BCE. The final story was put together by Valmiki, a holy man, in Sanskrit. Legend has it that Valmiki was a thief and a robber in his youth but was advised by a holy man to give up his evil ways and take to study. Whilst doing so he came into contact with Rama and Sita (see Photograph A), the main characters in the story.

The story of The Ramayana

The story bears many close similarities to that told in The Mahabharata. Prince Rama (see Photograph B) was the heir to the kingdom of Ayodyha but he was exiled when his step-mother tried to have her son made the heir in his place. Rama, Sita (his wife) and his brother (Lakshman) were sent away to the forest – home of the demons – for fourteen years. Whilst in exile Rama and his brother went out hunting one day leaving Sita at home on her own. She was kidnapped by Ravana, the king of Sri Lanka, who had come to the cottage disguised as a holy man. The deer, which had lured Rama and Lakshman away to hunt was, in fact, a demon.

Devastated by the disappearance of Sita the two brothers searched for her for many days without any success. Tired and dispirited they arrived at a kingdom whose ruler, Sugriva, had been deposed by his brother. Rama promised to help Sugriva regain his throne and, in return, Sugriva sent his monkey-general, Hanuman, to find Sita. She was located in the island kingdom of Sri Lanka surrounded by fierce female demons.

Rama and Sugriva gathered an army together and attacked Ravana's forces. In the final battle Rama killed Ravana and returned to Ayodyha with Sita and Lakshman. The people celebrated their return with great festivities. Rama was crowned but soon began to doubt that Sita had been faithful whilst separated from him, and so abandoned his pregnant wife.

The old hermit, Valmiki, took Sita in and she gave birth to twins, Lawa and Kusha. When they were old enough Valmiki told them the whole story. Some years later Valmiki went with the twins to the capital while Rama was performing a religious ceremony. The king was delighted to see them. Sita once again told the king that she was innocent and said that the earth would open up and swallow her if she had been pure all the time. The earth split open and Sita was lost for ever. Later Rama handed his kingdom over to his sons and gave up his earthly life.

FOR YOUR FOLDER

1 Imagine that a Hindu friend is finding life very difficult at the moment. Explain to them how the story told in The Ramayana shows that good will always triumph over evil at the end.

2 Explain how Hindus learn about the characters of their gods and goddesses from myths and stories. Refer to The Ramayana and to one other Hindu holy book in your answer.

A. Rama and Sita, from a nineteenth-century Bengali manuscript. How do you feel about the way that Rama treated Sita in the story?

The lessons of The Ramayana

The Ramayana is very popular because of the lessons that it still teaches Hindus today:

- Rama is both the ideal man and the ideal king. He is honest, trustworthy and loyal – although his treatment of Sita is a blemish on his character. Rama is considered to be the seventh 'avatar' (God descended to Earth) of Vishnu and one of the most widely worshipped gods in India. It is a characteristic of Hinduism that its gods are not expected to be perfect. When Rama returns to Ayodhya he is not only the rightful king but he sets up an ideal government. During his rule justice and happiness prevail for everyone.
- Sita is the ideal wife who is totally devoted to her husband. In the end her protestations of innocence are shown to be justified.
- Lakshman is the ideal brother who gives up living in a palace and is prepared to live in the forest out of loyalty to his brother.

B. A sixteenth-century statue showing an image of Rama. Why do Hindus look towards Rama as the ideal king?

DISCUSS

In the story told in The Ramayana, Rama is presented as the ideal man and king. Yet he treated Sita, his wife, very badly and placed his role as a king above that of a husband and father. Why do you think that Hindus are quite happy to tolerate flaws in the characters of their gods?

In the glossary: AVATAR; MAHABHARATA; RAMA; RAMAYANA; RAVANA; SANSKRIT; SITA; VISHNU.

God

Do Hindus believe in many different gods or in one God who takes many different forms?

FOCUSING QUESTIONS

Who is Brahman?

What are some of Brahman's characteristics?

What do the Rig Veda and the Yajur Veda say about Brahman?

From the scriptures

This story is told in The Upanishads to explain the relationship between God and the world. Read it through carefully:

'"Place this salt in water and then come to me in the morning." The son does as he is told. Uddalaka says to him; "My son, bring me the salt which you placed in the water last night." Looking for it, the son does not find it, for it is completely dissolved. The father says: "My son, take a sip of water from the surface. How is it?"

"It is salt."

"Take a sip from the middle. How is it ?"

"It is salt."

"Take a sip from the bottom. How is it?"

"It is salt."

"Throw it away and come to me." The son does as he is told, saying, "The salt was there all the time." Then the father says, "Here also, my dear, in this body, verily, you do not perceive Being [God] *but It is indeed there."'*

1 What do you think Hindus can learn about God and the world from reading this story?

2 How do you think that the Hindu ideas of God, expressed in this extract, compare to the beliefs about God that followers of other religions hold?

Amongst Hinduism's 550 million followers worldwide there are some Hindus who do not believe in God at all. They know that life itself depends on night following day; Summer coming after Spring and harvest following seedtime. They recognise that there is a principle of order in the universe that guarantees such things. They also believe that creation goes in cycles – a universe is created, flourishes and ends, to be replaced by another. This cycle takes an immense amount of time to work through – 4,320,000 years. The principle of order, however, guarantees that life will always continue and that death will always be followed by new life. People who believe this can still be good Hindus even though they find no place for God in their world.

The vast majority of Hindus do believe strongly in God – or should that be gods? Hindus themselves are often unclear on this point. The Rig Veda and other Hindu holy books, refer to thirty-three gods, but elsewhere the same books deny these gods real existence. The truth appears to be that there is one God in Hinduism who is worshipped under many different forms and images. This one God is Brahman.

Brahman

Hindus believe that Brahman, the Supreme Spirit, is beyond all human understanding, beyond time and space. Brahman is found throughout the universe, but is more than the universe. Brahman is the entire world around us – and yet it is also our inner world as well. This inner being is called the 'atman' (soul). Brahman and the soul are one. Heaven is reached when the human soul is reunited with Brahman.

The 'gods' which make Hinduism such a colourful religion each act to illuminate one aspect of the character of Brahman. Without this, Brahman would remain totally unknowable. Starting from the belief that God is One, and so there cannot be more than one God, the Rig Veda explains this: '*To what is one, sages give many a name, Agni, Yama, Matarisvan...*' to which the Yajur Veda adds '*For an awakened soul, Indra, Agni, Aditya, Candra, all these names represent only one basic power and spiritual reality.*' Hindus believe that it is the inability to grasp the truth that God and the world is one which leads to continual rebirths or reincarnations.

A. Meenakshi Temple in India. Describe the characteristics of some of the images of the gods that you can see in this Indian temple.

Gods and goddesses

All Indian words can be male, female or neuter, and Brahman is a neuter word. God is neither male nor female. Since Brahman embraces the whole of creation it can be represented by a male, a female, or by animals and birds. Some of the gods and goddesses who represent Brahman come and go. Indra, for example, is no longer worshipped. In the meantime, other gods have come to prominence, and many of them have been given consorts or wives. Sometimes a bird or an animal is placed alongside them as well. So Brahma, the creator-god, is always mentioned alongside Saraswati, the goddess of learning. Often a swan is placed alongside them. In fact, Saraswati has now become much more popular with worshippers than her consort.

FOR YOUR FOLDER

1

a) Why do you think that Hindus themselves sometimes find it difficult to know whether they believe in many gods – or just one God?

b) What do the Hindu holy books seem to teach?

c) Islam and Judaism are both strongly against giving God any kind of physical form. Hindus are encouraged to see their images as means of illuminating God – Brahman – who would otherwise remain unknowable. Do you think that such images are helpful – or are there dangers in allowing God to be represented in this way?

2 Describe what a Hindu believes about Brahman – the Supreme Spirit.

In the glossary: AGNI; ATMAN; BRAHMA; BRAHMAN; INDRA; RIG VEDA; SARASWATI; UPANISHADS; YAJUR VEDA.

Gods and the Trimurti

How *important are Brahma, Vishnu and Shiva in Hinduism?*

FOCUSING QUESTIONS

What is the trimurti?

Which two characteristics are brought together in the personality of Shiva?

What is an avatar?

Among the thousands of gods worshipped to a greater or lesser extent by Hindus three are most prominent. They are Shiva (called 'the Destroyer'),Vishnu ('the Preserver') and Brahma ('the Creator'). Together they make up the 'trimurti', Absolute Reality.

Shiva

Shiva, the Destroyer, is the most popular of the gods and his followers, called Shaivites, refer to him as Mahadeva meaning 'the Great God'. Shiva is a curious mix of characteristics. He is the god of death, destruction, and disease, yet he is also the god of dance and reproduction. He is, at once, both terrible and mild. He has been described as being *'ceaselessly active and eternally restful'*. Most Hindus see these very different characteristics in themselves – and in all human beings – and so feel very much at home with Shiva. Statues of Shiva often show him with four hands to demonstrate his supreme power over life, death, good and evil. He is 'the Lord of the Dance' (see Photograph A) whose energy keeps the universe in motion. Sometimes Shiva is shown dancing on the back of a demon – the demon of ignorance – that he is dedicated to destroying.

A. Shiva, the Lord of the Dance, surrounded by eternal flames. What overriding impression do you think that Hindus would get as they look at this statue of Shiva?

Vishnu

In contrast to Shiva, Vishnu is the preserver of life who, as the god of love and kindness, is dedicated to 'preserving' these qualities. Vishnu has immense concern for the human race which he has shown by appearing on Earth as an avatar (a form of God descended to Earth). Hindu tradition records nine occasions in which Vishnu has visited Earth either in animal or human form – as Gautama Buddha (the founder of the Buddhist religion) and Krishna among others. Each of the avatars appeared as chaos and wickedness seemed to be gaining the upper hand on Earth. One more avatar is expected before the world ends. This idea of Vishnu appearing on Earth is very important to Hindus since it suggests to them that God is keeping a watchful eye on what is happening.

B. A statue of Ganesha – the elephant god. What is the symbolic importance of the different parts of his body – including the missing tusk?

Brahma

Although one of the three members of the trimurti, Brahma is the least admired and worshipped. Few Hindus now would want to be known as worshippers of this god. Brahma is always shown with four heads to represent the four Vedas. His unpopularity stems from the story that he used his four heads to search for his daughter who had hidden from him when he wanted to seduce her.

Ganesha

Ganesha, the god of fortune and wisdom, is a much admired Hindu god. The popular image of Ganesha is with an elephant's head. He is often pictured with one broken tusk, which was lost in a fight, held in his hand. His whole tusk is said to represent Truth; the broken one represents the imperfect world, but both belong to the same body. His trunk is Brahman and his belly is full of created worlds. His ears are large enough to hear all prayers. There are several stories to explain why Ganesha has an elephant's head. One story describes how Ganesha was originally moulded from clay by the goddess Parvati to guard her bathroom door. Her husband, Shiva, was so furious when Ganesha stopped him entering that he cut off his head. Afterwards, to calm his wife, he cut the head off an elephant belonging to Indra, the rain god, and put it on Ganesha's body.

FOR YOUR FOLDER

1 Answer each of these questions in your own words:

a) How do his followers refer to Shiva – and why?
b) List four characteristics of Shiva.
c) How do you understand the description of Shiva as being '*ceaselessly active and eternally restful*'?
d) Why is Shiva often portrayed as the 'Lord of the Dance'?
e) Why is Shiva often portrayed as dancing on the back of a demon?
f) How has Vishnu shown his concern for the human race?
g) What is an avatar and how many avatars of Vishnu have there been? Are there any more to come?
h) Why do Hindus find the avatars of Vishnu so comforting?
i) There are only six temples dedicated to Brahma in the whole of India. Can you suggest why this is?

2 Hindus often bring together conflicting characteristics in the same god. Shiva is one classic example. The goddess Parvati is another. She is a peace-loving and gentle deity. As Kali, or Durga, however, she turns into a fierce tyrant. Explain, with reference to Shiva or Parvati, how Hinduism often combines two very different personalities in the same god or goddess. Why do you think they do this and what does it tell you about human nature?

3 Both Hinduism and Christianity hold the idea of God coming to Earth at the very centre of their beliefs. Do you think that this is feasible, or do you agree with those religions which maintain that it is totally impossible to think of God taking on human form?

In the glossary: Avatar; Brahma; Brahman; Durga; Kali; Ganesha; Indra; Krishna; Parvati; Shiva; Trimurti; Vedas; Vishnu.

The Path of Bhakti

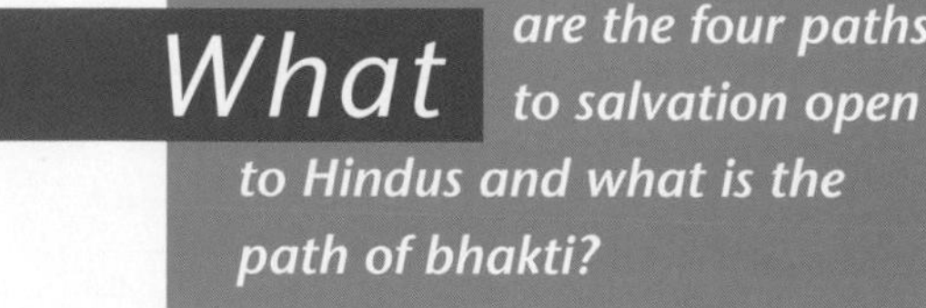

What are the four paths to salvation open to Hindus and what is the path of bhakti?

FOCUSING QUESTIONS

What are Hindus trying to escape from by following one of the paths open to them?

What is yoga?

What is the ishvara?

The four paths

Hindus do not start their understanding of human nature by stressing that human beings are sinners who need to be saved by God – as Jews and Christians do. Instead, each Hindu knows that he or she has a 'dharma' (a right way of life to follow) which will enable them to cope with 'dukkha' (the unsatisfactoriness/pain of life). Hindus are always aware, however, that the law of karma ('we only receive what we deserve') applies in this life and the next.

A. A personal deity in a shrine. Why do people who are following the path of bhakti need a personal god of their own to help?

The problem that each Hindu faces is not one of sin but that of maya (meaning 'not this' – an illusion). This is the name given to all visible things in the world which we assume to be real but which are not. Hindus believe that everything that does not exist for ever is unreal – an illusion. Only Brahman, the Supreme Spirit, is real since it alone is eternal. Hindus are offered four paths which will help them to distinguish between what is real (Brahman) and what is not (everything else). The four paths are:

- The path of bhakti – the path of love and devotion.
- The path of karma – the path of action.
- The path of jnana – the path of knowledge.
- The path of yoga – the path of communion.

The discipline required to follow one of these paths (yogas) is called a sadhana. There are different paths for different people. The householder, for example, is certain to follow a different path to the guru. The English word 'yoke' comes from 'yoga'. Yoga is a way of disciplining, or yoking, a person to bring them into unity with Brahman. Only by being yoked can someone obtain moksha – liberation.

Bhakti

The way of bhakti, devotion to a personal god, is the simplest way for the ordinary Hindu to move towards union with Brahman. In itself Brahman is a very difficult notion for people to grasp so they concentrate on their own personal god (the ishvara). This god can be Shiva, Vishnu, Rama,

From the scriptures

Lord Krishna speaks these words to Arjuna in The Bhagavad Gita: *'Whatever you do, eat, offer an oblation, give as a gift, or undertake as a penance, offer all that to Me, O Arjuna.'*

1 Who was the Lord Krishna?
2 What is The Bhagavad Gita?
3 What is bhakti and how can you tell that Krishna is speaking here of the path of devotion?
4 Why do you think that the path of bhakti is the most popular of all those followed by Hindus?

B. A Hindu family shrine. What is the Hindu worshipper expected to do after he or she has offered puja in front of the god?

Lakshmi or any of the thousands of other gods on offer. Those following the path of devotion want to have an image of their chosen god close to them and so they set up their own personal shrine in their home (see Photograph B). The ishvara represents some aspect of the Supreme Spirit to them.

The worshipper who is following the path of bhakti needs to have a deep faith in and love for his or her personal god, and to live a life based on:

- Keeping God at the front of the mind at all times – bowing in front of the statue and chanting God's name at every possible opportunity.
- Rejoicing every time there is an opportunity to hear the praises of God being sung.
- Serving God by offering puja (worship) in front of the shrine before going out to serve others selflessly.

The final goal of bhakti is to be so close to God that the human soul (atman) can gently merge with the spirit of God. This state, once reached, is one of perfect joy in which the soul will never be reborn. It will remain in union (oneness) with God for evermore.

FOR YOUR FOLDER

1 In the ways in which Hinduism encourages followers to reach God it is very different to Christianity, Judaism and Islam. Each of these religions offers one way to God and no other. Hinduism encourages its followers to choose the way that is best suited to them. Can you think of two advantages and two disadvantages for Hinduism in allowing this freedom of choice to its followers?

2 Explain the difference between sin (an act of wrongdoing against God) and maya.

3 Describe, in your own words: maya, the four paths, and bhakti.

In the glossary: Atman; Bhakti; Brahman; Dharma; Guru; Ishvara; Jnana; Karma; Lakshmi; Maya; Moksha; Puja; Rama; Sadhana; Shiva; Vishnu; Yoga.

The Path of Karma

What is karma and how does it affect the life of each person?

FOCUSING QUESTIONS

What are the ways in which the word 'karma' is used by Hindus?

How does the law of karma operate?

How can the law of karma be used to explain pain and suffering in this life?

The idea of karma is a very important one in Hinduism. There are two different ways in which the word can be used:

- Karma can cover every physical action – whether it is walking, running, sleeping, working, eating or thinking. It embraces everything that a person does, whether that action is a good one or a bad one.
- Karma can describe the total effect that a person's actions have on the world, on other people, and on themselves.

Usually both of these meanings are included in the word when it is used by a Hindu. The law of karma simply states that everything a person does in this life – in thought, word or deed – determines what happens to him or her in all future existences. There is no way that anyone can escape from this law and the way that it operates.

From the scriptures

In The Upanishads, one of the Hindu holy books, Yama, the god of death, states the belief of rebirth in this way:
'Well then...I shall tell you about this profound and eternal Brahman, and also about what happens to the Atman after meeting death. Some souls enter the womb for the purpose of re-embodiment and some enter into stationary objects – according to their work and according to their knowledge.'

1. After death, according to this quotation, the souls have two possible destinations. What are they?
2. What do you think this quotation means by *'stationary objects'*? Give two examples of *'stationary objects'*.
3. What part does karma play in deciding what happens to the soul after the body dies?

A. This person has a disability. How would a Hindu explain what has happened to him?

B. A low-caste leather worker's home in India. How would the law of karma explain the work that this man does?

DISCUSS

1 Do you think that every human action provides good or evil 'fruits'? Explain your answer.

2 What do you think about karma as a way of explaining suffering in the world? Does it always produce a convincing explanation?

3 Do you think that the law of karma offers comfort to people as an explanation of their present situation?

Hindus believe that every human action produces its own good or evil fruits. This means that a person's future life or lives will be decided by their karma now. It also means that, to some extent, a person's karma in this, and future lives is determined by karma from previous lives.

Pain and suffering

The law of karma is used by Hindus to explain many things. Hindus believe that pain, suffering and any kind of misfortune that a person experiences, has not been imposed on them by God – as some religions suggest. They are not even due to the actions of someone else, even though that may be their immediate cause. They are the result of a person's evil karma from a past existence. A person who, for instance, is born with a disability has suffered this misfortune because of the bad karma which has built up in a previous life.

Other lives

In common with Buddhists, Hindus do not think that this life is the end. Samsara (the whole process of rebirth or reincarnation) is based upon the assumption that everything living is subject to an almost limitless series of rebirths. All forms of life – human, animal or vegetable – are caught up in this process. The end of one life on this Earth simply heralds the beginning of another, and this new life will carry forward the inevitable consequences of karma. In this cycle of rebirths, reincarnation may take place at a lower or higher level than that enjoyed in a present existence. What determines the nature of the next rebirth is the law of karma. Inequalities brought about by birth, such as the caste that a person is born into, are explained, and justified by the law of karma which cannot be broken.

FOR YOUR FOLDER

1 The law of karma is one of the four paths that a Hindu can choose to take towards breaking the cycle of rebirths and reuniting with Brahman.

a) What do Hindus understand by the law of karma?

b) How do you think that a Hindu might use this particular path to reach his or her final 'liberation'?

c) Why do you think that few Hindus actually do choose the path of karma?

d) What makes the law of karma so difficult as a means of reaching liberation?

2 Many people say that a belief in karma locks Hindus into adopting a fatalistic attitude to life.

a) What is fatalism and how would you describe a fatalistic attitude to life?

b) Why should a belief in karma make people fatalistic?

c) What are the main arguments that can be put forward in favour of or against a belief in karma?

In the glossary: BRAHMAN; CASTE; KARMA; REINCARNATION; SAMSARA.

The Path of Jnana

What *is the path of jnana and why are very few Hindus able to follow it to salvation?*

FOCUSING QUESTIONS

What is jnana?

What place does a study of The Vedas and The Upanishads play in jnana?

What is the link is between the four ashramas and jnana?

Jnana, the path of knowledge or realisation, is the hardest, steepest and most difficult of all the paths to moksha (liberation) for someone to tread. Anyone who wishes to walk along this path must have a learned teacher (a guru), since it involves studying, and understanding the very difficult ideas in the smriti group of holy books – The Vedas and The Upanishads.

Following the path of knowledge

The Vedas and The Upanishads deal with the idea of the Supreme Spirit (Brahman); the individual soul, the nature of the universe in which human beings live, and the place that all human beings have in that universe. To follow the path of knowledge a man (few women have even attempted to walk this path) must study the sacred scriptures at great depth, since it is only through a knowledge of them that a person can free themself from an attachment to all material things. Such a study demands dedication and commitment. A person can only 'move on' to a higher spiritual level when they have broken their 'attachment' to the illusion (maya) that material things are part of the real world. They are not. Brahman alone is real. Everything else is illusion and blocks the way to God.

As a person tries to follow the path of knowledge, so they lose their attachment to things and people. They cease to care about them. They begin to use knowledge to help them to distinguish between what is real and what only appears to be real. If they try really hard they will find their real self, the atman, which amounts to finding Brahman. The white cow is held to be sacred by all Hindus since it is a symbol of the real self – the atman.

The four stages

The four stages (the ashramas) are particularly important for those people who are hoping to be freed from the cycle of death and rebirth by treading the path of knowledge. It all begins with the student stage when the foundations are laid – the thirst for learning and the building of a strong moral character. During the second stage, that of the householder, the quest for liberation is temporarily put 'on hold', as other concerns take its place.

A. Can you explain why this cow is regarded by Hindus as being particularly sacred and important?

B. If this old man is following the path of jnana what must he do to reach salvation?

Stage three, which begins when the first grandchild is born, is called vanaprastha (meaning 'retirement as a hermit to search for the truth') and marks the serious beginning of the search for union with Brahman. The vast majority of Hindus do not reach stage three. A mere handful go on to stage four – the stage of the sadhu, the holy man. For those who do advance to this stage the advice in The Laws of Manu is that the person must give no thought at all to the future and show himself to be totally 'indifferent' (see FROM THE SCRIPTURES) to the present. To show the world around that they have renounced it totally sadhus shave their heads and remove their sacred threads. Very few women have ever reached this stage.

FOR YOUR FOLDER

1
a) What is a sadhu?
b) Why do you think that so few people become sadhus?
c) What is the attitude of sadhus towards material things and members of their family?
d) Why do you think that holy men and women are expected to have this attitude?
e) Do you have any sympathy with the idea that material things, and even personal relationships, are not the real things in life?

2 In most Hindu extended families children are expected to look after their ageing parents until they die. What do you think that becoming a sadhu and turning one's back on the family does to the sadhu and to the family?

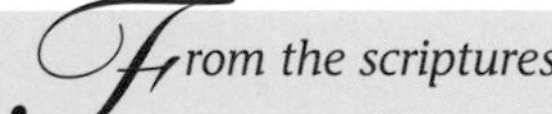

From the scriptures

This description of the life to be followed by the holy man or woman, the sadhu, comes from The Laws of Manu:
'Take no thought of the future and look with indifference upon the present. Departing from his house fully provided with the means of purification let him wander about absolutely silent and caring nothing for the enjoyments that may be offered to him. Let him always wander along, without any companion, in order to attain final freedom...he shall neither possess a fire, nor a dwelling, he may go into a village for his food but be indifferent to everything...Coarse worn-out garments, life in solitude and indifference towards everything, are the marks of one who has attained liberation...'.

1 Those who reach the stage of being sadhus are told that they must be '*indifferent*' to every material object. What do you think that it means in practice to be '*indifferent*' to something?
2 The advice is based upon the understanding that the sadhu must concentrate his or her mind totally on Brahman – and turn away from everything that would be a distraction. What aspects of modern life, in particular, do you think might act as a distraction to the sadhu?

In the glossary: Ashrama; Atman; Brahman; Guru; Jnana; Laws of Manu; Maya; Sacred Thread; Sadhu; Smriti; Upanishads; Vedas.

The Path of Yoga

What is yoga and why is it a very important way of approaching God?

FOCUSING QUESTIONS

What is the fourth, and final, path to liberation?

What does the final path help a human being accomplish so that he or she can reach moksha?

What does the word 'yoga' mean, and what does it involve?

The word 'yoga' comes from the Sanskrit word 'yuj' meaning 'to join or concentrate'. Yoga is one of the ways through which Hindus seek to release their soul and reunite it with God. By practising meditation Hindus surrender themselves to God by controlling their thoughts and their bodies. During meditation, they often find it helpful to chant the sacred syllable for God – AUM.

The eight steps

Raja yoga ('the kingly path') is the final of the four paths which can lead the Hindu to final reunion with Brahman and so break the cycle of birth, death and rebirth. It accepts the fact that life, for most people, becomes cluttered with things to do and problems to solve. Raja yoga offers a way to clear the head and calm the thoughts by following eight consecutive steps.

A. A person meditating in the Lotus position. Why do you think that people meditating are not encouraged to close their eyes, as Christians do when they are praying?

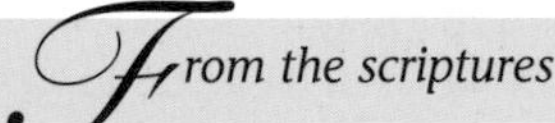

From the scriptures

The Bhagavad Gita underlines the Hindu belief that our attitude towards other people and God begin in the mind: *'The one whose mind views friends, comrades and enemies in the same way is outstanding.'*

1 What point do you think this quotation from The Bhagavad Gita is making?
2 Do you think that it is right?

Step one
Yama ('self-control') – this means that the person abstains from those things that are harmful and follows a life of compassion (ahimsa), speaking the truth (satya), celibacy (brahmacharya) and the rejection of greed and theft. This is the first, and very necessary, step on the pathway to moksha – reunion with God.

B. A Hindu sadhu meditates on the bank of the River Ganges, India. This person has reached the samadhi stage of meditation. How close are they to moksha?

Step two
Niyama ('observances') – this includes adopting pure and positive attitudes so that relationships with others and with God deepen and grow. If the first step was mainly concerned with abstinence, then the second calls on the worshipper to adopt a positive attitude towards God, others and his or her own life.

Step three
Asana ('positions for posture') – there are eighty-six different positions for the body to adopt during meditation. The Lotus position (see Photograph A) involves keeping the eyes half open and focusing on the nose or stomach. This allows the person to concentrate on meditation without distraction. From this position a person can begin to control their breathing which is essential for the next step.

Stage four
Pranayama ('controlled breathing') – for Hindus there is a very close link between a person's ability to control their breathing patterns and their ability to meditate on higher things.

Step five
Pratyahara ('being alone') – this stage is one of withdrawing the mind from things so that a person has complete mastery over the senses of touch, smell and hearing.

Step six
Dharana ('concentration') – mastering the mind so that it can be fixed on one divine thing rather than being allowed to wander from subject to subject.

Step seven
Dhyana ('meditation') – allowing the mind to have an unbroken flow of concentration on an object, so losing all sense of time and space.

Step eight
Samadhi ('contemplation') – this allows the person to appreciate the true nature of the object being contemplated, without being distracted by their own thoughts. Here the person discovers their real self, the atman, away from their normal worries and cares. Here the self exists in a state of complete isolation, like a lotus flower in a dirty pond, untouched by the dirt around. The next, and last stage is moksha – liberation.

FOR YOUR FOLDER

1 Write two sentences about each of the following: yama; niyama; asana; pranayama; pratyahara; dharana; dhyana; samadhi.

2 The fourth path, the way of yoga, is a very popular path to moksha. Why do you think that so many Hindus find that it offers them a real hope of reaching liberation?

3 Pursue the idea of a link between the control of one's breathing and the ability to meditate and clear the mind of all material matters and concerns. Discuss why many religions teach that people have to control their own bodies before they can hope to meditate successfully on God.

In the glossary: Ahimsa; Asana; AUM; Bhagavad Gita; Brahman; Celibacy; Dharana; Dhyana; Moksha; Niyama; Pranayama; Pratyahara; Samadhi; Sanskrit; Satya; Yama; Yoga.

Ahimsa

What do Hindus mean by ahimsa and how is the belief applied in Hinduism?

FOCUSING QUESTIONS

What is ahimsa?

What principle did Mahatma Gandhi adopt in his protest against the British Government in India?

Which element in Hinduism caused Gandhi deep unhappiness?

Hindus believe that Gautama Buddha (560 BCE – 480 BCE) was the ninth avatar of the god Vishnu. The Buddha, whose teachings gave birth to Buddhism, was one of the many Indian religious teachers who taught the doctrine of ahimsa.

Respect for life

In Sanskrit the word 'himsa' means killing or injury so 'ahimsa' is 'non-killing' or 'non-injury'. Along with truth and honesty, ahimsa is a very important everyday virtue which Hindus are expected to follow. By living by this principle Hindus express their respect and love for every form of life – birds, insects, animals, fish and human beings. To live by ahimsa a Hindu must give up every action which can lead to the spilling of blood or the taking of life. He or she must also avoid eating the flesh of any animal or insect.

Two important elements are involved for every Hindu who lives by the principle of ahimsa:

- to avoid causing any harm to other forms of life. For some Hindus this means that they do not intervene when they see other people causing harm, as long as they are not the direct cause.
- to avoid the shedding of blood or the taking of life. This does not extend to behaviour (such as greed) which might directly cause suffering for others.

At the heart of the Hindu's belief in ahimsa lies, of course, the belief in reincarnation. Hindus believe that they can be reincarnated in any form, and so it makes sense to treat those who have already done so with a large measure of respect.

From the scriptures

According to The Laws of Manu: *'a brahmin should make daily offerings, observe ahimsa, tell the truth, eradicate anger, and be trustworthy...'.*

How difficult do you think that it would be for a person to do all of the things listed in this extract? Do you think that a strongly held faith would help? If so, explain how.

A. What lies at the heart of the Hindu concern for all forms of life?

B. Gandhi leading the salt protest. In 1930, Gandhi launched a satyagraha against the Indian Government's monopoly of salt production – *'a commodity that was absolutely essential for poor Indians'*. Find out about another protest which Gandhi led against the authorities – and why the weapon of non-violence was so effective.

Mahatma Gandhi

The man who came to be known as Mahatma ('Great Soul') Gandhi was born in India in 1869. He became one of India's greatest political and religious leaders. He led the struggle for Indian independence from British rule by stressing non-cooperation and non-violence (ahimsa). He believed that this policy was capable of paralysing one of the most powerful governments on Earth – and he was right.

Gandhi believed that all resistance to authority should be based upon satyagraha (meaning 'truth-force') – a religious principle which he claimed to have learned from his wife. There are four elements to satyagraha :

- Truth. The cause must be a true one.
- Non-violence. Any form of protest is legitimate as long as it does not involve violence in any way.
- Self-control.
- Sacrifice.

The British soon realised that they were powerless against this non-violent form of protest.

Although Gandhi was a Hindu, he was interested in many religions – he studied The Bible as well as the teachings of Buddha – and was often critical of Hinduism. He was particularly unhappy about the Hindu teaching about 'untouchability' which he called *'a blot on Hindu religion'*. Gandhi renamed those people who belonged to the lowest 'untouchable' caste – Harijans, meaning 'Children of God'. He also fought for Hindu-Muslim unity.

FOR YOUR FOLDER

Here are two quotations from Mahatma Gandhi. Look at them carefully:

'What I want to achieve – what I have been striving and pining to achieve these thirty years – is self-realisation, to see God face to face, to attain moksha.'

'Man's ultimate aim is the realisation of God, and all his activities, political, social and religious, have to be guided by the ultimate aim of the vision of God...If I could persuade myself that I should find him in a Himalayan cave I would proceed there immediately. But I know that I cannot find him apart from humanity.'

a) What are the four paths by which Hinduism teaches that men can find God?
b) Do Gandhi's comments here suggest that he is hopeful of finding God by using one of these paths?
c) If not, which path does Gandhi hope will lead him to his ultimate aim of the *'vision of God'*?
d) What is the one ingredient which Gandhi accepts as being necessary in his quest for the *'vision of God'*?

In the glossary: AHIMSA; AVATAR; HARIJANS; REINCARNATION; SANSKRIT; VISHNU.

A

Agni The god of fire.

Ahimsa The belief in non-violence and respect for all forms of life.

Anyesti The funeral ceremony.

Asana The bodily position adopted for meditation.

Ashrama One of four stages in life.

Atharva Veda One of the four ancient books, The *Vedas*.

Atman The energy in every form of life, called the 'soul'.

AUM The sacred syllable.

Avatar The descent of a Hindu god to Earth.

B

Bhagavad Gita Meaning 'Song of the Lord'. The most popular of the Hindu scriptures.

Bhakti Love or devotion – an attitude of love towards God gained by reading the ancient books.

Brahma The Hindu creator-god; part of the *trimurti*.

Brahma Granthi The holy knot used during a sacred thread ceremony.

Brahman The Supreme Spirit, the holy power in the whole universe.

Brahmanas Hindu texts which are commentaries on The *Vedas*.

Brahmin The first of the four *varnas* from which priests are drawn.

C

Caste A division based upon a person's occupation within a *varna*. In recent years attempts have been made to dismantle this system , and during the government of V.P. Singh (1989-1990) a Reservation Policy was put into place, which reserved government jobs for members of the lower castes.

Celibacy A person's decision to live without sexual relationships. A married person can still choose this lifestyle.

D

Dassehra A festival at the end of the Autumn honouring the goddess *Durga*. Some Hindus celebrate this as Vijaya Dashami, which celebrates the victory of *Rama* over *Ravana*.

Dharana The beginning of meditation.

Dharma The religious or moral duty of a Hindu.

Dhoti A cotton garment worn to cover the lower part of the body.

Dhyana An important stage in meditation.

Divali The 'Festival of Lights', marking the end of the old year and the beginning of the new.

Dukkha Hindu teaching about suffering.

Durga A goddess and the wife of *Shiva*. Also called Parvati or Kali.

Durga Puja *See* **Navaratri.**

F

Fasting Going without food or drink for religious reasons.

G

Ganesha A Hindu god with the head of an elephant.

Ganges India's main river, considered sacred by Hindus.

Garbhagriha The inner room of a Hindu temple – the holiest part where the image of the god is installed.

Gayatri Mantra A hymn from the *Rig Veda*.

Guru A holy man, woman or teacher in Hinduism.

H

Harijans The name given to the 'untouchable' *caste* by Gandi, meaning 'children of God'.

Havan A form of worship involving a fire offering.

Hermit Someone who lives a totally solitary existence to seek God.

Holi The Spring festival of *Krishna*.

I

Indra The god of war, rain and thunder.

Ishvara A personal god worshipped by a Hindu in his or her own home.

J

Jnana One of the four paths to liberation, achieved by direct personal knowledge of God.

K

Kali *See* **Durga.**

Karma 'Action' or 'deed'. The actions that we do have an effect on us in this life – and the next.

Krishna One of the most popular of all Hindu gods, an *avatar* of *Vishnu*.

Kshatriya The second of four *varnas* – the ruling and warrior class.

Kumbha Mela A Hindu festival.

L

Lakshmi The goddess of fortune, and the wife of *Vishnu*.

Laws of Manu A code of behaviour attributed to Manu, the first man. Also called the Manusmriti.

M

Mahabharata The longest of the Hindu epic poems, and part of the sacred scriptures.

Mandala A symbolic diagram to indicate wholeness or perfection.

Mandir A Hindu temple.
Mantra A sacred formula or chant.
Maya The illusion that the world is real.

Meditation A spiritual exercise to centre the thoughts on God.
Moksha Final liberation from the cycle of rebirths, ending in reunion with *Brahman.*
Monotheism The belief in one God.

N

Navaratri A nine-day Hindu Autumn festival which precedes *Dassehra.*
Niyama A term used in *yoga* for observance of the rules of self-discipline – calm, study, prayer, etc.

P

Parvati *See* **Durga.**
Pranayama The control of the breath during *yoga.*
Prashad A blessed offering distributed to worshippers at the end of a *puja.*
Pratyahara The shutting out of the outside world during *yoga.*
Puja An act of worship.

R

Rama The hero of the epic The *Ramayana,* and one of the *avatars* of *Vishnu.*
Ramayana An epic poem which tells the story of *Rama* and *Sita.*
Ravana The demon-king of Sri Lanka, said to have had ten heads and twenty arms.
Reincarnation A belief that the soul survives death and is reborn in another form.
Rig Veda The first, the most ancient, and the most sacred, of the four ancient books, The *Vedas.*

S

Sacred thread A thread placed upon shoulder of Hindu boy when he becomes an adult.
Sadhana A course of spiritual discipline designed to lead to a fulfilment of life.
Sadhu A holy man or woman.
Sama Veda One of the four ancient books, The *Vedas.*
Samadhi Intense concentration during *yoga.*
Samsara The world – the place where the cycle of death and rebirth occurs.
Samskara The ceremonies associated with the life-cycle. The most important is the *sacred thread* ceremony.
Sanskrit The ancient language of India, used for Hindu scriptures.
Saraswati The wife of the creator-god *Brahma* and the inventor of the *Sanskrit* language.
Satya Truth.
Shiva One of the greatest Hindu gods who forms the *trimurti* with *Brahma* and *Vishnu.*
Shraddha The rituals performed by a Hindu after death.
Shudras The lowest of the four *varnas* in Hindu society.
Shruti Meaning 'that which is remembered'. This includes books such as The *Bhagavad Gita* which were remembered by holy men and written down.
Sita The wife of *Rama,* one of the main characters in The *Ramayana.*
Smriti Meaning 'that which was heard' – holy books transmitted to holy men by God and faithfully recorded by them.
Suttee Meaning 'good woman'. The practice, now outlawed, of a woman throwing herself on the body of her dead husband and perishing with him on the funeral pyre.

T

Trimurti Meaning 'three deities'. This refers to *Brahma, Vishnu* and *Shiva* who are believed to control the three gunas (goodness, passion and ignorance, which together form absolute reality). The trimurti should not be compared to the concept of Christian 'trinity'.

U

Untouchables The men and women without a *varna. See also* **Harijans.**
Upanayana The term for the *sacred thread* ceremony.
Upanishads Meaning 'to sit down near a teacher'. The holy book derived from sessions where disciples sat at the feet of their *gurus* listening.

V

Vaishya The third of the four *varnas* – devoted to commerce and industry.
Varanasi The most sacred pilgrimage destination of Hindu pilgrims.
Varna Meaning 'colours'. The four categories into which Hindu society is traditionally divided – white (*brahmins*), red (*kshatriyas*), yellow (*vaishyas*), and black (*shudras*).
Varuna The god of order in old Hindu myths.
Vedas Meaning 'knowledge'. The *Vedas* are made up of four books – the *Rig Veda*, the *Sama Veda*, the *Yajur Veda* and the *Atharva Veda*, which date from between 1500 and 800 BCE.
Vegetarian A person who does not eat the flesh of any living creature.
Vishnu The 'preserver' – associated with *Brahma* and *Shiva* in the *trimurti.*

Y

Yajur Veda One of the four ancient books, The *Vedas.*
Yama Self-control during *yoga.*
Yoga A spiritual exercise that combines physical and mental disciplines.

What is Judaism?

Who are the Jews?

FOCUSING QUESTIONS

What makes a person a Jew?

What is a non-Jew called?

Where does the word 'Jew' came from?

Jewish tradition teaches that a child born to a Jewish mother is a Jew – without anything else being taken into consideration. This means that a child born to a Jewish father and a non-Jewish (Gentile) mother is not a Jew – even if that person goes to the synagogue every week and keeps most of the Jewish traditions. On the other hand the son of a Jewish mother and a non-Jewish father is a Jew even if he is brought up in another religion and knows little about the Jewish faith.

The English word 'Jew' comes from the Hebrew word 'Jehudi' (meaning 'from the tribe of Judah'). Judah, the son of Jacob, gave his name to one of the twelve tribes of the Israelites. By the tenth century BCE, the twelve tribes had split into two kingdoms – the Northern Kingdom of ten tribes, called 'Israel', and the Southern Kingdom of two tribes, called 'Judah'. In 721 BCE the Assyrians conquered Israel and the people there were taken into captivity. From this time onwards all of the people, wherever they lived, adopted the name 'Judah', and from this grew the tradition of calling them 'Jews'.

PRAYER FOR THE
ROYAL FAMILY

He Who giveth salvation unto kings and dominion unto princes, Whose kingdom is an everlasting kingdom – may He bless

Our Sovereign Lady, Queen Elizabeth,
Elizabeth the Queen Mother,
Philip, Duke of Edinburgh,
Charles, Duke of Cornwall
and all the Royal Family.

May the supreme King of kings in His mercy preserve the Queen in life, guard her, and deliver her from all trouble and sorrow. May He put a spirit of wisdom and understanding into her heart and into the hearts of all her counsellors, that they may uphold the peace of the realm, advance the welfare of the nation, and deal kindly and truly with all Israel. In her days and in ours, may our Heavenly Father spread the tabernacle of peace over all the dwellers on earth; and may the redeemer come unto Zion; and let us say, Amen.

A. A prayer to the British Royal Family inscribed on a synagogue wall. Jewish people are found in almost every country in the world. In synagogues in Britain a prayer for the Royal Family is inscribed on the wall to show the loyalty of the Jewish community. Why do you think that this is thought to be so important?

Who are the Jews?

This is a difficult question to answer. There are four possible answers:

1 The Jews are a race of people. The Nazis in Germany in the 1930s were fanatically committed to the view that the Jews were an inferior race and this gave them the 'excuse' they needed to slaughter 6,000,000 of them between 1939 and 1945. Yet the Jews are not one race. Jews are found in every continent of the world, and share common racial characteristics with their fellow-countrymen whether they are Jews or not.

B. What names are given to those Jews who wish to leave the old traditions just as they are and those who wish to see some changes made?

2 The Jews are a 'religious community'. While many Jews have very strong religious views, there are many who do not believe in God at all. Those Jews without a religious belief (called 'secular Jews') are still proud of their 'Jewishness'.

3 The Jews are a nation. This cannot be an accurate description since only about 25 per cent of the world's Jews live in Israel, the only Jewish nation in the world. In Israel itself just over 3,000,000 Jews share Israeli citizenship with thousands of Christians and Muslims. In fact, at 5,000,000 plus, there are considerably more Jews in the USA than there are in Israel.

4 The Jews are a people. This is the most helpful, and accurate, description since it includes all Jews – those who live in Israel, and elsewhere, those who believe strongly in the one God of Abraham and Moses, and those who do not, those who keep the religious traditions faithfully, and those who rarely set foot inside a synagogue.

Having said this, however, it is religion which has helped Jews to keep their unique identity 'as a people' over the centuries. The Jewish faith has remained virtually the same for over 3,000 years. The Jewish community is however divided between those people who want to leave this faith untouched (called Orthodox Jews) and those who wish to make some changes (called Reform Jews).

FOR YOUR FOLDER

1 Explain, in your own words, the difficulties of speaking of:
a) The Jewish race.
b) The Jewish nation.
c) The Jewish religious community.

Why does it seem more helpful, and accurate, to speak of 'the Jewish people'?

2 Read this quotation through carefully:
'There is a river in the ocean. In the severest droughts it never fails, in the mightiest floods it never overflows. The Gulf of Mexico is its fountain and its mouth is in the Arctic seas. It is the Gulf Stream. Its waters are so distinctly marked that their line of junction with the sea-water may be traced by the eye. There seems to be a reluctance on the part of the waters of the Gulf Stream to mingle with the waters of the sea. There is a lonely river in the midst of the ocean of mankind. The fiercest fires of human cruelty have never caused it to dry up, although its waves for more than 2,000 years have rolled red with the blood of its martyrs, in Rome, in Greece, in Spain, in Russia, in Germany. The line which divides its billows from the ordinary waters of humanity is also plainly visible to the eye. It is the Jewish race.'

(By Hazel Broch. Quoted in 'Religion in the Multi-Faith School', edited by W. Owen Cole, published by Stanley Thornes and Hulton Educational, London. 1983.)

By drawing a comparison between the Gulf Stream and the Jewish people what important point is the writer making about Jews?

IN THE GLOSSARY: ABRAHAM; GENTILE; ISRAEL; ISRAELITES; JUDAH; MOSES; ORTHODOX JEW; REFORM JEW; SYNAGOGUE.

Abraham

Who was Abraham and why was he so important to the history of Judaism?

FOCUSING QUESTIONS

What happened to Abram in Ur which was to change the whole course of his life?

How did Abram show his devotion and dedication to God?

What is brit milah, and what does it signify?

The history of the Jews, or Hebrews as they were first called, is found in the Jewish Scriptures. The opening book of those Scriptures begins with a description of how the universe, the world, animals and human beings were created by God. Then it introduces us to the first Patriarch ('father-figure') of the Jewish people – Abraham (Abram).

Abraham's journey

Abram was born in Ur of the Chaldees (near the Persian Gulf) which, at the time, was a major centre for the worship of the Moon. Abram however rejected the gods that other people around him worshipped and came to believe in the one true God. We do not know how this happened, but Jewish tradition insists that it only came at the end of many years of searching by Abram for the truth. Around 1800 BCE, Abram made a covenant (agreement) with this God and was promised that his descendants would form the beginning of a new nation. In response to this promise Abram uprooted his family and travelled to Haran, and then on towards Canaan (the Promised Land, later called Palestine) where God made it clear to Abram that he would protect all of his descendants. (See Map A.)

A little later God – understood by Abram to be 'El Shaddai' (the Almighty) – repeated his earlier promise that Abram's descendants would be numerous. Abram was totally overwhelmed and bowed his face to the ground. To underline God's promise Abram's name was changed to Abraham – which means 'the father of many nations'.

A. A map showing the journey taken by Abraham and his family. Why did Abraham undertake the journey from Ur to Haran – and then on later to Canaan?

Circumcision

God repeated his promise to Abraham to give to him, and his descendants, the land of Canaan and told him to circumcise all the males in his household – including himself. In circumcision the foreskin, the loose skin at the end of the penis, is cut off. Nowadays most Jewish fathers do not carry out the circumcision themselves but they employ a mohel to carry out the 'brit milah' (covenant of cutting) for them. It is performed on every Jewish boy when he is eight days old. During the ceremony the father says: *'Blessed are you Lord...who has commanded us to enter him into the covenant of Abraham, our Father.'*

Its link with Abraham makes circumcision the oldest of all Jewish customs which are still performed. Then, as now, circumcision is an eternal sign 'in the flesh' of belonging to the people that God has chosen.

Isaac

Fulfilling God's promise, Sarah, Abraham's wife, gave birth to a son, Isaac, although she was past childbearing age. God asked Abraham to sacrifice Isaac by but, having proved his obedience, God supplied a ram for Abraham to sacrifice. To this day, to commemorate this event, a ram's horn, called a shofar, (see Photograph B) is blown in the synagogue on the morning of the Jewish New Year, Rosh Hashanah. Jews down the centuries have been so impressed by Abraham's willingness to sacrifice his son that, in an old Jewish tale, a man says that he does not want his son to become a famous scholar or saint but 'a simple Jew like our father Abraham'.

Eventually, however severe famine forced Jacob, Abraham' s grandson, to take his descendants to Egypt where they became slaves for over 400 years.

B. When is the ram's horn blown in the synagogue, and why?

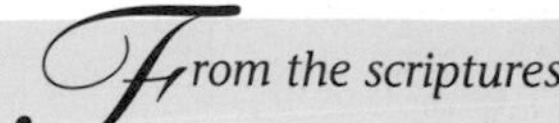

From the scriptures

This is how God's call to Abram is described in Genesis:
'Now the LORD said to Abram, "Go from your country and your kindred and your father's house to the land that I will show you. I will make you a great nation, and I will bless you, and make your name great, so that you will be a blessing. I will bless those who bless you, and the one who curses you I will curse; and in you all the families of the earth shall be blessed.'
(Genesis 12.1-3)

1 In this extract, what promises does God make to Abraham for the future?
2 Do you think that a Jew might feel that these promises have been fulfilled?

FOR YOUR FOLDER

1 Answer each of these questions in your own words:
a) What does Jewish tradition say about the time leading up to Abram's belief in the one, true God.
b) What did the agreement between God and Abram promise and why do you think that God repeated it?
c) What did Abram's new name symbolise?
d) Which is the oldest religious practice still carried out by Jews and what does it symbolise?

2 What is the link between Abraham, the story of Abraham's willingness to kill his son, the Jewish festival of Rosh Hashanah, and the scene shown in Photograph B?

3 Jews today look upon Abraham as the 'father of their people'. What do you think they mean by this description and what legacy did Abraham leave the Jewish people?

IN THE GLOSSARY: ABRAHAM; ABRAM; BRIT MILAH, HEBREWS; ISAAC; MOHEL; PALESTINE; PATRIARCH; PROMISED LAND; ROSH HASHANAH; SHOFAR; SYNAGOGUE.

Moses and the Exodus

How did the Israelites finally leave slavery in Egypt and what was the role played by Moses?

FOCUSING QUESTIONS

Why is Moses such an important figure in Jewish history?

How did Moses meet God whilst he was in Midian, and what he was told to do?

How was the pharaoh compelled to free the Israelites slaves?

Moses is an important figure in Judaism for two reasons. First, he led the Children of Israel (the Jews) out of Egyptian slavery to the very edge of the Promised Land (Canaan). Ever since Jews have re-lived the events of this journey, the Exodus, each year in their great festival of Pesach. Secondly, Moses was the teacher of the Torah (the Law), which he received from God on Mount Sinai. The Torah is often called by Jews 'the Torah of Moses'.

The life of Moses

According to Jewish tradition, soon after the birth of Moses, the Egyptian pharaoh, concerned that the Israelite slaves were becoming too numerous, decreed that every Israelite male child be put to death. Moses' mother hid him in the reeds of the River Nile to save him and it was here that he was found by the pharaoh's daughter. She adopted him as her son and he was brought up in the royal palace. When Moses grew up, however, he was horrified to see how his fellow Israelites were treated by their Egyptian task-masters. Seeing an Egyptian about to kill an Israelite Moses intervened and killed the Egyptian. As a result Moses was forced to leave Egypt and settle in Midian where he married. In a remarkable experience there, God spoke to him from a burning bush and told him to return to Egypt and demand that the Israelites be set free. Eventually, God told him, he would lead the Israelites to the land of Canaan, the land of their fathers.

FOR YOUR FOLDER

1 When the Israelites left Egypt they tasted freedom for the first time, since all of them had been born into slavery. Jewish people today call that night a 'leyl shimurim' – a night of watching for God and for the Children of Israel for ever. What do you think this means?

2 Before the Israelites were delivered from Egypt God made a series of promises to Moses. He said that: *'...I will free you from the burdens of the Egyptians and deliver you from slavery to them. I will redeem you with an outstretched arm and with mighty acts of judgement. I will take you as my people...I will bring you into the land that I swore to give to Abraham....'.* (Exodus 6.6-8)

a) There are five promises here altogether. What are they?
b) Every year, at Pesach, four cups of wine are drunk to correspond to the first four of the promises. Find out how the fifth promise is celebrated at Pesach.

A. This frieze shows the Israelites in the service of the pharaoh in Egypt. Why do you think that this period of slavery had such a profound effect on Jewish history?

The plagues

Moses did as God told him, but the pharaoh refused to let the Israelites go. To punish the pharaoh God sent ten plagues, of increasing severity upon the Egyptian people. After the last plague, the pharaoh begged the Israelites to leave. About 600,000 Israelite men, together with their families and livestock, left the country. They, and their ancestors, had been slaves there for 430 years.

The first thing that the Israelites did when they had left Egypt behind was to celebrate with a special meal – the Passover meal. This became the forerunner of the Jewish festival of Pesach. In his instructions for the meal God told Moses: *'...no foreigner shall eat of it, but any slave who has been purchased may eat of it after he has been circumcised...The whole congregation of Israel shall celebrate it.'* (Exodus 12.43, 44, 47.)

After the Israelites had left Egypt the pharaoh changed his mind and ordered his soldiers to pursue them. The Israelites were finally cornered on the shores of the Reed Sea (not the Red Sea) but God miraculously opened up a way through the waters so that the Israelites could pass through the waters to dry land. When the Egyptian soldiers tried to follow them, however, the waters closed up around them and the Egyptians were drowned. Moses led the Israelites in a song of victory.

THE TEN PLAGUES

1. The waters of the River Nile are 'turned to blood'.
2. A plague of frogs.
3. A plague of gnats.
4. A plague of flies.
5. Livestock are killed.
6. People and animals are covered in boils and sores.
7. Thunder and hail ruins crops.
8. A plague of locusts.
9. Darkness for three days.
10. All first born are killed.

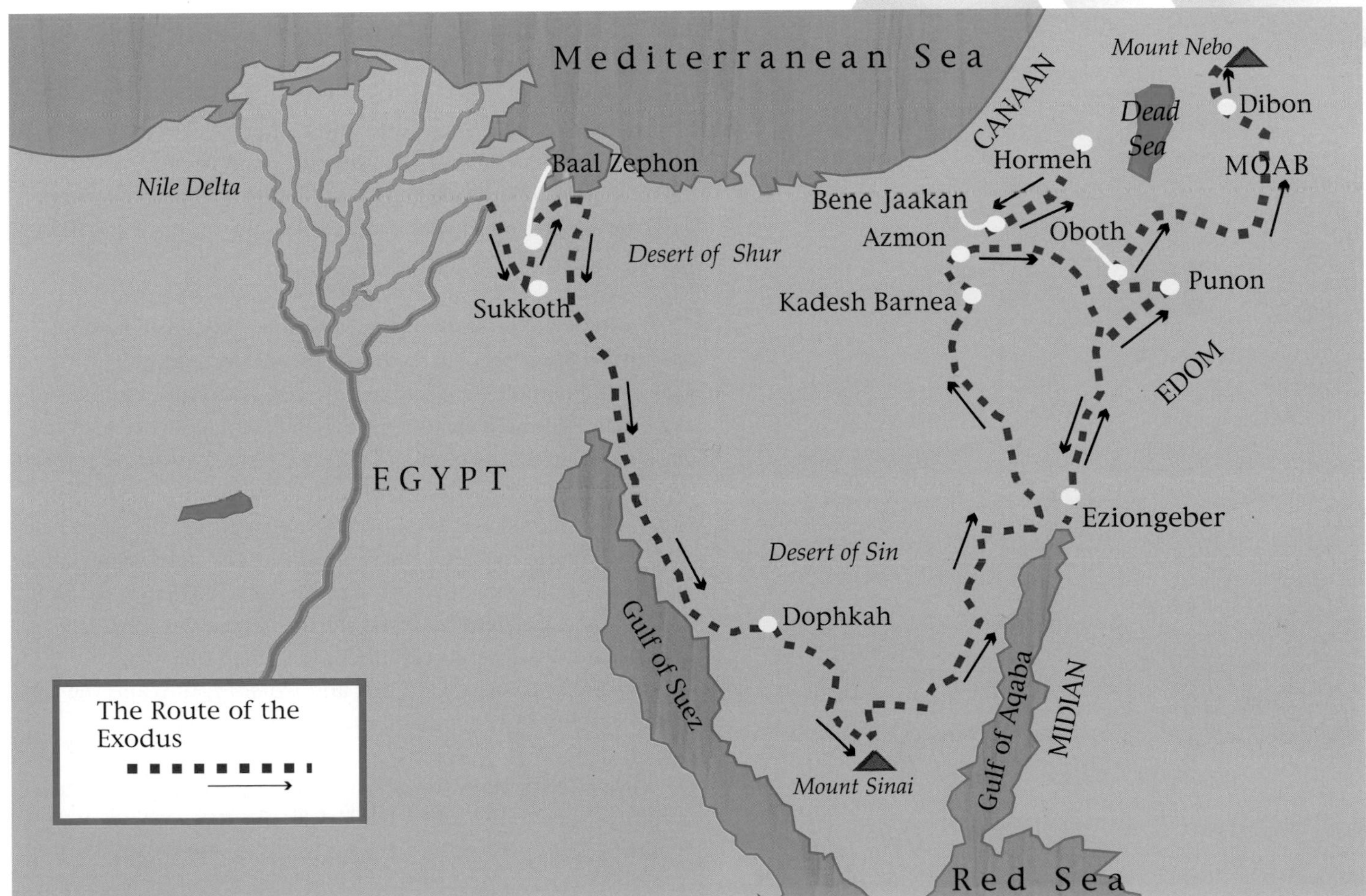

B. This map shows the route taken out of slavery towards the Promised Land. How does it show that God had many lessons to teach the Israelites on the journey?

IN THE GLOSSARY: CANAAN; EXODUS; MOSES; PESACH; PROMISED LAND; TORAH.

Moses and the Torah

What *happened to Moses on Mount Sinai and why is this event so important for all Jews?*

FOCUSING QUESTIONS

- What happened at Mount Sinai?
- What is the Torah?
- What are the Ten Sayings?

With Egypt behind them, the Israelites were optimistic that they could reach their Promised Land of Canaan quickly. According to the Jewish Scriptures, though, the journey took them forty years although this length of time need not be taken literally. The number could be a symbol for 'a very long time'.

Towards Mount Sinai

On their way to the Promised Land the Israelites camped at the foot of a mountain in the Sinai desert. The exact location of the mountain is unknown although local Bedouins have a tradition about a mountain that they call Jebel Musa – the mountain of Moses. According to Jewish Scriptures, what took place on the mountain is the most important event in Jewish history. Moses climbed up into the mountain to meet with God. For ancient people a mountain was always a place of mystery and fear – hence a suitable location in which to bring together the divine and the human.

The heart of the revelation that Moses received from God on Mount Sinai was the Ten Sayings – or the 'Ten Commandments'. These sayings are central to the teachings of the Torah, although the whole law-code which Moses received from God actually contains 613 laws. These laws can be found in Exodus 21-23; Leviticus 1-27 and Deuteronomy 5-31. They lay out the six fundamental human rights which lie at the heart of every civilised society: the right to life; the right to personal possessions; the right to clothing; the right to shelter; the right to work and the right to liberty. In the Ten Sayings two particular human responsibilities are spelled out – the responsibility to place God first and worship Him, and the responsibility to take care of one's neighbour.

Jews today look upon the Torah as God's greatest gift to them. Most of them still accept the need to live by its laws, although Reform Jews emphasise that some of the less important laws in the Torah no longer apply in modern times.

A. In almost all synagogues the first phrase of each of the Ten Sayings is to be found on the wall in Hebrew. Why do you think that this 'shorthand' version of the Ten Sayings is placed there?

B. The scroll of the Torah in use in a synagogue. What do Jews mean when they speak of the Torah?

The importance of the Torah

The Torah formed a covenant – a contract – between God and the Jewish people. Both sides were now bound by the terms of that contract. Moses became Moshe Rabbenu, Moses 'our teacher'. Tradition teaches that he received the whole Torah at one time from God and later wrote it down. The implication is that the Torah not only came from God but also existed from the beginning of creation. It marked the Jews out as God's people and gave to them all that they needed to know about God and their relationship with him. Anything that came later did not add to it but was simply a commentary on it. As a later prophet said: *'Remember the teaching of my servant Moses, the statutes and ordinances that I commanded him at Horeb* [Sinai] *for all Israel.'* (Malachi 4.4.)

FOR YOUR FOLDER

1 Some people argue that the Ten Sayings were designed to cope with a time of crisis in Jewish history. Other people say that they are suited to any group of people, and point to the fact that they have been used as the basis of many sets of moral and legal rules. Do you think that the Ten Sayings are a suitable basis for a community of people to live together happily? Could people realistically live by them, for instance, in this country?

2 A midrash is a short story which was told to put over an important truth. There is a midrash which portrays angels as moaning to God because it was Moses, and not they, who was given the honour of receiving the Ten Sayings from God. God told them that they had not been delivered from slavery and brought into freedom! Look at the Ten Sayings in Exodus 20.1-17 and explain what part you think over 400 years of slavery played in the ten laws that God gave to the Israelites. Look, in particular, at Exodus 20.2.

In the glossary: CANAAN; MOSES; PROMISED LAND; REFORM JEW; TEN SAYINGS; TORAH.

From the scriptures

The Ten Sayings are found in Exodus 20.1-17. This is a brief extract:

'...you shall have no other gods before me. You shall not make for yourself an idol...You shall not make wrongful use of the name of the Lord your God...Remember the sabbath day, and keep it holy...Honour your father and mother...You shall not murder...You shall not commit adultery...You shall not steal...You shall not bear false witness against your neighbour...You shall not covet your neighbour's house...'.

1 How does this set of rules show how important God is to the Jewish way of life?
2 What picture of God does the extract conjure up?
3 Why do you think that the Ten Sayings establish such a close link between honouring God and looking after one's neighbour? What does this suggest to you about the way that the Jewish people worship God?

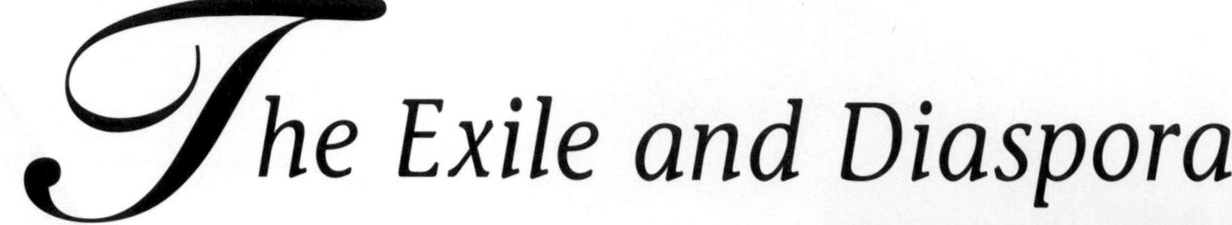

The Exile and Diaspora

What happened to the Israelites after they reached the Promised Land?

FOCUSING QUESTIONS

Who were the judges and what did they do?

Which king had a lasting effect on the Jewish people?

What do you understand by the word 'Diaspora'?

After forty years of nomadic life, the Jews crossed the River Jordan into the Promised Land of Canaan. They divided their new territory between the twelve tribes that had left Egypt, and each of the tribes established their own 'high place' (sanctuary) where God was worshipped. Each of the areas was ruled over by a 'judge'. These judges, including Gideon, Samson and Deborah, were really military leaders and, in the main, they managed to keep the various tribes safe against outside threats. Occasionally, though, enemies arose, like the Philistines, who were too powerful to be dealt with by a single tribe. This threat led to the tribes uniting and appointing their first king – Saul.

The time of the kings

Saul dealt with the menace of the Philistines but it was the second king, David, who was to make such a huge impression on the Jewish faith. David conquered the city of Jerusalem and set up his headquarters there. An enormous amount of feeling and emotion has been directed towards this city by Jews down the centuries. In 1967, the city came under Jewish control and today it is shared, uneasily, between Jewish, Muslim and Christian holy places. Jewish tradition credits David with writing many of the Psalms which play an important part in Jewish worship. Under David's son, Solomon, the kingdom was strengthened and a magnificent Temple (today called 'the First Temple') was built in Jerusalem. On Solomon's death, however, the kingdom split – with ten tribes forming Israel in the north, and two tribes forming Judah in the south.

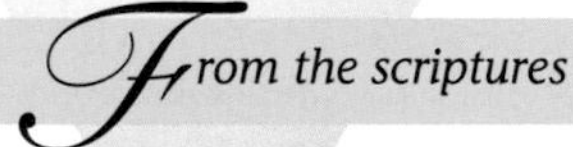

From the scriptures

These words were written by someone who was in exile in Babylon:
'By the rivers of Babylon – there we sat and there we wept when we remembered Zion [Jerusalem]. *On the willows there we hung up our harps. For there our captors asked us for songs, and our tormentors asked for mirth, saying, "Sing us one of the songs of Zion!"'*
(Psalm 137.1-3)

1 Why do you think that the remembrance of Jerusalem caused these exiles to weep and hang up their harps?
2 What do these verses tell you about the agonies of being in exile?
3 What do you think the Jews in exile missed most about their homeland?

Diaspora

In 722 BCE the Assyrians conquered Israel and deported the country's inhabitants. These people disappeared as a nation. In 586 BCE the Babylonians overran Judah and took many Jews to Babylonia. These people became known as the 'Diaspora' (the scattered ones) – a word which is used more than once in Jewish history. Despite being a scattered nation, these people retained their cultural identity. To people without a homeland, religion became an important means of maintaining this identity.

During the exile, men of God (prophets) explained to the people the riches that were to be found in the Torah. Prophets such as Isaiah, Jeremiah, Amos and Hosea denounced social inequalities and evil and condemned idolatry. Their job was to forth-tell (tell forth) God's will and so ensure that the exiled Jews did not forget their 'roots'.

When, in 538 BCE, King Cyrus Of Persia captured Babylonia, he allowed the exiled Jews to return home. Gradually they began to filter back to their homeland but, in 63 BCE, Israel fell under the domination of the Romans, who called it Palestine. The Jews drove out the Romans in 66CE, but in 70 CE the Romans recaptured the area, and Jerusalem and its Temple, were completely destroyed. A contemporary historian, Josephus, wrote that the destruction was so complete that *'not one stone was left standing on another'*. Soon there were many Jewish communities scattered throughout the Roman Empire and beyond. Jews did not return in large numbers to Israel until 1947.

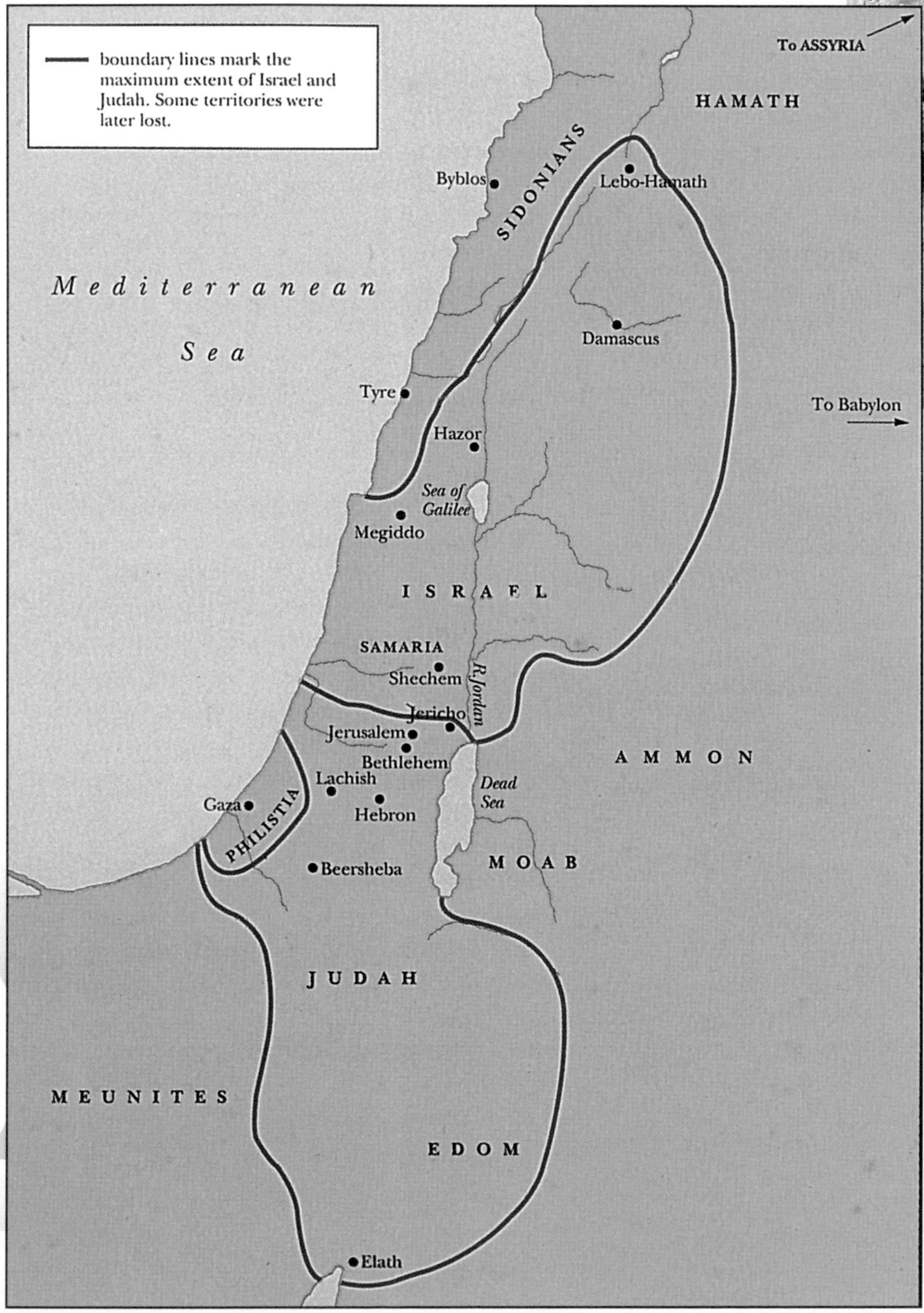

A. This map shows the kingdoms of Israel and Judah around 850BCE. What brought about this division into two countries?

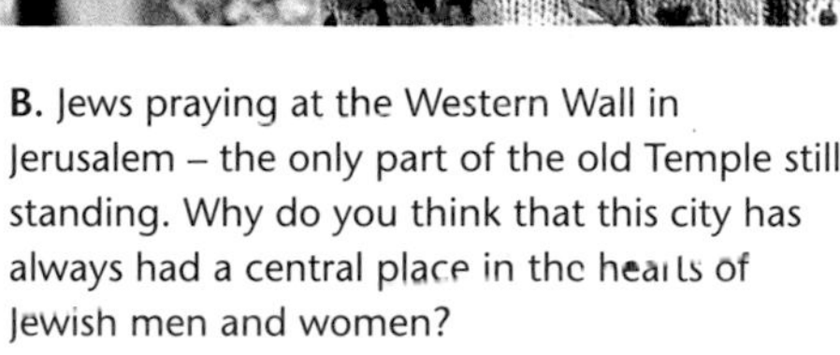

B. Jews praying at the Western Wall in Jerusalem – the only part of the old Temple still standing. Why do you think that this city has always had a central place in the hearts of Jewish men and women?

FOR YOUR FOLDER

1 When the Jews suffered their leaders said that it was God's judgement on them for breaking the covenant. Why do you think they said this rather than blaming it on God for letting them down?

2
- a) What was a prophet?
- b) What was the prophet's main task in Israel?
- c) Why do you think that God needed prophets to explain what He was doing and what He expected of the Israelites?
- d) What might have happened, do you think, in Israel if there had been no prophets to explain the ways of God?

In the glossary: David; Diaspora; Israel; Jerusalem; Judah; Judge; Palestine; Prophet; Psalms; Saul; Temple; Torah.

Antisemitism

What *is antisemitism and why has such hatred been directed against the Jews?*

FOCUSING QUESTIONS

What is antisemitism?

What is deicide, and why were the Jews accused of committing it?

How did the Christian reformer, Martin Luther, provide 'inspiration' for the Nazis in their attempt to eliminate all Jews?

Although the actual word 'antisemitism' (meaning a hatred of all things Jewish) was not coined until 1875 it is clear that such hatred has existed almost from the beginning of Judaism itself. Greek and Latin authors, for instance, ridiculed Jews as 'atheists' because they would not worship the ancient gods of Greece or Rome. One example of early antisemitism was the popular claim that the Israelites were driven out of Egyptian slavery because they were lepers. Another was that the Jews kept the Shabbat as one of total rest because they were too lazy to work.

The Christian Church and antisemitism

Most of the early followers of Jesus (the founder of the Christian faith) were Jews, and for some time the fledgling faith of Christianity remained as an off-shoot of Judaism. Distance grew between the two religions, however, when the new Church began to argue that it had replaced the Jews in the affections of God. Indeed, early Christians often accused the Jews of 'deicide' – the killing of Jesus, who they believed to be God in human form. Later Jews were accused of killing Christian babies and using their blood to make the unleavened bread which they used in the festival of Pesach. This charge, first made at Norwich in 1154, became known as the 'blood libel' and was the direct cause of thousands of Jews being put to death by 'Christian' mobs in the twelfth and thirteenth centuries. Then, during the time of the Black Death, in the fourteenth century, Jews were accused of poisoning the wells and bringing about the deaths of many Christians. All of these claims were, of course, nonsense.

A. What was 'deicide' and why were Jews accused of committing it?

Preis 30 Pfennig

Ritualmord-Nummer

Der Stürmer

Deutsches Wochenblatt zum Kampfe um die Wahrheit

HERAUSGEBER: JULIUS STREICHER

Sonder-Nummer 1 | Nürnberg, im Mai 1934 | 12. Jahr 1934

Jüdischer Mordplan

gegen die nichtjüdische Menschheit aufgedeckt

Das Mördervolk

Judenopfer

Durch die Jahrtausende vergoß der Jud, geheimem Ritus folgend, Menschenblut
Der Teufel sitzt uns heute noch im Nacken, es liegt an Euch die Teufelsbrut zu packen

Die Juden sind unser Unglück!

B. The front page from the infamous 'Der Stuermer', which shows the blood of the German people pouring onto the plates of the Jews. The editor, Julius Streicher, blamed all German misfortunes on the 'greed' of the Jews. What do you think was the purpose of such lies?

Antisemitism in Europe

By the Middle Ages antisemitism was rife throughout western Europe. The Crusaders slaughtered thousands of Jews, and by the thirteenth century Jews had been expelled from most countries in Western Europe. In the sixteenth century Martin Luther led the Reformation which broke the power of the Roman Catholic Church over Christians everywhere. To begin with Luther hoped that the Jews would be his allies in this by converting in large numbers to the Christian faith, but they showed no interest in doing so. In a fit of pique Luther wrote leaflets inciting Christian mobs to burn down Jewish synagogues and to show the Jewish people no mercy.

In the years that followed, Luther's wishes were put into practice. When the Nazis in Germany put their plan to eliminate the Jews ('the Final Solution') into operation in the 1930s they claimed the support of Martin Luther for what they were doing. This led many Christians in Germany to support them – at least at the beginning. The Nazis burnt many synagogues to the ground; humiliated Jewish children at school; rounded up Jews into ghettos, and gave them the most degrading public work to do. All of these measures had been suggested by Luther in his writings. Even he, though, could not have imagined the 'Final Solution' that the Nazis planned – the total elimination of the Jews from the face of the Earth. This event is known as the Holocaust.

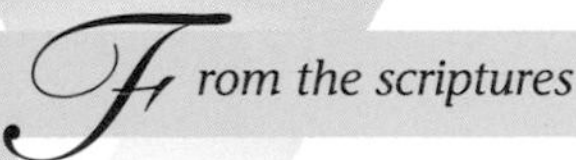

From the scriptures

There are several examples of antisemitism in the New Testament; part of the Christian holy Scriptures. Perhaps the most important of these is in Matthew's description of the events leading up to the death of Jesus. Jesus stands in front of Pontius Pilate, the Roman governor:
'So when Pilate saw that he could do nothing, but rather that a riot was beginning, he took some water and washed his hands before the crowd, saying, "I am innocent of this man's blood; see to it yourselves." Then the [Jewish] people as a whole answered, "His blood be on us and on our children!"'

(Matthew 27.24-25)

These words have caused more Jews to be killed than any others in Jewish history. Yet it is very doubtful whether they were ever said by the Jewish crowd in the first place. The Roman authorities were responsible for the death of Christ. Why, then, would a Christian writer want to suggest that the Roman governor was innocent and that the Jewish crowd swayed him?

FOR YOUR FOLDER

1 Explain in your own words:
a) The meaning of the word 'antisemitism'.
b) The meaning of the 'blood libel'.
c) What Martin Luther hoped for from the Jews and why he turned against them so strongly.
d) The link between Martin Luther and the Nazis.

2 Most, but not all, of the hatred which Jews have experienced over the centuries has come from Christians. Bearing this in mind what do you think the attitude of Jews towards Christianity should be today?

In the glossary: ANTISEMITISM; DEICIDE; HOLOCAUST; PESACH; SHABBAT; SYNAGOGUE.

The Holocaust

What was the Holocaust and why was it the most terrible event in Jewish history?

FOCUSING QUESTIONS

What was the Holocaust?

What are the facts are about the Holocaust?

Why did the Holocaust take place?

The Holocaust was the murder of over 6,000,000 Jews by the Nazis during the Second World War (1939-45). No-one knows who coined the word 'Holocaust' to describe this most terrible of all events in Jewish history. The word, meaning a 'burnt-offering', was used because of the crematoria in which the bodies of the victims were burned. Jews themselves prefer to use one of two different Hebrew words to describe what happened – Shoah ('Catastrophe') or Hurban ('Desolation').

A. This memorial to the victims of the Holocaust is erected at Yad Veshem – a Holocaust museum. What does it show, and do you think it acts as a suitable reminder of the Holocaust?

The facts

Unbelievably there are still people who deny that the Holocaust ever happened. The simple facts about this horrifying event and its aftermath, however, are beyond dispute. They are that:

- Six million people (about 1/3 of the Jews in the world) were murdered in Nazi Concentration Camps in six years. At the end of the war about 11.5 million Jews remained. Over 5,000,000 of these lived in the USA, 250,000 Jews were living in Displaced Persons Camps in Europe, and 1,500,000 were without any home. 650,000 of these people went to live in the new State of Israel.

- One million of those who died were children.
- There were twenty-eight Concentration Camps at the height of this atrocity, and the most horrific of these, such as Auschwitz and Treblinka, were killing over 5,000 Jews each day.
- The German intention was to wipe out all of the Jews in Germany and then, by winning the war in Europe, to eliminate them in a much wider area. This is called genocide.

Why did the Holocaust happen?

Many of the reasons for the Holocaust were the same as those which have resulted in the persecution of Jews and other peoples throughout history – because they held too many positions of responsibility in the country; they were too successful in business; the German people owed them too much money, or because people thought that Jewish allegiance belonged to their religion rather than to their country. As with all bigotry and hatred, people find it easy to be jealous, envious, or afraid of those who are believed to be 'different' in some way. Added to this was the desire of Hitler, and the Nazis, to create a 'pure' Aryan race. Amongst those persecuted along with the Jews were gypsies and homosexuals – both of whom were said to threaten the purity of the German race.

A response to the Holocaust

For the average person in Britain, and elsewhere, the Holocaust came as a tremendous shock when the news broke in 1945. The Jewish community was numbed and shocked into silence. It then determined that no-one should be ever allowed to forget what had happened. Days of memorial and remembrance were organised, Concentration Camps were opened to the public as a reminder of what had happened in them, special prayers were written and said, and a special memorial was built at Yad Veshem in Jerusalem (see Photograph A). The name Yad Veshem means 'a place and a name' and the names of the different camps are inscribed on the floor. A line of trees, 'the Avenue of the Righteous', commemorates all of the Gentiles who risked their lives to help Jewish men and women during the Holocaust.

FOR YOUR FOLDER

1 An inscription at Dachau, one of the worst of the Concentration Camps, says '*Never Again*' in four languages. Can you think of three ways in which the world could make sure that the events of the Holocaust are never repeated?

2 Explain, in a paragraph, what you understand by: genocide; the Holocaust; Yad Veshem.

3 Imagine that you are a Jew living in 1945. You have found out the extent of the Holocaust and you begin to wonder about the meaning of what has happened. Three members of your own family have died at the hands of the Nazis.

a) What questions would you want to ask God about the Holocaust if you had the chance?
b) What questions would you want to address to other members of the Jewish community?
c) Do you think that your own faith in God and in the Jewish way of life would survive the experience of what you, and others, had been through?

B. This Star of David is surrounded by barbed wire in this Holocaust memorial. The full truth about the Holocaust is only just beginning to emerge – over fifty years later. Why do you think it has taken so long?

In the glossary: GENOCIDE; HOLOCAUST; HURBAN; SHOAH.

The State of Israel

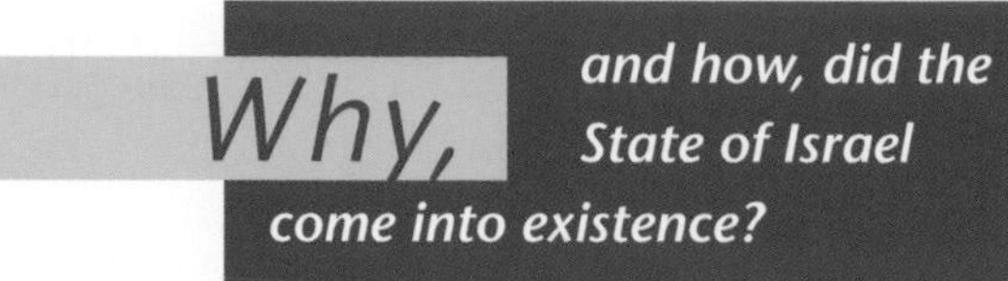

Why, and how, did the State of Israel come into existence?

FOCUSING QUESTIONS

What was Zionism and why was the movement formed at the end of the nineteenth century?

What happened in Palestine between the two World Wars?

How was the State of Israel formed?

Jews were dispersed from the land of Israel when the Romans destroyed the country in 70 CE. In the centuries that followed a few moved back to the Holy Land but the vast majority found homes elsewhere. Jews everywhere, though, prayed and worked for a return to Israel. The Pesach service has always included the prayer that, next year, the festival might be celebrated in the holy city of Jerusalem.

Zionism

The word 'Zion' is a synonym for Jerusalem and, at the end of the nineteenth century, a movement called Zionism was born which campaigned for the Jews to be given their own homeland in Palestine. Many Jews believed that they would never be safe from persecution, or free to practise their own religion, until they had a homeland of their own. Zionism, though, met strong opposition from other Jews who objected to the fact that it was a political organisation. They argued that it was their religious faith which bound all Jews together on every continent of the world. Others argued that the Jews must wait until God sent the promised Messiah to lead them back to their Promised Land.

A. A nineteenth-century illustration showing the search for leaven before Pesach. What prayer at the annual festival of Pesach kept alive the hope that Jews would return to their homeland?

DISCUSS

Two thousand years have elapsed between the Jews losing and reclaiming their homeland. How was the dream kept alive during this time?

In 1897, a Jewish religious leader, Theodore Herzl, called for a Jewish State to be set up in Israel. This Eretz Israel ('Land of Israel'), the Promised Land, was given a boost when the city of Tel Aviv began life early in the twentieth century as the first entirely Jewish city. A much greater boost to the Zionist's cause came in 1917 when the British Foreign Secretary, Lord Balfour, issued a Declaration saying that Britain supported the idea of the Jews having their own homeland (the Balfour Declaration).

Between the wars

After the First World War ended in 1918, Palestine (the biblical Holy Land) which the Jews knew as Canaan, came under British control. The Jews began to move back to the country in greater and greater numbers – the Jews in Palestine increased from 55,000 in 1918 to 450,000 in 1939. As their numbers increased to thirty per cent of the total population so the Arabs who lived there began to complain to the British authorities that the country was being overrun by Jews. In the 1930s and the 1940s the British, under pressure from the Arabs, tried to stop Jewish emigration. Terrorist activity by the Jews, however, forced the British out of Palestine in 1947, and in 1948 the United Nations was called upon to divide the land between the Arabs and the Jews. After much discussion the Jews established their own government and this insisted on Orthodox Jewish standards being applied throughout the country – no public transport on Shabbat, kosher food throughout the army, etc. The Jewish State of Israel had been born.

The Promised Land

A number of events in Jewish history are seen as significant by those Jews who see the land of Israel as their birthright and homeland. They are:

- The Exodus from Egypt. On this journey God promised all Jews that the Promised Land would be theirs.
- The building and destruction of the Temple in Jerusalem. Even today, although the site is now covered by a mosque, Jews gather at the ruined Western Wall in Jerusalem, the only part of the old Temple left standing, to pray for the reconstruction of this ancient centre of worship.
- The horrors which the Jewish people have endured over 2,000 years, which culminated in the Holocaust. Those centuries of bloodshed and hardship underline the importance of the Declaration made on May 14th 1948 that the State of Israel had been formed. From this moment onwards hundreds of thousands of Jews returned to Israel to live. Palestine was no more. The State of Israel had replaced it.

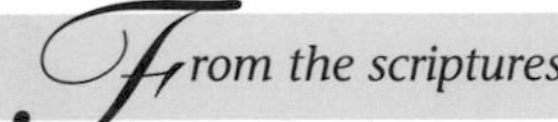

In the long time between being dispossessed and once again living in their homeland the Jews always believed that God would fulfil his promise to give them the land of Israel. Here is one of the promises that helped to sustain them:

'Thus says the LORD: Keep your voice from weeping, and your eyes from tears; for there is a reward for your work, says the LORD: they shall come back from the land of the enemy; there is hope for your future...your children shall come back to their own country.'
(Jeremiah 31.16-17)

1 According to this extract, how were the Jews living in exile told to remember what had happened in the past and to hope?
2 If the generation listening to Jeremiah were not to return to their homeland who was?

FOR YOUR FOLDER

1 One of the groups fighting for Israel to be given to the Jews did so under the slogan *'The land of Israel for the people of Israel under the Torah of Israel'*.

a) What moral or religious right did the Jews have to claim the land of Israel for themselves?
b) Who were the *'people of Israel'* when this claim was being made?
c) On what foundation were the laws of the country of Israel established?

2 When the State of Israel was formed in 1948 thousands of Arabs became refugees – themselves without a home. Can you find out what has happened to them since?

In the glossary: Canaan; Exodus; Holocaust; Israel; Jerusalem; Messiah; Palestine; Pesach; Promised Land; Temple; Zion; Zionism.

Orthodox Jews

Who *are the Orthodox Jews and what makes their approach to Judaism distinctive?*

FOCUSING QUESTIONS

Who are the Hasidism and what makes them distinctive as a religious group?

What makes Orthodox Jews distinctive?

What are the major differences between the Ultra-Orthodox and Orthodox Jews?

There are about 350,000 Jews living in Britain today and ninety per cent of this number belong to an Orthodox synagogue. Orthodox Jews fall into two separate categories – Ultra-Orthodox Jews and Orthodox Jews.

Hasidism

Ultra Orthodox Jews refer to themselves as the Hasidism, meaning 'those who fear God'. This description is based on a verse from the Jewish Scriptures (Isaiah 66.5) which says *'Hear the word of the LORD, you who tremble at his word'*. One characteristic of this group is that they often tremble as they pray. Ultra-Orthodox Jews try to put two basic principles into practice believing that:

1 The world is a dangerous place for those who believe in God, and so must be kept at arm's length. To emphasise this they wear nineteenth-century Eastern European dress (see Photograph A) and only speak Yiddish (an everyday version of the traditional Hebrew language) among themselves. Within the home television is either banned altogether or severely rationed. Children are only sent to Ultra-Orthodox Jewish schools where, from the beginning, a clear distinction is drawn between the education of boys and girls. Boys undergo a rigorous education following a curriculum laid down over 2,000 years ago. Jewish girls, however, are expected to become loyal and dedicated mothers and homemakers and their education is directed towards training them to fulfil this future role.

2 Everything in life is based on the laws found in the first five books of the Jewish Scriptures – the Torah. All of these laws are kept scrupulously and it is this, more than anything else, that distinguishes Ultra-Orthodox believers from other Jews.

The traditional Jews

Many Orthodox Jews prefer to call themselves 'traditional' because they see themselves following a religion which has remained virtually unchanged for centuries. The Orthodox Jews accept, and live by, the teachings in The Tenakh (the Jewish Bible), The Talmud, and The Midrash (commentaries). All of them are read as the revealed 'Word of God' and so are binding on all Jews. This means that a Jew

FOR YOUR FOLDER

1 Write a paragraph on Ultra-Orthodox Jews and Orthodox Jews.

2 Write a one sentence definition of: a synagogue; the Torah; Hebrew; Abraham; Moses; the Shabbat.

3 The Mitzvah on which Orthodox and Ultra-Orthodox Jews base their lives are now 3,500 years old. Do you think that a set of laws can be given 'once and for all' or does the rapid pace of change in the modern world make these old laws obsolete?

is committed to believing in:

- The one God who created the world, sustains it, and brought the human race into being.
- The God who called Abraham and Moses, and through them created the nation of Israel. He made a covenant (agreement) with Abraham which still extends to Jewish people today. God promised that He would be their God if they remained faithful to Him and kept His laws.
- The God who gave Moses the most precious of all gifts to the Jewish people – the Torah or the Law. This He did on Mount Sinai and a record of this is found in the first five books of the Jewish Scriptures – Genesis, Exodus, Leviticus, Deuteronomy and Numbers. No part of the Torah can be changed – every part is binding on the Jewish people. Its 613 instructions ('mitzvah') must be interpreted and obeyed. These instructions cover all aspects of behaviour including diet.

A. Ultra-Orthodox Jews, in Jerusalem, Israel. What makes these Ultra-Orthodox Jews distinctive? Why is it important to them to maintain this distinctiveness?

Shabbat

Celebrating the Shabbat is an important element in Orthodox Judaism. The very strong prohibition on any work being carried out on the Shabbat is maintained unless life is at risk. Only men and sons attend the synagogue on the Friday evening for prayers although the whole family go on Shabbat morning. For this service, though, women and girls take their seats in the gallery and play no active part in the service. Men alone are able to take part in the prayers and the readings from the Scriptures.

B. You can see the balcony quite clearly in this photograph of a synagogue. This is the place where women and girls sit during worship on Shabbat. Do you think that it is right to maintain rules like this in the twentieth century, and why do you think it is still done? Look at it from the point of view of men and women in the Jewish community.

In the glossary: ABRAHAM; HEBREW; ISRAEL; MIDRASH; MITZVAH; MOSES; ORTHODOX JEW; SHABBAT; SYNAGOGUE; TALMUD; TORAH; ULTRA-ORTHODOX JEWS;

Reform Jews

What is Reform Judaism and how does it differ from Orthodox Judaism?

FOCUSING QUESTIONS

Why was the setting up of the first Reform synagogue in Hamburg such a big step for Jews to take?

How did the early Reform Jews reinterpret the traditional belief that God would send a Messiah to deliver them?

What did the Reform Jews set out to do to the traditional Jewish faith?

FOR YOUR FOLDER

1 You are invited to take part in a debate on the relative merits of the Orthodox and Reform approaches to being a Jew.

a) Make a list of the main arguments that both sides might put forward to support their argument.

b) Which of the two approaches do you think makes most sense as we approach the beginning of the twenty-first century?

2 An Orthodox Jew would argue that he or she finds a great sense of security in belonging to a faith which has been unchanged for centuries. A Reform Jew would argue that religious faith, like everything else, has to change as life itself changes. Where do your sympathies lie in this debate – and why?

There is a very good reason for agreeing with the claim of Orthodox Jews that their understanding of the faith goes back to the birth of Judaism. Reform Jews make no such claim. They trace their movement back to the eighteenth century when the Haskalah Movement, under its leader Moses Mendelssohn, tried to integrate Jews into the wider society in Europe. The Jewish community tried to change whilst leaving their central beliefs and religious activities untouched.

The Hamburg Reform synagogue

The first Reform synagogue was established in Hamburg in 1818 and was called the Hamburg Temple. Until then all Jews had looked forward to the coming of the Messiah – a figure promised in their Scriptures as a leader who would deliver them from all their enemies. The early Reform Jews said that this was a mistaken hope. The promise of the Messiah was a dream which was now being realised in the opportunity which Jews had for social and educational improvement – and a freedom which they had never enjoyed before.

Real changes were introduced. For centuries Jews had looked forward, when the Messiah came, to a return to Zion (Jerusalem) and the rebuilding of the old Temple there. This dream was built into many of their prayers, but the Hamburg synagogue removed all such references. Prayers and sermons were expressed in German rather than the traditional Hebrew. In another departure from tradition an organ was introduced to accompany the singing in the synagogue.

Reform Beliefs

During the 1840s leaders of several different Reform synagogues met together to try to agree on a set of beliefs for the movement. They saw themselves as offering a 'spring-cleaning' to the Jewish community by sweeping away outdated laws and rituals. This also led to the introduction of new ideas, although some of the suggestions put forward were seen as too radical. One group, for instance, wanted to abolish circumcision (brit milah) but few Jews were prepared to go that far. Amongst the beliefs that characterise Reform Jews are the following:

- A new understanding of revelation – the way in which God makes himself known to his people. For Orthodox Jews the Torah is the revealed will of God and this remains true until the end of time. The Jew must keep all of the demands of the Torah because it expresses the will of God for all Jews. Reform Jews, on the other hand, speak of 'progressive or gradual revelation' with God, in every generation, leading them into a new understanding of the Torah which must be incorporated into belief and worship.

- A redefinition of work. For Orthodox Jews the law against working on Shabbat is absolute and covers all work unless a life is at stake. Reform Jews, though, allow important work to be done on the holy day whilst still insisting that it is a day of rest. That, they maintain, is the real reason for the laws surrounding the day anyway.

- A refusal to accept the laws in the Torah relating to purity. This includes the teaching in Leviticus 18.19 that a married couple stop all physical contact as soon as a woman starts to menstruate. Orthodox synagogues still have a mikveh (See Photograph A), which is a special pool in which a woman immerses herself after menstruating before she can resume normal sexual relations. Reform Jews believe that this practice has no value in the present time.

- A change in the traditional Jewish practice relating to marriage and divorce. Under the traditional system a Jewish woman is only able to divorce her husband once she has received a 'get' (a document of divorce) from him. He can withhold this document if he so chooses and the wife cannot divorce – or remarry. In the Reform community a marriage can be annulled even if there is no get forthcoming.

In the Reform community, then, the central beliefs and practices of Judaism are followed just as they are in the Orthodox community. The main difference is that the Reform community dispenses with 'minor' practices, and beliefs, that it does not consider to be relevant any longer. Instead of placing its whole emphasis on the Torah the Reform synagogues stress that God continues to reveal himself today.

A. A mikveh bath in an Orthodox synagogue. What is this bath traditionally used for and why would you not find one in a Reform synagogue?

DISCUSS

Reform Jews believe that God continues to 'reveal' Himself today. What do you think that they mean by this?

B. A female rabbi takes a service in a Reform synagogue. This has only been allowed since 1972. How might this fit in with the Reform idea of 'progressive revelation'?

In the glossary: BRIT MILAH; GET; HEBREW; JERUSALEM; MESSIAH; MIKVEH; ORTHODOX JEW; REFORM JEW; SYNAGOGUE; TEMPLE; TORAH.

The Synagogue

What is a synagogue and what part does it play in the Jewish community?

FOCUSING QUESTIONS

What roles does the synagogue play in the Jewish community?

Why was the first synagogue built?

What is the focal-point of a synagogue and why?

A synagogue (meaning 'bringing together') is the place where Jews meet to offer their communal worship to God. To the Jewish community however, it is more than that. It is the 'bet ha knesset' – a place of assembly, a community centre. This is the most popular description for synagogues in Israel. In fact the Israelis call their parliament the 'Knesset' – the place of assembly. Synagogues are also seen as the 'bet ha midrash' – the 'shul' or place of study. In Britain, Jews usually call the synagogue the shul. Studying is a very important activity for all Jews and this often draws them into the shul. Finally, the synagogue is the 'bet ha filah' – the house of prayer. Prayer is the most important religious activity for all Jews, and communal prayer takes place in the shul although, in Orthodox buildings, women play little part in it.

Synagogues provide the facilities for all of these activities but they are not, strictly speaking, Jewish places of worship since Jewish worship is home-centred rather than synagogue-centred.

A. This photograph shows the inside of a typical synagogue. How many of the features in the photograph can you recognise?

The need for a place of worship

It seems that Jews first began to build synagogues when they were exiled to Babylon in the sixth century BCE, since they could no longer regularly visit the Temple in Jerusalem. Whilst the Temple still existed, Jews in Israel went to Jerusalem three times a year for the 'Pilgrimage festivals' – Pesach, Shavuot and Sukkot. When the Temple was finally destroyed by the Romans in the first century CE it was never rebuilt. Since then Jewish worship has revolved around the synagogue and the home.

Inside the synagogue

The Ark, the focal-point of a synagogue, is in the eastern wall of the building facing eastwards to Jerusalem (see Photograph A). The scrolls of the Torah – the 'sefer Torah' – are stored in the Ark, and are usually hidden from view by curtains. This is in obedience to the instructions in Exodus 26.31-34 which describe the furnishings of the first portable Ark used when the Jews were in the wilderness. Each of the scrolls in the Ark has been copied out by hand by a scribe in Hebrew. It is mounted on two wooden rollers ('trees of life') with silver heads and bells on the crown which represent God's sovereignty. Whilst in the Ark the scroll is wrapped in velvet with a breast plate to represent the breastplate worn by the High Priest in biblical times. When a scroll becomes too worn to use it is not destroyed – it is buried just like a human being.

B. These scrolls are the holiest objects in the synagogue. How is this holiness recognised when a scroll reaches the end of its life?

There is a raised platform (the 'bimah') in every synagogue from which the scroll of the Torah is read during the service. In Orthodox synagogues this platform is in the middle of the building, but in most Liberal and Reform synagogues it is on the same level as the Ark. This means that the leader of the service (the cantor or the rabbi) prays facing the Ark in Orthodox synagogues whilst in other buildings he or she faces the congregation.

Above the Ark shines the 'ner tamid' – the lamp of perpetual light. This light burns all the time to represent the continuity of the Jewish community, and the fact that God is always present with His people. This tradition goes back to the event which marks the inception of the Jewish festival of Hanukkah.

Somewhere in the synagogue you are also likely to see two tablets of stone which contain the first two Hebrew words for each of the Ten Sayings. The symbol of Judaism, the Star of David, is also likely to be prominently displayed somewhere in the synagogue.

FOR YOUR FOLDER

1 Here are three Hebrew phrases which describe important aspects of the role which the synagogue plays in the life of the Jewish community. Explain each one of them: bet k'nesset; bet ha midrash; bet t'filah.

2 Describe why the Jewish community first built synagogues and what the word means.

3 You will find each of the following in a synagogue. Explain their significance: the Ark; the curtain covering the Ark; the scrolls; the ner tamid; the Star of David.

In the glossary: Ark; Cantor; Hebrew; Jerusalem; Hanukkah; Ner Tamid; Pesach; Rabbi; Sefer Torah; Shavuot; Synagogue; Temple; Torah.

DISCUSS

How is the holiness of God recognised and symbolised in the synagogue?

Prayer

What *part does praying play in the life of the Jewish community?*

FOCUSING QUESTIONS

What are the mitzvah?

What is the tallit, and when it is worn?

What is the yamulkah?

Prayer is the most important activity for every committed Jew, being identified in Hebrew as a mitzvah (meaning a commandment or duty). There are 613 mitzvah in the Torah and Jews keep these commandments as their part of the covenant that God made with their ancestors.

The mitzvah bring every aspect of daily religious and non-religious life under the control of God, by giving every action a purpose and a meaning – even the smallest detail of everyday life. As an old rabbi put it:
'Even unregulated actions, such as eating and drinking, sitting, standing, intercourse, talk and all the needs of the body, everyone of them should be directed to the service of the creator, or as a means leading to service unto Him.'

DISCUSS

1 Why do you think that Jews have prayers to cover every aspect of life? What do you think they learn about God from this?

2 Why is it important that such prayers are old and traditional?

Daily prayer and special prayer

Holy Jews are those people who are constantly aware of God's presence and are always ready to praise Him. Judaism provides three orders of daily prayer – in the morning, at noon and in the evening to help them do this. Besides these opportunities, special times of prayer are also assigned to events such as eating meals, celebrating holy days, reading the Torah, enjoying the different months of the year and so on. Nearly all prayers are 'formal' in that they are written down and have been used for centuries. Reciting old prayers is believed to correspond with the cycle of nature – always the same yet ever new. Saying these prayers links each Jew with the Jewish community, both past and present.

A. A worshipper wearing the tallit, tefillin and yarmulkah. Can you identify each of these important objects?

B. The tefillin are laid out ready for prayer. What do they contain?

The order of daily prayer

The Shema is the most important Jewish prayer of all and is recited during every Jewish act of worship. The order of daily prayer in the Jewish prayer book, the Siddur, also stipulates that two benedictions (blessings) must be said before the Shema is recited and nineteen benedictions (originally eighteen) be said afterwards. These benedictions are known as the 'Amidah' (standing), and are to be said standing without leaning on anything. Each order of daily prayer finishes with the 'Aleinu' meaning 'upon us is our duty'. This prayer is made up of two paragraphs – the first meditates on the special responsibilities which every believer has towards God and the second looks forward to that time when every person will enter into God's kingdom which will be set up on Earth. Jews believe that God's promised Messiah will come to do this.

The symbols of prayer

One unique feature of Jewish prayer is the importance which is attached to different symbols which are used. The most important of these symbols are:

- **The tallit.** This is the robe in which the worshipper wraps himself during prayer and which is often called the 'prayer shawl'. This four-cornered garment has fringes, called tzizit, attached to each of the corners, in keeping with the instructions found in Numbers 15.37-40. The tallit is worn by males at morning prayer only and is draped across the back and across the shoulders leaving the ends dangling at the front and back. In Reform synagogues the tallit is also worn by women.

- **The tefillin** (also called phylacteries – see Photograph B). These are cube-shaped leather boxes, containing four passages from the Scriptures, which are attached to the head and arm and worn during morning prayer. The tefillin are not worn on Shabbat or festival days.

- **The yarmulkah** – skull-cap. This head-covering is worn by Jewish men as it is believed that to pray or study with a bare head shows disrespect for God. Most Orthodox Jews cover their heads at all times, not only during prayer or study. Reform Jews usually pray without wearing a yarmulkah or any head covering.

FOR YOUR FOLDER

1 Moses Maimonides, an important Jewish philosopher from the twelfth century, had this to say about the tefillin:
'Great is the sanctity of tefillin for as long as the tefillin are upon man's head and arm, he is humble and God-fearing and is not drawn after frivolity and idle talk, and does not have evil thoughts, but directs his heart to words of truth and righteousness. Therefore a man should try to have them on all day...Even though they should be worn all day it is a greater obligation to wear them during prayer...'.

a) What are tefillin?
b) Where are the tefillin always worn? Can you suggest reasons for this?
c) What is contained in the tefillin?
d) What is, according to Moses Maimonides, the effect upon a man of wearing the tefillin?

2 This quotation is taken from the Amidah:
'O Lord, our God, hear our cry! Have compassion on us and pity us; Accept our prayer with loving favour...For You mercifully heed Your people's supplication. Praised are You, O Lord, who is attentive to prayer.'

How does this prayer combine a recognition of God's greatness with the worshipper's great sense of unworthiness?

In the glossary: Aleinu; Amidah; Messiah; Mitzvah; Orthodox Jew; Reform Jew; Shabbat; Shema; Tallit; Tefillin; Yarmulkah.

The Shema

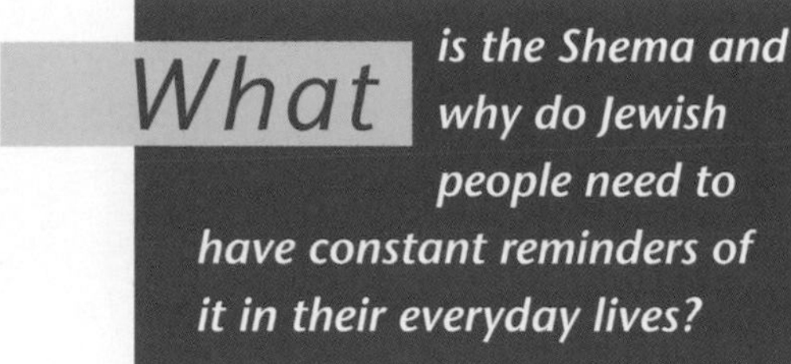

What is the Shema and why do Jewish people need to have constant reminders of it in their everyday lives?

FOCUSING QUESTIONS

What is the Shema?
When do Jews say the Shema?
What is a mezuzah?

The Shema is not so much a prayer as a statement of belief in God. It is addressed to the Jewish people ('Israel') and is found in the Torah.

The Shema, in Deuteronomy 6.4-9, 11.13-21 and Numbers 15.37-41 makes two very important statements. It begins with the most basic teaching of the Jewish religion – that there is only one God: *'Hear, O Israel: The LORD is our God, the LORD alone* [is one].*'* To emphasise this the people are told to *'Hear'* (Shema) the belief which is at the very heart of Judaism. It is so important that everything else in the faith stems from it.

A. This stained-glass window shows a small part of the Shema in Hebrew. What does the whole prayer say in English?

The second statement is one which worshippers are expected to respond to wholeheartedly, in a way that leaves no doubt about their total commitment to the one God: *'You shall love the LORD your God with all your heart, and with all your soul, and with all your might.'* (Deuteronomy 6.5).

The Shema in life and worship

It is the custom in Jewish families to teach children to say the first words of the Shema as soon as they begin to talk. From then onwards the saying of it forms an essential part of every day. In Deuteronomy, the people are told to say the Shema *'when you lie down and when you rise'* (6.7). This has been taken by Jews for centuries to mean that they should say the words in the morning and the evening, although some have taken this literally to mean that it is to be said when they are reclining in bed or getting up.

At home or in the synagogue devout Jews cover their eyes while they recite the Shema to help them concentrate on the awe-inspiring theme of God and His sovereignty in the world and over their own lives. Orthodox Jews sit while they say the words and whisper them quietly. Other Jews, though,

B. Why is this man is covering his eyes as he recites the Shema?

shout it out as if they are calling out to their fellow-worshippers to listen to what they are saying. There are records of Jewish martyrs reciting the Shema as they went to their deaths. Most Jews hope that the Shema will be the last words that they are able to utter when they sense that their soul is about to leave their body.

Reminders

A Jewish person is constantly reminded of the Shema in two ways:

1 It is on one of the scrolls included in the tefillin that he wears as he prays.

2 It is in the mezuzah (see Photograph C). This is a small scroll (about seven and a half centimetres long), encased in wood or metal and secured on the doorposts of all Jewish homes. Inside the scroll the Shema is inscribed in Hebrew to symbolise God's presence in the home.

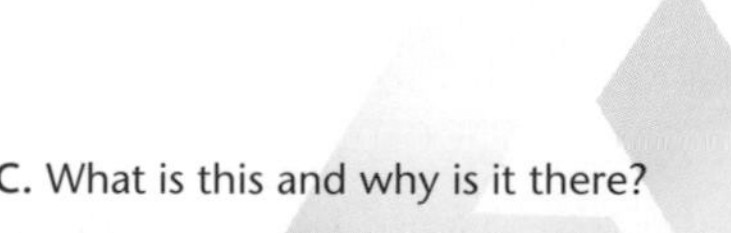

C. What is this and why is it there?

From the scriptures

These words are found in Deuteronomy 6.6-9:
'Keep these words that I am commanding you today in your heart. Recite them to your children and talk about them when you are at home and when you are away, when you lie down and when you rise. Bind them as a sign on your hand, fix them as an emblem on your forehead, and write them on the doorposts of your house and on your gates.'

1 What are *'these words'* which are being referred to here?
2 How are these words kept alive from one generation to another?
3 How do Jews understand the command to recite the words *'when you lie down and when you rise'*?
4 When are *'these words'* bound *'as a sign'* on the hand and fixed *'as an emblem'* to the forehead?
5 How do Jewish people write the words on the doorposts of their houses and on their gates?
6 Why are these words so important to all Jewish people?

FOR YOUR FOLDER

1 What does the word 'Shema' mean?

2 What very important statement is made in the Shema about God, and why does this matter so much to all Jews?

3 How is the two-way responsibility of the covenant between God and Israel reflected in the Shema?

In the glossary: MEZUZAH; ORTHODOX JEW; SHEMA; SYNAGOGUE; TEFILLIN; TORAH.

Shabbat

What is Shabbat and why has it been so important to the Jewish community?

FOCUSING QUESTIONS

What is meant by 'Shabbat'?

How is Shabbat welcomed into a Jewish home?

What is meant by Havdalah?

The life of a Jewish person builds up through six week days to reach its climax on the seventh day – the Shabbat. The Jewish Shabbat begins at sunset on the Friday evening and lasts until night falls on the Saturday evening. It is a day of rest but it is much more than that – it is a 'holy' day which reminds all Jews of the Covenant between God and their people made by Moses. Because of this, no part of Judaism is treated with greater awe or respect than the Shabbat. The Shabbat is the institution which has contributed most to the survival of Judaism through to the present day.

What is Shabbat?

The fourth of the Ten Sayings (Deuteronomy 5.12-15) says this:
'Observe the sabbath day and keep it holy, as the Lord your God commanded you. Six days you shall labour and do all your work. But the seventh day is a sabbath [Shabbat] *to the Lord your God; you shall not do any work...'.*

There are two reasons why Jews refrain from all kinds of work to keep the Shabbat – because they believe that God himself rested after spending six days creating the world, and because God commanded the Jews to keep the day special after bringing them out of slavery in the land of Egypt.

From the scriptures

In a version of the Ten Sayings found in Exodus 20 8-11 we read:
'Remember the sabbath day, and keep it holy...For in six days the LORD made the heaven and earth, the sea, and all that is in them, but rested the seventh day; therefore the LORD blessed the sabbath day and consecrated it.'

How do Jewish people attempt to keep the 'sabbath day' (the Shabbat) *'holy'*?

A. How is Shabbat welcomed into every Jewish home?

B. The Shabbat table is laid (left). Why do you think that Shabbat starts with a meal?

C. What do you think is happening in this photograph?

Keeping Shabbat holy

In most Jewish families celebrating Shabbat is made up of several elements. First, on the Friday evening, Shabbat is welcomed. At home, the woman of the house or one of her children lights special candles and asks for God's blessing on her household while the man of the house pronounces a special blessing (a 'kiddush') over wine and bread. A father's blessing on his family has always been very important in Judaism. This is followed by a festive meal which brings together all the family and which is brought to an end by songs and the saying of grace.

On the Saturday morning, the whole family attends the synagogue for thanksgiving. During the service, for which in Orthodox synagogues males and females are separated, seven people are 'called up' to the bimah to follow the reader. He reads the prescribed portion from the Torah and offers a prayer to thank God for the gift of Shabbat. An eighth person then reads from the Nevi'im (the Prophets) and the service is closed by a sermon based on the Torah.

A symbolic ceremony in the home, called 'Havdalah' (meaning separation or distinction) draws Shabbat to a close. A lighted candle is extinguished in wine by the youngest member of the family while a spice box (often in the form of a tower) is passed around for all members of the family to sniff. This reminds them of the sweetness of Shabbat as it draws to a close. The ceremony also acts as a 'distinction' between the Shabbat, which is ending, and the rest of the week which is about to begin.

FOR YOUR FOLDER

1
a) Why do Jews treat Shabbat as special?
b) A popular Jewish saying goes: *'More than Israel kept the Sabbath, the Sabbath kept Israel.'* What do you think this means?

2 The order of service for the Shabbat includes the words: *'The Sabbath day is a sabbath of the Lord your God...and you shall remember that you were a slave in the land of Egypt.'* What do you think that Jews today might gain from remembering events that happened so long ago?

3 This prayer of blessing is said by each Jewish father over his family on Shabbat:
'Blessed are you, O Lord our God, ruler of the universe who makes us holy through doing his commandments and has commanded us to light the Shabbat candles.'

a) What does the word 'Shabbat' mean and how does this affect the way that the day is celebrated?
b) Why do you think that the people are reminded on Shabbat that God is the ruler of the universe?
c) What do you think the candles on the Shabbat table remind each Jew about?

In the glossary: Bimah; Kiddush; Moses; Nevi'im; Shabbat; Synagogue; Ten Sayings; Torah.

Kashrut

What *are the special laws in Judaism relating to diet and why are they an important part of worship?*

FOCUSING QUESTIONS

What is kosher food?

What is treyfah?

What is a kosher kitchen like?

FOR YOUR FOLDER

1
a) Explain the difference in meaning between kosher and treyfah.
b) How can Jews tell which is a kosher and which is a treyfah animal?
c) List four kosher animals and four treyfah animals.
d) What is special about a kosher home, and how would you recognise one?

2
a) What is meant by shechita?
b) What is a shochet and why is he an important member of the Jewish community?
c) What is special about the way that animals are killed for Jews to eat?
d) What do you think that the special regulations which govern the killing of animals in the Jewish community are intended to prevent?

Kashrut, the dietary rules, play an important part in the everyday lives of most Jews. Because the laws go back over 3,000 years, to the time when the Torah was given to Moses, it is not now possible to explain why many of them were first introduced. Jews today simply accept them as part of the whole system of holy living and worship introduced by God. They have to be followed because that is what the Torah, God's Word, demands.

The food laws

All food is placed in one of two categories by the Torah:

1 Food which is kosher – suitable to eat. The basic law laid down in the Torah is that animals may be eaten if they have *'... divided hoofs and is cleft-footed and chews the cud...'* (Leviticus 11.3). Included in this category of permissible animals are oxen, goats, cows, sheep, gazelles and domesticated animals like chicken, ducks and geese. Fish that have both fins and scales, such as salmon and cod, are also acceptable. Milk can only be drunk from kosher animals, and the same applies to eggs.

2 Food which is treyfah – forbidden. Any mammal which does not meet the basic requirement of having split hooves and eating the cud is forbidden. The pig, in particular, is singled out as being treyfah, as are birds of prey, such as eagles and kestrels. Fish without fins and scales, such as shell-fish, are also forbidden.

Slaughtering animals

Kosher food must meet the basic slaughtering regulations, called 'shechita', before it is acceptable for Jews to eat. The main requirements are that the death of the animal must have been brought about in the most humane way. Death must be at the hands of a specialist, (the 'shochet'), who must use a very sharp knife to cut the animal's throat, severing its arteries, veins and windpipe at one stroke so that the blood drains out rapidly. Death must be instantaneous, so this rules out the trapping, shooting and hunting of animals for food. After death the shochet must examine the animal for any signs of disease or damage, since a damaged animal cannot be eaten. It is very important that all of the blood is drained out of the animal. When this has happened the person selling the meat must wash and soak the carcass in salt to remove any traces of congealed blood. Only then is the animal considered kosher.

A kosher home

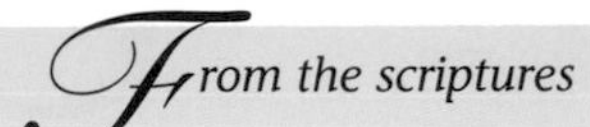

In a kosher home, meat and dairy products may not be cooked, served or eaten together, nor may butter be spread on bread if meat is being served at the same meal. Several hours after eating meat must pass before a glass of milk can be drunk. Two complete sets of cooking utensils, dishes, and cutlery are needed to make sure that there is no possible contact between meat and dairy products. As Jews only eat unleavened products at Pesach so a further two sets are employed to keep leavened and unleavened products apart. (Unleavened foods contain no yeast or any substance which ferments in dough or batter and causes it to rise.)

Trained rabbis supervise and make rulings on all matters relating to kashrut. All committed Jews, however, share the responsibility of maintaining these laws. The shochet , the butcher who sell the products, and the person who uses them all accept their obligation, under Jewish law, to live by the kashrut laws, and they do so in the joyful belief that they are carrying out a sacred and holy duty – a mitzvah.

After laying out the various kosher laws, the author of the book of Leviticus wrote:
'This is the law pertaining to land animal and bird and every living creature that moves through the waters and every creature that swarms upon the earth, to make a distinction between the unclean and the clean, and between the living creature that may be eaten and the living creature that may not be eaten.'
(Leviticus 11.46-47)

1 Can you put forward two practical reasons why the kosher laws might have been introduced originally?
2 Explain why Jews still keep the kosher laws today, although the original reason for keeping them has long since disappeared.

A. How do Orthodox Jews look upon the obligation to keep the Jewish dietary laws?

In the glossary: KASHRUT; KOSHER; MITZVAH; MOSES; PESACH; RABBI; TORAH.

Rosh Hashanah and Yom Kippur

Why *are Rosh Hashanah and Yom Kippur such important Jewish festivals and what is the link between them?*

FOCUSING QUESTIONS

Why is Rosh Hashanah is also called 'the Day of Judgement'?

How is Rosh Hashanah celebrated?

How is Yom Kippur celebrated?

The Jewish New Year, Rosh Hashanah, is the most serious festival in the Jewish religious year and is followed ten days later by the most solemn day of all, Yom Kippur. Celebrated at the beginning of the month of Tishri (September/October), these ten days draw to a close a period of repentance which began a month earlier (called 'the Days of Awe').

Orthodox Jews follow tradition and celebrate Rosh Hashanah over two days but Reform Jews set aside a single day. Yom Kippur lasts for twenty-five hours.

The Day of Judgement

The Talmud calls Rosh Hashanah the 'Day of Judgement' since, on this day, the fate of everyone is settled for the coming year. At the same time, it is also a 'Day of Remembrance' – the day on which God remembers all of His creatures and their needs. Over the centuries, rabbis have taught that Rosh Hashanah is the day on which three books are opened in Heaven. These books record the deeds of every individual and, when they are opened, the righteous are rewarded with life and the wicked are punished by death. Those 'in between' are given ten days between Rosh Hashanah and Yom Kippur to show that they are worthy of Heaven. This is why, on Yom Kippur, Jews will often greet each other with the words '*May you be inscribed and sealed for a good year*'.

Celebrating Rosh Hashanah

The main symbol associated with this festival is that of the shofar – the ram's horn. This is blown at the end of morning prayer every day during the month preceding Rosh Hashanah to remind worshippers that the solemn festival is approaching. Then it is blown 100 times during the festival service making three different, symbolic, sounds:

- a long, drawn-out sound which calls on everyone to listen;
- a broken, plaintive sound which represents the repentant people of Israel;
- a sharp, staccato sound which is reminiscent of the crying of repentance.

On this day the people also look forward to the time when God's Messiah will come to Earth and set up his kingdom. Because of this the service ends with the words *'May God's universal sovereignty be over humans and nature, for the arrival of God's kingdom in which mankind will be joined in universal brotherhood to do the divine will with a perfect heart.'*

From the scriptures

These verses describe the inauguration of the festivals of Rosh Hashanah and Yom Kippur:

'The LORD spoke to Moses, saying: Speak to the people of Israel, saying: In the seventh month, on the first day of the month, you shall observe a day of complete rest, a holy convocation commemorated with trumpet blasts. You shall not work at your occupations...Now, the tenth day of this seventh month is the day of atonement; it shall be a holy convocation for you...and you shall do no work during that entire day...'.

(Leviticus 23.23-27)

1. When do Jews celebrate Rosh Hashanah?
2. What is the main symbol associated with Rosh Hashanah?
3. How long elapses between Rosh Hashanah and Yom Kippur?
4. What is the other name for Yom Kippur and what does this name mean?

A. Traditionally Moses came down from Mount Sinai (above) on Yom Kippur with the Ten Sayings. How is this event linked to the theme of forgiveness on Yom Kippur?

Day of Atonement

Yom Kippur is the great and holy day on which the people of Israel meet with their God. Traditionally, it was on Yom Kippur that Moses came down from Mount Sinai with the tablets of stone containing the Torah. The people knew then that God had forgiven their sins, and Jews today spend Yom Kippur asking for forgiveness for wrongdoings. During the evening service in the synagogue worshippers sing the 'kol nidrei', which asks God for absolution for vows which they have failed to keep in the previous year.

Although Yom Kippur is a day of fasting, spent almost entirely in the synagogue, it is a day of rejoicing as well. On Yom Kippur, Jews do not eat, drink, wash, have sexual intercourse, anoint their bodies with oil or wear sandals or leather shoes. In this they attempt to following the example of God's angels who do not eat or drink but spend their entire time praising Him. In the end they share the delight of the angels in God's presence.

In the glossary: Messiah; Moses; Rosh Hashanah; Shofar; Talmud; Torah; Yom Kippur.

FOR YOUR FOLDER

1 In the first century CE a Greek philosopher noted that: *'Yom Kippur is observed not only by the pious and holy but also by those who never act religiously in the rest of their life.'* This is still the case. Synagogues are usually full on Yom Kippur. Can you suggest why?

2 The prophet Amos, in the Jewish Scriptures, said: *'Is a trumpet blown in the city, and the people are not afraid?'* (Amos 3.6)

a) What is blown in the synagogue during Rosh Hashanah and Yom Kippur?
b) What are the people afraid of when they hear its sound?

3 According to Moses Maimonides, the purpose of blowing the shofar is to say: *'Awake from your slumbers, you who have fallen asleep, and reflect on your deeds'.*
Why do you think the Jews are encouraged to *'reflect on their deeds'* on Rosh Hashanah?

Sukkot and Simchat Torah

What features are distinctive about the festivals of Sukkot and Simchat Torah?

FOCUSING QUESTIONS

What were the three pilgrimage festivals and why were they so called?

How is everyone in the synagogue involved in the festival of Sukkot?

What happens to the scrolls of the Torah during Simchat Torah?

In ancient Israel there were three 'pilgrimage' festivals which drew Jews from all over Israel to the Temple in Jerusalem. The harvest festival of Sukkot was one of these festivals, and celebrated the forty years that the Israelites had spent wandering in the desert after they left Egypt. This completed the story told at the other two pilgrimage festivals – Pesach at which the journey out of slavery was re-enacted, and Shavuot which commemorated the giving of the Torah on Mount Sinai.

The Feast of Tabernacles

A. This stained-glass window expresses the harvest theme of Sukkot. How is this theme expressed in the celebrations on this day?

The Feast of Sukkot (meaning 'tabernacles' or 'booths') begins just five days after Yom Kippur and continues for eight days (seven in Reform synagogues). Sukkot has always been an occasion for rejoicing since it originally marked the harvest festival of thanksgiving when booths (temporary shelters) were erected as makeshift dwellings for the farmers at harvest-time. Whilst this agricultural link remains (see Photograph A), Sukkot follows other major festivals in being linked with an important event in Jewish history. Sukkot reminds Jews of the booths that the Israelites lived in for forty years in the desert. During Sukkot Jewish people erect tabernacles, or booths, in their own gardens and spend some time in them. Deliberately the roofs of the booths are left open to the heavens – and to God. Booths are also erected in synagogues for those people unable to put them up at home. Special services are held in the synagogue on the first two and last two days of the festival.

The original harvest theme of the festival is underlined by the four symbols, or 'species' as they are called, which are most closely identified with Sukkot. These four symbols are:

1 The 'fruit of the goodly tree' ('etrog') which is citrus and looks rather like a lemon.

2 The branch of the date palm ('lulav').

3 A bough of a leafy tree, with twigs of myrtle ('hadas').

4 Sprigs of willow ('aravah').

These four 'species' are brought to the sanctuary in the synagogue and bound together. Worshippers then walk around the building carrying and waving them. As they do so, the Psalms of Thanksgiving, Psalms 113-118, are recited.

DISCUSS

What themes are expressed in the festivals of Sukkot and Simchat Torah? Why are these themes very important to Jewish worshippers?

Rejoicing in the Torah

B. What is special about these scrolls of the Torah and how is this expressed during Simchat Torah?

Simchat Torah follows on as soon as Sukkot has finished. Every year, during synagogue services, the Torah is read all the way through in sections. The final section (see Deuteronomy 33 and 34) is read on Simchat Torah. On the same day, the first portion of the next cycle, from the book of Genesis, is read. To express the strong Jewish belief that the Torah is eternal, without beginning or end, it is important that there is not even a breath taken between the ending of the old reading and the beginning of the new. The person who has the honour of being called up to read the passage from Deuteronomy is called the 'Hatan Torah' (meaning the Bridegroom of the Torah) to show that the Jews are 'married' to the Torah. The person who reads the opening passage from Genesis is called the 'Hatan Bereshit' which is taken from 'In the beginning' – the first words in the Torah.

During a service in the synagogue on Simchat Torah all of the Scrolls are taken out of the Ark (see Photograph B) and carried in procession seven times around the synagogue – and sometimes out into the street as well. The people accompany the scrolls dancing and singing. Children kiss the scrolls, carry banners and receive sweets. Often the 'Bridegrooms' provide drinks and cakes for the congregation. The honour is sometimes extended to women in Reform synagogues where they are called the 'Bride of the Torah' and the 'Bride of Genesis'.

FOR YOUR FOLDER

1 Explain:
a) Why the festival of Sukkot is also called 'the Festival of Tabernacles'.
b) The link between the harvest festival of Sukkot and the forty years that the Israelites spent in the desert.
c) What the four species are.
d) Why the reading from the last part of the Torah and the first part of the Torah proceeds without a breath being taken.

2 Some Jewish festivals are very solemn whilst others are full of thanksgiving. What do you think that Jewish people today might learn from these two very different kinds of celebrations?

3
a) How would you describe the significance to the Jewish community of the festivals of Sukkot and Simchat Torah?
b) What do you think Jewish people might learn from celebrating them?

In the glossary: Ark; Jerusalem; Pesach; Shavout; Simchat Torah; Sukkot; Synagogue; Temple; Torah.

Hanukkah

What miracle forms the basis of the Hanukkah celebrations and what do these celebrations involve?

FOCUSING QUESTIONS

What makes Hanukkah unique amongst all the many Jewish festivals?

Which two important events are being recalled at Hanukkah?

How do Jewish people celebrate Hanukkah?

The festival of Hanukkah (meaning 'Dedication') is a minor Jewish festival that lasts for eight days in December. Hanukkah is unique amongst Jewish festivals since it is the only one that is not mentioned in the Jewish Scriptures. It is, however, recorded in the books of 1 and 2 Maccabees which are part of the Apocrypha.

The background to Hanukkah

The festival is based on a legend that comes from the second century BCE when a Jewish revolt took place against the Seleucid king, Antiochus IV. The king had issued several decrees in his kingdom designed to eliminate the Jewish religion altogether. The Jews who opposed the king on this matter were tortured and killed, and Antiochus had a pagan altar set up in the Temple in Jerusalem. This sparked an uprising in 168 BCE. After three years of heavy fighting the army of the king was driven out of Palestine. This important event in Jewish history is known as the Maccabean revolt since the leader of the uprising was Judas Maccabeus.

When the Maccabeans came to rededicate the Temple to God they could only find a small pot of consecrated oil with which to kindle the menorah, the seven-branched candelabrum which was lit daily in the Temple. The jar contained enough oil for just one night but, by a miracle, it lasted for eight nights until fresh oil could be produced. When Jews, therefore, celebrate Hanukkah today they are recalling both the victory of the Maccabeans over their enemies, and the miracle of the oil. Because of this, Hanukkah is also sometimes called the 'Festival of Lights'.

A. A hanukiah candelabrum, used during the festival of Hanukkah. Why is the festival sometimes called the 'Festival of Lights'?

B. Children playing with dreydels. What might this family learn about the festival of Hanukkah by playing with dreydels together?

Celebrating Hanukkah

According to Jewish tradition, lights are lit in every Jewish house during the eight days of Hanukkah. These lights are kindled in a special nine-branched candelabrum which is called a hanukiah (see Photograph B). Whilst most Jews now use candles to light the candelabrum some still use olive oil. One light is kindled on the first day and so on through the festival. An additional light is used to do the kindling and this is called the Shamash ('servant'). Two blessings are then given.

Traditionally, at Hanukkah, the children play with dreydels. These are spinning tops which have a different Hebrew letter on each of four sides. The letters are the initial letters of four Hebrew words which mean 'a great miracle took place there' and this refers, of course, to the miraculous supply of oil.

Hanukkah is very much a festival that is celebrated with the family. The people eat food cooked in oil, like doughnuts, to remind them of the single jar of oil in the Temple. They also enjoy a traditional Jewish chip, also cooked in oil, known as a 'latkes' (or 'levitot'). Presents are given and received on Hanukkah – sometimes on each of the eight days of the festival.

DISCUSS

Why do you think that the festival of Hanukkah is important, whether or not the event upon which it is based actually happened?

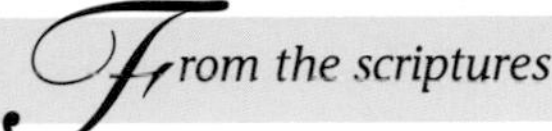

From the scriptures

This description explains why the festival of Hanukkah is celebrated:
'They also rebuilt the sanctuary and the interior of the temple, and consecrated the courts. And they made new holy vessels, and brought the lampstand, the altar of incense, and the table into the temple. They offered incense on the altar and lit the lamps on the lampstand and these gave light in the temple...Then Judas and his brothers and all the assembly of Israel determined that every year at that season the days of dedication of the altar should be observed with joy and gladness for eight days...'.
(1 Maccabees 4.48-50, 59)

What rules are laid down here for the celebration of Hanukkah?

FOR YOUR FOLDER

1 Jewish legend records that when Judas and his supporters entered the Temple they found the menorah damaged beyond repair. They immediately built a makeshift menorah out of their spears. What spiritual lessons do you think Jews might draw from this event today?

2 After the lights have been kindled on each night of Hanukkah the following declaration is made by everyone present:
'We kindle these lights on account of the miracles, the deliverances and the wonders which Thou didst work for our fathers, by means of Thy holy priests. During all the eight days of Hanukkah these lights are sacred, neither is it permitted to make any profane use of them; but we are only to look at them, in order that we may give thanks unto Thy name for Thy miracles, Thy deliverances and Thy wonders.'

a) What do you think *'...these lights are sacred, neither is it permitted to make any profane use of them'* means?
b) What do you think that time spent looking at the lights of the hanukiah might lead Jewish people to appreciate?

In the glossary: APOCRYPHA; DREYDEL; HANUKIAH; HANUKKAH; JERUSALEM; MENORAH; TEMPLE.

Purim

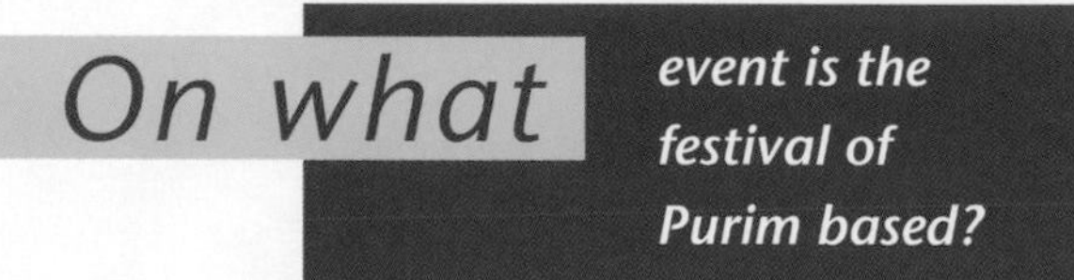

On what event is the festival of Purim based?

FOCUSING QUESTIONS

What is the story behind the Jewish festival of Purim?

What is unusual about the book of Esther in the Jewish Scriptures?

Why does The Talmud encourage Jews to drink a lot of wine on Purim?

Just like Hanukkah the festival of Purim (also known as the 'Festival of Lots') is a minor celebration in the Jewish religion but it is one which does have a foundation in the Jewish Scriptures. The celebration takes place in late Winter (February/March) and commemorates the events which are recorded in the Book of Esther. In this book, set in ancient Persia, the Jews were saved from destruction by the God-inspired actions of Esther.

The background to Purim

The story of Esther revolves around the actions of four main characters: the Persian king, Ahasuerus; his wife, the Jewish queen Esther; the king's commander-in-chief, Haman; and Esther's Jewish uncle, Mordecai.

According to the Book of Esther, Haman's jealousy of Mordecai, and the favour he had found with King Ahasuerus made him determined to discredit all of the Jews living in Persia. Accordingly, he told King Ahasuerus that the Jews were plotting his overthrow. Outraged, the king ordered that lots be drawn to determine the day on which the Jews were to be killed. Haman's plans were only defeated by courage of Esther who, refusing to separate herself from her people, finally convinced her husband that it was Haman not the Jews who were the real threat to his empire. In the end, Haman was hanged on the very gallows that he had built to execute Mordecai.

The unusual feature of the Book of Esther is that it is the only book in the Jewish Scriptures in which the name of God is not mentioned at all. This troubled Jews until the Middle Ages when they began to see that God was still active in the story, even if His name wasn't mentioned. Now the festival is taken to celebrate not only the deliverance of the Jews from danger under Esther, but also at different times throughout history.

DISCUSS

Which important lesson do Jews learn about God by celebrating the festival of Purim? How is this lesson brought out in the way that the festival is celebrated?

Celebrating Purim

The central part of the Purim celebration in the synagogue is the reading of the 'Megillah' (scroll) as the Book of Esther is called. During the morning service, the reading of the Torah deals with the 'blotting out' of the memory of Am'alek, who was an ancestor of Haman (see Exodus 17.8-16). It has long been the custom for the children in the service to 'blot out' Haman's name by making loud noises with rattles or whistles whenever his name is mentioned during the reading of the Megillah.

A. This stained-glass window commemorates the festival of Purim but why is this festival celebrated?

From the scriptures

In this description from the Book of Esther the queen is pleading with the king to stop Haman from carrying out his plan to kill all the Jews:

'..."*If it pleases the king, and if I have won his favour, and if the thing seems right before the king, and I have his approval, let an order be written to revoke the letters devised by Haman...which he wrote giving orders to destroy the Jews who are in all the provinces of the king. For how can I bear to see the calamity that is coming on my people? Or how can I bear to see the destruction on my kindred?*"'

(Esther 8.5-6)

Do some further research, and answer the following questions:

1 How had Esther come to marry the Persian king?
2 What was the plan that Haman had devised against the Jews?
3 How did the festival of Purim receive its name?
4 What is the most important theme to come out of the festival of Purim – and how is this theme kept alive in the way that the festival is celebrated today?
5 What is the spiritual significance of the festival of Purim?

Purim is also a time for thinking of others, and for giving gifts. The Book of Esther speaks of sending gifts to friends and the poor at Purim (Esther 9.22) and this is a widespread custom during the festival. The rule, stated in The Talmud, is that each person must send a gift of at least two items of food to a friend and give at least one donation to two poor men.

In The Talmud people are encouraged to drink as much wine as possible on Purim until they are not aware whether they are 'blessing Mordecai or cursing Haman'. The reason for this curious commandment is that King Ahasuerus killed his first wife because he was drunk, and if he had not done so Esther would not have become queen – and the Jewish nation would have been wiped out. A few ultra-Orthodox Jews may still carry this out, but the majority of Jews do not.

FOR YOUR FOLDER

1 There is a popular Jewish saying: *'A high temperature is not an illness and Purim is not a festival.'* What do you think this is saying about Purim?

2 Carry out a little further research into the Purim story and then write notes on the part played by: King Ahasuerus; Haman; Mordecai; Esther.

In the glossary: ESTHER; HANUKKAH; MEGILLAH; PURIM; SYNAGOGUE; TALMUD; TORAH.

Pesach

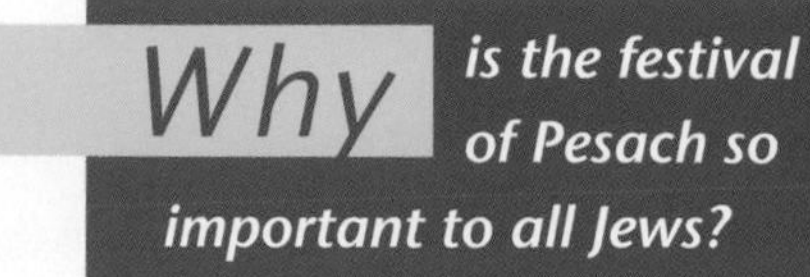

Why is the festival of Pesach so important to all Jews?

FOCUSING QUESTIONS

Why is Pesach also sometimes called 'Passover' or the 'Feast of Unleavened Bread'?

What is the Seder meal?

Which four questions are asked at the Seder meal and how are they answered?

Pesach, or Passover, is the oldest and most important festival in Judaism. This Spring festival, celebrating the release of the Israelites from Egypt, lasts for eight days (seven days in Israel). The word 'Pesach' comes from the paschal lamb which was offered to God as a sacrifice on the eve of the festival in the old Temple. The English title 'Passover' comes from the fact that the Angel of Death 'passed over' the house of the Israelites while killing the first-born in every Egyptian household in the last of the ten plagues. In the Jewish Scriptures, the festival is called 'The Feast of Unleavened Bread' because of the command to eat unleavened bread ('matzah') and not leavened bread ('hametz') on this festival.

The Seder meal

Pesach is very much a family festival with the most important part of the celebrations taking place in the home. Before it begins, the house is thoroughly cleaned to remove all traces of leavened bread. This search is turned into a game, and pieces of leavened bread, are hidden for the children to find. Then, on the eve of Pesach, the whole family sits down to eat a special Seder meal. This meal follows a traditional pattern, as described in The Hagadah, which is the book which tells the story of the liberation of the Jews from slavery.

A. A Seder plate. What items will be put on this dish, and what is their symbolic significance?

B. A stained-glass window celebrating the festival of Pesach. How does wine play an important part in this festival?

The Seder meal starts with the blessing of the wine. During the evening four glasses of wine are drunk to remind everyone of the four promises that God made to Moses. There are a number of symbolic items on the table to help each member of the family to recreate, and so relive, the events of the Exodus from Egypt. Two of the items on the Seder plate are not eaten – a roasted shank-bone, which represents the lamb which was slaughtered each year in the Temple, and a roasted egg, which recalls the Passover sacrifice. Neither of these acts have been carried out since the Romans destroyed the Temple in Jerusalem in the first century CE. The other items on the table, however, are tasted to remind everyone of the Exodus. They are:

- Three matzah loaves. When the Jews left Egypt they did so in such a hurry they could not take any leavened bread with them.
- Maror or bitter herbs which recall the bitterness of 430 years of slavery in Egypt.
- A green vegetable, usually parsley, which is dipped into salt water to remind everyone of the tears that the Israelites shed while they were in captivity.
- Haroset – a mixture of nuts, wine and apple – which symbolises the cement which the Israelites were forced to make to build cities for the Egyptians.

A fifth cup of wine also stands on the table although no-one drinks from it. This represents the belief that, at some future time, the old prophet Elijah will return to Earth to herald the arrival of God's promised Messiah. At the meal, the youngest child asks four questions which are laid down in The Hagadah:
'Tonight, why do we only eat matzot?'
'Tonight why do we eat bitter herbs?'
'Tonight why do we dip twice?'
'Tonight why do we lean [as we eat]*?'*
and the father answers them by reading the story of Exodus from The Hagadah.

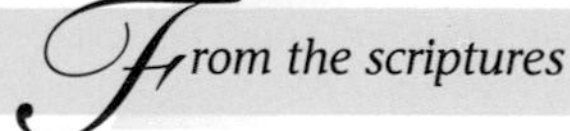

From the scriptures

Here is an extract from the Torah:
'You shall observe the festival of unleavened bread; as I commanded you, you shall eat unleavened bread for seven days at the appointed time...for in it you came out of Egypt.' (Exodus 23.15)

1 What is unleavened bread?
2 Why is the eating of unleavened bread such a central feature of the celebration of this festival?

FOR YOUR FOLDER

1 These words are taken from The Hagadah: *'In every generation everyone should regard himself as if he had personally come out of Egypt'.*

a) What is The Hagadah?
b) How is the celebration of Pesach intended to help each Jew to relive the events of the Exodus as if he or she had personally been there?
c) Why do you think that it is important for Jews to relive the event in this way?

2 The festival of Pesach is a reminder of the events of the Exodus, but it is more than that. It is a festival of freedom. What do you think this means?

In the glossary: Elijah; Exodus; Hagadah; Matzah; Messiah; Moses; Pesach; Prophets; Seder; Temple; Torah.

Shavuot

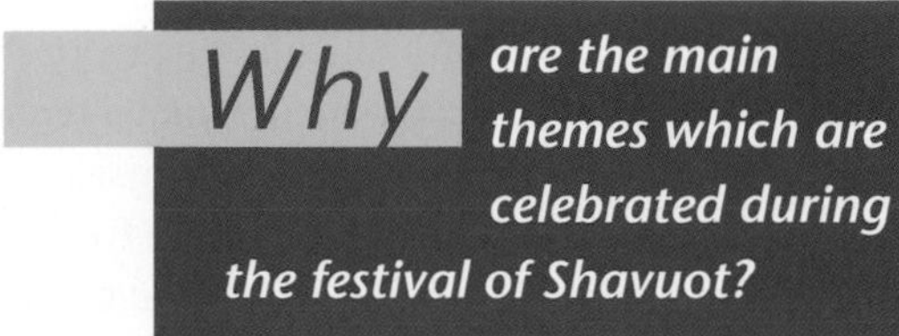

Why are the main themes which are celebrated during the festival of Shavuot?

FOCUSING QUESTIONS

What is the importance of the links between the festivals of Pesach and Shavuot?

How are the old agricultural roots of the festival of Shavuot kept alive during modern celebrations of the festival?

How do Jews remind themselves of the giving of the Torah to Moses at Shavuot?

Shavuot was one of three 'pilgrimage festivals' in ancient Israel, during which Jews visited the Temple in Jerusalem. The other Pilgrimage Festivals were Sukkot and Pesach. The old rabbis spoke of Shavuot being the 'complement' to Pesach. As with the other two festivals, Shavuot celebrated two events – harvest and the giving of the Torah to Moses on Mount Sinai.

On the second day of Pesach, a measure of barley, called an omer, was brought to the Temple and, during the forty-nine days that followed, the Jews counted the days between the presentation of the omer and the start of Shavuot – a period called sefirat hamer. This meant that the festival of Shavuot followed fifty days after the start of Pesach and it still does. The importance of this dating is underlined by the name which the festival is given in the Jewish Scriptures, the 'Feast of Weeks', since it comes seven weeks after Pesach.

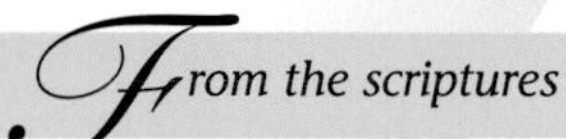

From the scriptures

These words about Shavuot are found in the Book of Leviticus: *'And from the day after the sabbath, from the day on which you bring the sheaf of the elevation offering, you shall count off seven weeks; they shall be complete. You shall count until the day after the seventh sabbath, fifty days: then you shall present an offering of new grain to the LORD.'*

(Leviticus 23.15-16)

1 What is the *'sheaf of the elevation offering'* called?
2 Another name for the festival of Shavuot is the 'Feast of Weeks'. Explain why.
3 What is the *'offering of new grain'* that is presented to God on Shavuot called, and why is it given?
4 How is the old tradition of presenting the *'offering of new grain'* still maintained today?

A harvest festival

During the original festival of Shavuot farmers brought the 'first-fruits' of their harvest to the Temple, where they offered them as a token of their thankfulness to God. They were only allowed to eat the produce themselves after the first gift had been made to God. In Israel today many farmers still maintain this tradition by bringing their baskets of 'bikkurim' (ripe first-fruits) to a central collecting area. In Britain, this link to the agricultural roots of the festival is maintained by synagogues being beautifully decorated for Shavuot with fresh fruit, plants and flowers. Some Jews have complained that is too similar to the Christian harvest festival, but the tradition remains.

The giving of the Torah

The link between the festival of Shavuot and the giving of the Torah (the Law) to Moses is what really matters to Jews today. The Torah is believed to be God's greatest gift to the Jews, and their greatest treasure. At Mount Sinai a weary, and dispirited, group of ex-slaves accepted the Torah and was transformed into the nation which has survived over 3,000 years. The secret of that survival has been the Torah with its 613 laws, including the Ten Sayings. Traditionally Jews stay up all night on Shavuot reading the Torah, keeping themselves awake by drinking large quantities of coffee and eating cheesecake. They also eat other milk products to remind themselves that the Torah, like milk, nourishes young and old alike.

Honeycake is a also a popular food to remind everyone that the Torah is sweet to the spiritual tastebuds.

Apart from the reading from the Torah of the giving of the Ten Sayings (Exodus 20.1-17) all Jews read the lovely Book of Ruth on Shavuot. This love-story from the Scriptures tells how Ruth, a Gentile woman, was converted to the Jewish faith after helping with the gleaning at harvest-time. Ruth is taken as the supreme example of someone who accepted the teachings of the Torah of her own free-will. According to Jewish tradition King David was a descendant of Ruth, and as he died on Shavuot this provides another reason for reading the book on this day. Often young boys will begin their study of the Torah on Shavuot.

A. In Israel many farmers still bring the 'first-fruits' of the harvest to the synagogue during Shavuot. How does this reflect the origins of the festival?

DISCUSS

Which important Jewish themes are brought out during the festival of Shavuot?

FOR YOUR FOLDER

1 Harvest festivals are important in many religions. Why do you think this is? Do you think that thanking God for a successful harvest is an important activity today? Might your answer to this question depend on where in the world you live?

2 Answer each of these questions in your own words:

a) Why was the giving of the Torah to the Jews such an important event and how does this justify an annual celebration of the event at Shavuot?
b) What is the significance of the first night of Shavuot?
c) Why is the reading of the Book of Ruth from the Jewish Scriptures an important part of the celebrations of Shavuot?

In the glossary: David; Gentile; Jerusalem; Moses; Pesach; Sefirat Hamer; Shavuot; Sukkot; Temple; Ten Sayings; Torah.

Brit Milah

What is brit milah and why does it happen?

FOCUSING QUESTIONS

Who, according to Jewish tradition, is involved in the birth of every new baby?

What is circumcision?

What does brit milah indicate within the Jewish community?

DISCUSS

What do you think that Jewish men today expect to enjoy as a result of having been circumcised?

Jewish tradition teaches clearly that three people are involved in the creation of new life – the mother, the father and God. An old Jewish saying says that '*the whole world rejoices at the birth of a baby*'. Every new baby is welcomed into the Jewish community as a gift from God but only boys go through a special initiation ceremony – called brit milah or circumcision. Since this custom can be traced all the way back to Abraham, circumcision is the oldest religious practice still followed by the Jews.

A token of the Covenant

Circumcision is always carried out on a baby boy on the eighth day after birth and involves the removal of the foreskin of his penis. The justification given in the Jewish Scriptures for this practice is that it is a 'token of the Covenant' which God first made with Abraham and then renewed with Moses. Circumcision is the outward, physical sign that the child is a member of the Jewish people and so a partaker of the Covenant. No male can belong to this community of people unless they carry this outward sign.

Originally the father in the Jewish family was charged with the responsibility of circumcising all of his sons. Abraham, for instance, was given the responsibility of circumcising all the males in his family including himself! Today, though, the operation is usually carried out by a trained Jewish circumciser – called a 'mohel' – although it can be performed in a hospital if a rabbi is present. Orthodox Jews prefer for it to be carried out in the synagogue or in the home for which a quorum of ten males have to be present.

Circumcision

The child is carried into the gathering by his godmother and is then held by his godfather who is usually the 'sandek' – the person who will hold the baby during the ceremony. Before performing the operation the mohel says: *'Blessed art Thou, O Lord our God, King of the universe, who has sanctified* [made us holy] *with Thy commandments, and hast given us the command concerning circumcision.'*

The mohel removes the foreskin from the penis with a quick stroke of the knife, wipes off the blood and then secures the skin to prevent any further growth. The father of the child then says the blessing : *'Blessed are You, O Lord our God, ruling*

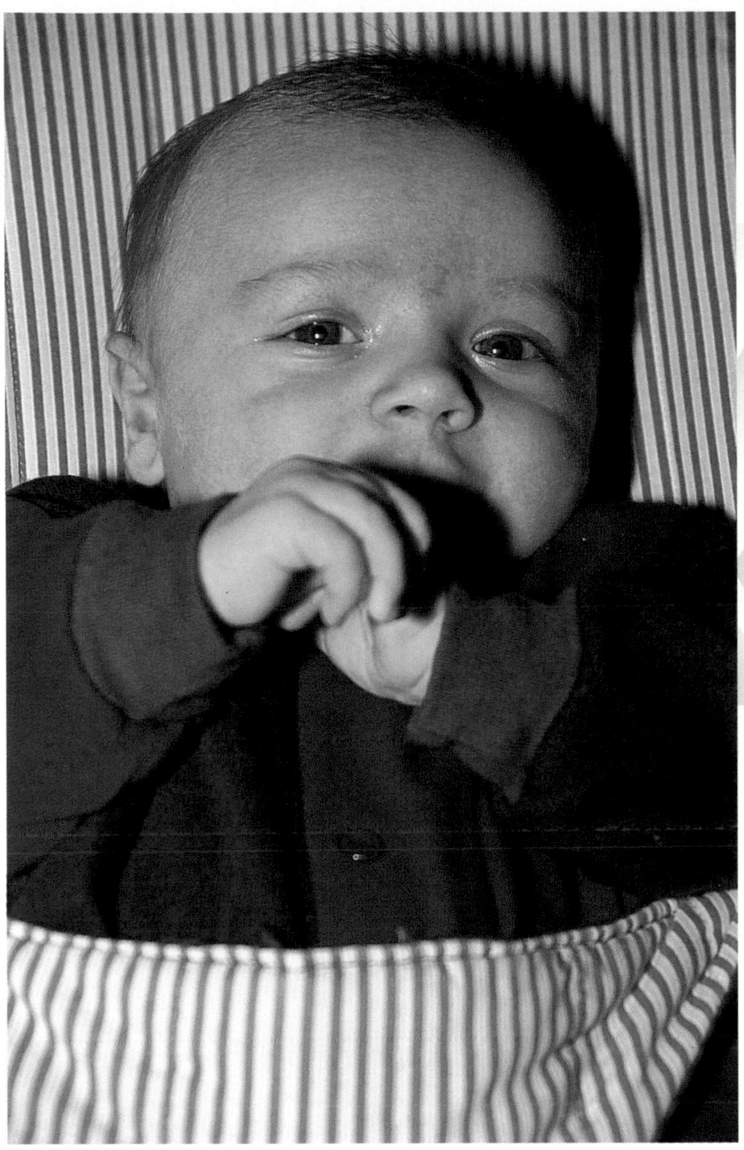

A. Why do you think the circumcision of this baby is a very important occasion for the whole Jewish community?

From the scriptures

When God made the original Covenant with Abraham he told him:
'This is my covenant, which you shall keep, between me and you and your offspring after you: Every male among you shall be circumcised. You shall circumcise the flesh of your foreskins, and it shall be a sign of the covenant between me and you. Throughout your generations every male among you shall be circumcised when he is eight days old...'.
(Genesis 17.10-12)

1. What is the relationship between the Covenant that God made with Abraham and the ritual of brit milah?
2. What spiritual benefit does circumcision place on a Jew today?

Spirit of the Universe, who has commanded us to enter our son into the Covenant of our father Abraham.'

Those present respond by saying: *'As he entered the Covenant, so may he enter into the love of the Torah, into the marriage canopy and into a life of good deeds.'* At this point the child is given his name, a blessing is made over a glass of wine, and a drop of wine is placed on the baby's lips. The father drinks some of the wine that remains before sending the rest to the baby's mother who waits in a separate room during the ceremony.

The reasons for circumcision

There are three reasons why circumcision is carried out on every Jewish boy:

- It is an act of complete obedience since it removes something from the body because God commanded it.
- Jews accept circumcision as a sign for every man that he is a member of God's chosen people – the Jews.
- It provides the opportunity for the child to receive the blessing of his father – always a very important event in the life of each member of a Jewish family.

FOR YOUR FOLDER

1
a) During the brit milah ceremony everyone present says: *'As he entered into the Covenant, so may he enter into the love of the Torah, into the marriage canopy and into a life of good deeds.'* According to this, when does the child enter into the Covenant?
b) Why do you think these other three blessings are singled out for the life ahead of the child?

2 At the time of the early Jews, those who were not Jewish were described as the 'uncircumcised'. It was a term of abuse. Why do you think that the Jews placed such importance on circumcision?

In the glossary: ABRAHAM; BRIT MILAH; MOHEL; MOSES.

Bar Mitzvah and Bat Mitzvah

What is a Bar Mitzvah and Bat Mitzvah, and what do they signify?

FOCUSING QUESTIONS

How does a Jewish boy prepare to become Bar Mitzvah?

What happens when a boy becomes Bar Mitzvah?

What are Bat Mitzvah and Bat Chayil?

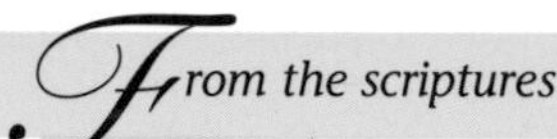

Parents are given this advice in The Talmud: *'When a child begins to speak his father should speak with him in the holy tongue and teach him Torah. If he does not do so it is as if he buries him.'*

What do you think this means?

A Bar Mitzvah, meaning a 'son of Commandment', is a Jewish boy who has reached, at the age of thirteen, the time when he takes religious responsibility for his own actions. The training of the boy to take on these responsibilities started at a very early age (see Photograph A) when he was taught to read and speak Hebrew, the language in which all Orthodox synagogue services are conducted. He was introduced to those mitzvah ('commandments') which tell him how he should behave when he becomes an adult. He also memorised the Shema since The Talmud teaches that: *'As soon as a male child can speak, his father teaches him the Torah.'*

The Bar Mitzvah ceremony

The ceremony which accompanies a boy becoming Bar Mitzvah takes place, if possible, on the first Shabbat following his thirteenth birthday. The ceremony itself is comparatively recent, and was probably first introduced in the thirteenth or fourteenth centuries. It is not, in itself, particularly important. The boy would still become a Bar Mitzvah even if the ceremony did not take place. The ceremony does, though, give the Jewish community an opportunity to show that they now accept that the boy has become an adult.

During the service, the passage for the day is read from the Sefer Torah. In most synagogues the boy is called up to the bimah (reading platform) to read this passage, although sometimes he is asked to read from the Prophets instead (see Photograph B). The boy reads the passage in Hebrew but, before he does so, his father recites the blessing: *'Blessed be He who has freed me from responsibility for this child.'* Up until this point, the father has been held responsible for any sins that his son has committed. Now the father is delivered from this responsibility and the son must answer for his own actions. The most important of these responsibilities are spelled out in the Ten Sayings. From now on, the Bar Mitzvah is able to wear his tallit and tefillin, be called up to read from the Torah in the synagogue, and be accepted as part of the quorum – the group of ten males who have to be present during all services in an Orthodox synagogue.

A. What is a Jewish boy expected to learn before his Bar Mitzvah?

B. What is meant by 'Bar Mitzvah'?

C. What is meant by 'Bat Mitzvah'?

The Bat Mitzvah ceremony

Girls become Bat Mitzvah ('daughters of Commandment') at the age of twelve, although only Reform synagogues offer this. While a boy marks his 'coming of age' by wearing the tefillin and reading from the Torah there were not, until recently, any special ceremonies connected with Bat Mitzvah. In recent years, though, this has changed, and many Reform synagogues have introduced special prayers during the service and a party to follow. In Reform synagogues the Bat Mitzvah girl can now read a portion from the Torah just as a boy does at his Bar Mitzvah.

Bat Chayil

Girls brought up in most Orthodox synagogues have the opportunity of becoming Bat Chayil – meaning 'daughters of valour'. This service takes place in the synagogue any time after the girl's twelfth birthday. Usually held on a Sunday, the service often celebrates more than one girl reaching this landmark. Before this time the girl spends time studying what it means to be a woman in the Jewish tradition. As only men read from the Torah in the synagogue, the girl is likely to read a poem or another piece of spiritual writing as part of the service.

FOR YOUR FOLDER

1 Make a list of three ways in which the Bar Mitzvah ceremony differs from that of the Bat Mitzvah.

2
a) Look at Photographs B and C. Describe what is happening in each photograph.
b) What responsibility is the father thankful to have been delivered from because his son has reached his Bar Mitzvah?

3
a) In what ways does the ceremony of Bat Chayil differ from that of Bat Mitzvah?
b) Read Proverbs 31.10-31 which provide the basis for a woman being described as 'a daughter of valour'. Make a list of those characteristics which, according to the extract, a daughter of valour is expected to show.

In the glossary: BAR MITZVAH; BAT MITZVAH; BAT CHAYIL; BIMAH; HEBREW; MITZVAH; PROPHETS; SEFER TORAH; SHABBAT; SHEMA; SYNAGOGUE; TALMUD; TEN SAYINGS; TORAH.

Marriage

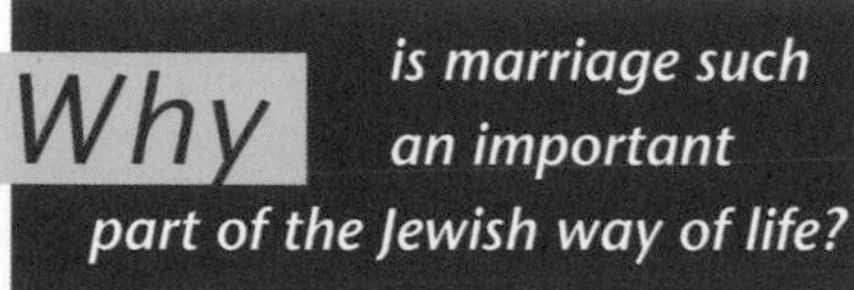

Why *is marriage such an important part of the Jewish way of life?*

FOCUSING QUESTIONS

How does the Jewish community view marriage?

What is needed before a Jewish marriage can be carried out in a synagogue?

How is a divorce granted in the Jewish community?

In every Jewish holy book marriage is considered to be the ideal state for everyone. Although the first purpose of marriage is to provide a home for children to be brought into, it also exists, in the words of one of the marriage blessings, *'to give joy and gladness, mirth and exultation, pleasure and delight, love, peace and friendship'* to the couple.

The marriage service

Although Reform Jews have changed a few minor details, both Orthodox and Reform marriage services are essentially the same. According to Jewish law, the marriage must involve both a Jewish man and a Jewish woman if it is to be carried out in a synagogue. Marriages involving just one Jewish person can be performed elsewhere. Jewish marriages cannot be performed on Shabbat or any festival day.

A Jewish marriage service begins with the signing of the wedding document – the ketubah (see Photograph A) – in front of two witnesses. The contract sets out the man's marriage responsibilities but does not contain any promises from the woman, since the whole intention of the document is to offer the bride future security.

DISCUSS

Judaism is not the only religion which spells out the responsibility of the man in the marriage relationship. Do you think this is a good idea and, if so, why?

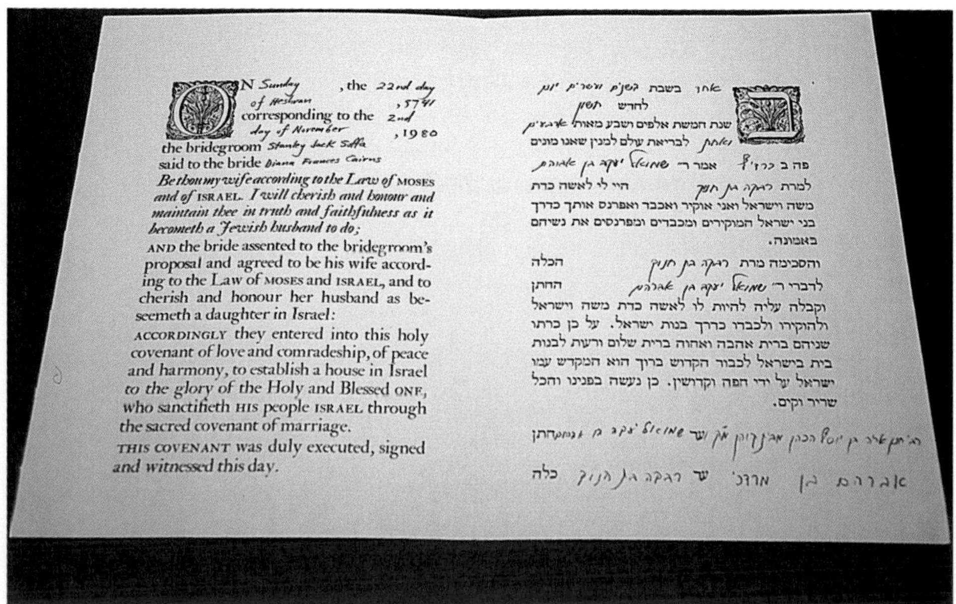

ON Sunday, the 22nd day of Heshvan, 5741 corresponding to the 2nd day of November, 1980 the bridegroom Stanley Jack Saffa said to the bride Diana Frances Cairns

Be thou my wife according to the Law of MOSES *and of* ISRAEL. *I will cherish and honour and maintain thee in truth and faithfulness as it becometh a Jewish husband to do;*

AND the bride assented to the bridegroom's proposal and agreed to be his wife according to the Law of MOSES and ISRAEL, and to cherish and honour her husband as beseemeth a daughter in Israel:

ACCORDINGLY they entered into this holy covenant of love and comradeship, of peace and harmony, to establish a house in Israel to the glory of the Holy and Blessed ONE, who sanctifieth HIS people ISRAEL through the sacred covenant of marriage.

THIS COVENANT was duly executed, signed and witnessed this day.

A. Why is the signing of the ketubah (shown, right) a very important part of the Jewish wedding service – especially for the bride?

B. What do you notice about this huppah?

Following the signing, the couple are escorted by their parents to stand under the wedding canopy – the huppah (see Photograph B). The canopy symbolises the home that the couple are going to set up together. The parents remain at their side throughout the ceremony. The marriage ceremony begins with a recitation of Psalm 100 and other Psalms and then a blessing: *'He who is mighty, blessed and great above all, may He bless the bridegroom and the bride.'*

Next, the person conducting the ceremony recites a blessing over a glass of wine. The bride and groom sip the wine and the groom then places a simple ring on the bride's right hand and says: *'Behold thou art consecrated to me by this ring, according to the law of Moses and Israel.'* The ketubah is then read aloud.

A further blessing is made over the wine and seven benedictions are then pronounced. In these, God's blessing is called down on the bride and bridegroom and a prayer for Zion (Jerusalem) is included. The bride and groom again sip the wine and the groom stamps on a wine glass and shatters it. The purpose of this is to remind the bride and couple on their happy day of the destruction of the Temple in Jerusalem. The Psalmist (the author of the Psalms) in Psalm 137.6 pledges that Jerusalem will never be forgotten – even in the midst of joy.

There are no vows made in a Jewish wedding as there are in a Christian service. It is understood that the provisions in the ketubah will be carried out and that the husband and wife will remain faithful to each other until death separates them. Jewish tradition frowns upon oaths and vows as a way of making people carry out their obligations.

Divorce

If a marriage breaks down, Jewish tradition lays down a procedure for a divorce without either person having to prove 'guilt' or responsibility for the breakdown of the marriage. After the divorce has been approved by the civil courts, the couple appear before the bet din (the 'house of judgement') which is made up of three rabbis. Only the bet din can grant a religious divorce, and a person cannot remarry unless the bet din grants them a 'get' (a bill of divorce).

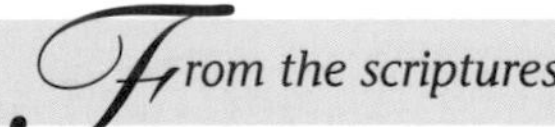

From the scriptures

In Psalm 137.6, the Psalmist writes from exile in Babylon and laments over the destruction of the city of Jerusalem. This verse is recalled during the wedding service: *'Let my tongue cling to the roof of my mouth, if I do not remember you, if I do not set Jerusalem above my highest joy.'*

1 Why does the city of Jerusalem occupy such an important place in the hearts of Jewish people?
2 How is the promise of the Psalmist brought to mind during the wedding service?

FOR YOUR FOLDER

1
a) What is the Jewish wedding document called?
b) How many people must witness the signing of this document and when does this signing take place?
c) What is contained in the ketubah?
d) Why is the signing of the ketubah, and not any spoken vow, so important?

2 During the wedding service, when the groom gives the ring to his bride, and says: *'Behold you are sanctified to me with this ring, according to the law of Moses and Israel'.*
What do you think these words mean?

In the glossary: HUPPAH; GET; JERUSALEM; KETUBAH; MOSES; RABBI; REFORM JEW; SHABBAT; TEMPLE; ZION.

Death

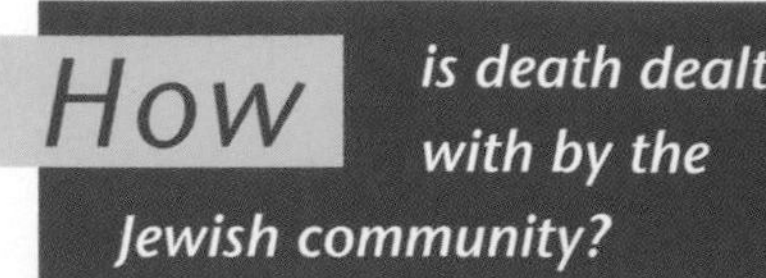

How is death dealt with by the Jewish community?

FOCUSING QUESTIONS

What is the Chevra Kadishah ?

How do Jews treat the body of someone who has just died?

What is the Kaddish prayer?

DISCUSS

1 Why do you think that the Jewish community appoints a special group of people to deal with death?

2 What reason can you put forward for the tradition of not leaving the body unattended between death and burial?

The Psalmist leads all Jews to believe that they can hope to live for eighty years (Psalm 90.10) and this is the hope of every believer. Moses, though, lived, according to the Jewish Scriptures to the age of 120 years and Jewish people often wish one another 'until 120' on their birthday. For Jews life is seen as a gift from God which is to be cherished and valued. Death is seen as a tragic, though inevitable, event.

Dealing with death

The rabbi is not expected to be present as life draws to a close. Each synagogue has its own Chevra Kadishah ('holy fellowship') – a group of men and women who are noted for the holiness of their lives. They stay with the person who is dying and then take care of the body once death has occurred. Belonging to the Chevra Kadishah is a great honour. The voluntary act of love which its members show to the dying is a true mitzvah since it is carried out without any thought of reward.

It is Jewish tradition that a body should not be left unaccompanied from the moment of death to its burial and the Chevra Kadishah guarantee this. Following death the corpse is placed on the ground, since this is symbolic of where the body came from originally and to which it shall shortly return. They wash it and dress it in simple white linen garments to emphasise that all people, rich and poor, are equal in the sight of God. The body of a man is likely to be wrapped in the tallit which he used to pray. The body is then placed in a simple wooden coffin with the head resting on earth that has been brought specially from the Holy Land. A heavy black shroud is also placed over the coffin to make sure that everyone is treated exactly the same.

The funeral

Jewish tradition requires that burial takes place as soon as possible after death, usually within twenty-four hours. People who die within the Orthodox tradition are always buried, but cremation is allowed for members of the Reform synagogues. The larger synagogues often have their own burial-grounds but often a special area is set aside in general graveyards. The funeral itself is essentially simple, with the rabbi delivering a eulogy in praise of the dead person. Psalms from the Jewish Scriptures are chanted and the Kaddish prayer is recited:
'Let the glory of God be extolled, let His great name be exalted in the world whose creation

He willed. May His kingdom prevail, in our own day, in our own lives, and the life of all Israel. Let us say, Amen...May the source of peace send peace to all who mourn and comfort to all who are bereaved. Amen.'

The body is carried by pallbearers to the place of burial, stopping seven times on the way to remember the seven 'vanities' listed in the Book of Ecclesiastes. The coffin is lowered into the ground with the immediate family, and then other mourners, shovelling earth on top. Everyone then washes their hands as they leave the cemetery. This act shows that they are free from any guilt for the person's death, and encourages those present to turn their back upon death now and get on with living. This is very much the emphasis of the Jewish faith. As The Talmud teaches, the deceased has now set off on its journey into eternity while the living must, with God's help, carry on with their lives. The laws governing mourning in the Jewish community are designed to help them do this as soon as possible.

FOR YOUR FOLDER

1 A very important element in the way that the Jewish community deals with death is the way that the equality of all people is emphasised.

a) Describe two ways in which Jewish funerals underline this message.

b) Why do you think that this is a very important element in the Jewish approach to death?

2 This is the last prayer which every Jewish person hopes that he or she will have the strength to say before dying:

'My God and the God of my fathers, accept this prayer; do not ignore my supplication. Forgive me all the sins I have committed in my life-time and may it be your will to heal me. Yet, if you have decreed that I should die...may my death atone for all my sins and transgressions which I have committed before you...Grant me a share in the life to come...into your hands I commend my spirit.'

What do you think the words: *'...if you have decreed that I should die...may my death atone for all the sins and transgression which I have committed before you...'* mean?

3 The earth and the soil are very important symbolic elements in the Jewish approach to death. Why do you think that they are so important?

A. This stained-glass window has been erected in a synagogue in memory of someone who has died. Such memorials cannot be erected until at least a year has passed after the person's death. Can you suggest why?

In the glossary: CHEVRA KADISHAH; MITZVAH; MOSES; PSALM; RABBI; SYNAGOGUE; TALMUD.

Mourning

What *are the traditions within the Jewish community concerned with mourning the death of someone close?*

FOCUSING QUESTIONS

What is an Onan?

What is Shiva?

When does the period of mourning end in a Jewish family?

The Jewish religion lays a strong emphasis on the need that everyone has to mourn the death of a close relative – a father, mother, son, daughter, brother, sister, husband or wife. Jewish tradition has determined that mourning should pass through three or possibly four stages altogether. Moses Maimonides, the great Jewish teacher of the twelfth century, taught that it is foolish to exceed these stages since that would show a reluctance to accept that death comes to all of us. Not to mourn at all, though, is unfeeling since it shows that the dead person was not really loved. The traditions about mourning try to strike the balance between the two.

The four stages

Stage one

The short period between the death and the funeral, during which time the mourner, known as the Onan, is released from all other religious responsibilities. During this period, the close family of the dead person is fully supported by the Jewish community whilst the Chevra Kadishah takes full care of the funeral arrangements. The Jewish community emphasises the importance of people mourning together.

Stage two

The Shiva which lasts for seven days from the moment of burial. To show their intense grief the close relatives put a tear in one of their outer garments, remove their shoes, and sit on the ground or low stools at home. They do not shave, bathe or cut their hair during Shiva. All of the mirrors in the home are covered as no-one should pay any attention to their personal appearance at this time. Mourners must not have any sexual contact, study the Torah (because to do so is a great delight to all Jews), go to work or attend to their business affairs. The only time that mourners leave their homes during Shiva may be to go to the synagogue to recite the Kaddish prayer. Generally, however, they arrange for a quorum of ten males to come to their home where the Kaddish prayer is said three times each day.

A. It is normal to have a candle lit in the home throughout Shiva. Can you suggest why?

Within the Jewish community, it is seen as an important responsibility to look after mourners during Shiva. Members of the community will therefore often cook meals, or shop for bereaved families. When visitors enter the bereaved families home they offer words of consolation and comfort saying, as they arrive, *'May the Omnipresent comfort you in the midst of all other mourners over Zion and Jerusalem.'*

There are just two exceptions to these rules about Shiva. First, people are expected to go to the synagogue on Shabbat as usual but are spared from being called up to read from the Torah or from carrying out any other responsibility. Secondly, if a festival falls during Shiva then the mourning is suspended, since the responsibility to celebrate the festival takes precedence over everything else.

Stage three

The Sheloshim period. This lasts for another twenty-three days making the time of mourning thirty days in all. During Sheloshim, mourners do not shave or have a haircut, listen to music, go to weddings or parties. They do, however, gradually begin to return to normal. At the end of Sheloshim the time of mourning is over for everyone except those who are grieving the loss of a parent.

Stage four

The mourning time for those who have lost a parent ends one year after their death. Following this there is an annual remembrance day, Jahrzeit. The closest relative has recited Kaddish in the synagogue for the first eleven months, and now does so on the anniversary of the person's death – on which occasion a candle is also lit in the home (see Photograph A). A memorial stone to commemorate the deceased can now be erected on the grave (see Photograph B).

Orthodox Jews observe these mourning laws very strictly. Reform Jews observe some of them but do not accept that all of the laws are binding on them. They rather see some of them as useful in helping people to overcome their grief and these are the ones that they observe.

B. What is the link between the erection of a headstone on a grave and the end of the period of mourning?

FOR YOUR FOLDER

1 There are strict laws about mourning in most religions – with the notable exception of Christianity. Many people believe that these laws help them to come to terms with the death of someone close.

a) Do you think that the way that Christians deal with death is helpful or not?
b) Do you think that Christians would find it helpful if there were traditions about mourning that people could follow?

2 It is normal to have a candle burning in the house throughout Shiva. Explain why by looking at Proverbs 20.27

3

a) What are the three stages of mourning through which a Jewish family is expected to pass?
b) What additional period of mourning is expected of those who have lost a parent?
c) Why do you think that the loss of a parent requires extra time to be spent in mourning?
d) Do you think that it is a good idea to have these recognised stages of mourning? How do you think that they might benefit the people involved?

DISCUSS

The various stages of mourning in Judaism are intended to help a person to come to terms with their grief. Do you think that they achieve their aim?

In the glossary: CHEVRA KADISHAH ; ORTHODOX JEW; REFORM JEW; SHABBAT; SYNAGOGUE; TORAH.

The Tenakh

Which *three parts go to make up The Tenakh and what is the significance of each of them?*

FOCUSING QUESTIONS

Into which three sections are the Hebrew Scriptures divided?

What is contained in the Torah?

What are the Ketuvim and the Nevi'im?

The Hebrew holy Scriptures, The Tenakh, is divided into three parts – the Torah, the Nevi'im (the 'Prophets') and the Ketuvim ('Writings'). Tenakh is often spelt TeNaKh, the capital letters standing for each of these three sections:

The Torah

The Torah, meaning 'guidance' or 'teaching' is at the beginning of the Jewish Scriptures and contains five books – Genesis, Exodus, Leviticus, Deuteronomy and Numbers – whose authorship has traditionally been ascribed to Moses. They are often called the 'Books of Moses' as tradition asserts that God gave them to Moses on Mount Sinai and he wrote them down directly. Of these books:

- Genesis (meaning 'Beginnings') deals with the beginning of life on Earth, the great Flood, and the lives of Abraham, Jacob and Joseph.
- Exodus describes the time the Israelites spent in slavery, the call of Moses to lead them out of Egypt (the Exodus), the encounter of Moses with God on Mount Sinai, and the journey of the Israelites to the Promised Land of Canaan.
- Leviticus lays down rules on, amongst many other things, the work of the priests.
- Numbers outlines Jewish history from the time that the Jews left Mount Sinai until they approached Canaan, and shows how Moses built their community into a nation.
- Deuteronomy (the 'second book of the Law') reviews the material in the other books and provides a second account of the giving of the Ten Sayings (Deuteronomy 5.1-22). It also includes some strong statements by Moses on how Jews ought to live.

No part of the Jewish Scriptures is as valuable to Jews as the Torah. Throughout Jewish history it has been hailed as the most precious gift of God to the Jewish people. The Midrash (rabbinical commentaries on the Scriptures) says that the Torah was created before the world which was then made by God using the Torah as his blueprint. When God told his angels that he was giving the Torah to Israel they objected strongly – they wanted to keep it for themselves! Psalms contains many statements in praise of the Torah. The longest psalm,119, uses each letter of the alphabet eight times in praise of the Torah and contains the words: *'O how I love your law! It is my meditation all day long'* (verse 97).

From the scriptures

Here are some extracts from Psalm 119:
'Happy are those whose way is blameless, who walk in the law of the LORD, Happy are those who keep his decrees...I shall not be put to shame, having my eyes fixed on all your commandments...I treasure your word in my heart...I delight in the way of your decrees...Your word is a lamp to my feet and a light to my path...'.

1 When the Psalmist talks about delighting in God's decrees what is he actually talking about?
2 On what does the Psalmist, the author of the Psalms, fix his eyes?
3 What do you think the Psalmist means when he says: *'Your word is a lamp to my feet and a light to my path'*?

A. A Torah scroll being read. What do you think the Psalmist meant when he said '*It* [the Torah] *is my meditation all day long*'?

B. What does the word Torah mean?

The Nevi'im

The Nevi'im is made up of two kinds of books:

1 History books which cover the story of the Jews from the time of Joshua onwards. During this time various holy men, called prophets, explained about God to the Jews and tried to guide them in their worship.

2 Books which contain the prophecies of such people as Isaiah, Jeremiah and Ezekiel. These were prophets whose message was, in the main, rejected by the people.

The Ketuvim

These books are considered to be of less value than the Torah or the Nevi'im, but the writings do contain the Psalms which are used regularly in synagogue worship. Other readings from the Ketuvim do take place – usually on festival days.

FOR YOUR FOLDER

1 Answer these questions about the Torah in your own words:

a) What does the word 'Torah' mean?
b) What are the five books which make up the Torah and where would you find them in the Hebrew Bible?
() What would you expect to read in the Book of Genesis?
d) Where would you look for details about the work of the priests in Israel?
e) Which books contain the Ten Sayings?
f) Which book is also called 'the second book of the Law'? Why?
g) What evidence is there that the Jews have always held the Torah in the highest possible regard?

In the glossary: ABRAHAM; CANAAN; EXODUS; KETUVIM; MIDRASH; MOSES; NEVI'IM; PROPHET; PSALMS; SYNAGOGUE; TENAKH; TEN SAYINGS; TORAH.

The Talmud and the Midrash

What *are The Talmud and Midrash and what is their importance to the Jewish community?*

FOCUSING QUESTIONS

How were the comments of the early rabbis on the Torah and the other books in the Jewish Scriptures kept 'alive' before they were written down?

What is the relationship between The Talmud, the Mishnah and the Gemara?

What is the difference between The Talmud and the Midrashim?

The books in the Jewish Bible, The Tenakh, were completed and put together by the at the Synod of Jamnia held in 96 CE. By this time, great changes had taken place within Judaism and these changes gave rise to a whole series of new interpretations of the holy books being expressed by the rabbis of the time. These opinions were not originally written down but were passed on by word of mouth. Although Judaism strongly believed that the Torah was supreme as God's greatest gift it also supported these interpretations which became known as The Talmud and The Midrash.

A. These Jews are studying the Jewish holy texts. What might they hope to find there?

Teachings and spiritual guidance

The Talmud is a collection of rabbinical teachings compiled between the destruction of the city of Jerusalem in the first century CE, and the end of the fifth century. After the five books of the Torah, it is regarded as the highest legal authority in Judaism.

The first part of The Talmud is called the Mishnah. The second, and much longer, part is called the Gemara. The Talmud was brought together by two rabbis in the fifth century. The result amounts to 6,000 pages and 3,000,000 words drawn from some 1,000 contributors.

The Talmud provides legal rulings – covering laws on topics such as agriculture, the Temple and its sacrifices, cleanliness and impurity, and criminal and civil law. It also contains humorous sketches, parables and short sayings about the meaning of life, as well as giving the reader a glimpse into the nature of ancient Jewish life. For Jews living in the modern world, however, it also offers a range of moral insights and spiritual values which are still very relevant. It advises Jews on the way that they should lead their lives at home, among their families, and in the outside world. The Talmud still forms the basis of study in seminaries, where rabbis are trained, and in traditional Jewish schools.

From the scriptures

Here are just three examples of midrashim:
'Why was man created a solitary human being, without a companion? So that it might not be said that some races are better than others.'

'If two men claim your help, and one is your enemy, help him first.'

'A man is forbidden to eat anything until he has fed his beast first.'

Imagine situations, or questions, which might have arisen and led to the making up of these three midrashim.

Illustrations

Ancient Jews often used midrashim (the plural of midrash) to illustrate the meanings of certain passages from the Scriptures. Rabbis would give sermons in which they commented on passages from the Scriptures using parables, legends, myths and stories to explain the important points. In doing this, the rabbis were also attempting to 'search out' meanings in the Torah which were not immediately apparent. In this, the rabbis claimed to have the authority of the Scriptures, and they turned to Ezra, a Jewish leader from the fifth century BCE, as an example: *'For Ezra had set his heart to study the law of the LORD, and to do it, and to teach the statutes and ordinances in Israel'* (Ezra 7.10).

The word 'midrash' means 'to seek' or 'to enquire', and this search for meaning has been extended beyond commentaries on the books of the Torah to every book in the Jewish Scriptures. Most of these 'illustrations' were collected together between the first and the eighth centuries, although some came to light as late as the fourteenth century.

DISCUSS

The Talmud was not completed for over five centuries after the books of The Tenakh were put together. Do you think that this long gap makes the teachings in The Talmud less useful?

FOR YOUR FOLDER

1
a) The Talmud still forms the basis of study in Jewish academies and schools. Do you think that judgements made about different matters almost 2,000 years ago can still be useful in governing behaviour today? Explain your decision.
b) Do you think that it makes any difference to the authority of a holy book if the real meaning of certain passages needs to be 'searched' out?

2 Each of the following are important words used in this spread. Explain, in your own words, what each of them mean: Talmud; Mishnah; Gemara; Midrash.

3 How did The Talmud come to be written? What do you think that its value is to Jews today?

In the glossary: GEMARA; JERUSALEM; MIDRASH; MISHNAH; RABBI; TALMUD; TORAH.

God

What do Jews believe about God and how has this belief given them a distinctive way of looking at the world?

FOCUSING QUESTIONS

What is the basic Jewish belief about God?

How do the Jewish Scriptures explain the existence of life?

What does the Shema say about God?

It is very difficult to imagine someone being a Jew without believing in God yet, for many Jews, this belief represents a real stumbling-block. A whole series of reasons have led many Jewish people to abandon the traditional Jewish understanding of God. Questions like 'How could God, if he is good and all-powerful as Jews believe, allow an event like the Holocaust to take place?' have forced many Jews to conclude that there is no God. Many of them, though, still wish to keep their Jewish identity and remain a part of the Jewish community.

God

The Jewish Scriptures describe how Abram came from a city in which many gods were worshipped yet he, and his family, became convinced of the existence of one God alone who 'spoke' to him. This belief in one God is the focal point of the Jewish Scriptures and is vindicated by the existence of the universe which the one God has created, and in the history of the Jews to whom the one God has often revealed himself.

A. There are many aspects of life which Jews take to be 'signs' that God exists. Do you think they are right and, if so, which signs do you think point most clearly to God?

God in the world

The Jewish faith teaches that the universe did not create itself, nor has it always existed. The world is not the result of chance or an accidental collision of atoms. It was created by God. God is the source of all life in the universe and He actively intervenes in daily events. God has a purpose for the whole of life and the power to bring that purpose about. This is why many Jews praise God each morning with the words:

'Praised are You, O Lord our God, King of the universe. You fix the circles of light and darkness; You ordain the order of all creation, You cause light to shine over all the earth. Your radiant mercy is upon its inhabitants...Praised are you, O Lord, Creator of the heavenly bodies'.

Jews see the reality of God revealed in all the force, and wonder, of nature. God has infinite power and authority. He did not come into existence since nothing or no-one could possibly create God. God is eternal – there was never a time when He did not exist.

B. What do you think a Jewish person hopes to gain by studying the holy books?

Yet this all-powerful God turned from creating the universe to make a covenant (an 'agreement' or 'contract') with one family – that of Abram, who is called 'The Friend of God'. In this covenant, God promised that he would remain faithful to the descendants of Abraham, the Jews, and would treat them as his special people. They, in turn, would be expected to remember God at all times, serve Him and keep all of His laws. The Jewish Scriptures are full of occasions when God intervenes in human affairs to keep his side of the Covenant.

The Shema

Each morning and evening Jewish people recite a prayer called the Shema (meaning 'hear'). The Shema is the closest that Jews come to expressing their belief about God. The full Shema can be seen in three passages:

1. Deuteronomy 6.4-9. There is one God and no other. Everything that a Jew believes about God is based on this core belief. Throughout the Scriptures the Jews are forbidden from making any physical representation (an idol) of this God to worship. God is way beyond human understanding and thought – how can He be represented in wood or stone?

2. Deuteronomy 11.13-21. God has entered into a binding agreement with the Jewish people. This agreement still exists today.

3. Numbers 15.37-41. It was God who delivered the Jews from slavery in Egypt and gave them their Promised Land of Canaan. God's purpose for the Jews is still being worked out.

FOR YOUR FOLDER

A powerful ruler wanted Rabbi Joshua ben Hananiah, who lived in the first century CE, to let him see God: *'"You cannot," replied the rabbi. "But I insist," repeated the Emperor. The rabbi's response was to point up to the blinding light of the noonday sun. "Look into the sun," he said. "I cannot," answered the Emperor. "If you cannot look at the sun, which is one of the servants who stands in the presence of the Holy One, praised be He," said the rabbi, "then is it not even more evident that you cannot see God?"'*

What point do you think the rabbi was making about God ?

In the glossary: Abraham; Canaan; Promised Land; Shema.

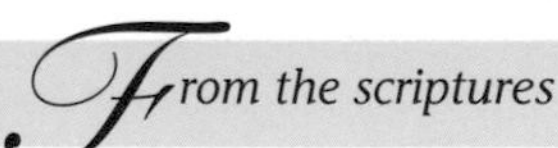

rom the scriptures

Read this quotation from the Psalms carefully:
'Who is like the LORD our God, who is seated on high, who looks far down on the heavens and the earth? He raises the poor from the dust, and lifts the needy from the ash heap, to make them sit with princes, with the princes of his people. He gives the barren woman a home, making her the joyous mother of children.'
(Psalm 113.5-9)

Describe the two Jewish beliefs about God that are expressed here.

Human Destiny

How *do Jews understand the nature and destiny of the human soul?*

FOCUSING QUESTIONS

What do Jews mean when they talk about the human soul?

What are the different stages in life through which a person passes?

What do Jews believe about life after death?

The Jewish understanding of human nature begins with the belief that God created the first human being *'in his image'* (Genesis 1.27). The Torah explains that man is God's finest creation and bears a close likeness to God with the authority of govern the Earth. Human beings can perfect or destroy the world. They must live with this responsibility and this makes them different from all of the other forms of life on Earth.

The soul

Jews believe that the image of God in human beings refers to their spiritual dimension. When a person is born their body comes from the earth but their spiritual capacity (their soul) comes from God. One Jewish prayer puts it like this: *'The soul You have given me is pure, my God. You created it. You formed it. You breathed it into me and You preserve it in me. You will take it from me...'.*

Human beings are complete creations – body and soul. The soul does not exist separate from the body. Salvation with God can only be found through the soul, whilst the body is the source of all wrongdoing. When he responds to his spiritual nature man resembles the angels, but when he gives in to his body he becomes an animal. Most of the time he moves between the two. The rabbis of old explained it in this way: *'As the Holy One* [God] *fills the entire world, so the soul fills the entire body. As the Holy One sees but is not seen so the soul sees but is not seen. As the Holy One sustains the whole world, all of it so the soul sustains the entire body. As the Holy One is pure so the soul is pure.'*

A. Jewish people are expected to study for their whole lives – starting when they are very young. Why do you think that it is important that children should study the holy books from a very early age?

The stages of life

Judaism believes that human growth and development should be directed towards helping the image of God to grow in everyone. This involves pursuing a lifetime of studying the Torah (see Photograph A), acting morally, marrying and creating a family, and growing throughout adulthood right up to death. The rabbis always considered marriage to be an essential part of life – *'When a man is without a wife, he lives without joy, without blessing, without good.'* The age of eighteen was considered the ideal time to marry – yet a man should establish his financial future before taking a wife. People marrying can expect that God will bless their relationship

B. So much of a human being's destiny is wrapped up in family life in the Jewish community. How might this affect someone who comes from a broken home?

From the scriptures

A midrash tells a story of what happened in the beginning: *'When the Holy One created the first man, He took him and led him around all the trees of the Garden of Eden, and said to him: "Behold My works, how beautiful, how splendid they are. All that I have created, I created for your sake. Take care that you do not become corrupt and thus destroy My world. For once you become corrupt, there is none after you to repair it."'*

According to this midrash God has given almost unlimited power to the human race. Is that how you see it?

with children. The relationship between parents and children is similar to that between God and the Jews and is covered by the commandment, *'Honour your father and mother, so that your days may be long in the land that the LORD your God is giving you'* (Exodus 20.12). Then, when life draws to a close, they can expect their eldest child to take responsibility for their welfare.

Death and the afterlife

There are some places in the Jewish Scriptures which suggest that death is the end of everything. When Adam is being punished by God for committing the first sin he is told: *'By the sweat of your face you shall eat bread until you return to the ground, for out of it you were taken; you are dust, and to dust you will return'* (Genesis 3.19). A later passage (*'If mortals die, will they live again?'*; Job 14.14) also suggests that death is the end. Elsewhere, though, there is the suggestion that there is a state after death into which all the dead descend – called Sheol. This is a place of darkness and gloom in which everyone shares the same fate. The dead already in Sheol greet newcomers with a description of what they will find – *'...maggots are the bed beneath you, and worms are your covering'* (Isaiah 14.11). Only one verse from the Scriptures offers a hopeful message for those who die: *'...the dust returns to the earth as it was, and the breath returns to God who gave it'* (Ecclesiastes 12.7).

FOR YOUR FOLDER

1 The relationship between a child and parent is said to be similar to that between God and the Jews. What do you think this means?

2 Explain, in your own words:
a) What it means to say that man has been made 'in the image of God'.
b) What authority God has given the human race and what responsibility it carries.
c) What it means to speak of the spiritual nature of human beings.

3 Martin Buber, the Jewish philosopher, said *'In every man and woman there is something precious which is in no-one else'.*
a) What do you think this *'something precious'* is?
b) Do you agree with this statement?

In the glossary: Rabbi; Sheol; Torah.

The Chosen People

Why *do Jews believe that they have a special relationship with God and what is the nature of this relationship?*

FOCUSING QUESTIONS

What was the response of the Israelites when God offered to make a covenant with them?

What sign God did God give to Abraham to show that the Covenant was real?

What mission did God have in mind for the Jews when He chose them?

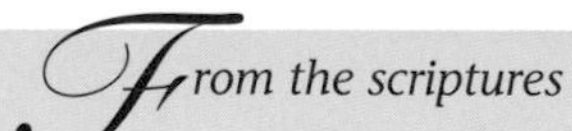

From the scriptures

These words were spoken by God to Moses on Mount Sinai: *'Now therefore, if you obey my voice and keep my covenant, you shall be my treasured possession out of all the peoples. Indeed, the whole earth is mine, but you shall be for me a priestly kingdom and a holy nation.'*

(Exodus 19.5-6)

1 As their part of the agreement with God the Israelites were expected to *'keep my covenant'* What did that really mean?
2 What do you think the phrases *'a priestly kingdom'* and *'a holy nation'* meant?

The destiny of the Jewish people was settled when Moses came down from Mount Sinai, having received the Torah, to tell the people waiting for him that God had offered them a covenant. The people answered: *'Everything that the LORD has spoken we will do'* (Exodus 19.8). The agreement was made. The books of Exodus and Leviticus go on to record everything that was expected of the Jews following their agreement to the Covenant.

Children of the Covenant

The idea that the Jews were the Chosen People of God began with Abraham who was promised that he, and his descendants, would inherit a new country – the Promised Land. As a sign of this promise, or covenant, God demanded that Abraham circumcise himself and all of the men in his household – 318 of them altogether. Circumcision has been the physical sign that someone belongs to the Chosen People ever since. The clearest demonstration that God intended to keep His covenant with the Jews came much later when He delivered them from slavery in Egypt. Before they reached the Promised Land of Canaan Moses told the Jews: *'...you are a people holy to the LORD your God; the LORD your God has chosen you out of all the peoples on earth to be his people, his treasured possession'* (Deuteronomy 7.6). The religious rituals of the Jews keep alive this idea that God has chosen them to be special. All of the festivals – Pesach, Shavuot, Sukkot, Rosh Hashanah and Yom Kippur – begin with the blessing over the wine which says: *'Blessed are You, Lord our God, King of the universe, who has chosen us from among every nation, exalted us above every language and sanctified us by Your commandments.'*

A. This child belongs to what the Jewish Scriptures call 'the Chosen People'. What precisely does that mean?

B. A truck-load of bodies in a Nazi concentration camp. The bodies were about to be burnt, in an attempt to hide the 'evidence' of the Nazi atrocities, when the camp was liberated by the U.S. 3rd Army. The greatest example that the Jews have offered the rest of the world is the way they have dealt with unbelievable suffering. What do you think that other nations could learn from this example?

Why the Chosen People?

A question many Jews throughout the ages have asked is why God should choose them as His people. One or two Jewish prayers, such as the Aleinu, try to answer this by suggesting that God deliberately created differences between Jews and non-Jews, and that the destiny of the Jews is different from that of other peoples. Most Jews, however, feel very uncomfortable with any suggestion that they are 'better' than the Gentiles. This is why the prophets of the Jewish Scriptures introduced another idea altogether – that the Jews had been chosen by God to show the superiority of the Torah. Gradually prophets such as Isaiah added another element to this. Isaiah believed that whilst the Torah belonged to Israel, its message was for everyone: *'I will give you* [Israel] *as a light to the nations, that my salvation may reach to the end of the earth'* (Isaiah 49.6).

The Jews, then, are called to be an example, by the quality of their belief in God, to all the nations of the world. That is why they have been chosen by God. The hostility that Jews have faced over the centuries has been part of the price to be paid for being 'Children of the Covenant'. Jews today still believe that they have been chosen by God, although they still disagree among themselves as to what this means exactly. Most Jews remain convinced that, if their people remain faithful to the Torah and carry out its commandments, then God will continue to treasure them. They are sure that they must be a *'light to the nations'* by leading efforts to bring about a better world.

FOR YOUR FOLDER

1 The Jewish prayer, the Aleinu, begins by thanking God for choosing the Jews to be his special people and ends with the hope that the day will arrive when all people will recognise God – Jews and Gentiles. What part are the Jews expected to play in bringing this about?

2
a) Why do you think that many Jews are reluctant to speak of themselves as belonging to the 'Chosen People'?
b) What does it mean to speak of the Chosen People as being intended by God to be a *'light to the nations'*?
c) What new twist did the prophet Isaiah offer to the traditional description of the Jews as being the Chosen People?

In the glossary: ABRAHAM; ALEINU; CANAAN; CIRCUMCISION; ISAIAH; MOSES; PROMISED LAND; PROPHET; TORAH.

Suffering

Why *has the problem of suffering always troubled the Jews, and how have they dealt with it?*

FOCUSING QUESTIONS

In which belief did Job find comfort when he had lost everything?

Who was the Suffering Servant, and how might this be used to explain the suffering of the Jewish people?

How have Jewish people come to terms with the fact that their loving and good God has allowed them to suffer so much?

Everyone who believes in God must be concerned about human suffering. Among Jews, however, the problem of suffering has a particular significance. Throughout the centuries Jews have suffered more than any other group of people. At times this suffering has stretched their belief in a good and loving God almost to breaking-point. For some it has destroyed that belief altogether.

God's judgement on the wicked

Many passages in the Jewish Scriptures are an attempt to come to terms with a God who has made an eternal agreement with the Jewish people and yet who allows His Chosen People to suffer great hardships. In the earliest days the Jews, like everyone else, saw human suffering in terms of God's punishment for wickedness and sin. When, therefore, hardships did not obviously fall on the wicked people were puzzled. Many, including the prophets, took seriously their responsibility of reminding God that, whilst the innocent were suffering, the wicked were clearly prospering.

The most well-known study of suffering in the Jewish Scriptures is found in the Book of Job. In the story, Satan receives God's permission to test Job's faith in God by taking away his family, his possessions and his health. When this happens three friends ('Job's comforters') try to persuade him to turn against God, but Job refuses to do so. Job concludes that as God has created everything that exists then the wisdom of God also created a reason for suffering. Human beings make a very serious mistake if they think that they can even begin to understand the actions and motives of God.

Other parts of the Jewish Scriptures sought a different answer to the 'fairness' of human suffering by pointing out that people must wait for God to punish the guilty and the wicked. God works on a different time-scale to human beings. The author of the Psalms, the Psalmist, even pointed out that 1,000 years in God's sight were but a single day (Psalm 90.4).

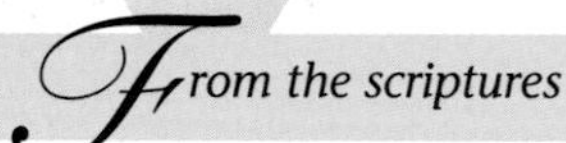

From the scriptures

Jeremiah, an important Jewish prophet, asked God:
'Why does the way of the guilty prosper? Why do all who are treacherous thrive?...Pull them out like sheep for the slaughter, and set them apart for the day of slaughter.'
(Jeremiah 12.1-3)

Words like these are found constantly throughout the Jewish Scriptures. In the light of the Covenant He had made with Israel do you think that the people were right to expect God to punish the wicked? Is that something that you would expect God to do?

Bitterness and hope

When the Jews were forced into exile in 721 BCE and 586 BCE the suffering brought about caused an intense bitterness. Many Jews felt confused and 'betrayed' – they had lost the homeland which God had promised would always be theirs.

A. One of the many buildings damaged by a recent earthquake in Mexico, which left thousands of people dead or injured. What questions do you think should be asked of God after undeserved suffering on this scale?

This bitterness can be seen particularly in some of the Psalms. In the centuries that followed, however, the Jewish community came to some conclusions about the suffering that it had been experiencing:

Conclusion One. Whatever the suffering, and however undeserved it was, God remained God and could be trusted. The story is told how, during the Second World War, when millions of Jews were being murdered by the Nazis, the Jewish inmates of one concentration camp held a trial. God was put in the dock and accused of doing nothing to help them and was found guilty. By the time the verdict was reached, however, it was early evening and sentence was never passed. The Jewish elders simply said, 'It is time for evening prayers'.

Conclusion Two. Judaism must accept the suffering of the Jewish people as a divine test and not see it as a punishment because they have been wicked. As God's Chosen People the Jews have had their faith tested continually throughout history.

Conclusion Three. The Jews have turned to an example from their Scriptures to help them understand suffering. In Isaiah 53 the Suffering Servant is despised and rejected by his fellow-men but, through his suffering, the Servant redeems and saves others. Many Jews have seen their Jewish community as the Suffering Servant.

FOR YOUR FOLDER

1 Someone has described the conclusion of Job, and the answers offered to explain his suffering, as being '*totally inadequate*'. Imagine that Job was around today. What questions would you wish to ask him about the answer that he put forward to explain his suffering?

2 The text on these pages suggests that at least three different explanations have been put forward to suggest why God has let the Jews suffer so much through history. Explain, in a paragraph:

a) The earliest explanation put forward.
b) The explanation which is suggested by the Book of Job.
c) The later explanation suggesting an answer to the obvious fact that the wicked often seemed to prosper.

In the glossary: Job; Prophet; Psalms; Satan.

The Messiah

Who ***is the Messiah and what do Jews believe that he will be like?***

FOCUSING QUESTIONS

What is meant by the word 'Messiah'?

How was the idea of the Messiah born?

For thousands of years Jews have believed in the Messiah, 'God's Anointed [chosen] One', who would be sent by God to usher in a new age on Earth. In this new age all people will worship the one true God, and peace will reign on the Earth. This is a very important idea since it underlines the Jewish belief that 'eternal life' will be lived here on Earth and not in heaven.

The anointed one

DISCUSS

What do Jews believe about the nature of the kingdom that the Messiah will establish?

The idea of the Messiah grew out of the despair that so many Jews felt when they were taken into exile in 722 and 586 BCE. It appeared to many Jews that God had totally abandoned them and, as the Jewish Scriptures record many times, they often cried out in despair to him. In response to their despair the prophets began to talk of a special messenger that God would send to deliver the Jews from their enemies. The Messiah would not be divine, but an exceptional human being – possessing extraordinary righteousness, wisdom and powers of leadership. This individual would be descended from Israel's most perfect king – David – and would set up a perfect kingdom of peace on Earth. As Isaiah tells us, in the Messiah's kingdom even natural enemies in the animal world would be at peace: *'The wolf shall live with the lamb, the leopard shall lie down with the kid, the calf and the lion and the fatling together, and a little child shall lead them'* (Isaiah 11.6). (See Photograph A).

A. In this embroidery, two natural enemies are friends. What lesson was this intended to teach about the kingdom of the Messiah?

When the Messiah comes he is expected to scatter Israel's enemies and restore the Jews to their homeland. This will be a clear sign to everyone that God is with the Jews and that the Jews are His Chosen People *'They shall know that I, the LORD their God, am with them and that they, the house of Israel, are my people, says the LORD GOD'* (Ezekiel 34.30). This, at least, is how most Jews have always thought of their Messiah. Orthodox Jews still believe this today. Reform Jews, however, believe something rather different.

B. 'Shalom', meaning peace – here represented by the dove of peace. What will God's new kingdom be like?

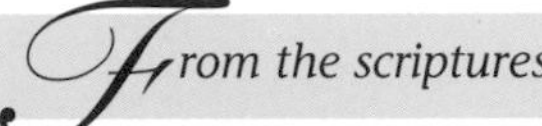
From the scriptures

These two quotations really belong together since they are talking of the same event – the coming of the Messiah and the kind of kingdom he will set up on Earth:

'The days are surely coming, says the LORD, when I will raise up for David a righteous Branch, and he shall reign as king and deal wisely, and shall execute justice and righteousness in the land.'

(Jeremiah 23.5)

'In the days to come the mountain of the LORD's house shall be established as the highest of the mountains, and shall be raised above the hills; all the nations shall stream to it. Many peoples shall come and say, "Come, let us go up to the mountain of the LORD...that he may teach us his ways and that we may walk in his paths."'

(Isaiah 2.2-3)

Make notes about all of the information that these two passages tell you about the Messiah and his kingdom.

The Reform Jews and the Messiah

Reform Jews see the Messiah, not as one individual person who will save the Jews from their enemies, but as all people everywhere who, together, will usher in paradise on Earth. In this new kingdom, in which Jews and Gentiles will share, there will be peace, justice and kindness. Although Reform Jews might disagree with the Orthodox Jews on some aspects of their beliefs about the new kingdom, most would agree that:

- When the new kingdom comes Jews will return from all over the world to their homeland.
- The new kingdom will abolish unrighteousness and immorality.
- This new society will be based on justice and truth.
- A new, universal religion will begin, with all people united in their belief in the one true God of the Jews.

Jews have always been discouraged by the rabbis from trying to work out when this new kingdom will come. Although many people over the ages have claimed to be, or have been believed to be, the promised Messiah, Orthodox Jews are still waiting for him to appear.

In the glossary: DAVID; ISAIAH; MESSIAH; ORTHODOX JEW; PROPHET; RABBI; REFORM JEW.

FOR YOUR FOLDER

1
a) What do Jews believe the Messiah will do when he comes?
b) How did the Jewish belief in the Messiah develop out of great despair?
c) What do Jews believe about the kind of person that the Messiah will be?
d) What do both Orthodox and Reform Jews believe about the Messiah?

2
a) Why do you think that the idea of the Messiah continues to be attractive to Jewish people even though they have been waiting for him for thousands of years?
b) Do you think that it is totally unrealistic to look forward to a time when all people will live together in harmony and peace? If it is still realistic, how do you think it might be brought about?

A

Abraham The father of the Jewish people.
Abram The name by which *Abraham* was originally known.
Aleinu A prayer which is said at the end of the three daily *synagogue* services.
Amidah A series of eighteen blessings which are at the centre of Jewish worship.
Antisemitism A hatred of all things Jewish.
Apocrypha Meaning 'hidden' - books which are not included in the Hebrew Scriptures.
Ark The place in the synagogue where the scrolls of the *Torah* are kept.
Atheism The belief that God does not exist.

B

Bar Mitzvah Meaning 'son of Commandment'. The name given to boy who has passed his thirteenth birthday.
Bat Chayil Meaning 'daughter of valour'. The name given to some girls who have passed their twelfth birthdays in the *Orthodox* community.
Bat Mitzvah Meaning 'daughter of Commandment'. The name given to girl who has passed her twelfth birthday. Bat Mitzvahs usually only take place in *Reform* synagogues.
Bimah The desk or platform in a *synagogue* from which the *Torah* is read.
Brit Milah Meaning 'covenant of cutting'. Also called circumcision, this is an operation performed on an eight-day-old boy to remove the foreskin of his penis. Circumcision is viewed as the outward sign of God's covenant with His Chosen People.

C

Canaan The Jewish *Promised Land* which later became *Israel*.
Cantor The person who leads the singing in a *synagogue*.
Chevra Kadishah The group of people who look after the dead and arrange for their burial.
Circumcision *See* **Brit Milah**.

D

David The second king of *Israel* and considered to be the 'perfect' king.
Deicide The word used to describe the killing of Jesus, who Christians believed was God.
Diaspora Meaning 'the scattered ones'. In 586 BCE the Babylonians overran *Judah* and took many Jews to Babylonia. These people became known as the Diaspora.
Dreydel A spinning-top with four sides, played with on *Hanukkah*.

E

Esther The queen who saved the Jewish people, and whose story forms the basis for *Purim*.
Elijah A *prophet* in the Scriptures. It is believed that he will return to Earth before the *Messiah* comes.
Exodus The journey of the *Israelites* out of slavery, also the name of book in the *Torah*.

F

Feast of Tabernacles Another name for the festival of *Sukkot*.
Feast of Unleavened Bread Another name for the festival of *Pesach*.
Feast of Weeks *See* **Shavuot.**
Festival of Lights Another name for *Hanukkah*.
Festival of Lots Another name for *Purim*.

G

Gemara Commentary on the *Mishnah*. The *Mishnah* and the *Gemara*, make up *The Talmud*.
Genocide The word used to describe the whole-scale murder of an entire nation or race of people.
Gentile Anyone who is not a Jew.
Get A Jewish note of divorce.

H

Hagadah Meaning 'telling'. This is the book used during the *Seder meal* to recount the story of the *Exodus* from Egypt.
Hanukiah A nine-branched candelabrum used during the festival of *Hanukkah*.
Hanukkah The eight-day festival celebrating the victory of Judas Maccabeaus over Antiochus 1V. Also called the Festival of Lights.
Hebrew The language in which the Jewish Scriptures are written. Services in an *Orthodox synagogue* are conducted in Hebrew.
Hebrews An early name for the *Israelites* who then became known as Jews.
Holocaust Meaning 'burnt-offering'. This is one of the words used to describe the murder of 6,000,000 Jews by the Nazis between 1939 and 1945 CE.
Huppah The canopy at the front of a *synagogue* under which a wedding is performed.
Hurban Meaning 'destruction'. One of the preferred Jewish terms for the *Holocaust*.

I

Isaac The son of Abraham and Sarah; one of the three *patriarchs*.
Israel The name given to the ten tribes (called the Northern Kingdom) descended from Jacob. The modern state of Israel was formed on 14th May 1948. *See also* **Palestine**.
Israelites The people who left Egyptian slavery, later called Jews.

J

Jerusalem The city captured by *David*, which became the centre of Jewish religion. Jerusalem is also considered sacred by Christians and Muslims.
Job A book in the Scriptures which looks at the problem of suffering.
Judah The fourth son of *Isaac*. Also the name of the Southern Kingdom. In 721 BCE the Assyrians conquered Israel, and all of the displaced people adopted the name 'Judah'. From this grew the word 'Jew'.
Judge A men or women who ruled over the tribes of Israel when they first entered *Canaan*.

K

Kosher Meaning 'fit' or 'proper'. Used to describe food which is judged fit to eat under the Jewish dietary laws.
Kashrut Laws from the Scriptures which govern Jewish diet.

Ketubah A Jewish wedding certificate.
Ketuvim Meaning 'Writings'. One of the three divisions into which The *Tenakh* is divided – the others being the *Torah* and the *Nevi'im*.
Kiddush A prayer of sanctification said at the start of a *Shabbat* service.

M

Matzah Unleavened bread used during *Pesach*.
Megillah The scroll which contains the books of *Esther* and Ruth amongst others.
Menorah The seven-branched candelabrum which was lit daily in the *Temple* in *Jerusalem*.
Messiah Meaning 'anointed one'. The leader for whom the Jewish people have waited for centuries.
Mezuzah Small cases containing passages from *the Torah*, attached to door-posts in Jewish homes.
Midrash The teachings and commentaries of old Jewish *rabbis*.
Mikveh The baths in some *Orthodox synagogues* used by women to purify themselves after they have had a period.
Mishnah A collection of Jewish law which forms the main part of The *Talmud*.
Mitzvah The obligations or duties required of Jews.
Mohel A man trained to circumcise Jewish boys.
Moses The leader who led the *Israelites* out of Egypt and gave them the *Torah*.

N

Ner Tamid Meaning 'the eternal lamp', which stands above the *Ark*.
Nevi'im Meaning 'Prophets'. One of the three divisions into which The *Tenakh* is divided – the others being the *Torah* and the *Ketuvim*.

O

Orthodox Jew A Jew who believes the traditional teachings of Judaism.

P

Palestine The name given to the land of *Canaan* by the Romans, after the destruction of *Jerusalem* in 70 CE. In 1948 Palestine was split into an Arab state and the new State of *Israel*.
Passover *See* **Pesach**.
Patriarch An early 'founding father' of the Jewish nation. This title was given to *Abraham*, *Isaac* and Jacob.
Pesach The name of the most important Jewish festival which commemorates the deliverance of Jews from Egyptian slavery. Also sometimes called Passover or the Feast of Unleavened Bread.
Promised Land The land promised to *Abraham* by God, later called *Israel*.
Prophet A man or a woman in the Jewish Scriptures who was believed to have been sent by God to pass on His message to the people.
Psalm A song used in worship.
Psalms A collection of religious songs in the Scriptures.
Prophets *See* **Nevi'im**.
Purim The festival held to celebrate *Esther's* saving of the Jewish nation. Sometimes called the Festival of Lots.

R

Rabbi The teacher responsible for leading a Jewish congregation.
Reform Jew A Jew who does not believe that all the old laws of Judaism have to be followed exactly.
Rosh Hashanah Meaning 'head of the year'. The name for the Jewish New Year.

S

Satan One of the names for the tempter of *Job*.
Saul The first king of *Israel*.
Seder Meaning 'order'. The order of service followed during the *Seder meal* at *Pesach*.
Seder meal A special *Pesach* meal containing elements symbolic of the liberation of the Jews from slavery in Egypt: three *matzah* loaves, maror (bitter herbs) a green vegetable, which is dipped into salt water, and haroset – a mixture of nuts, wine and apple.
Sefer Torah The scroll of the *Torah* kept in the *Ark*.
Sefirat Homer Meaning 'counting', referring to the counting of the days between *Pesach* and *Shavuot*.
Shabbat The holy day of rest for all Jews. Sometimes called the Sabbath.
Shavuot A festival celebrated fifty days after *Pesach*.
Shema The most important statement of Jewish belief about God.
Sheol The destination of those who have died.
Shoah Meaning 'desolation'. One of the preferred Jewish names for the *Holocaust*.
Shofar The ram's horn blown in the *synagogue* during *Rosh Hashanah* and *Yom Kippur*.
Simchat Torah Meaning 'rejoicing in the Law'; a festival marking the end of one cycle of *Torah* readings and the beginning of another.
Sukkot One of the three 'pilgrimage festivals'. The Jewish Fest of Tabernacles.
Synagogue A Jewish place of worship, study, and a community centre.

T

Tallit A prayer-shawl made of white or blue linen with tassels. Usually worn by men in the *synagogue*.
Tefillin Two black leather boxes containing passages from the Scriptures worn on the arm and forehead.
Temple The place of worship in *Jerusalem* first built by Solomon and then, much later, rebuilt by Herod the Great.
Ten Sayings The ten laws given to the *Israelites* by *Moses*. Also called the Ten Commandments by Christians.
Tenakh Or TeNakh. Spelt this way the capitals represent the three divisions of the Jewish Bible – the *Torah*, the *Nevi'im* and the *Ketuvim*.
Torah The five books of the Law, given to *Moses* by God on Mount Sinai. The Torah forms part of The *Tenakh*.

U

Ultra-Orthodox Jews The strictest group of Jews.

W

Writings *See* **Ketuvim**.

Y

Yarmulkah A head-covering worn by male Jews.
Yom Kippur Meaning 'the Day of Atonement'. The most solemn day in the Jewish year.

Z

Zion A name for the city of *Jerusalem*.
Zionism A political movement which pressed for the land of *Israel* to be given to the Jewish people.

Who are the Christians?

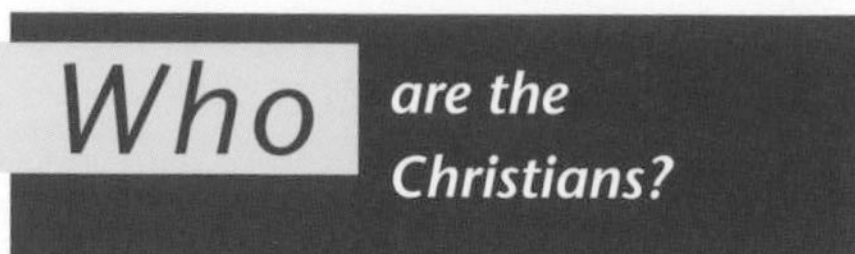

FOCUSING QUESTIONS

Who are the Christians?

What are 'denominations' – and how many of them are there?

How do the different Christian Churches organise themselves?

In the two thousand years since Jesus died the Christian religion has grown from a small off-shoot of Judaism to a religion which has followers in every continent. Christians are people who try to follow the example and teachings of Jesus; share a common core of beliefs with other Christians, and apply common principles to their ways of worshipping and expressing their religious faith.

A diverse community

Throughout the world there are thought to be about $1^1/_2$ billion Christians – 1 in 4 of the world's population. This makes Christianity the world's largest religion. Of this number 1 billion Christians are Roman Catholics and the rest belong to the various Protestant and Orthodox churches.

In the course of the long history of the Christian religion, disagreements about beliefs and forms of worship have caused the Christian Church to 'split'. Although all Christians share the same core beliefs, there are now thought to be around 21,500 different 'denominations' or Churches within the Christian faith, and the variety which these various groupings bring to Christian worship is quite staggering. Anyone, for instance, visiting a Zulu church in Africa, a Russian Orthodox church in Moscow, a parish church in rural East Anglia, or a West Indian community church in the East End of London might be forgiven for wondering whether all these churches really belonged to the same Christian faith – yet they do. For some people such variety is one of the greatest strengths of Christianity, but others wonder why all Christians cannot worship God in the same way.

A. These Christians are leaving a church after Sunday morning worship. What do you think binds this group of people together into a community?

Differences

The various Christian Churches organise themselves very differently. Roman Catholic, Protestant and Orthodox Churches are led by Archbishops and Bishops, although the Orthodox Church prefers to call their leaders Patriarchs. At grass-roots level, leadership comes from priests who are responsible for one, or several, churches, and they are often assisted by curates (trainee priests) and deacons. In some Churches, such as the Quaker community, no single person is responsible for leading the worship. Most Christians come together to worship in a cathedral, church, chapel or citadel. An increasing number, however, worship in House Churches.

The central act of worship in most churches is the service in which the members of the congregation remember the death of Jesus. Roman Catholics call this service 'Mass' and hold it daily. Anglicans call this remembrance 'Holy Communion' or the 'Eucharist'. Other denominations, like the Baptists, hold the service which they call 'the Breaking of Bread' or 'the Lord's Supper', twice a month. During this service, however, all Christians, whichever Church they belong to, eat a small piece of bread and take a sip of wine to help them to remember the crucifixion of Christ. The Salvation Army and the Quakers do not hold this service at all.

The point of unity

In recent years many different churches have started to meet, pray, worship and work together. The fact remains, though, that on many issues, they still have very different beliefs. In the past, and occasionally today, these differences have led to violence and bloodshed. What, then, is the link that binds most of these groups together, under the overall label of 'Christian'? The common focus which they all share, to a greater or lesser extent, is a common loyalty to a man who lived and taught on Earth; was crucified and buried; rose again from the dead and returned to his Father (God) in Heaven. That man was Jesus of Nazareth.

FOR YOUR FOLDER

1 Do you think that the variety of beliefs and forms of worship within the Christian community is a strength or weakness? Would the Church benefit and grow if it was united under the same umbrella?

2 Find out more information about: the Protestant Church; the Roman Catholic Church; the Orthodox Church; the Salvation Army; the Quakers.

3 Find out about the differences between a cathedral, a church, and a chapel.

4 In which Churches would you celebrate: Mass; Holy Communion or the Eucharist; the Breaking of Bread or the Lord's Supper?

DISCUSS

Why do you think that the Christian religion has been so successful? Do you think that it would be as easy to 'spread the faith' today as it used to be – or are people inclined to be less 'religious' in general?

B. Here you can see Christians praying together, although they also pray when they are on their own. Why do you think they place such an importance on this activity?

In the glossary: Archbishop; Bishop; Breaking of Bread; Cathedral; Chapel; Church; Denomination; Eucharist; Holy Communion; Jesus; Judaism; Lord's Supper; Mass; Orthodox; Patriarch; Priest; Protestant; Quaker; Roman Catholic; Salvation Army.

Jesus of Nazareth

***What** do Christians consider to be the most important aspects of the life and teaching of Jesus of Nazareth?*

FOCUSING QUESTIONS

What happened to the information about Jesus before the first Gospel was written?

Which event began the public ministry of Jesus?

Where did the main opposition to Jesus came from – and why?

A. An icon showing Mary and Jesus. Which two Gospels refer to the Virgin Birth?

Apart from one or two brief references to someone who may have been Jesus by contemporary Roman and Jewish historians, the only record of the life, teaching and death of Jesus of Nazareth is found in the four Gospels in the New Testament. The first of these, Mark's Gospel, was not written until about forty years after his death, whilst the last, John's Gospel, did not appear until Jesus had been dead for sixty-five years. In the intervening period between the death of Jesus and the writing of the first Gospel all of the information about Jesus was kept alive and passed down by word-of-mouth (called 'oral transmission').

The country of Palestine had been under Roman occupation for over half a century when an unmarried Jewish couple, Mary and Joseph, received the news that they were going to be the parents of God's Son. For many Christians the conception of Jesus was miraculous since two of the Gospels, Matthew and Luke, say that he was conceived by the Holy Spirit in the womb of Mary. This belief is called 'the Virgin Birth'.

DISCUSS

The first Gospel was not written down until forty years after the death of Jesus. Do you think that this makes it unreliable?

The work of Jesus

Christians believe that, after being baptised by John the Baptist in the River Jordan at the age of thirty, Jesus began a public ministry that was to last three years. He began by choosing twelve disciples with whom he was to share the rest of his life. Jesus spent much of his time either teaching the disciples so that they could continue his work after he was gone, or travelling through Palestine helping and healing those in need. During this time, Jesus is described as performing a number of miracles. Many Christians believe these to be actual events, while others believe that they are allegories (stories where events are used to symbolise a deeper spiritual meaning). The miracles that Jesus is described as performing can be divided into three categories:

1 Miracles of physical healing – a man with leprosy (Matthew 8.2-3); a paralysed man (Mark 5.25-29); two blind men (Luke 18.35-43).
2 Miracles over the destructive force of nature – calming a storm (Matthew 8.23-27); walking on the water (John 6.19); turning water into wine (John 2.1-9).
3 Bringing people back to life – Jairus' daughter (Mark 5.22-42); a widow's son (Luke 7.11-15); Lazarus (John 11.1-44).

The teaching of Jesus

The main theme of the teaching of Jesus was the coming of God's kingdom on Earth. To everyone's amazement he taught that the religious leaders would not be the first to enter this kingdom – if they entered it at all! Ahead of them would be such social outcasts as tax-collectors, the poor and the prostitutes. He taught largely in the form of parables, which were everyday stories which carried a religious and a moral meaning. Matthew brought together much of the teaching of Jesus into a collection known as the Sermon on the Mount (Matthew chapters 5-7).

Jesus was a Jew and much of his teaching brought him into conflict with the Jewish religious leaders of the time – especially since he directed much of it against them (Matthew 5.20; 16.6; 23.13). The two most important religious groups of the time were the Pharisees and the Sadducees and they began to plot against Jesus. The extent to which they were involved in bringing about his death, though, is disputed since the main responsibility for this must be carried by the Romans.

Death and the Resurrection

A very large proportion of the material in the Gospels is concerned with the last week in the life of Jesus. Although the Jewish leaders had Jesus arrested, the final decision to execute him could only be taken by the Roman procurator of the region, Pontius Pilate. Christians believe that Jesus was put to death on a hill outside the city of Jerusalem, called Calvary or Golgotha, probably around 29 CE. Three days later, according to the Gospels, God brought him back to life. This event, the 'Resurrection', is considered to be the most important Christian belief.

B. Why do you think that Christians claim that the death of Jesus was a triumph not a disaster?

FOR YOUR FOLDER

1 What do you think a miracle is ?
a) Do you think that miracles can happen or are they totally impossible?
b) How important do you think miracles were in the life of Jesus? Would they drastically affect our understanding of Jesus if they were removed from the Gospels?
c) If Jesus did perform miracles, what do you think they tell us about him?

2
a) What is meant by the Virgin Birth?
b) Whether or not Jesus was born to a virgin, the belief does make an important point about Jesus. What is it?

3 Find out more about Jesus by looking up these references and making your own notes: the birth of Jesus (Luke 2.1-20); Jesus begins his public ministry (Mark 1.14); the teachings of Jesus (Matthew chapters 5-7); the parables of Jesus (Luke 8.4-15; 14.15-24; 15.11-32); the miracles of Jesus (Matthew 8.28-34; 9.18-34); the death of Jesus (Mark chapters 14 and 15); the resurrection of Jesus (Mark 16.1-8).

In the glossary: Calvary; Disciple; Golgotha; Gospel; Holy Spirit; Jerusalem; Jesus; John's Gospel; John the Baptist; Joseph; Luke; Mark's Gospel; Mary; New Testament; Palestine; Parable; Pilate, Pontius; Sermon; Virgin Birth.

Understanding Jesus of Nazareth

What do Christians believe about Jesus?

FOCUSING QUESTIONS

How did Jesus meet his death – and who was responsible?

How important is the resurrection of Jesus to Christian beliefs?

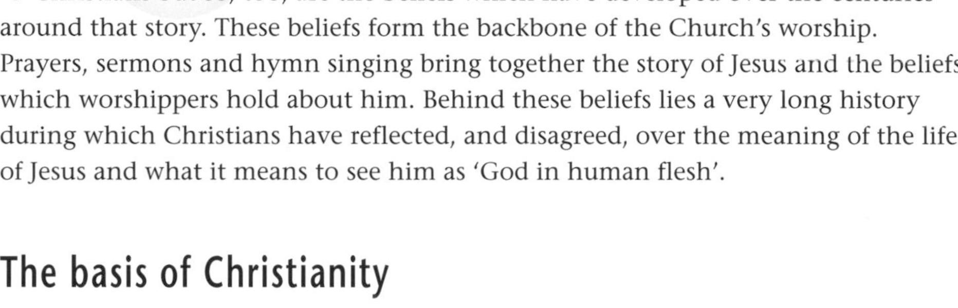

The details of the life-story of Jesus of Nazareth are very important to all Christians but so, too, are the beliefs which have developed over the centuries around that story. These beliefs form the backbone of the Church's worship. Prayers, sermons and hymn singing bring together the story of Jesus and the beliefs which worshippers hold about him. Behind these beliefs lies a very long history during which Christians have reflected, and disagreed, over the meaning of the life of Jesus and what it means to see him as 'God in human flesh'.

The basis of Christianity

Most Christians believe that:

- Jesus was God's only Son. This conclusion comes from one of the earliest episodes in the life of Jesus when he was baptised by John the Baptist in the River Jordan. A voice from Heaven told Jesus: *'You are my own dear son. I am pleased with you'* (Mark 1.11). Christianity is based on the belief that God is a 'Trinity' – God the Father, God the Son (Jesus) and God the Holy Spirit.

- Jesus was conceived in Mary's womb by the power of the Holy Spirit. This belief has caused considerable debate within the Christian community. Was Jesus conceived in the normal way through sexual intercourse or was he conceived supernaturally? Christians may disagree over this, but all share the belief that Jesus was God in human form (the 'Incarnation').

- Jesus grew up, taught and ministered to the needs of the people in the country of Palestine. He was born in either 4 BCE or 5 BCE and died thirty-three years later. Jesus was tried, condemned, crucified and buried at the express orders of Pontius Pilate, the Roman procurator. Pilate ruled over Palestine at the behest of Caesar Augustus between 26-36 BCE. The Bible, though, makes it clear that the death of Jesus was not an unfortunate fact of history, but part of God's plan to save the human race (see Photograph B). In the teaching of Paul it is designed to bring the human race back into a relationship with God (the 'Atonement' or "making one'). At no time did Jesus imagine that a Church would grow up to keep his message alive.

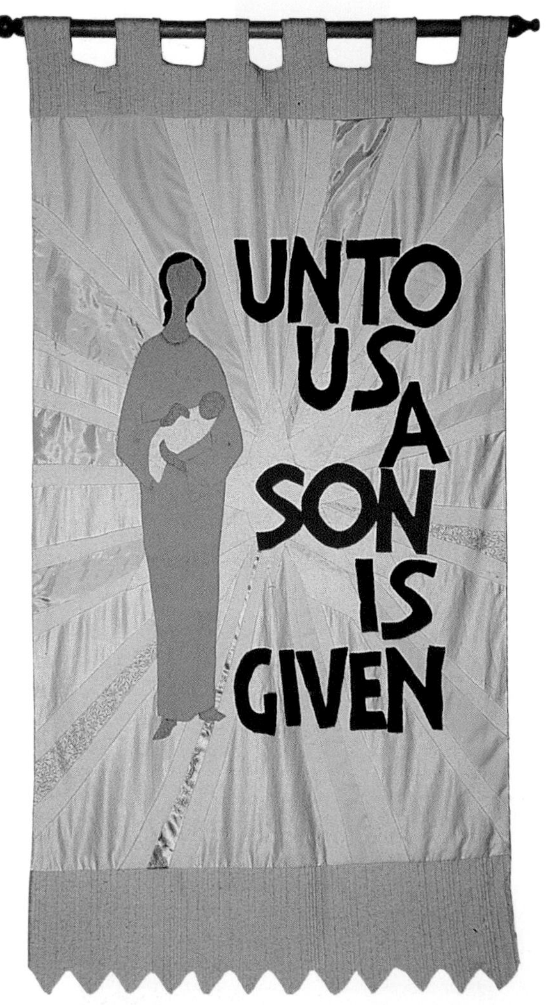

A. Each year, at Christmas, Christians celebrate the birth of Jesus, God's Son. Both Judaism and Islam strongly reject the idea of God being born on Earth. Why do you think they find this idea so unacceptable?

B. This Station of the Cross in a Roman Catholic church shows Jesus dying on the cross. How does The Bible explain the death of Jesus?

- Jesus came back to life three days after being crucified. This event, the Resurrection, stands at the very centre of the Christian faith. Without it, Paul said, the Christian faith would not exist. Forty days later Jesus ascended into Heaven (see Photograph C). Within a short time the Holy Spirit had been given to the early disciples of Jesus and the Christian Church was born. The beliefs of the early Christians was set out in the preaching of such people as Peter, Stephen and Paul. It was to be centuries, however, before the Church could be sure as to exactly what its beliefs were. During the fourth century CE it set these beliefs out in two important Creeds which are still used in Christian worship today – the 'Apostles' Creed' and the 'Nicene Creed'.

- Jesus will come back to the Earth at some future time to set up God's kingdom. The early Christians expected this to happen in their lifetime and there is every reason to believe that Jesus thought so too. Many Christians continue to believe that Jesus will return to the Earth at a time known only to God.

C. In this stained-glass window, Christ ascends into Heaven at the end of his life. Why do you think many Christians find this difficult to accept?

FOR YOUR FOLDER

1 Each of these terms is extremely important for Christian belief. Explain, in your own words, what each of these phrases means: the Holy Spirit; the Virgin Birth; the Incarnation; the Atonement; the Trinity; the Second Coming of Christ.

2 This extract comes from Matthew's Gospel:
'"What about you?" he asked them. "Who do you say I am?" Simon Peter answered, "You are the Messiah, the Son of the living God."' (Matthew 16.15-16)

According to the Gospel of Matthew, this incident took place at Caesarea Philippi and is one of the most important events in the New Testament. Look up the full account in Matthew 16.13-28, and write about the occasion when this declaration was made and the response of Jesus to it.

In the glossary: Apostles' Creed; Atonement; Bible; Disciple; Holy Spirit; Hymn; Incarnation; John the Baptist; Mary; Nicene Creed; Palestine; Paul; Peter; Pilate, Pontius; Resurrection; Sermon; Trinity; Virgin Birth.

The Church is Born

How was the Christian Church born and who were its earliest leaders?

FOCUSING QUESTIONS

Where is the only record of the birth of the Christian Church found?

What two symbols are associated with the giving of the Holy Spirit to the early disciples and why they are appropriate?

Who were the two leaders who led the early Christian Church, and what happened to them?

The Jewish festival of Pesach (Passover), during which Jesus was put to death was followed, fifty days later, by the annual festival of Pentecost (the 'Feast of Weeks'). Luke described what happened at this particular Pentecost in the Acts of the Apostles – the fifth book in the New Testament. We have no other record of the birth of the Christian Church. The Acts of the Apostles was written towards the end of the first century CE by Luke, who also wrote one of the Gospels. In fact, there is good reason to think that Luke originally set out to write a two-part history of the beginnings of the Christian Church but the two books became separated.

The Day of Pentecost

For some weeks after the death of Jesus his followers huddled together in Jerusalem waiting for the spiritual power from Heaven that Jesus had promised them: *'But when the Holy Spirit comes upon you, you will be filled with power, and you will be witnesses for me in Jerusalem, in all Judea and Samaria, and to the ends of the earth'* (Acts 1.9). In the supernatural experience that followed two images are used to describe the indescribable. First, a sound from Heaven *'like a strong wind blowing'* (Acts 2.2) filled the house where the disciples were meeting. Then, flames, *'like tongues of fire'* (Acts 2.3), came to rest upon each of them (see Photograph A).

Peter's sermon

The arrival of God's Spirit marked the birth of the Christian Church. People had come from all over the Roman Empire to be in Jerusalem for Pentecost and now many of them heard the disciples speaking in their own languages – 'speaking in tongues'. On that day alone, Luke tells us, 3,000 people were added to the Christian community. The same people then returned to their own widely scattered homes and began to spread the Christian Gospel. The work of winning converts to the Christian Church (called 'evangelisation') had begun, and this work still continues today.

A. What do you think that the images of wind and fire used to describe the arrival of God's Spirit were intended to convey?

In the sermon that he delivered later that day Peter, the leader of the disciples, made four points about Jesus. He told the people that:

- Jesus was the Messiah promised by God in the Jewish Scriptures (Acts 2.36).
- The Messiah had been crucified and brought back to life by God (Acts 2.24).
- Jesus had now been given the highest place in Heaven (Acts 2.33).
- All those who repent of their sins and believe the Gospel will be forgiven by God (Acts 2.38).

This same message has been the one preached by the Church ever since. Christians refer to it as the 'Gospel'.

B. How are these Christians carrying on the tradition established by the early followers of Jesus?

The message spreads

To begin with the leader of the Christian community was Peter who, according to the promise of Jesus, was to be the rock on which the Church was going to be built. Peter undertook preaching tours but, as a Jew, seemed unable to accept that non-Jews (Gentiles) should be welcomed into the Church on equal terms. After a time, Peter was superseded by Paul who had ruthlessly persecuted the Christians but had been converted. Paul became a tireless traveller, preacher and letter-writer in the Christian cause. He made three missionary journeys to the furthest reaches of the Roman Empire and was put to death by the Emperor Nero in Rome in 64 CE – the same fate as Peter.

FOR YOUR FOLDER

Read Acts 2.1-42.

a) What did the *'last days'* (Acts 2.17) refer to and what had God promised to do in them – and where?
b) How did the early Christians know that Jesus was God's Messiah?
c) Why was Jesus put to death and who, according to the writer of the Acts of the Apostles, was responsible?
d) Why was Jesus raised from the dead?
e) What did Peter tell the crowd to do?

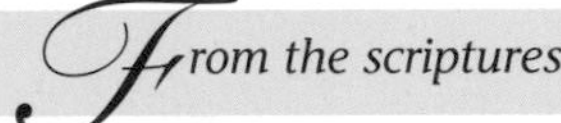

From the scriptures

Peter was the first disciple to recognise that Jesus was the Messiah. At Caesarea Philippi, Jesus told him:
'"...this truth did not come to you from any human being, but it was given to you directly by my Father in heaven. And so I tell you, Peter: you are a rock, and on this rock foundation I will build my church...I will give you the keys of the Kingdom of heaven...".'
(Matthew 16.17-19)

1 Can you find out which Christian Church claims to have a direct line of descent back to Peter through its leaders – and why?
2 Can you find out what importance this has for this particular Church today?
3 What power did Jesus promise Peter?
4 Why was it important to establish that Peter's insight about Jesus was divinely inspired?

In the glossary: Acts of the Apostles; Disciple; Gentile; Gospel; Jerusalem; Luke; Messiah; New Testament; Passover; Paul; Pentecost; Peter.

Paul

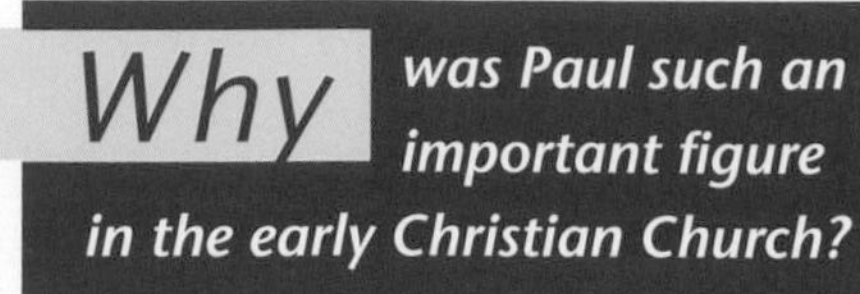

Why was Paul such an important figure in the early Christian Church?

FOCUSING QUESTIONS

Who was Stephen and why was he was important?

How did Paul became a leader of the early Church instead of its persecutor?

How did Paul lead the early attempts by Christians to spread the Gospel?

The first Christian martyr was Stephen who was appointed as a deacon to look after a charity for widows in the early Church. Some Jews came up from Cyrene and Alexandria and accused Stephen of preaching against the law of Moses (the Torah). Stephen was taken in front of the High Priest and the Jewish Council (the Sanhedrin) and the long speech that he made there is fully reported in the Acts of the Apostles. The Jewish leaders were infuriated by what Stephen said and they arrested him, hounded him out of the city, and stoned him to death (Acts 6.8-7.60). Today some churches celebrate the martyrdom of Stephen on December 26th.

Saul of Tarsus

At the same time that Stephen was being put to death, Saul of Tarsus was creating havoc in the early Church by hounding the Christians – and putting many of them in prison. The High Priest in Jerusalem granted him permission to travel to Damascus, round up Christians, and bring them back to Jerusalem. All that we know about the background of Saul is that he was a Pharisaic Jew, a strict observer of the Jewish Law, a student of the great Jewish rabbi, Gamaliel, and a Roman citizen.

A. Read the account of Paul's three missionary journeys in the Acts of the Apostles (13-14; 15-18 and 18.24-20.36) and follow them on this map.

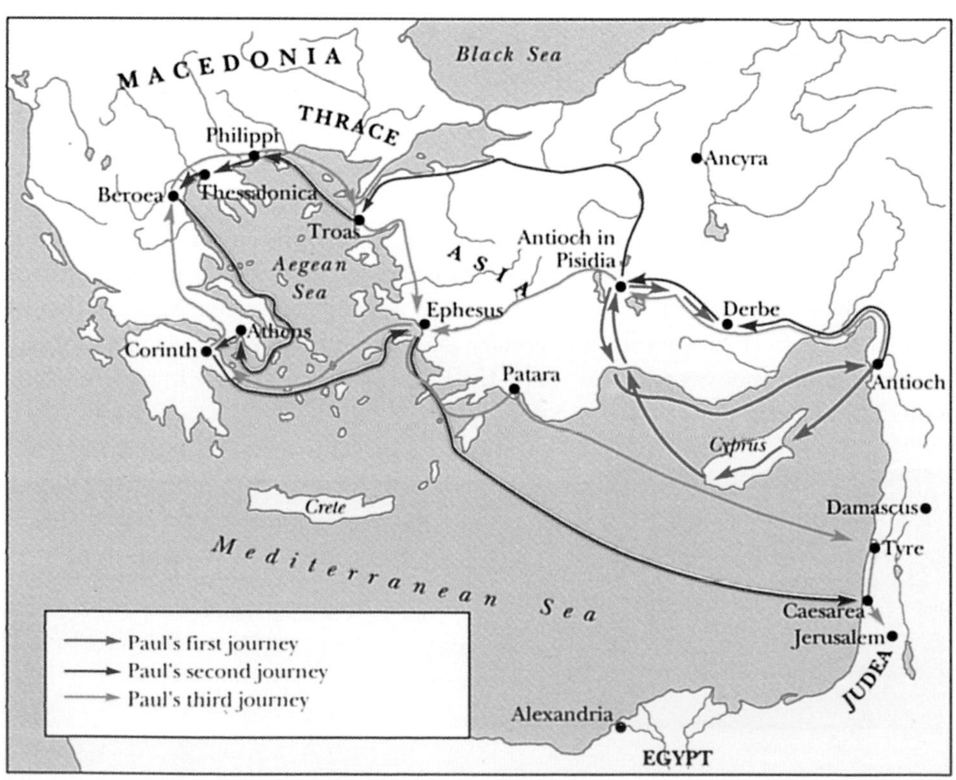

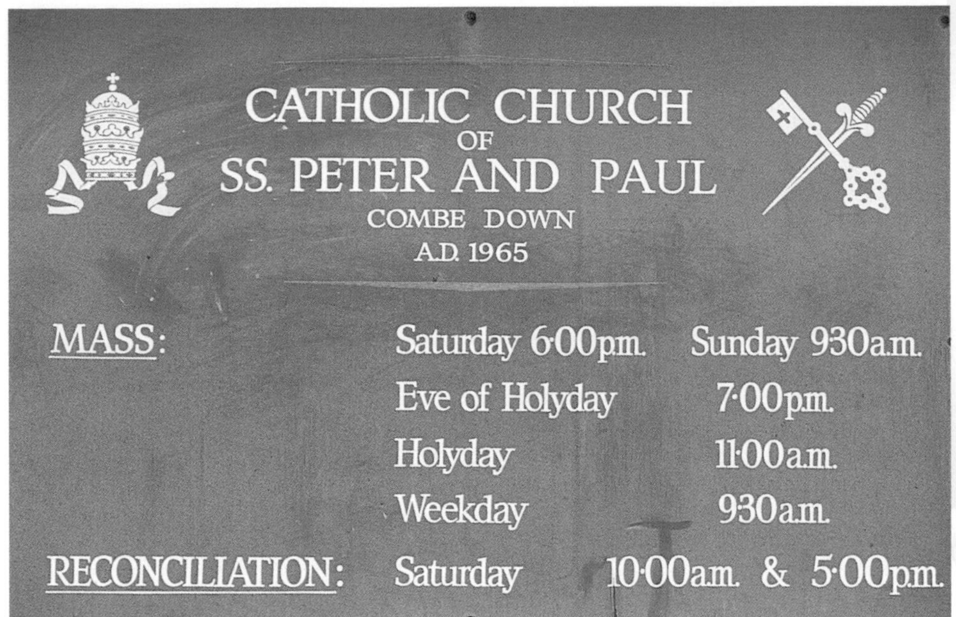

B. Many churches are dedicated to the memories of these two early Church leaders. Why do you think they still inspire Christians today?

It was on his way to Damascus that Saul was struck down by a blazing light out of which he heard Jesus speaking to him commanding him to stop persecuting the Church. Saul was struck blind and entered Damascus unable to see (Acts 9). After a little time Saul was cured of his blindness by Ananias and received into the Church. Straight away he began to preach that 'Jesus is the Son of God' and went on to become the dominant personality in Church history. His enormous legacy to the Church was felt in three ways:

1 As a missionary. In around 45 CE Paul set out with Barnabas to undertake his first missionary journey. He made two subsequent journeys before returning to Jerusalem in 58 CE (see Map A). Prior to this he had taken part, in 51 CE, in the so-called Council of Jerusalem at which the early Church leaders had debated the issue which was troubling the Church more than any other – whether non-Jews who become Christians should also accept some of the rules followed by Jewish Christians. The outcome of the Council was to open the Church up to Gentiles without expecting them to live as Jews.

2 As a church planter. The Christian Church grew very quickly in Paul's lifetime and many new churches were established after he had visited an area. Paul worked tirelessly to teach and encourage the new Christians so that they could play an active part in the fledgling church. As most of the new converts came from a pagan background their whole life-style needed to change before they could play an active part in spreading the Christian Gospel.

3 As a letter-writer. Paul wrote many letters (called 'Epistles') to churches and individual Christians with whom he had a close relationship, and some of these are preserved in the New Testament. Some of these letters were written to solve a problem within a church or to explain some aspect of Christian belief. Some of the letters are long and complex such as Romans and 1 Corinthians, whilst others, such as Philemon and Titus, are brief. These letters were clearly greatly valued because they were saved and circulated amongst other churches in the area.

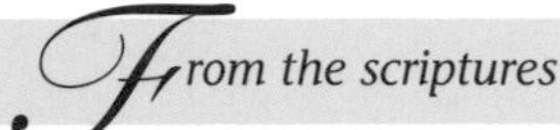
From the scriptures

In one of his letters Paul wrote a vivid description of his own missionary travels:
'Five times I was given the thirty-nine lashes by the Jews; three times I was whipped by the Romans; and once I was stoned. I have been in three shipwrecks, and once I spent twenty-four hours in the water. In my many travels I have been in danger from floods and from robbers, in danger from fellow-Jews and from Gentiles; there have been dangers in the cities, dangers in the wilds, dangers on the high seas, and dangers from false friends.'
(2 Corinthians 11.24-26)

If you were to ask Paul why he had run such danger what do you think his answer would be?

FOR YOUR FOLDER

Read Acts 15.1-35. This tells the story of the Church Council meeting in Jerusalem.

a) Who attended the Council in Jerusalem and when did it take place?
b) Why was this Council called?
c) What did Paul and Barnabas tell the believers in Phoenicia and Samaria – and what was their response?
d) What did Peter tell the Council?
e) What advice did James give to the Council?
f) What was in the letter sent out to all non-Jewish believers from the Council? Why do you think that this directive has been called 'an uneasy compromise'?

In the glossary: Acts of the Apostles; Epistle; Gentile; Jerusalem; New Testament; Paul; Peter; Saul of Tarsus.

Three Churches – One Family

What are the main groups of Christian Churches and how did they come into existence?

FOCUSING QUESTIONS

What led to the early Church breaking up?

What happened in 1054?

Who started the Reformation – and how?

The Christian Church started as a small off-shoot of Judaism in the country of Palestine, but it soon spread throughout the Roman Empire – and beyond. Over the centuries that followed the Church – the name used to describe the community of Christians – broke up into a number of different Churches. These 'denominations' fall into three broad groups – the Orthodox Church, the Roman Catholic Church and the Protestant Church.

The Great Schism

After the fall of the Roman Empire in 410 CE the real power in the Church shifted from the West to the East. A Council of bishops meeting at Chalcedon in 451 CE, however, passed a resolution that many of the Eastern Christians could not accept and the Church began to show the first signs of disintegration with the formation of the Eastern Oriental Church. It was not until 1054, when the 'Great Schism' (split) took place, and the Orthodox (meaning 'right belief') Church broke away from the Catholic (meaning 'universal') Church that this split became permanent. There were three main points of difference between the two branches of the Church:

- The claim of the Pope, the head of the Roman Catholic Church in Rome, to have supreme authority over the whole Church.
- The desire of Rome to become the centre of Christianity.
- The Catholic Church charged the wording of the Nicene Creed – a statement of faith which Eastern Christians considered unalterable.

So the Christian community split into two distinct Churches. After centuries of hostility and silence these Churches held an historic meeting in 1964, and have since begun talks with one another.

A. What does the word 'Orthodox' mean?

____

B. The outside of an Anglican church (left). How did the Anglican Church come into existence?

C. This Baptist Church is a Nonconformist Church. What does this mean?

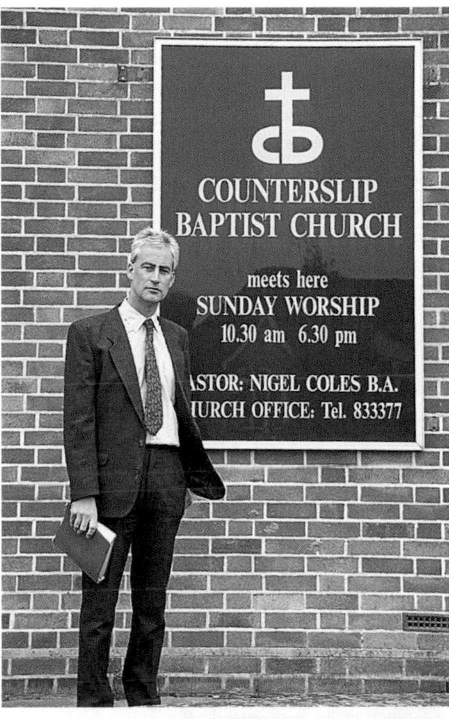

The Reformation

In the centuries that followed the Schism dissatisfaction began to build up in the Roman Catholic Church. Matters came to a head in 1517 when Martin Luther, a Catholic monk, nailed a list of ninety-five theses ('grievances'), to the door of his church in Wittenburg in Germany. In them Luther argued that a Christian did not need to buy salvation through purchasing indulgences but simply through faith in Christ and that anyone could pray to God directly without needing to go through a priest. The Bible, Luther argued, and not the Church was the supreme authority for all Christians.

This protest led to the birth of the 'Protestant' movement and a further splintering of the Church. Luther was excommunicated (excluded from taking part in communion), but churches sprang up based on his teachings. In Britain King Henry VIII fell out with the Pope over the Church's refusal to grant him a divorce and declared himself to be the Head and Protector of the Church in England and its Supreme Governor. The Church of England grew up under Elizabeth I and became the 'established' (official) church in England. Churches which grew out of the Church of England are called Anglican.

The Nonconformists

Before long the Church of England itself began to splinter and divide into smaller Churches. These new Churches were called 'Nonconformists' because they did not 'conform' to the teaching of the Church of England. They were also called 'Free Churches' for the same reason. Among the early Nonconformist Churches were: the Baptist Church, the Quakers, the Methodist Church, and the Salvation Army.

FOR YOUR FOLDER

1 Write a paragraph about each of the following: the Great Schism; the Reformation; the Orthodox Church; the Church of England; the Nonconformists.

2
a) There are a staggering number of different Christian Churches. Why do you think the number of Churches is growing all the time?
b) Someone has said that the wide variety of Churches is a strength of Christianity. What do you think? What are some of the advantages and disadvantages of there being so many different denominations?

In the glossary: Baptist; Bible; Church of England; Creed; Denomination; Great Schism; Judaism; Methodist; Monk; Nonconformist; Orthodox; Palestine; Pope; Protestant; Quaker; Reformation; Roman Catholic; Salvation Army.

The Roman Catholic Church

What is distinctive about the beliefs and worship of the Roman Catholic Church?

FOCUSING QUESTIONS

Who is believed to be the Bishop of Rome in the Catholic Church – and why?

What is meant when the Pope is said to be speaking infallibly?

Why is the Catholic Church called 'Roman'?

There is considerable debate amongst Christians over whether Peter, the disciple of Jesus, ever became the first Bishop of Rome. Certainly, by the fifth century CE, the Bishop of Rome was claiming to have authority over the whole Christian Church – a claim much disputed by bishops in places such as Alexandria and Constantinople. It was this claim that later led to the eventual split between the Western and Eastern branches of the Church and the power of the Pope being confined to churches in the West.

Why Roman Catholic?

There are 1 billion 'Roman Catholics' in the world today, representing about sixty per cent of all Christians. Catholics are called 'Roman Catholics' for two reasons:

1. The name 'Roman Catholic' is preferred because it recognises that the Pope (meaning 'father'), who is the Bishop of Rome, is its leader. Catholics believe that the authority of the Pope goes all the way back to Peter who was appointed to be the first leader of the Church – and Bishop of Rome. The powers which Jesus gave to Peter are thought to have been transferred to each successive Pope by the 'laying on of hands'. The authority passed on from one Pope to another is called 'Papal Succession'. This authority allows the Pope to speak, from time to time, infallibly (without error). This only happens when he is speaking about matters of religious belief and delivers his statement 'ex cathedra' (from the throne). When he does this, any statement he makes is incorporated into the Church's official teaching. This happened as recently as 1950 when Pope Pius XII declared that Mary (the mother of Jesus) did not die but was taken bodily into Heaven (called the 'Bodily Assumption of the Virgin Mary').

2. The Church is 'Catholic' because it is universal, although it is strongest in North America, South America and Europe. Catholics see themselves as belonging to the one, true Church with Christians in other Churches being 'separated brethren'.

A. This stained-glass window shows a representation of Peter holding the keys to the kingdom of Heaven. What is the link between the Apostle Peter and the Roman Catholic Church?

Beliefs and practice

Roman Catholic beliefs are rooted in the teachings of Jesus and his Apostles and in Church tradition. At the centre of worship is the Mass. This is the time when the death of Christ on the cross as a sacrifice for everyone is re-enacted on the altar. At the most solemn part of the Mass Catholics believe that the bread and wine become the actual body and blood of Jesus – a belief which is called 'transubstantiation'.

The Roman Catholic Church also places great importance on the saints and the Virgin Mary (see Photograph C). Mary, the mother of Jesus, is believed to 'intercede' (plead) with God on behalf of each Catholic believer when they pray.

B. What did the Second Vatican Council decide about the Mass – and why do you think its decision was important for members of the Catholic Church?

Vatican II

The beliefs of the Church cannot be changed since they have been passed down by successive popes speaking infallibly. The worship life of the Church, however, can be altered as the result of a Church Council which draws together the Pope, cardinals and bishops from all over the world. The last such Council was called by the much-loved Pope John XXIII in 1962 to '*open the windows and let the wind of change blow through the Church*'. This Council decided that the Mass should be celebrated in the language of the people and not Latin, that everyone should be involved in the decision-making of the Church, that the Church should forge new links with other Christian Churches and people from other faiths, and that the Church should re-think its attitude to such matters as abortion, contraception, euthanasia and poverty. Some, but by no means all, of these changes have been made.

C. There is a statue of the Virgin Mary in every Catholic church. Find out as much as you can about her and the important part that she plays in Roman Catholic devotion and prayer.

FOR YOUR FOLDER

1 Find out five pieces of information about each of the following and record what you have discovered in your folders: Peter; the Pope; the Virgin Mary; a cardinal; a bishop.

2
a) What is the service called at which Catholics celebrate the death of Jesus?
b) What do Catholics mean when they speak of transubstantiation?
c) What do Catholics mean when they say that the Virgin Mary 'intercedes' with God on their behalf?
d) Who called the Second Vatican Council – and why?
e) How did the Second Vatican Council attempt to change the Church?

3 The Roman Catholic Church traces its origins back to the disciples of Jesus – and through them to Jesus himself. Why do you think this is important?

In the glossary: Apostle; Bishop; Bishop of Rome; Ex Cathedra; Heaven; Hell; Mary; Mass; Peter; Pope; Purgatory; Rosary; Transubstantiation.

The Orthodox Church

What is distinctive about the Orthodox Church?

FOCUSING QUESTIONS

What does the name 'Orthodox' mean?

What two broad 'families' is the Orthodox Church divided into?

What do members of the Orthodox Church call the sacraments?

Within a few centuries of the death of Christ cities such as Antioch, Alexandria, Constantinople and Rome had already become important centres of Christianity. During this time, however, the churches in the East were developing very different attitudes to many issues compared to those in the West. This culminated in 1054 when the two branches of the Christian Church split. The Church in the East has maintained a fierce independence from the Western Church ever since, although some moves towards greater co-operation have begun recently.

FOR YOUR FOLDER

1 Photograph B shows the iconostasis which acts as a barrier between the people and the altar. The people can just see the priest when he is at the altar preparing the bread and wine. Can you suggest why the people are cut off in this way from the altar?

2
a) Which two sources does the Orthodox Church recognise for its authority?
b) Why do you think that it is important for the Orthodox Church to be able to trace its beliefs and traditions back to the earliest days of Christianity?
c) Why has it been important for each Orthodox Church to be independent – taking its name from its country of origin?

3 The two branches of the Orthodox Church are due to unite shortly. Why do you think they have taken so long to reach this decision ?

In the glossary: ANOINTING THE SICK; BISHOP; CONFIRMATION; DIVINE LITURGY; EASTERN ORTHODOX; HOLY COMMUNION; INFANT BAPTISM; MYSTERIES; ORDINATION; ORTHODOX; PATRIARCH; PENANCE; ROMAN CATHOLIC; SACRAMENT; TRINITY.

The Eastern Church

The Orthodox Church today has about 150 million members worldwide, with each member Church being totally self-governing. Most member Churches are found in Eastern Europe, Russia and around the Eastern Mediterranean. Each Church is led by a senior bishop who is known as a 'patriarch'. Among the patriarchs special honour is given to the Patriarch of Constantinople (now Istanbul in Turkey) who is the spiritual leader of the whole Orthodox community. He is called the 'Ecumenical Patriarch'. The two broad 'families' into which the Orthodox Church is divided are:

1 The Oriental Orthodox Church which includes the Coptic, Syrian and Ethiopian Orthodox Churches. This branch of the Orthodox Church has about 30 million members.

2 The Eastern Orthodox Church which has about twenty different Churches as members. Among the Churches in this community are the Russian, Romanian, Bulgarian, Serbian, Georgian and Greek Orthodox Churches. This family has a membership of over 120 million people.

Beliefs

The basic belief of the Orthodox Church is conveyed in its name – 'orthos' meaning 'right' and 'doxa' meaning 'belief'. Orthodox Christians are those believers who see themselves as 'rightly glorifying God'. They draw their beliefs from the Holy Scriptures and from the traditions of the Church. All Orthodox Christians believe that:

- God is a Trinity – God the Father, God the Son and God the Holy Spirit – three Persons within the Godhead. This is a belief that Orthodox Christians share with almost all Christian believers. It was this Creed however, and the addition made to it by the Catholic Church that was one of the causes of the split between East and Western Churches.

A. Icons, holy pictures, are very important aids to worship for Orthodox believers. Why do you think that they constantly want to be surrounded by reminders of the Virgin Mary and Child, and the saints?

- Jesus Christ, the second Person of the Trinity, was born as a baby and lived on Earth to help men and women to understand God. Whilst he was here Jesus was both fully human and fully divine.

- All worship must centre around the Sacraments – or 'Mysteries' as the Orthodox Church prefers to call them. The Divine Liturgy, at which the death of Jesus is celebrated, is the central act of worship in an Orthodox church. For Orthodox believers this service is a 'window into Heaven' since the liturgy (the form of service) never changes. Through it they believe that they are able to glimpse God the Father, God the Son and God the Holy Spirit. The Orthodox Church – as the Roman Catholic Church – celebrate seven Sacraments in all – Holy Communion, Infant Baptism, Chrismation (confirmation), Marriage, Penance, Ordination to the Priesthood, and Anointing the Sick. To Orthodox Christians the holy Church includes the living and the dead – those on Earth and those in Heaven.

B. The iconostasis in an Orthodox church

The Church of England

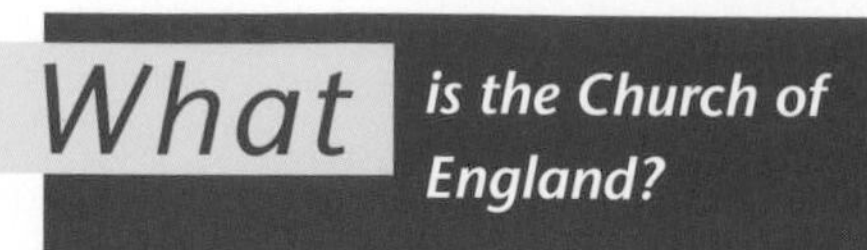

What is the Church of England?

FOCUSING QUESTIONS

What happened at the Synod of Whitby in 664 CE?

How did the Pope lose his authority over the Church in England?

What are The Book of Common Prayer and The Alternative Service Book?

In 597 CE, the monk Augustine was sent by the Pope to bring the British Christians back under the control of the Church in Rome. Christianity had been brought to Britain during the Roman occupation, but the form of Christianity that Augustine found there was very different to that in Rome. Celtic Christianity was very close to nature, the seasons and the earth, and it wasn't until 664 CE, at the Synod of Whitby, that the British finally accepted Augustine's much more disciplined form of Christianity.

Protector of the Faith

The Church in England continued to recognise the authority of the Church in Rome until 1534 when King Henry VIII declared himself to be the 'Especial Protector' and head of the Church in England. This action was the result of a quarrel between Henry and the Pope, who refused to grant him a divorce. The Church of England, or the Anglican Church as it is usually called, was born.

Although Henry made no major changes to Church belief, two Acts of Parliament, in 1536 and 1539, brought about the dissolution of the monasteries – the real seats of Roman power in England – and the placing of copies of the Miles Coverdale Bible in English in every church. It was Elizabeth I, though, who made the Church of England the Established Church with leaders, such as the Archbishop of Canterbury, being appointed by the Prime Minister. This remains the case today and distinguishes the Church of England from other Protestant Churches. Later, in 1662, The Book of Common Prayer became the official service book of the Church of England. In 1980, The Alternative Service Book was authorised.

A. What is the main difference between the Church of England and other Protestant Churches?

Beliefs

The Church of England, the Anglican Church, is committed to believing in the Scriptures 'as containing all things that are necessary for salvation'. This was the distinguishing mark of the Reformation and the Church of England is a 'reformed' Church. The Church of England is also a 'catholic' Church, because it is part of the 'universal' Church established by Jesus. The beliefs of the Church of England are found in the Thirty-Nine Articles which were drawn up in the sixteenth century and in two Creeds – the Apostles' and the Nicene. The Church of England only recognises two sacraments – Holy Communion and Baptism – and accepts the authority of bishops over the Church. This makes it an 'episcopal' Church.

C. A stained-glass window showing the image of a bishop. What does it mean to call the Church of England an 'episcopal' Church?

B. The Bible (above) plays a central role in worship in the Church of England. Why was the Miles Coverdale Bible so important?

FOR YOUR FOLDER

1

a) What does it mean to call the Church of England 'the Established Church'?
b) Outline two ways in which the Church of England is treated differently from other Churches in this country.
c) Can you think of two advantages and two disadvantages for the Church to be linked with the State in this way?

2

a) Do some further research and describe, in your own words, how and why the Church of England came into existence.
b) What are the main beliefs held by members of the Church of England?

In the glossary: Alternative Service Book; Anglican; Apostles' Creed; Augustine; Bishop; Book of Common Prayer; Episcopacy; Established Church; Holy Communion; Infant Baptism; Monastery; Monk; Nicene Creed; Pope; Priest; Reformation; Sacrament; Thirty-Nine Articles.

The Nonconformists

What *are Nonconformist Churches and what makes them different from the other Christian Churches?*

FOCUSING QUESTIONS

What is meant by the word 'Nonconformist' and which are the main Nonconformist Churches?

Which two Churches were the first to combine in Britain and what was the name of the new Church which was formed?

How did the Quakers obtain their name?

The Nonconformists, or Free Churches, are those Churches which have been formed because their members could not agree with the teachings of the Church of England – they could not 'conform' to it. After the Act of Uniformity, in 1662, demanded strict observance of The Book of Common Prayer some 2,000 clergy were ejected from the Church of England and lasting divisions resulted.

The Presbyterians

The Presbyterian Church has always been strongest in Scotland and believes in the supreme authority of The Bible, the importance of local church government, and a simple form of worship based on readings from The Bible, hymns, spoken prayers and a sermon based on a biblical passage. In 1972 the Presbyterian Church in England joined with the Congregational Church to form the United Reformed Church.

The Quakers

The founder of this denomination, George Fox, wanted his followers to return to the simple faith and worship of the early Christians. He called it 'The Society of Friends' because he wanted his followers to be friends of Christ and each other. They were called 'Quakers' by a judge who, at Fox's trial in 1650, was told to *'tremble* [quake] *at the voice of the Lord'*.

A. From this photograph of a Quaker meeting what do you think are the distinctive features of this meeting and how does a meeting house differ from a church?

B. A Methodist church service.
How did the Methodist Church come into being?

The Baptists

In the seventeenth century many churches were opposed to the baptism of babies. They insisted that only adults who believed in Christ for their salvation could properly be baptised. The 'Baptists' were persecuted in the seventeenth century but have since become a worldwide denomination with some 40 million members.

The Methodists

Methodism came into existence through the preaching and teaching of an English clergyman, John Wesley (1703-1791). The name 'Methodists' was first applied to Wesley and his friends when they were studying at Oxford because of the 'methodical' way that they studied and read The Bible. Wesley became a minister in the Church of England but then had a spiritual experience which convinced him that God had taken away his sins. He travelled across Britain preaching to immense crowds and founding many churches.

The Salvation Army

Founded as the 'Christian Mission' in 1865 by William and Catherine Booth, the Salvation Army received its name in 1878. Its basic aim has always been the conversion of the poor and social outcasts to Christianity. From the beginning the Army has been run along military lines with ranks such as General, Colonel and others, and with everyone wearing a distinctive uniform. Today it runs open-air meetings, helps released prisoners, searches for missing persons and carries out other practical work.

FOR YOUR FOLDER

1 Why do you think that Nonconformist Churches are also called 'Free Churches'?

2
a) What do you think are the main advantages and disadvantages of organising the Salvation Army along military lines?
b) How does this name illustrate the kind of work that William Booth was trying to do through the Salvation Army?

In the glossary: Baptist; Bible; Book of Common Prayer; Booth, William; Church of England; Denomination; Established Church; Fox, George; Free Churches; Hymn; Meeting House; Methodist; Minister; Nonconformist; Presbyterian; Quaker; Salvation Army; Sermon; Society of Friends; United Reformed; Wesley, John.

The Evangelicals

Who are the Evangelicals and what is distinctive about them?

FOCUSING QUESTIONS

What is an Evangelical Christian?

What does it mean, in practice, to be an Evangelical Christian?

What does it mean to call The Bible, 'inerrant' and 'inspired'?

Evangelicals do not form a single Church but can be members of any Protestant church which believes that a Christian life begins when a person commits him or her self to Jesus Christ as a Saviour. Called a 'conversion' experience this can be as dramatic as that experienced by Saul on the road to Damascus, or simply a quiet personal commitment. Evangelical Christians now represent a significant percentage of Christian believers.

Beliefs and practices

The beliefs of Evangelicals are more closely defined than those of any other Christian group (see Photograph A). Evangelicals believe in:

- Placing The Bible at the centre of worship and life. Evangelical Christians believe that The Bible is the 'inspired' and 'inerrant' Word of God, which came into being because its many writers were inspired by the Holy Spirit as they

DISCUSS

Evangelicals are the only part of the Christian Church which has expanded in the last decade. Can you suggest why?

WHAT WE BELIEVE

About God:
God is the Creator of all things. He is powerful, loving and pure, and He is one God in three Persons- Father, Son and Holy Spirit.

About Jesus Christ:
He is Gods Son, and is both fully human and fully divine. He died on the cross in the place of sinners, He rose again from the dead, He is alive today, and He will one day personally return to earth as the Judge of every person.

About the Holy Spirit:
He is fully divine and makes the work of Jesus Christ real in the lives of believers.

About Ourselves:
Every person is a sinner by nature and therefore separated from God and under his judgment, God invites every person to turn from their sin and trust in Jesus Christ as Saviour. All who believe in Him are saved, but those who do not turn to Him in repentance and faith remain under Gods judgement.

About the Bible:
The Bible is Gods living Word and is therefore totally true. Through it He speaks to the world today, It contains all that we need to know about God, and about how we can be made right with Him and live to please Him.

A. This Creed has been posted outside an Evangelical church. Why do you think that it is there?

wrote, and so could only tell the truth. The Bible can, therefore be wholly trusted, and Evangelical Christians spend much time reading and studying it. They usually set aside time each day to pray and find ways to put the teachings of the Bible into practice (called a 'Quiet Time').

- The value of preaching and proclaiming 'the Word of God' (The Bible). This is why the sermon is usually longer than in other church services since Evangelicals firmly believe that it is through this that people come to believe in Christ. It is The Bible itself, presented in the power of the Holy Spirit, which is able to convince people of their sinfulness and offer them God's forgiveness. This is why Evangelicals often meet together to study The Bible. Special groups are held regularly in church or people's homes to help them to understand The Bible.

- A God who is able and willing to constantly intervene in international, national, social and personal affairs. Stemming from this is the Evangelical belief in the power of prayer. As Evangelicals point out, Jesus encouraged everyone to ask God for the things that they need.

- The need for everyone to respond individually to the Gospel (God's Good News of salvation), so the message of that Gospel needs to be presented at every opportunity. The work of sharing the Gospel is called 'evangelism' and this evangelism takes place through meetings, in church services, on the streets, in youth clubs and through personal contacts. Whatever the method chosen Evangelicals are constantly seeking to introduce other people to Jesus.

B. Why do you think that Evangelical Christians stress the need for each person to read their Bible daily?

FOR YOUR FOLDER

1 Can you explain what Evangelicals mean when they speak about:
a) A person being 'converted'?
b) The Bible as being the 'Word of God'?
c) God intervening in human affairs to answer prayer?
d) The Christian 'Gospel'?
e) The work of 'evangelism'?

2 Look closely at Photograph A. Make a list of the Creeds in your book and try to explain three of them in your own words.

3 The Evangelicals offer a much simpler form of the Christian Gospel than other groups. Why do you think this appeals to more and more people?

In the glossary: Bible; Evangelism; Gospel; Holy Spirit; Protestant; Quiet Time; Sermon; Word of God.

Worship

What are the distinctive elements in most acts of Christian worship?

FOCUSING QUESTIONS

Which two elements are brought together in each act of worship?

What is the liturgy?

What acts as a focal-point in Roman Catholic and Nonconformist churches?

In every genuine act of Christian worship two elements must be present:

1. God must always remain unknowable and mysterious. It is God's 'transcendence' (otherness) which places Him totally beyond human reach. At best, human language, expressed in hymns or sermons, can only provide a 'picture' of God.
2. Worship, through its language and actions, attempts to bring God within the reach of those who are worshipping.

A. What 'picture' of God do you think might be suggested to worshippers by this cathedral?

Different forms of worship

Christian acts of worship can be very different. Some Churches – the Roman Catholic, Anglican and Orthodox – set out their services in a Prayer Book. The Book of Common Prayer and The Alternative Service Book are used in the Church of England, and The Missal is used in Roman Catholic churches. The distinctive pattern of each Church's worship (the liturgy) emphasises ritual and the sacraments. For this reason the focal-point in these Churches is the altar since that is the place where most of the sacraments, such as Holy Communion, are celebrated.

Nonconformist Churches do not use a set form of worship, preferring to rely on the guidance of the Holy Spirit. They place a greater emphasis on singing, extempore prayers, reading The Bible, and the giving of sermons. Whilst Baptism and Holy Communion are important services, the emphasis is very much on the spoken word and this is underlined by the central position of the pulpit – from which the 'Word of God' (The Bible) is preached.

House Churches

In recent years some Christians have become dissatisfied with the traditional Churches and have formed small fellowship groups which meet in each other's homes or in halls (called House Churches). As they study The Bible, sing hymns, pray, and break bread together so they believe that they are following the same pattern of worship as the early Christians in the New Testament.

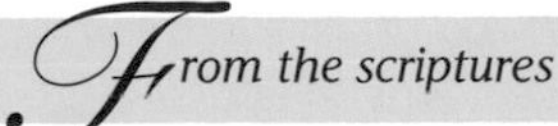

This extract describes the response of the people to the message of Peter on the Day of Pentecost:
'Many of them believed his message and were baptized, and about 3,000 people were added to the group that day. They spent their time in learning from the apostles, taking part in the fellowship, and sharing in the fellowship meals [Holy Communion] *and prayers.'*
(Acts 2.41-42)

Which four activities were carried out by the early Christians and how do they correspond to Christian worship today?

B. Why is the pulpit the focal-point in a Nonconformist church?

FOR YOUR FOLDER

1
a) Which Churches use a Prayer Book in their services and what are they called?
b) How do services in the Roman Catholic and Anglican Churches differ from those in Nonconformist Churches?

2 The philosopher Rudolf Otto described God as *'Mysterium, Tremendum et Fascinans'*. Do some research to find out what this Latin phrase means and how this is reflected in Christian worship.

In the glossary: ALTERNATIVE SERVICE BOOK; ANGLICAN; BAPTISM; BIBLE; BOOK OF COMMON PRAYER; CATHEDRAL; CHURCH; HOLY COMMUNION; HOLY SPIRIT; HOUSE CHURCH; HYMN; LITURGY; MISSAL; NEW TESTAMENT; NONCONFORMIST; ORTHODOX; PULPIT; ROMAN CATHOLIC; SERMON.

Inside an Anglican Church

What *are the distinctive features of an Anglican church and what part do they play in worship?*

FOCUSING QUESTIONS

What forms the focal-point in an Anglican church?

What is the nave in a church?

Why is the altar such an important part of an Anglican church?

Although Christians have always been free to worship God anywhere they soon began to build cathedrals, churches and chapels. Many of them have used the size, architecture and furnishings of their places of worship to express their beliefs about God.

Inside the building

Most traditional Church of England or Anglican (Churches which grow out of the Church of England) churches are built in the shape of a cross or an oblong, although some modern buildings offer worship 'in the round'. In older churches the font, which holds the water which is used when a baby is baptised, is located just inside the door to indicate that a person 'enters' the Church through Baptism. Modern churches, though, often have portable fonts which can be placed in the middle of the church. This shows that, through Baptism, the child is being

A. What beliefs about God do you think the builders of this church were trying to express?

B. Look at the altars shown in these two photographs. Both come from Anglican churches. Can you notice any differences between them?

welcomed into the Christian community, and that members of the church will play their part in the spiritual growth of the child.

The nave and the chancel

The nave is a passage-way which runs almost the entire length of the church. On either side of the nave are the pews, where the 'congregation' of worshippers sit during the service. The nave ends at the chancel which runs across the top of the church at right angles to the nave, giving most churches their characteristic cross shape. Two important pieces of furniture are situated on either side of the chancel:

- The pulpit. This is a platform which is usually reached by steps. The priest goes into the pulpit to deliver his or her sermon, during which a passage from The Bible is explained and discussed.
- The lectern. This a free-standing ledge on which a copy of The Bible is placed.

The altar

Usually, altars are made of stone and are situated at the east end of the church, although new churches sometimes place a simple wooden altar or Communion table in the centre. This indicates a change in the attitude of many Anglicans who now see Holy Communion as a fellowship meal in which all share, rather than a sacrifice offered to God by the priest for the people. The altar represents the table where Jesus shared the Last Supper with his disciples.

Within the Church of England there are those worshippers who favour a more Roman Catholic form of worship, and those who prefer a more Evangelical approach. The type of altar found in a church is usually a good indication of whether the church is 'High' (Anglo-Catholic) or 'Low' (Evangelical). Generally, High Church altars resemble those found in Catholic churches – with several candles and a crucifix. Low Church altars are simple with little more than a cross, an open Bible and some flowers. These obvious differences reflect deep differences in belief and worship between the two groups in the Anglican Church (see Photograph B).

FOR YOUR FOLDER

1 Explain, in your own words, the meaning of each of the following: the font; the nave; the chancel; the altar; the pulpit; the lectern. What part do the font, altar, pulpit and lectern play in Christian worship?

2 Can you explain why:

a) Baptismal fonts are now often placed in the middle of the congregation for an infant baptism?

b) The altar is now often placed in the middle of the congregation rather than in front of the east wall?

c) The lectern often has the carving of an angel on the front of it?

In the glossary. ALTAR; ANGLICAN; ANGLO-CATHOLIC; BAPTISM; BIBLE; CATHEDERAL; CHANCEL; CHAPEL; CHURCH; CHURCH OF ENGLAND; CRUCIFIX; DISCIPLE; FONT; GOSPELS; HOLY COMMUNION; LECTERN; NAVE; PRIEST; PULPIT; SERMON.

Inside a Roman Catholic Church

What are the main features of a Catholic church and what part do they play in worship?

FOCUSING QUESTIONS

Why is there a strong similarity in design between traditional Anglican and Roman Catholic churches?

Why is infant baptism so important to Roman Catholics?

What role do candles play in Roman Catholic worship and what do they signify?

As most of the Anglican churches were taken from the Roman Catholics at the time of the Reformation in the sixteenth century there is a strong similarity between the older buildings of these two denominations. The older Roman Catholic churches were built in the shape of a cross or oblong but newer ones, such as Liverpool Cathedral and Clifton Cathedral in Bristol, have the congregation gathered in a semi-circle or a circle around the altar. This stresses the strong Catholic belief that the altar is the place where God meets with His people during Mass – when believers remember the sacrifice of Jesus. It is therefore appropriate for it to be in the middle of the congregation with the Church 'family' gathered around it.

Inside the door

Just inside the door of a Catholic church is a container of holy water into which worshippers dip two fingers as they enter church before tracing the 'sign of the cross' on their bodies. This water, which has been blessed by the priest, symbolises the new life which all worshippers find in the Church. This new life is also symbolised by the font, since the traditional teaching of the Roman Catholic Church stresses that 'there is no salvation outside the Church' and so baptism into the Church is essential for the future salvation of every child.

The high altar

The high altar stands, with crucifix and candles, in the middle of the east wall of the church so, when worshippers face the altar, they are also facing the holy city of Jerusalem (see Photograph A). A tabernacle (cupboard) stands behind the altar or in a side-chapel holding the 'Reserved Sacrament' (blessed bread) which is used every time that the Holy Communion – called Mass in Roman Catholic churches – is celebrated. As the central act of worship in every Catholic church, the Mass is celebrated each day.

A. Why is the altar at the centre of Roman Catholic worship?

The Stations of the Cross and the Virgin Mary

Around the church there are carved statues or paintings showing the 'Stations of the Cross' illustrating the different places at which, according to the Gospels and Church tradition, Jesus stopped on his way to crucifixion. Worshippers process around each Station during Lent and Holy Week, pausing to say a prayer and remember the sufferings of Jesus (see Photograph B).

Statues of the Virgin Mary and other saints occupy an important place in most Catholic churches. Mary was the mother of Jesus who, Catholics believe, entered the world sinless and was taken up into Heaven at the end of her life without dying. Worshippers often light candles in front of her statue as they pray when they are seeking help or guidance. Elsewhere in the church anyone who simply wishes to say a prayer is encouraged to light a votive candle – candles symbolising the light of God which shines eternally in the world and in the hearts of all believers.

B. One of the Stations of the Cross. What do these Stations illustrate?

FOR YOUR FOLDER

a) Look at Photograph **B.** What are the Stations of the Cross and where would you expect to find them in a Roman Catholic church?
b) What do you think is happening in the Station shown in the photograph?
c) Find out what is represented on each of the fourteen Stations of the Cross.
d) What part do the Stations play in the devotions performed in church during Holy Week?
e) What other reminders of the death of Jesus are found in Roman Catholic churches? Why do you think that Catholic worshippers are reminded so often of the death of Jesus?

2 What do you think the old Catholic statement 'there is no salvation outside the Church' means? How does this affect the position of the font in a Roman Catholic church?

DISCUSS

Roman Catholic churches are full of symbols to remind worshippers of Jesus and the Virgin Mary. Why do you think that the Catholic church believes that this is necessary, when other Christian denominations do not?

In the glossary: Altar; Anglican; Baptism; Crucifix; Denomination; Font; Gospels; Holy Week; Jerusalem; Lent; Mary; Mass; Priest; Reformation; Roman Catholic; Saint; Sign of the Cross.

Inside an Orthodox Church

What ***symbolism is to be found in an Orthodox church and what does it express?***

FOCUSING QUESTIONS

What is the meaning of the symbolism of the dome and floor in an Orthodox church?

What is the iconostasis?

What do the two icons on either side of the Royal Doors symbolise?

The Orthodox Church worldwide is made up of a 'family' of self-governing Churches which are found mainly in Eastern Europe, Russia and around the eastern side of the Mediterranean Sea. Only a tiny fraction of the Orthodox Church's 170 million believers live in Great Britain, but there are still many distinctive places of worship in this country.

A. What is your overall impression as you look at this photograph of an Orthodox church? Do you think that beautiful buildings help people to worship God?

The church

The usual shape of an Orthodox church is that of a cross (the basic symbol of Christianity) with a dome above the centre to represent the heavens which are stretched out over the Earth. A painting of Christ the Pantocrator – the ruler over all things in the heavens, the universe and Earth – is found on the ceilings of most Orthodox churches. The floor of the church represents the earth, with the people standing in the nave as they worship God. The choir, out of sight in the transepts (the side arms of the cross), plays an important part in worship since musical instruments are not used.

B. What do Orthodox believers consider icons to be?

Icons

Orthodox Christians believe that God is all-powerful and so beyond the reach of human understanding. Normally this would make it impossible for any human being, no matter how holy, to worship God. Icons, though, are religious pictures which bring God within the reach of those who wish to worship Him, and for this reason they are used widely as devotional aids in both the church and the home (see Photograph B). Each icon is believed to be an earthly copy of a heavenly image, and so the painting of them demands a high level of devotion and holiness from the artist for which he or she receives special training. Icons are usually painted on wood in bright colours and depict, in a formal way, saints, the apostles or members of the Holy Family – especially Mary and the infant Jesus. There are icons around the walls of the church building and candles often burn in front of them. Worshippers usually light one of the candles and kiss the icon before taking their place in the church congregation.

Iconostasis

The altar in an Orthodox church is separated from the worshippers by a screen called the iconostasis – because it is decorated by icons. The iconostasis symbolises the unbridgeable gulf which separates God and human beings, Heaven and Hell. The icons covering the iconostasis often represent an important religious theme, such as God rescuing the human race from sin. Two 'Royal Doors' in the centre of the iconostasis are opened to allow the priest to pass through during the Divine Liturgy (Holy Communion). On either side of the doors are icons. The one of the left depicts the 'incarnation' (Jesus born to the Virgin Mary) while the one on the right shows the promised Second Coming of Christ. During the Divine Liturgy the Communion bread and wine are brought to the people through the Royal Doors. Otherwise the doors stay closed, symbolising the belief that it is only through the Liturgy, and the intercession of the priest, that sinful human beings can approach God. The people believe that Christ is present in the church through the bread and wine, so bringing together the icons on either side of the door.

FOR YOUR FOLDER

1 Explain, in your own words, the symbolic meaning of the following: the dome; the icons; the iconostasis; the Royal Doors; the bread and wine at the Divine Liturgy.

2
a) What is an icon?
b) How does the preparation of icons indicate their special nature?
c) How do people often show their respect for icons when they are in church?
d) How would you describe the symbolic importance of icons in religious worship?

In the glossary: ALTAR; APOSTLE; CHURCH; DIVINE LITURGY; ICON; ICONOSTASIS; INCARNATION; MARY; NAVE; ORTHODOX; PRIEST; ROYAL DOORS; SAINT.

Inside a Nonconformist Church

What is distinctive about Nonconformist worship and how is this reflected in the different places of worship?

FOCUSING QUESTIONS

When did the growth in the Nonconformist Church occur who was its most prominent leader?

What are the differences between citadels and other Nonconformist places of worship?

How would you distinguish between a citadel, a meeting house and a Baptist church?

Although the Quakers and the Baptist Church began in the seventeenth century, real growth in the Nonconformist Church took place in the eighteenth and nineteenth centuries. This was largely due to the very effective preaching of John Wesley, the founder of Methodism. His brother, Charles, made an equally important contribution to Nonconformist Church by writing more than 1,000 hymns, many of which are still used in worship today.

Meeting houses

Quakers (members of the Society of Friends) gather in places of worship called 'meeting houses'. The simplicity of their worship is reflected in the rooms in which they meet – simple and bare with the chairs arranged in a square or circle around a table which usually contains a Bible and some flowers – nothing else.

Citadels

Members of the Salvation Army worship in citadels (see Photograph A). The word 'citadel' means a small, fortified city, and the Salvation Army citadels are felt to offer spiritual and physical safety from the evil world outside. These buildings are similar to other Nonconformist places of worship, but they do not have a Communion table as the Salvation Army does not celebrate Holy Communion. The hall is divided into two sections:

- The upper part, the rostrum, where the band sits. At the front of this is a reading desk from which the officer conducts the service.
- The lower part where the congregation sit. The 'mercy-seat' or 'penitent's form' (a long bench) is in front of the congregation, and anyone can come forward and kneel at it if they wish to seek God's forgiveness or help. The flag of the Salvation Army is displayed prominently in the citadel.

DISCUSS

How have different Nonconformist buildings been built to reflect the different kinds of worship that takes place in them?

Chapels and churches

Baptist and Methodist churches are sometimes called chapels. There is no altar in a Nonconformist church but the pulpit, a raised platform at the front of the building, is the focal-point. This is because the emphasis in Baptist and Methodist worship is

A. What are the main features of a Salvation Army citadel?

on the preaching of the 'Word of God' (The Bible) and not on the sacraments. The sermon, when the minister goes up into the pulpit to explain some passage from The Bible, is the most important part of the service.

Two other features are particularly noticeable in Baptist and Methodist churches:

- A Communion table is at the front of the church. This holds the individual glasses and pieces of bread which are taken to the people in their pews during Holy Communion, which Nonconformists call the Lord's Supper. During the service the minister and the elected deacons or elders of the Church sit behind the table facing the people.

- In Baptist churches there is a baptismal pool at the front which is opened up and filled with water for the service of Believer's Baptism. At other times the pool is emptied and covered.

Singing plays a very important part in Nonconformist worship and in many churches this is led by an organist – although a piano or a music group are just as likely to be used in modern churches. In recent years much new music has been written which places the emphasis very much upon the participation of all the congregation in the worship.

FOR YOUR FOLDER

1
a) Why is there a pool of water at the front of Baptist churches?
b) Why do music and singing play an important part in Nonconformist worship?

2 Look at Photograph A.
a) Explain why there is no Communion table in this Salvation Army citadel.
b) Explain what happens in the 'mercy-seat'.

In the glossary: Altar; Baptist; Believer's Baptism; Bible; Chapel; Church; Citadel; Deacon; Hymn; Lord's Supper; Meeting House; Mercy-Seat; Methodist; Minister; Nonconformist; Pulpit; Quaker; Salvation Army; Wesley, Charles; Wesley, John.

Protestant Churches and Holy Communion

***What** emphasis do the different Protestant Churches bring to the celebration of Holy Communion?*

FOCUSING QUESTIONS

How do Nonconformists celebrate the Breaking of Bread?

What is the 'Peace'?

How do High and Low Church Anglicans differ in their understanding of the significance of Holy Communion?

From the birth of the Christian Church believers met together to 'break bread' as Jesus had told them to do – words which are recorded in all four Gospels and 1 Corinthians 11.17-34. Most Anglican churches 'break bread' twice a week, but Nonconformist churches do so twice a month.

The Eucharist

The Anglican Eucharist, usually called 'Holy Communion', is a 'meal' in which members of the church come together to thank God for the death of Jesus and to celebrate their oneness and love for each other. People express this love when, during the Eucharist, they say to each other *'The Peace of the Lord be with you'* as they kiss or shake hands. Then, once the bread and the wine have been consecrated (made holy) by the priest, the people come to kneel before the altar. The priest hands them a piece of bread with the words *'The body of our Lord Jesus Christ'* and then a communal chalice (goblet) of wine saying *'The blood of our Lord Jesus Christ'*.

A. What do Low Church Anglicans believe about the wine in this chalice?

B. This photograph shows the 'Breaking of Bread' service in a Baptist church. Why do you think that the deacons usually take the bread and wine to the people in their seats?

From the scriptures

This is what Paul wrote about Holy Communion:
'For I received from the Lord the teaching that I passed on to you: that the Lord Jesus, on the night that he was betrayed, took a piece of bread, gave thanks to God, broke it, and said, "This is my body, which is for you. Do this in memory of me." In the same way, after supper, he took the cup and said, "This cup is God's new covenant, sealed with my blood. Whenever you drink it, do so in memory of me".'
(1 Corinthians 11.23-25)

What reason is given in this extract for celebrating Holy Communion?

For Anglo-Catholic members of the Church of England (the Anglican Church) these words carry the same meaning as they do for Roman Catholics – that the bread and wine are turned into the actual body and blood of Jesus (a belief called 'transubstantiation'). For Low Church (Evangelical) Anglicans, however, the bread and wine remain just symbols to help them to re-live the death of Jesus. This is the meaning attached to the bread and wine by Nonconformist Churches as well.

The Breaking of Bread

When Nonconformists come together to celebrate the Holy Communion, which they call the 'Breaking of Bread' or the 'Lord's Supper':

- They begin by confessing their sins to God and listening to a passage from The Bible.
- The bread and wine are then consecrated as the minister reads the words that were spoken by Jesus at the Last Supper (Mark 14.22-25).
- The bread is taken by the deacons (leaders) of the church to the people in their pews followed by individual glasses of wine (see Photograph B).
- Most Methodist churches, however, follow the Anglican custom of people coming forword to kneel and accept the bread and wine. The people eat the bread at once to underline the Protestant belief that Christ makes claims on each person individually. The people then hold their glasses until everyone has been served before drinking together to express their 'oneness in Christ'.

FOR YOUR FOLDER

This prayer is at the heart of the Protestant Communion service:
'...Who in the same night that he was betrayed, took bread and gave you thanks; he broke it and gave to his disciples, saying, Take, eat; this is my body which is given for you, do this in remembrance of me. In the same way, after supper he took the cup and gave you thanks; he gave it to them, saying, Drink this, all of you; this is my blood of the new covenant, which is shed for you and for many for the forgiveness of sins. Do this, as often as you drink it, in remembrance of me'.'

Why did Jesus tell his disciples to eat the bread and drink the wine?

In the glossary: Altar; Anglican; Bible; Breaking of Bread; Deacon; Eucharist; Evangelical; Gospel; Holy Communion; Last Supper; Lord's Supper; Minister; Nonconformist; Peace; Priest; Protestant; Roman Catholic; Sacrament;

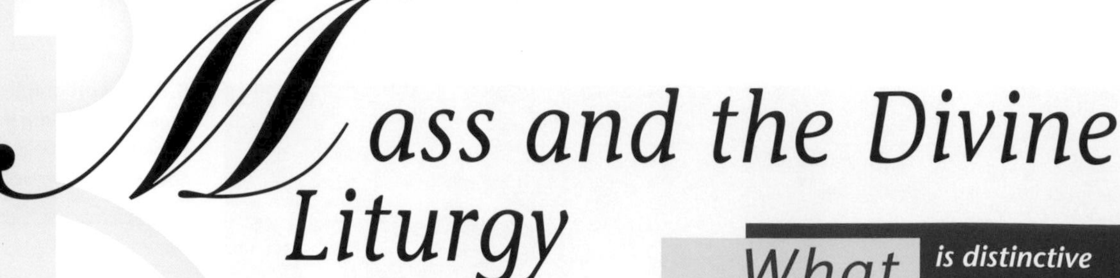

Mass and the Divine Liturgy

What is distinctive about the Mass and the Divine Liturgy?

FOCUSING QUESTIONS

How did the word 'Mass' probably originate?

How does the service of the Divine Liturgy begin?

How are the bread and the wine taken in the Divine Liturgy?

The origin of the word 'Mass' is difficult to unravel but it seems to come from the very last words of the old Latin Mass – 'Ite Missa Est' (meaning 'go in peace'). Two beliefs underlie the Catholic approach to this service and these distinguish it from the Protestant Holy Communion, and its variants. First, Roman Catholics believe that the Mass is a sacrifice. Each time it is celebrated Christ renews the sacrifice that he made for the sins of the world when he was crucified. Secondly, Roman Catholics believe that the bread and wine change, when they are consecrated in the Mass, into the actual body and blood of Jesus. This belief, called transubstantiation, is one of the most important differences between most Protestants and Roman Catholics.

The Mass

The priest begins the Mass by making 'the sign of the cross' and leading the people in repentance before God. On every Sunday, apart from those in Advent and Lent, the Gloria Patri ('Glory to God in the highest and peace to his people on earth') is either said or sung. Then the Liturgy of the Word takes place. Readings are taken from the Old Testament, the Gospels and Epistles and these are followed by a homily (sermon or discourse) from the priest. Following this, the gifts of bread and wine are brought to the altar by members of the congregation. The priest washes his hands to symbolise his cleansing before he offers the Mass.

The priest then offers the Eucharistic prayer. Through the Holy Spirit the priest asks that the bread and wine might become the body and blood of Jesus and this is followed by the breaking and sharing of bread. As the priest holds up the host (a wafer of bread) he invites the people to receive the gift which God has given them with the words: *'This is the Lamb of God who takes away the sins of the world. Happy are those who are called to his supper'* (see Photograph A). To this the worshippers reply: *'Lord, I am not worthy to receive you, but only say the word and I shall be healed'.* When the Mass is over the priest dismisses the people with the words: *'Go in peace to love and serve the Lord'.*

FOR YOUR FOLDER

1 Explain, in your own words, the main difference in understanding Holy Communion between the Roman Catholic Church and the Protestant Churches.

2 Why do you think that in the Orthodox Church, as in the Roman Catholic Church, the priest takes the bread and wine before they are offered to the people?

3
a) Why do you think that the Mass ends with the people being 'sent' out into the world to serve God and help other people?
b) What do you think is the symbolic importance of the bread being dipped in wine and then being placed directly on the back of the tongue with a silver spoon in the Divine Liturgy?

The Divine Liturgy

In the Orthodox Church the Divine Liturgy – the Orthodox version of Holy Communion – follows an ancient ritual which begins with the carrying of the Gospels above the priest's head through the Royal Doors into the nave of the

A. A Roman Catholic priest holds the host up during the Mass. What does the host represent in the Mass, and why do you think that the priest is holding it up above the altar?

B. The full text on this banner would read: 'The Lamb of God who takes away the sins of the world.' What is the link between this message and the Roman Catholic Mass?

church. After a reading from it the book is then returned to the altar through the iconostasis.

The Liturgy itself is performed by a priest at the altar, standing behind the iconostasis, although the people can see enough to follow it. The wine and bread are prepared for communion, blessed, and then brought through the Royal Doors to the people who are kneeling at the front of the church. Each 'communicant' waits to receive a piece of bread dipped in wine which is placed at the back of the mouth on a long, silver spoon by the priest.

In the glossary: ALTAR; DIVINE LITURGY; GLORIA PATRI; GOSPELS; HOMILY; HOST; ICONOSTASIS; MASS; NAVE; ORTHODOX; PRIEST; PROTESTANT; ROMAN CATHOLIC; ROYAL DOORS; SIGN OF THE CROSS; TRANSUBSTANTIATION;

Prayer and Meditation

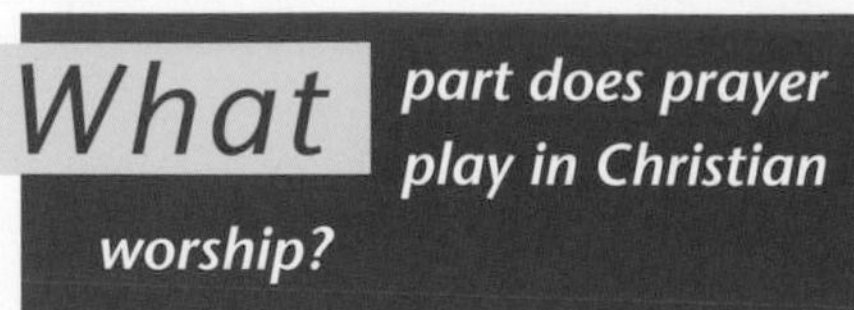

FOCUSING QUESTIONS

Why does private prayer lie at the heart of a Christian's private devotions?

What is 'Quiet Time'?

What is contemplation?

Although prayer plays a very important part of Christian worship it is private prayer which lies at the heart of each Christian's spiritual life. This is not surprising. In the most important collection of the sayings of Jesus in the Gospels, the Sermon on the Mount (Matthew chapters 5-7), Jesus told his followers not to pray to gain the admiration of others but to *'...go into your room, close the door, and pray to your Father, who is unseen'* (Matthew 6.6).

Prayer

There are few set prayers which are common to all Christian traditions although the Lord's Prayer (called the 'Our Father' by Roman Catholics) is the exception. Most Christian prayers, however, do contain common ingredients:

- The praise and adoration of God. All genuine prayer begins as the Christian thanks God for the world He has created and the faculties of health and strength to enjoy it.
- A confession of any sins committed and the seeking of God's forgiveness.
- Requests to God to intervene in their own personal life or in the lives of others. Prayers for others are called 'intercessions' and these form an important part of both private and public prayer (see Photograph B).
- Thanksgiving for all the blessings that have already been received from God.

All of these elements are brought together in the Lord's Prayer (see FROM THE SCRIPTURES) which Jesus taught all of his followers to use.

Unlike several other religions there are no set times for prayer in the Christian tradition – although this is not true for monks and nuns. Many Christians, though, do feel the need to start each day with a 'Quiet Time' when they set time aside to read their Bible and pray, and they may well end the day in the same way as well.

A. Why do you think that personal prayer plays such an important role in a Christian's religious life?

B. Part of this congregation's praying is called 'intercession'. What does this mean?

Meditation

Meditation is an activity which is found in many religions and some Christians use it as part of their own spiritual devotions. Meditation is a mixture of silent and audible prayer. Some Christians read a passage from The Bible and try to 'visualise' it to discover its true meaning. The parables of Jesus, in particular, lend themselves readily to this. 'Contemplation' is a spiritual activity which goes a stage further – being a kind of 'internal conversation' between a person's spirit and God in which words are unnecessary.

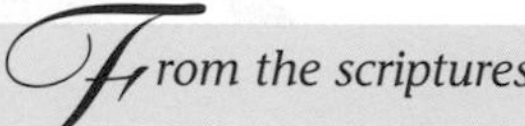

The 'Lord's Prayer' was given by Jesus to his disciples as a 'model prayer':
'This, then, is how you should pray: 'Our Father, in heaven: May your holy name be honoured; may your Kingdom come; may your will be done on earth as it is in heaven. Give us today the food we need. Forgive us the wrongs we have done, as we forgive the wrongs that others have done to us. Do not bring us to hard testing, but keep us safe from the Evil One.'

(Matthew 6.9-13)

1 Christian prayer traditionally includes praise, regret for sin, intercessions for oneself and others, and a thanksgiving. How are these different ingredients included in this prayer that Jesus taught his disciples to pray?

2 Do you find any phrases in this prayer surprising and, if so, which?

FOR YOUR FOLDER

The 'Hail Mary' is a very important Roman Catholic prayer. It says:
'Hail Mary, full of grace, the Lord is with thee. Blessed art thou among women, and blessed is the fruit of thy womb, Jesus. Holy Mary, Mother of God, pray for us sinners, now, and at the hour of our death. Amen'.

a) Why do Roman Catholics often pray to God through the Virgin Mary?
b) This prayer says something very important about the Virgin Mary. What is it?

In the glossary: Bible; Gospels; Hail Mary; Intercessions; Lord's Prayer; Meditation; Monk; Nun; Our Father; Parable; Quiet Time.

Aids to Prayer

What ***do some Christians use to help them in their prayers and meditations?***

FOCUSING QUESTIONS

What is a rosary?

What is a crucifix?

What is the difference between a cross and a crucifix in a church?

FOR YOUR FOLDER

1 Do some research and make a complete list of the joyful, sorrowful and glorious mysteries.
a) Why do you think they are called 'mysteries'?
b) All but two of the 'mysteries' are mentioned in the New Testament. Which are the odd ones out?
c) Why do you think these particular events have been singled out to be remembered whilst using a rosary?

2 The Gloria is a very brief but important Roman Catholic prayer: *'Glory be to the Father, and to the Son, and to the Holy Spirit, as it was in the beginning, is now and ever shall be, world without end. Amen.'*
a) Can you find any link between the Gloria and the Our Father?
b) What do you think is the basic belief behind the Gloria?
c) How does the Gloria take in the whole of history?
d) How do you understand the phrase '*world without end*'?

The majority of Protestant Christians do not make use of any aids to help them to pray. Others, mainly Roman Catholics and Orthodox Christians, find aids such as the rosary, the crucifix, and icons particularly helpful.

The rosary

The rosary is a traditional Roman Catholic way of meditating on the key events in the life of Jesus (see Photograph A). On the circle of beads there are five sets of ten beads, separated by single larger beads. A crucifix, on a short set of four beads, is attached to the end. Holding the beads between their fingers as he or she prays the worshipper is reminded of several prayers. The Hail Mary is repeated with each single bead and the Our Father (the Pater Noster) is recited when a large bead is reached. At the end of each set of ten beads the Gloria Patri is recited. On working their way through each set of beads the worshipper meditates on one event (called a 'mystery') in the life of Jesus. In all, there are five joyful mysteries, five sorrowful mysteries, and five glorious mysteries.

The crucifix

The cross is the most important of all Christian symbols and is to be found in almost all churches. In Roman Catholic and Orthodox churches, though, it is likely to have the figure of Jesus on it (crucifix) representing the sufferings of Jesus on the cross. An empty cross, found, for example, during the festival of Easter, represents the resurrection of Jesus. Many Christians pray in front of a crucifix at home or in church since this centres their minds on the death of Jesus.

Icons

As a sacred picture painted on wood, the icon carries many significant symbolic features and is to be found both in Orthodox churches and homes. Not only are there symbolic features associated with the figures painted, such as one of the saints or Mary, but even the style and paint are important. Most Orthodox believers prefer to pray in front of an icon or to have one close at hand.

A. What prayers are repeated by this Roman Catholic worshipper when using the rosary?

B. Why do you think that the crucifix is such a powerful and moving symbol for so many Christians?

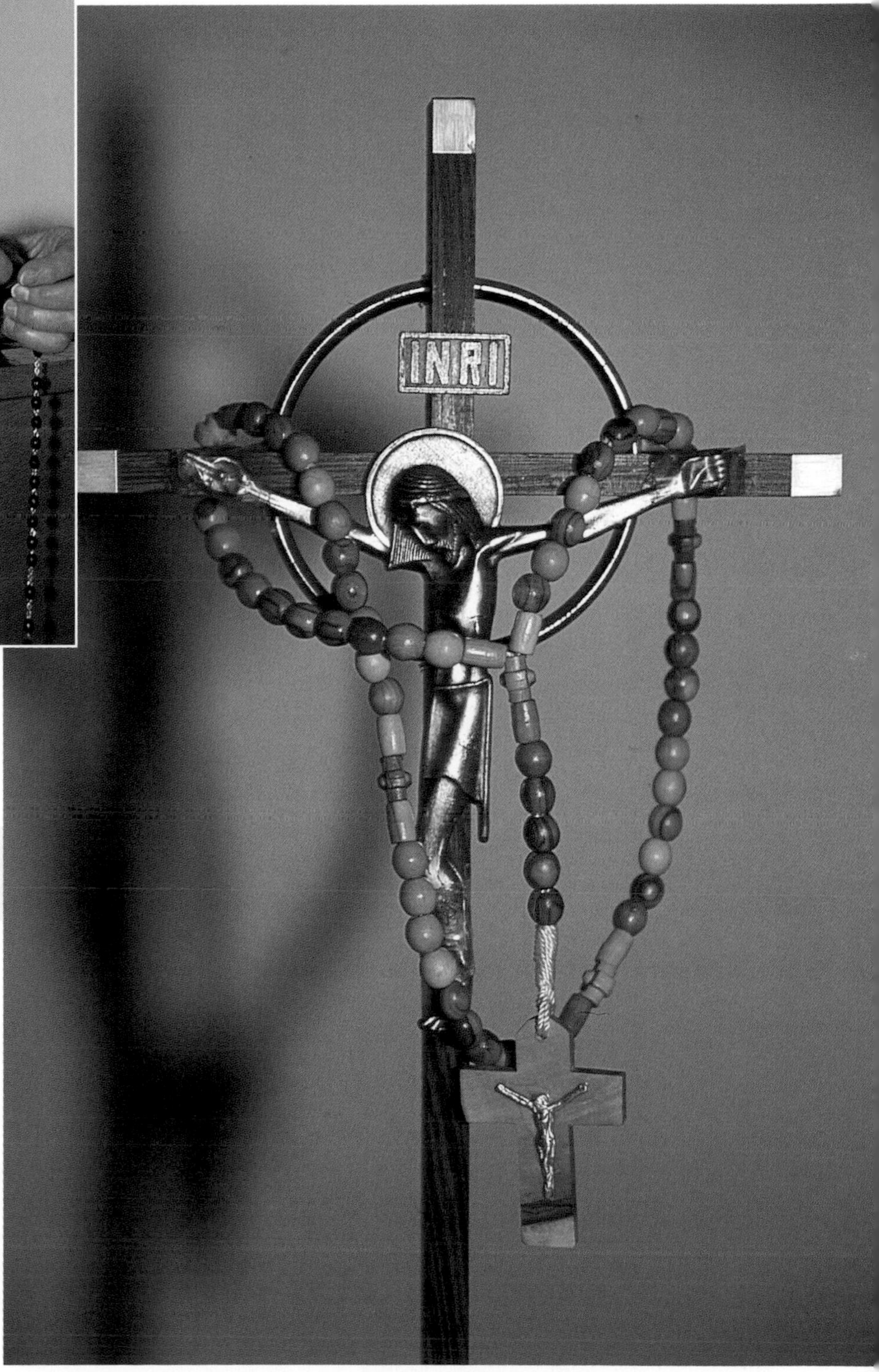

DISCUSS

The use of the rosary, crucifix or icon by Christians seems to suggest that many find prayer 'difficult'. Do you agree? If so, why might prayer be 'difficult', and how could these different objects help?

In the glossary: CHURCH; CRUCIFIX; EASTER; GLORIA PATRI; HAIL MARY; ICON; MARY; ORTHODOX; OUR FATHER; PROTESTANT; RESURRECTION; ROMAN CATHOLIC; ROSARY; SAINT.

From Advent to Epiphany

What do Christians celebrate at Advent, Christmas and Epiphany?

FOCUSING QUESTIONS

Why is Advent sometimes called the season of 'comings'?

How do Christians celebrate the birth of Jesus?

What do many Christians celebrate at Epiphany?

Advent

The Christian year in Roman Catholic and Anglican churches begins with the first Sunday in Advent, which is the fourth Sunday before 25th December (Christmas). For 1,400 years many Christians have marked this as a period of spiritual preparation before the celebration of the birth of Jesus. For Christians, Advent, 'the time of coming', remembers:

- The coming of the Angel Gabriel to the virgin Mary, who announced that she was to give birth to Jesus (the 'Annunciation').
- The coming of John the Baptist to prepare the people for Jesus, the Messiah.
- The coming of God's Son, Jesus.
- The Second Coming of Jesus at the end of time.

A. What does the 'voice' of Advent say to many Christians?

Christmas

At the festival of Christmas Christians celebrate a very important part of the faith. They believe that God became a man in the form of Jesus of Nazareth – the 'Incarnation' – and this began with the birth of a baby in a stable in Bethlehem. Many Christians believe that Jesus was not conceived by any human father but by God in the form of the Holy Spirit – an event called the Virgin Birth. Christians see Jesus as God's greatest gift to the human race, and the celebration of this gift in church as the clock strikes midnight on Christmas Eve (Midnight Mass) is the cause of great thanksgiving. The church is lavishly decorated for this service which is, in most churches, the best attended of the year.

Epiphany

Epiphany (meaning 'showing forth') is a festival which celebrates a number of different events. In the Anglican and Roman Catholic Churches Epiphany is celebrated on January 6th, and is the time when Christians remember the coming of the Wise Men – the first non-Jews (Gentiles) – to visit the infant Jesus and the 'showing' of Jesus to them. In the Orthodox Church, the festival of Epiphany celebrates three events:

1 The birth of Jesus when he was 'shown' to be the awaited Messiah. Before Christians adopted the Gregorian calendar, they celebrated Christmas on January 6th, and this is still followed by Orthodox Christians.

B. This scene reminds Christians of the 'Incarnation'. What does this word mean?

DISCUSS

For some Christians the idea of Jesus being born to a virgin is an essential part of Christianity. Why do you think that this belief is so important to many believers?

2 The Baptism, when Jesus was 'shown' to be God's son.

3 The first miracle performed by Jesus which took place, according to John's Gospel, at Cana in Galilee. When he changed the water into wine at the wedding feast he 'showed' that God's power was with him.

FOR YOUR FOLDER

1 Explain, in your own words, what Christians mean by: Advent; Christmas; the Incarnation; Epiphany.

2
a) Which four events, three in the past and one in the future, are celebrated by Christians during Advent? What link can you suggest between the four events?
b) What do Christians mean when they speak of the 'Virgin Birth'?
c) How do the Orthodox, Roman Catholic and Anglican Churches differ in their understanding of the celebration of the festival of Epiphany?

3 Using material in this unit to help you, draw up a chart of the main Christian festivals as follows:

Festival . . . .

When held . . . .

What is celebrated . . . .

In the glossary: ADVENT; ANGLICAN; ANGEL GABRIEL; BETHLEHEM; CHRISTMAS; EPIPHANY; GENTILE; INCARNATION; JOHN'S GOSPEL; JOHN THE BAPTIST; MARY; MESSIAH; MIDNIGHT MASS; ORTHODOX; ROMAN CATHOLIC; SUNDAY; VIRGIN BIRTH.

Lent

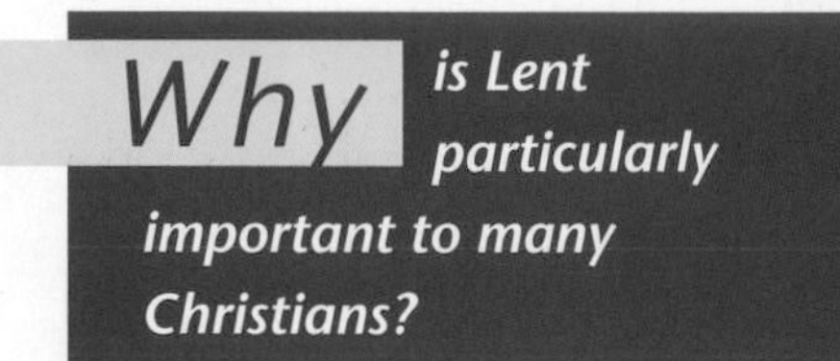

Why is Lent particularly important to many Christians?

FOCUSING QUESTIONS

What is the link between the time that Jesus spent in the wilderness being tempted and the festival of Lent?

How do Christians celebrate Lent today?

What do churches celebrate on Palm Sunday?

Lent is the period of penitence and preparation that precedes the most serious of all the Christian festivals – Easter. Lent itself lasts for forty days but it is, in the Orthodox Church, preceded by four weeks of fasting called 'the Great Fast'. The biblical precedent for this is found in the descriptions in the Gospels of the time that Jesus spent in the wilderness immediately after he had been baptised by John the Baptist. According to the Gospel of Matthew, Jesus was led by the Spirit of God into the wilderness (Matthew 4.1-11) where he was tempted by Satan for forty days.

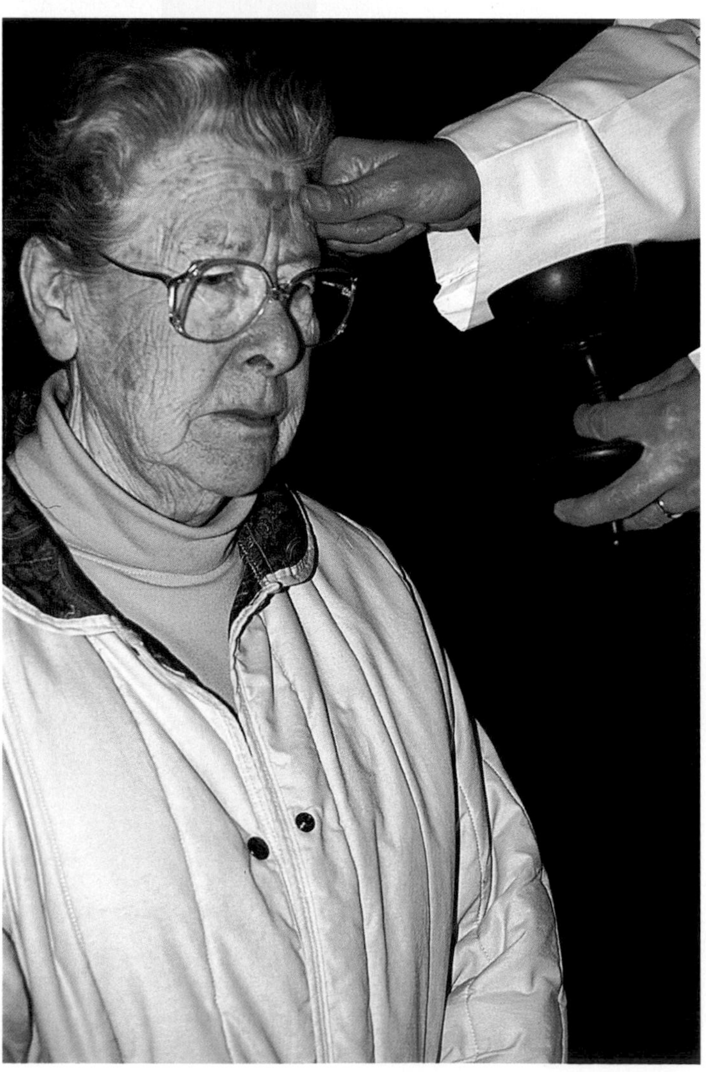

Penitence and preparation

Lent begins with Ash Wednesday on which ash is used to make the sign of the cross on the foreheads of worshippers in church (see Photograph A). The ash is obtained from burning the palm crosses from the previous year's Palm Sunday celebrations. The priest applies the ash as he says *'Dust thou art and unto dust thou shalt return'*. Lent continues until Easter Sunday. Few Protestant Christians now fast during this time, although some Christians, particularly Roman Catholics, still carry out some form of self-denial, often giving up a particular food and donating the money saved to charity.

In most churches, Lent is now a time set aside for serious thought, prayer and Bible-study with congregations being broken down into small study-groups in which people try to deepen their own understanding of God.

Holy Week

During the last week of Lent, known as 'Holy Week', Christians try to relive many of the events which took place at the end of the life of Jesus – leading up to his suffering and death. Two days are particularly important:

- Palm Sunday (also called Passion Sunday) is when Christians recall the triumphant entry of Jesus into

A. How do the forty days of Lent begin for many Christians – and why?

Jerusalem when, riding on a donkey, he was welcomed by jubilant crowds throwing their cloaks on the road and waving palm branches. In many churches, palms are blessed and people wave them in the streets as they follow a donkey in procession – often carrying a small child.

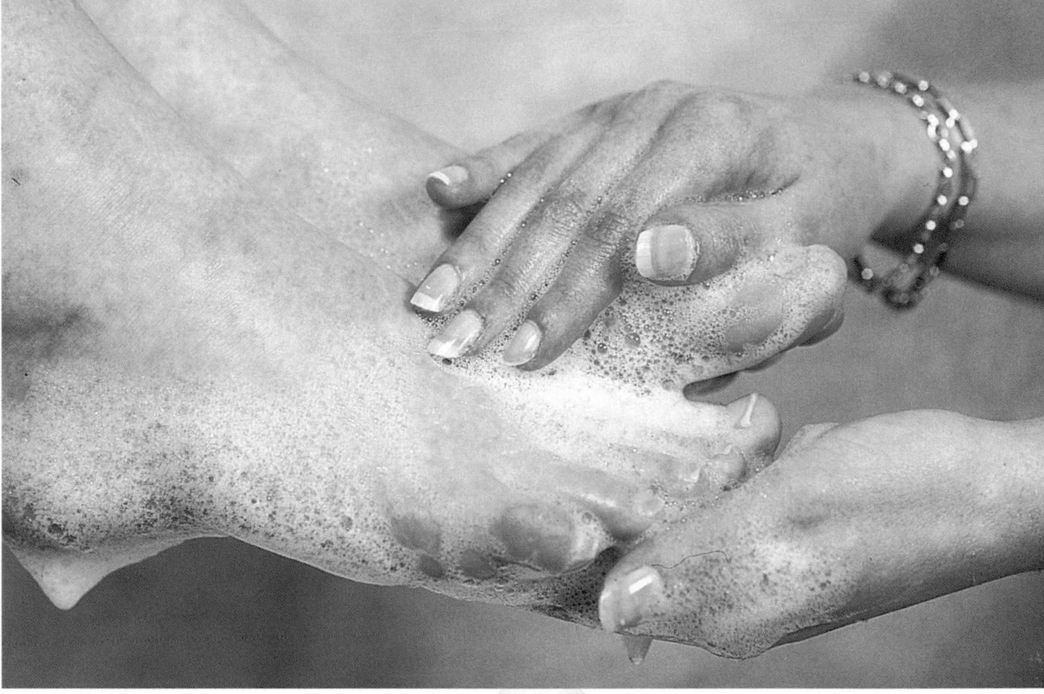

- Four days after Palm Sunday, on Maundy Thursday, a special Holy Communion reminds everyone of the last meal that Jesus ate with his disciples before he was crucified. During the 'Last Supper' Jesus instructed his followers to break bread and drink wine in his memory. This is the origin of the service of Holy Communion which stands at the heart of Christian worship. Also, on this day, Jesus washed the feet of his disciples (see Photograph B) to remind them to serve one another and this tradition is continued by some Christian groups. In Britain on this day specially minted 'Maundy money' is given to the poor by the Queen.

B. In some churches on Maundy Thursday, Christians re-enact Jesus' washing of his disciples feet. What do you think that Christians might learn from continuing this tradition?

FOR YOUR FOLDER

1 The words which the priest speaks to each worshipper on Ash Wednesday '*Dust thou art and unto dust thou shalt return*' are also used in the burial service.

a) What do you think is the link between these two events?

b) Why do you think these words are spoken to remind everyone of repentance and penitence on Ash Wednesday?

2

a) Find out a little about the religious practice of fasting.

b) Why do you think that many religious people see a link between denying themselves food and their spiritual journey?

c) Why do you think that few Christians fast these days, although the practice is still common in some other religions, especially Islam?

d) Why do you think that, in the past, fasting was thought to be appropriate before Easter?

3 Read about the temptations of Jesus in Luke 4.1-13.

a) Which event came immediately before the temptations and what reason did Luke give for Jesus going into the wilderness?

b) Which three temptations were directed towards Jesus and why do you think that each of them was attractive?

c) Lent begins with the temptations of Jesus and ends with his death. What link can you see between these two events?

In the glossary: Ash Wednesday; Bible; Church; Disciple; Easter; Fasting; Gospels; Holy Communion; Holy Week; Jerusalem; John the Baptist; Last Supper; Lent; Maundy Thursday; Orthodox; Priest; Satan; Sign of the Cross.

Easter

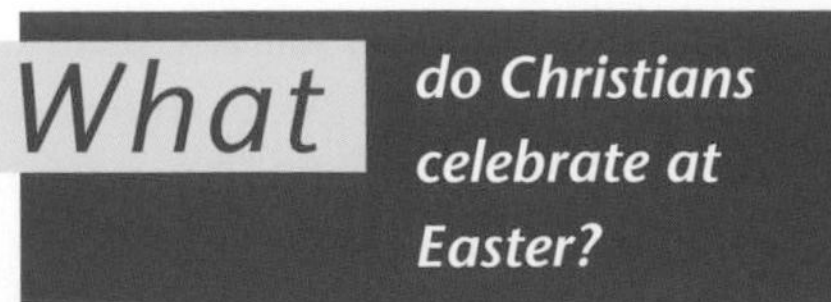

What do Christians celebrate at Easter?

FOCUSING QUESTIONS

How do many Christians spend the time between noon and 3.00 am. on Good Friday – and why?

What are the 'Stations of the Cross'?

What part do the symbols of light and darkness play on Easter Sunday?

At Easter Christians of all denominations seek to gain a deeper understanding of the sufferings, death and resurrection of Jesus. Between Good Friday and Easter Sunday their emotions swing from intense sadness to overwhelming joy as the events of the first Easter are re-lived.

Good Friday

On the day after Maundy Thursday, Good Friday, Christians remember the trial of Jesus and his death at the hands of the Romans. On this, the most solemn of all days, special services are held in church to meditate on the crucifixion whilst marches and Passion Plays spread the message of Good Friday to others. The main service in most churches lasts for three hours from 12 noon – the time when the Gospels say that the Earth was plunged into darkness by the impending death of Jesus. This time of meditation is called a 'vigil' as those present seek to 'watch' with Jesus. They do this by singing hymns, reading the accounts of the crucifixion in all four Gospels and taking part in a silent or guided meditation. In addition to their 'Celebration of the Lord's Passion' Roman Catholics may visit each of the fourteen Stations of the Cross (see Photograph A). These are placed around the church and illustrate places where Jesus is believed to have stopped on his way to his execution. As they stop at each of the Stations worshippers pray. In Orthodox churches an icon showing the dead Christ is carried around the inside and outside of the building in a funeral procession.

Easter Saturday and Sunday

Easter Saturday, the Great Sabbath, is the last day of Holy Week and a time of quiet anticipation for many Christians as they look forward to Easter Sunday. Churches are cleaned and new altar-cloths are laid out for the following day as some time is spent contemplating the burial of Jesus in the tomb.

A. This photograph shows the fourth of the fourteen Stations of the Cross. Why do Stations of the Cross play an important part in Roman Catholic services during Holy Week?

B. How does this help Christians to remember the trial, death and resurrection of Jesus?

Easter Sunday is the most important day in the Christian calendar, and Orthodox and Roman Catholic churches begin their celebrations at midnight as candles and lamps are handed from one to another in the darkened church. This symbolises the rolling away of the stone from the door of Jesus' tomb – as the cry goes up *'Christ* [Jesus] *is risen'*. A large Paschal Candle is carried through the church to represent the light of Jesus shining in a darkened world. Often a baby is baptised, another symbol of new life, before everyone celebrates a special Communion together. Many Christians in Anglican and Nonconformist Churches come together early on Easter morning for a 'sunrise service'. This recalls the discovery of the Resurrection, when the women went to Jesus' tomb to anoint his body at the end of the Jewish Sabbath Day and found that it was empty.

C. Why do you think that Easter Day is the most important day in the Christian year?

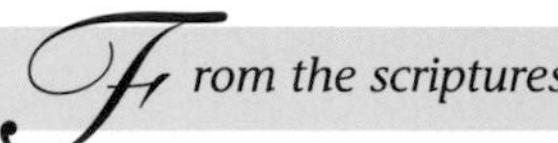
rom the scriptures

Paul wrote:
'But the truth is that Christ has been raised from death, as the guarantee that those who sleep in death will also be raised. For just as death came by means of a man [Adam], *in the same way the rising from death comes by means of a man* [Jesus].'
(1 Corinthians 15.20-21)

What does Paul say about the resurrection of Christian believers – and the link this has with the resurrection of Jesus?

FOR YOUR FOLDER

1 Look at Photograph B.
These Christians have erected crosses on a hill to celebrate the death of Jesus. Why do you think that they feel this is an appropriate thing to do on Good Friday?

In the glossary: Anglican; Bible; Church; Easter; Easter Saturday; Easter Sunday; Good Friday; Gospels; Holy Communion; Holy Week; Hymn; Icon; Orthodox; Paschal Candle; Protestant; Roman Catholic; Vigil.

From Pentecost to Harvest

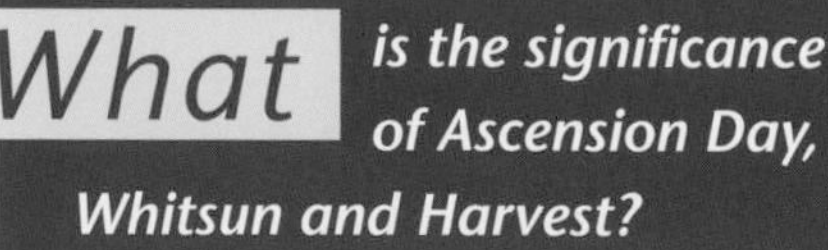

What is the significance of Ascension Day, Whitsun and Harvest?

FOCUSING QUESTIONS

Which event gave birth to the Christian Church?

Why is the festival of Pentecost also sometimes called Whitsun?

Why do most churches celebrate Harvest?

Between Easter and Christmas many minor festivals are celebrated by different Christian Churches – especially the Roman Catholic Church which has several dedicated to the Virgin Mary and other saints. Three festivals – Ascension Day, Whitsun and Harvest are celebrated widely, if not universally.

Ascension Day

Ascension Day comes forty days after Easter Sunday since Christians believe that Jesus spent this time after he rose from the dead appearing to his disciples before leaving the Earth altogether. Always falling on a Thursday, there are no special traditions associated with this day although it is celebrated in Anglican and Roman Catholic churches with a Communion service. Nonconformist Churches do not celebrate Ascension Day.

Pentecost

This festival, also known as 'Whitsun', commemorates the birth of the Christian Church. The early followers of Jesus were in Jerusalem to celebrate the Jewish Festival of Pentecost (the 'Feast of Weeks') which commemorates the giving of the Ten Commandments, and the rest of the Jewish law, to Moses on Mount Sinai. Although it was fifty days since Jesus had been crucified the disciples were still frightened that the Romans would arrest them and so they locked and bolted the door. According to the Acts of the Apostles, however, the Holy Spirit came down upon them and transformed them into fearless preachers. This event gave rise to the birth of the Christian Church and is one of the most important dates in the Christian year.

A. Carry out some research to find out why the dove is the most widely-used symbol of the Holy Spirit.

B. Why do you think that Harvest has become a popular celebration in almost all churches since the middle of the nineteenth century?

Traditionally, Easter and Pentecost were the favourite times for baptising new converts to Christianity and this explains the other name for the festival, Whitsun ('White Sunday'), since those baptised wore white robes for the occasion – which, if the ceremony took place at Easter, were worn through to Whitsun.

Other Festivals

The Roman Catholic Church believes in transubstantiation and because of this they show great respect for the host (the bread used in the Mass). On the feast of Corpus Christi, Catholics kneel as a procession carrying the host passes by. Roman Catholics also celebrate six separate festivals commemorating various aspects of their belief in the Virgin Mary – including her birth and the time she was visited by the Angel Gabriel.

Since the middle of the nineteenth century many churches have also celebrated Harvest Festival in September or October (see Photograph B). For this festival the church is decorated with harvest produce which is distributed to the poor after the service. The festival provides an opportunity for worshippers to thank God for all that He has provided for them in the natural world.

FOR YOUR FOLDER

1 Read the accounts given in Luke 24.36-53 and Acts 1.3-9 of the ascension of Jesus to Heaven. Why do you think that many Christians have difficulty understanding, and celebrating, this event?

2 In The Bible several symbols are used to represent the Holy Spirit – most particularly wind, fire and the dove. Each of these symbols is intended to underline one different quality or characteristic of the Holy Spirit. What do you think these qualities are?

In the glossary: Acts of the Apostles; Angel Gabriel; Anglican; Ascension Day; Disciples; Easter; Holy Spirit; Host; Jerusalem; Mary; Nonconformist; Pentecost; Ten Commandments; Transubstantiation.

Monastic Communities

What *is a monastic community and what have been the main religious Orders?*

FOCUSING QUESTIONS

How and why were the first monastic communities formed?

What is the 'Rule of St Benedict' and why it has been so important for the monastic movement?

Which religious Order was founded by Bernard of Clairvaux – and what did he teach his monks?

The monastic movement in the Christian Church began in the fourth century CE when men and women began to make their way into the desert to dedicate their lives to prayer and solitude. They believed that they were following the example of Jesus who, according to the Gospels, spent forty days in the wilderness being tempted by Satan at the start of his work. These people adopted a life without any material comforts and, to begin with, lived as solitary hermits. Later, though, they joined with other hermits to form monastic communities.

The Rule of St Benedict

The founder of the monastic movement was probably St Benedict (480-547 CE) who became the first abbot of the community of monks and nuns at Monte Cassio in Italy. He laid down a series of 'rules' for the monks and these rules (later called 'The Rule') were adopted by other monastic orders. They were:

- To live in absolute poverty with no personal possessions. Any possession which the person brought with them when they joined were given over to the community.
- To live a life of chastity – abstaining from all sexual contact and intercourse. For nuns in the different Orders this took the form of being 'married' to God and this was signified by the wearing of a ring.
- To live a life of absolute obedience to God and to the leader of the community, the abbot or Mother Superior, who was elected from among the monks or nuns.

A. Monasteries try to strike a balance between community prayer, work and relaxation. Why do you think that working within the community, and outside, is given a high priority in monastic life?

St Benedict laid a great emphasis upon the importance of communal prayer which he said should take place seven times a day: 3.00 am (morning prayer); 6.00 am (prime); 9.00 am (terce); midday (sext); 3.00 pm (none); early evening (vespers); end of the day (compline). The remainder of the day should be spent in study, work and recreation. Monks and nuns today follow a similar timetable although the number of compulsory prayers has been reduced in most Orders.

B. In recent years the number of men and women feeling a 'vocation' (calling) to live in a monastery or convent has gone down. Can you suggest any reasons for this?

The later monastic orders

By the end of the thirteenth century there were about 2,000 religious monastic houses following a life based upon Benedict's Rule. Apart from the Benedictines there were other Orders which became influential in the life of the Roman Catholic Church especially.

The Cistercians
This Order was founded by Bernard of Clairvaux in 1098. Bernard taught his monks that three beliefs were very important: the centrality of the Virgin Mary in devotions and worship; the importance of private prayer and meditation; and the value of private rather than public penance and confession.

The Franciscans
During the twelfth and thirteenth centuries, an Italian nobleman, Francis of Assisi, decided to imitate the simple lifestyle of Jesus preaching a straightforward message of repentance, trust and respect for the whole of God's creation. At the same time a similar Order of nuns was founded, the Order of Poor Clares, which followed the same principles. The friars and the nuns were dedicated to absolute poverty, the renunciation of all worldly pleasure, the preaching of the Gospel, and caring for the sick and needy.

The Dominicans
This is a Roman Catholic teaching Order of nuns and friars founded in 1215. At first this Order, known as the Black Friars because of the colour of their habits, were 'mendicants' (a begging Order), but from 1425 they were supported by the Roman Catholic Church. The aim of the Dominicans has always been to teach 'truth' and the Order is divided into three branches – monks who teach, nuns who live totally within the confines of a convent and share a life of prayer and contemplation, and people who follow lives outside the monastery or convent but who share in its life – called 'tertiaries'.

Other orders
Over the centuries, many other Orders grew up. The Carmelites and the Augustinians placed themselves at the disposal of the Pope, offering preaching and confession to the people and setting up many foreign missions. In the sixteenth century St Teresa of Avila and St John of the Cross set up a reformed Order of Carmelites called the 'Discalced' (meaning barefoot). They intended to follow a stricter way of life than the original Order.

FOR YOUR FOLDER

1
a) Why did many men and women make their way into the desert to spend time alone with God? What was the attraction of the desert?
b) What is the difference between a hermit and a monk? Why do you think that people stopped following solitary lives and formed themselves into communities?
c) Why do you think that the three parts of the 'Rule' were thought to be desirable for those people seeking God together in a religious community?

2 Why do you think that many Christians have gained inspiration from the monastic movement over the centuries?

In the glossary: Abbot; Bernard of Clervaux; Gospels; Hermit; Mary; Monk; Nun; Order; Penance; Rule; Satan.

Taizé and Iona

What is distinctive about the community life in Taizé and Iona?

FOCUSING QUESTIONS

Why was Iona considered to be a holy place by the eigth century?

Why is the religious community on Iona unusual and what commitments are its members asked to make to it?

What is universal about the religious community at Taizé?

Although the old monastic Orders and traditions still survive, many Christians today have turned to more modern communities such as that at Iona, revived in the 1930s, and Taizé, founded at the end of the Second World War. These communities embrace many of the old monastic ideals but bring them into line with twentieth-century ways of worshipping.

Iona

After founding many monasteries in Ireland in the sixth century, St Columba sailed, with twelve companions, to the Scottish island of Iona where he founded another monastery. Columba used the island as his base for carrying the Christian message to the people of northern England. Much has been written of Columba's attractive personality, his skill as a bard (song and poetry writer) and scribe, of his visions, prophecies and miraculous deeds, one of which was the expulsion of a 'water monster' from the river Ness by making the sign of the cross.

A. A view of the Abbey at Iona. Visitors can be seen camped in the grounds to the right. What is distinctive about the work of the Iona community?

From the time of Columba onwards Iona came to be regarded as a holy place. During the Middle Ages a larger monastery was built on the island but this was closed down by Henry VIII. In 1899 the eigth Duke of Argyll, who owned the island, gave it to the Church of Scotland and during the 1930s it again became a place of pilgrimage. In 1938 the Rev. George MacLeod from Glasgow arrived on the island with a group of unemployed people to rebuild the monastery. From the beginning church ministers and working people went to Iona together, spent a short time there talking and praying, and then returned to their work physically and spiritually refreshed – and this continues today. Hundreds of young people also go to summer camps on the island each year to pray, discuss important social issues, work and make many friends.

B. A Celtic cross outside of Iona Abbey. How does this cross reflect the long history of Iona?

Iona is unlike almost any other religious community since there are no monks or nuns attached to the community. Instead there are 200 full-time and 800 associate members who have made an agreement to spend a minimum of one week a year on the island as part of the community and to pray regularly for the community. Each member also agrees to follow a way of life which is in keeping with the ethics of the community – to live a life of love and service; one devoted to the welfare of all God's creatures and the struggle for justice and peace in the world. They also 'tithe' by giving ten per cent of their income to the Church and to the community.

Taizé

Taizé, like Iona, is a religious community which offers spiritual refreshment to people drawn from a wide range of denominations – including Protestants, Roman Catholics and Orthodox believers. The community was founded in south-eastern France in 1940 by Brother Roger, who had sheltered many Jewish refugees in his home from the Nazis. His vision was to provide a Christian community where young people could spend time together to worship and pray. In 1949 he was joined by several other men who took the normal monastic vows and so bound themselves together into a community. Today, hundreds of young people travel to Taizé each year to join in the worship of the community of some eighty monks. They worship in the Church of Reconciliation which was built by Germans in 1962 as a token of reconciliation (bringing together) between Germany and the rest of the world after the Second World War.

FOR YOUR FOLDER

1
a) What is the word which sums up the basic message of Taizé and which is symbolised in the church?
b) How was this key-word particularly appropriate at the time when the Taizé community was founded?
c) How does the mixture of different backgrounds from which the monks are drawn reinforce this message?
d) The monks at Taizé have been described as *'...signs of the presence of Christ amongst men and women and the bearers of joy'.* What do you think this means?

2 The Iona community was first set up because George MacLeod did not think that the Church was offering anything to people who spent their lives struggling in the inner city areas of Glasgow. What do you think that time spent on a beautiful Scottish island might offer to people who spend the rest of their lives in the middle of Glasgow – or any other large city?

3 Here is a sentence from the Rule of Taize, which differs from the Rule of St Benedict:
'For them [my fellow brothers] *I will become all things to all, and even give my life, for Christ's sake and the Gospel's...'.*
a) What do you think is meant by this extract?
b) What is the striking difference between this Rule and the Rule of St Benedict?

In the glossary: DENOMINATION; MONASTERY; MONK; NUN; ORTHODOX; PROTESTANT; ROMAN CATHOLIC; SIGN OF THE CROSS; TITHE.

Pilgrimages

What *is a pilgrimage and why do many Christians, especially Roman Catholics, undertake one?*

FOCUSING QUESTIONS

How did the idea of Christians making a pilgrimage to a holy place begin?

What are relics and what link do they have with the idea of Christians making a pilgrimage?

Where are the main pilgrimage centres?

Pilgrimages are a very important part of many religions, particularly Islam and Hinduism. In the past, they were also considered important by the Christian Church and many Christians have made arduous and hazardous journeys to holy places over the centuries, either as a way of atoning for their sins or for their own spiritual reasons. Many modern Christians still undertake pilgrimages which they see as an important part of their own 'spiritual journey', as well as taking them to places where, it is believed, God has revealed Himself to fellow believers in the past.

Places of pilgrimage

Christian pilgrimages started in the fourth century when Helena (250-330 CE), mother of the Roman Emperor Constantine, claimed to have discovered three crosses in Jerusalem. No-one was sure which of them was the original cross on which Jesus died so they were each laid, in turn, on the body of a sick woman. According to the story, when the original cross touched the woman's body she was miraculously cured. From this time onwards 'relics' such as this became important focuses for worship, and places where holy relics were found or kept, or places which were linked to the life of Jesus, (and later the saints) became centres of pilgrimage. Rome, in Italy, especially became a very popular pilgrimage destination due to its links with St Peter who Roman Catholics believe was the first Pope (Bishop of Rome). Today thousands of pilgrims crowd into St Peter's Square in Rome on Easter Sunday to receive the blessing of the present Pope delivered in their own language (see Photograph A).

A. The Pope blessing the crowd in St Peter's Square, Rome. Why have these pilgrims travelled to Rome to receive the Pope's blessing?

B. The Church of the Holy Sepulchre, Chapel of Calgary, Jerusalem, Israel. Jerusalem is a popular place for pilgrims to visit. Why?

In England the most important early place of pilgrimage was the shrine of St Thomas à Beckett (1118-1170) in Canterbury Cathedral. His brutal murder by four knights on the altar-steps of his own cathedral shocked the Christian world and the king was held responsible. Beckett's shrine became one of the most visited in the Christian world and many miracles were reported to have occurred there. Similar miraculous events were reported from the shrine at Walsingham after it was built by Lady Richeldis as a result of a vision she had received from the Virgin Mary.

During the Middle Ages churches competed, often violently, against each other for possession of similar relics, since possession of one guaranteed that the church would be visited by many pilgrims and this brought considerable wealth. The pilgrims came in their thousands for a variety of reasons and many of the same reasons still compel people to undertake pilgrimages today:

- To seek spiritual guidance and refreshment.
- To thank God, the Virgin Mary, or one of the saints for blessings or a healing that they had received in answer to their prayers.
- To seek healing from God in a place which has been associated with such miraculous occurrences in the past. The most well-known shrine of this kind is Lourdes, in southern France, where the Virgin Mary is thought to have appeared to a peasant girl, Bernadette.
- To perform an act of penance (repentance) to show their sorrow for a sin that they have committed.
- To follow in the footsteps of Jesus in the Holy Land of Palestine. Christians today still visit Israel to see the places associated with the life, teaching and death of Jesus (see Photograph B). In particular, they visit the places associated with his birth (Bethlehem, Nazareth) at Christmas time and those linked with his death (in and around Jerusalem) at Easter.

DISCUSS

There have been recent attempts to revive many of the holy sites. Do you think that visiting them could be helpful to people today?

FOR YOUR FOLDER

1

a) What are the main reasons that Christians make pilgrimages?
b) To what extent do you think that a pilgrimage needs to be physically as well as spiritually demanding? Does the fact that many modern pilgrimages can be undertaken in relative comfort negate their spiritual benefits?
c) Why do you think that many Christians feel that it is spiritually desirable to visit different sites associated with Jesus? What do you think that they might hope to gain from going to them?

2

a) Although thousands of sick pilgrims travel to holy places seeking a cure each year very few of them are healed. Does this surprise you?
b) Why do you think that people continue to go to holy places if there is little chance that they will be healed?
c) Do you think that people in need of healing might receive something important from a pilgrimage even if their body is not cured? If so, what do you think this is?

In the glossary: Altar; Beckett, Thomas à; Bethlehem; Bishop of Rome; Cathedral; Christmas; Easter; Jerusalem; Mary; Nazareth; Palestine; Penance; Peter; Pope; Relic; Roman Catholic; Saint.

Holy Places

Why are Walsingham and Lourdes special places of pilgrimage for many Christians?

FOCUSING QUESTIONS

What is the link between the Virgin Mary and the shrines at Walsingham and Lourdes?

How did the shrine in Walsingham come to be built – and what miracle is associated, by tradition, with it?

How did the pilgrimage centre of Lourdes achieve its reputation as a place of healing?

A pilgrimage is a journey to a holy place undertaken through devotion to God to receive supernatural help or to act as a means of thanksgiving or penance. For Roman Catholics in Britain two such holy places, Walsingham and Lourdes, both of which have a strong link with the Virgin Mary, are particularly important places of pilgrimage.

Walsingham

Walsingham, in Norfolk, is known as 'England's Nazareth' since it was there, in the eleventh century, that a replica of the Virgin Mary's home in Nazareth was built. The Lady of the Manor in Walsingham, Richeldis de Faverches, had a vision of the home and was told to construct an identical building in her own village. One legend relates that the ground-plan for such a building was traced out in dew in two different places and that the builders constructed the building in the wrong place. Deeply upset about this Richeldis spent the whole night in prayer to the Virgin only to find that the building had miraculously transferred itself, with the help of some angels, to the right site in the night! Myths of this nature are often attached to the most holy sites – raising their level of importance in the minds of many people.

A. A Seventeenth-century travel book, showing Christian pilgrims on their way to Jerusalem. Do you think that the reasons that a Christian might undertake such a pilgrimage have changed since this illustration was drawn?

Augustinian monks became the guardians of the shrine in 1169 and it became popular because English pilgrims found their way to the 'Holy Land' (Palestine) blocked by Muslim soldiers. A statue of Our Lady of Walsingham (the Virgin Mary) and a phial said to contain milk from Mary's breasts drew pilgrims to Walsingham instead. The road taken by pilgrims from London became known as the 'The Milky Way'. Until the sixteenth century different kings provided money to keep and maintain the shrine and endless miracles were recorded as taking place there. The shrine was destroyed by King Henry VIII in 1538, but was restored by Anglo-Catholics in the Church of England in 1897. It is now the centre of a national pilgrimage each year during Spring Bank Holiday and separate shrines are maintained in the town by the Anglican, Roman Catholic and Orthodox Churches.

FOR YOUR FOLDER

1 Explain what you understand by: a pilgrimage; a pilgrim; a shrine; a relic.

2 Someone has said that: *'The only pilgrimage that really matters is the inner journey of the soul towards God'.* What do you think they meant?

3 In Walsingham there is a restored statue of our Lady of Walsingham holding the infant Jesus. Many Christians find that it is more meaningful to pray for unity between the different Christian Churches in front of this statue than anywhere else. Why do you think this is?

Lourdes

Lourdes, in the south of France, is the most popular destination for Christian pilgrims in the twentieth century. It was in Lourdes, in 1858, that Bernadette Soubirous, a fourteen-year-old girl, claimed to have had a series of visions of the Virgin Mary who appeared to her in the grotto of Massbielle predicting that a spring of water would rise up from the grotto floor. When the spring appeared it was soon reported to have healing properties and a church was built on the rock. Both church and spring became international centres of pilgrimage (see Photograph B). Today Lourdes attracts over 2,000,000 pilgrims a year, mostly Roman Catholic, who come seeking healing for all kinds of diseases and illnesses. They believe that they must be lowered into the water to be healed and a whole army of helpers exist to help them to do this. Roman Catholic churches from all over the world take parties of needy people to Lourdes each year.

B. A view of Lourdes, France, showing the Basilica. Why do pilgrims visit Lourdes, and what might they gain from their visit?

Bernadette entered the convent of the Sisters of Notre-Dame at Nevers at the age of twenty-two and remained there for the rest of her life nursing, for a time, the wounded of the Franco-Prussian war from 1870 onwards. She died on April 10th 1879, confirming the truth of her visions on her deathbed. She was canonised (declared to be a saint) in 1933 and this only served to increase the respect in which Lourdes was held within the Roman Catholic Church. A feast-day to St Bernadette is celebrated in many Catholic churches on April 10th.

In the glossary: Anglican; Canonisation; Church of England; Convent; Jerusalem; Mary; Nazareth; Orthodox; Penance; Roman Catholic.

Infant Baptism

How do many Christians celebrate infant baptism and what significance is the service believed to have?

FOCUSING QUESTIONS

Why is the font traditionally placed inside the door of a church?

Why are modern fonts often put in the middle of the congregation?

What are the responsibilities of parents and godparents towards the baby who has been baptised?

Infant Baptism is an important sacrament in Anglican, Roman Catholic and Orthodox Churches. The ceremony usually takes place in very early childhood and in the Catholic Church is thought to be necessary for salvation – it is a serious matter, therefore, if a child dies unbaptised. Nonconformist Churches, with the exception of the Methodists, do not believe in Infant Baptism.

Protestant and Roman Catholic Churches

The parents of the baby choose relatives or friends to be its godparents and their role is to make sure that the child is brought up in the Christian faith. The parents, baby and godparents gather with the priest around the font which is traditionally placed just inside the door of the church. This is a symbolic reminder that the child is entering the Church through Baptism. Some modern churches have portable fonts which can be placed in the middle of the congregation to show that the whole Church 'family' is welcoming a new member.

The priest begins the service by saying to the parents, *'You have asked to have your child baptised. In doing so you are accepting the responsibility of training him/her in the practice of the faith...Do you clearly understand what you are undertaking?'* whilst to the godparents he or she says *'Are you ready to help the parents of this child in their duty as Christian parents?'* Parents and godparents are then challenged, point by point, on their own Christian beliefs by being asked six questions.

A. A baby being baptised in an Anglican church. What is the spiritual significance believed to be of the service of Infant Baptism?

B. Why have the clothes of this baby been taken off before it is baptised?

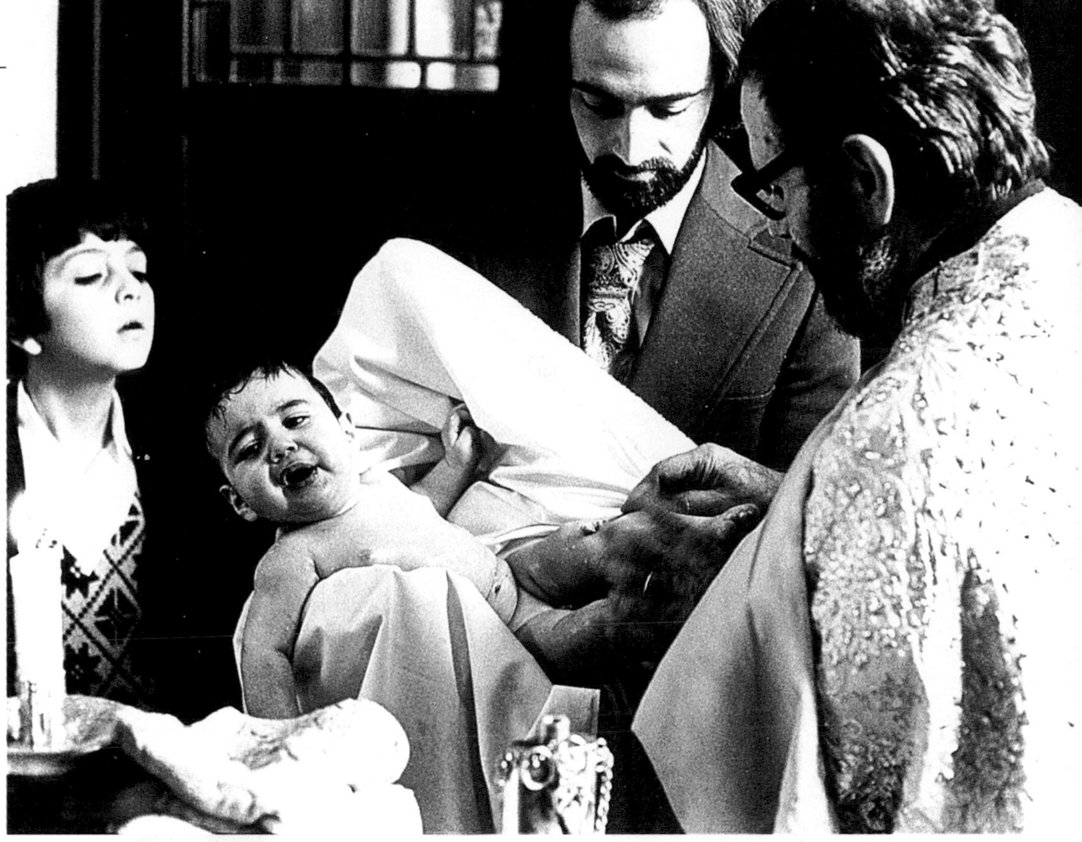

The priest uses water from the font to make the sign of the cross (a mark of Christ's death) on the baby's forehead. The priest then takes the baby into his or her arms, names it and says the words *'I baptise you in the name of the Father and of the Son and of the Holy Spirit'* before sprinkling the baby with water three times (see Photograph A). Christians believe that this ceremony marks the spiritual rebirth of the child as others renounce all evil and repent of sin on its behalf. The child can return much later, at Confirmation, to make the same vows for himself or herself.

The Orthodox Church

In an Orthodox church, after blessing the water in the font with a prayer and breathing on it, the priest anoints the baby with the 'oil of gladness'. The baby is placed in the font facing eastwards. This is the direction of the rising Sun, and therefore symbolises new life. The baby is then completely undressed and immersed beneath the water three times (see Photograph B). The ceremony of 'chrismation', anointing the body with oil, is carried out immediately afterwards to complete the baptism. The baby is then dressed in new clothes to symbolise the new life ahead which has been received through baptism.

DISCUSS

What is the link between Infant Baptism and Confirmation? Why do you think that the two services 'need' each other?

FOR YOUR FOLDER

This extract is taken from The Alternative Service Book:
'Children who are too young to profess the faith are baptised on the understanding that they are brought up as Christians within the family of the Church.'

As many parents who have their children baptised do not go to church afterwards do you think they should be refused Baptism for their children? Write down the reasons for your answer.

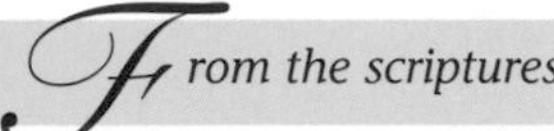

From the scriptures

This passage is often read during an Infant Baptism service:
'Some people brought children to Jesus for him to place his hands on them, but the disciples scolded the people. When Jesus noticed this, he was angry and said to his disciples, "Let the children come to me and do not stop them, because the Kingdom of God belongs to such as these. I assure you that whoever does not receive the Kingdom of God like a child will never enter it." Then he took the children in his arms, placed his hands on each of them, and blessed them.'

What do you think is the link between this passage and Infant Baptism?

In the glossary: CHRISMATION; CHURCH; CONFIRMATION; FONT; HOLY SPIRIT; INFANT BAPTISM; METHODIST; ORTHODOX; PRIEST; PROTESTANT; ROMAN CATHOLIC; SIGN OF THE CROSS.

Church Membership

***What** is Confirmation and why is it an important ceremony in many Churches?*

FOCUSING QUESTIONS

How do many Christians believe that the Holy Spirit is received – and what this has to do with the early Christians?

Which questions are asked by the bishop of each person wanting to be confirmed?

How do Churches other than Roman Catholic or Anglican admit people into their membership?

According to the New Testament, the first Christians received the Holy Spirit after Christ left them, and Confirmation is based on the belief that the Holy Spirit can still be received through the laying-on of the bishop's hands during Confirmation. Although Roman Catholic and some Anglican churches admit children to Communion before they are confirmed, Confirmation bestows full membership of the Church and provides an opportunity for a person to renew the vows that others took for them when they were baptised.

Confirmation

During the Confirmation service the bishop asks each candidate three questions and they are expected to respond positively:
'Do you turn to Christ?'
'Do you repent of your sins?'
'Do you renounce evil?'

A. What is the bishop doing in this Confirmation service and what is the significance of his action?

The bishop then tells the candidates, *'You must now declare before God and the Church that you accept the Christian faith into which you were baptised and in which you live and grow'* before asking them three questions about their Christian belief. They are asked whether they believe and trust in God who made the world, in his Son, Jesus Christ, who redeemed mankind, and in the Holy Spirit who gives life to the people of God. If they answer 'yes' to these questions then the bishop lays his hands on their head and prays: *'Confirm, O Lord, your servant with your Holy Spirit. Defend, O Lord, your servant with your heavenly grace until they come into your heavenly kingdom. Amen'.*

In the Roman Catholic Church the bishop anoints each person with special oil (called 'chrism') and says to them, 'Be sealed with the Holy Spirit'. Many Christians believe that they receive the Holy Spirit when the hands of a bishop are laid upon them. Others believe this has already happened when they became a Christian and the laying-on-of-hands is merely a 'confirmation' of this.

Orthodox and Nonconformist Churches

In the Orthodox Church, Infant Baptism and Confirmation (called 'chrismation') take place at the same time. In the Methodist Church, a person who has been baptised becomes a church member when the hands of the minister are laid upon them. Each year after this they sign their ticket of membership (see Photograph B) and renew their covenant at the annual service held on the first Sunday of each new year. The Baptist Church extends the 'right hand of fellowship' to those who have been baptised as adults.

B. A 'membership ticket' for someone who is a full member of the Methodist Church.

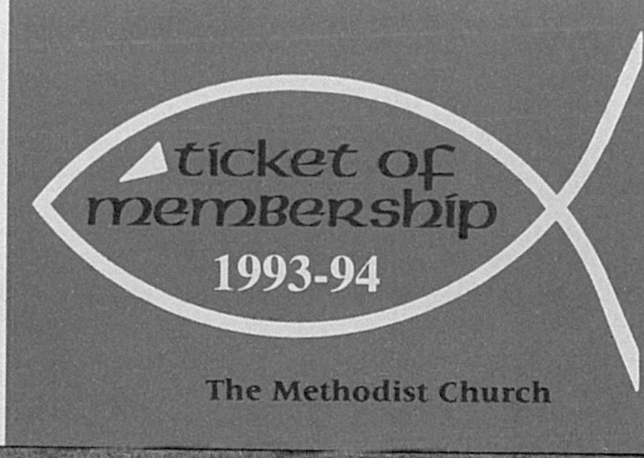

FOR YOUR FOLDER

1
a) Look at Photograph **A.** What is this ceremony called?
b) In which two Churches could this ceremony be taking place?
c) This ceremony is always conducted by a bishop. Can you suggest why?
d) Describe what happens in this service.
e) What does Confirmation demand of a person and at what age do you think they are old enough to meet those demands?

2
a) See Photograph **B.** This 'membership ticket' spells out the responsibilities of Church membership for each Methodist. What does God and the Church expect from each new member?
b) Methodists renew their commitment to God and to the Church each year? Why do you think that this could be a very valuable experience for them?

In the glossary: ANGLICAN; BAPTIST; BISHOP; CHRISM; CHRISMATION; CONFIRMATION; HOLY COMMUNION; HOLY SPIRIT; INFANT BAPTISM; METHODIST; MINISTER; NEW TESTAMENT; ORTHODOX; ROMAN CATHOLIC; SACRAMENT; SUNDAY.

Believer's Baptism

Why *do some Churches baptise adults rather than children and what is the symbolism behind the service?*

FOCUSING QUESTIONS

Why do Baptists argue that only believing adults should be baptised?

What do people usually do in a Baptist church before they go down into the water to be baptised?

What happens to the baptised person on the first Lord's Supper after their baptism?

DISCUSS

How does the service of Believer's Baptism illustrate the importance of symbolism in the Christian faith?

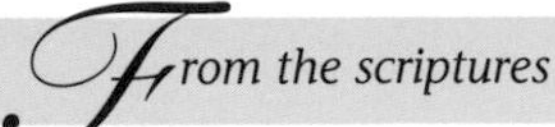

From the scriptures

This extract describes what happened when Paul was in Corinth:
'Crispus, who was the leader of the synagogue, believed in the Lord, together with all his family; and many other people in Corinth heard the message, believed, and were baptised.'

(Acts 18.8)

1 What is the link in this extract between baptism and believing in Christ?
2 How is this link stressed in the modern service of Believer's Baptism?

Baptists believe that the Church is a community of believers who have accepted that Jesus died and rose again to forgive their sins – and that a person cannot be baptised until this has happened. They point out that Jesus was baptised by John the Baptist in the River Jordan (Matthew 3.13-16) when he was thirty-years-old and that the message of Peter and others in the early Church was that people *'...should turn away from their sins and be baptised...'* (Acts 2.38). Clearly only adults could do this.

Believer's baptism

Those being baptised usually wear white, the symbol of purity, since this was the custom in the early Christian Church. Each person must repent of their sins and turn to God to receive forgiveness. Before they descend into the pool to be baptised by the minister (the leader) of church they speak publicly of their faith in front of the whole church.

What follows next is a highly symbolic 'picture' of that spiritual 'rebirth' which has already taken place:

- Going down into the pool shows that the person is leaving their old sinful life behind. A parallel is drawn between the death of the believer to their old sinful life and the death of Jesus on the cross.
- Being submerged beneath the water symbolises the break between the old and the new life. As they spend a moment beneath the water each person is symbolically 'buried with Christ' (Christians believe that Jesus spent three days in the tomb before being resurrected).
- By coming out of the water, and leaving the pool by different steps, the believer is showing that he or she is sharing 'the resurrection life of Christ'. Just as Christians believe that Jesus rose to enjoy eternal life with God, so the person being baptised enters a totally new life which stretches forward into eternity.
- The person is received into full membership of the church at the first Lord's Supper (Holy Communion) after their baptism when they receive 'the right hand of fellowship' from the minister. From now onwards the person is expected to play an active role in spreading the Christian Gospel.

A. A man going down into Baptismal pool. What must this person have done before he can be baptised?

FOR YOUR FOLDER

1 In the early years of the Christian Church adult Baptisms were only performed at Easter and Whitsun. Can you suggest reasons why these festivals were thought to be particularly appropriate times for people to be baptised?

2 Explain in your own words how parallels are drawn between the three stages in the Baptism of believers and three events in the life of Jesus.

B. What symbolic meaning does this part of Baptism carry for the believer?

C. What is the person 'sharing' as he leaves the Baptismal pool?

In the glossary: BAPTISM; BAPTIST; BELIEVER'S BAPTISM; EASTER; GOSPEL; HOLY SPIRIT; JOHN THE BAPTIST; LORD'S SUPPER; MINISTER; PAUL; PETER; WHITSUN.

Marriage

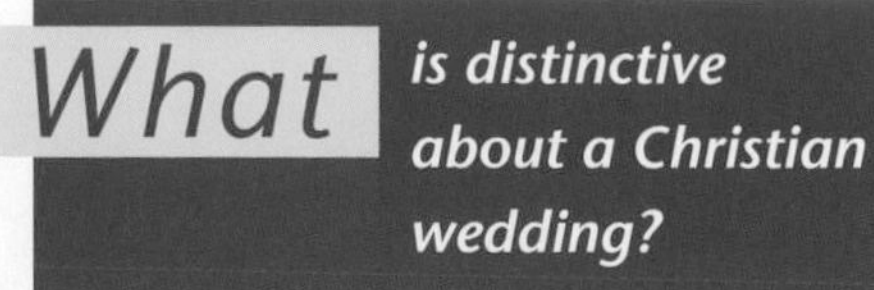

What is distinctive about a Christian wedding?

FOCUSING QUESTIONS

Why do Christians believe that marriage is a reflection of the relationship between Christ and his Church?

How does the sacrament of marriage differ from the other sacraments?

Why do the bride and groom wear wreaths during the Orthodox wedding service?

The Church believes that the marriage between a man and a woman is a reflection of the union between Christ and the Church – in The Bible, Christ is described as a *'bridegroom'* and the Church as his *'pure, spotless bride'*. All wedding services emphasise that marriage is a life-long commitment and that the couple can expect to be blessed by God with children.

The wedding service

In the Anglican wedding service three reasons are given for the importance of marriage – and these are shared by Christians of all denominations:

- It is the best possible relationship in which two people can love and care for each other.
- It provides the most suitable relationship in which sexual intercourse can take place.
- It provides a loving and stable home in which children can best be brought up.

During the wedding service the couple promise *'to love, comfort, honour and protect each other in sickness and in health as long as they both shall live'*. The man places a ring on the third finger of the bride's left hand saying: *'I give you this ring as a sign of our marriage. With my body I honour you, all that I am I give to you, and all that I have I share with you, within the Love of God'*. In all denominations the ring, a perfect and unbroken circle, is a symbol of that love which will, if genuine, last for eternity. The priest pronounces the couple husband and wife with the words: *'That which God has joined together, let not man divide'*.

Two important variations to this understanding of the wedding service are found in different Churches:

- In the Catholic Church marriage is regarded as a sacrament. In the other sacraments, though, the blessing of God is bestowed on the people by the priest. Marriage is unique in that the sacrament is bestowed by the man and the woman on each other. This is why they offer each other the bread and wine in the Nuptual Mass at the end of the wedding service.

- In the Orthodox Church, during the service the priest crowns the couple with wreaths showing that they are to become a king and queen over the own small kingdom – the house that they will set up together. To symbolise their unity they share a glass of wine and walk, three times, hand-in-hand around a table in the middle of the church.

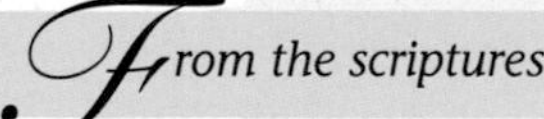

From the scriptures

According to the Gospel of Mark, these are the words of Jesus:

'But in the beginning, at the time of creation, 'God made them male and female,' as the scripture says. 'And for this reason a man will leave his father and mother and unite with his wife, and the two will become one.' So they are no longer two, but one.'

(Mark 10.6-8)

Sum up just what this extract is saying about marriage.

A. What do weddings performed in a church emphasise?

FOR YOUR FOLDER

This extract is taken from the Methodist wedding service:

'...marriage is the lifelong union in body, mind and spirit, of one man and one woman. It is his [God's] will that in marriage the love of a man and a woman should be fulfilled in the wholeness of their life together, in mutual companionship, helpfulness and care. By the help of God this love grows and deepens with the years. Such marriage is the foundation of true family life, and when blessed with the gift of children, is God's chosen way for the continuance of mankind and the bringing up of children in security and trust.'

According to the extract:

a) When two people marry what is being brought together?
b) What does God intend should be fulfilled in every marriage?
c) What happens to genuine love as a marriage continues?
d) What is God's chosen way to ensure the continuation of the human race?

In the glossary: ANGLICAN; BIBLE; DENOMINATION; METHODIST; ORTHODOX; PRIEST; ROMAN CATHOLIC; SACRAMENT.

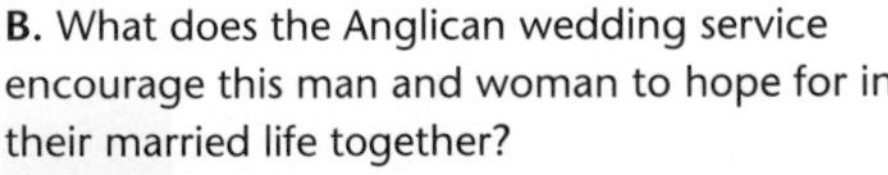

B. What does the Anglican wedding service encourage this man and woman to hope for in their married life together?

Death

What *beliefs do Christians express through their burial services?*

FOCUSING QUESTIONS

What are the basic Christian beliefs about death and life after death?

What is distinctive about an Orthodox funeral?

What is distinctive about a Roman Catholic funeral?

Christianity strongly maintains that death is not the end and that the soul (the spiritual part of each person) lives for ever. A Christian believes that, at the end of time, the body of each believer will be resurrected to share in Christ's own victory over death – this belief is at the heart of the funeral service.

An Orthodox funeral

In the Orthodox community, as soon as a person has died, their body is washed, dressed in new clothes and placed in an open coffin which is positioned at the front of the church. It remains open during the service to remind everyone that death is an unnecessary tragedy, since it is God's punishment for human sin. Yet, the tragedy of death is accompanied by the hope of resurrection and this is symbolised by the candles that are burning and the incense which is sprayed over the coffin. The readings from The Bible emphasise the resurrection of the dead and the hope that is shared by all believers in God.

A. In many churches the coffin is left in the church on the day before its burial. Can you suggest any reason for this?

Protestant and Roman Catholic funerals

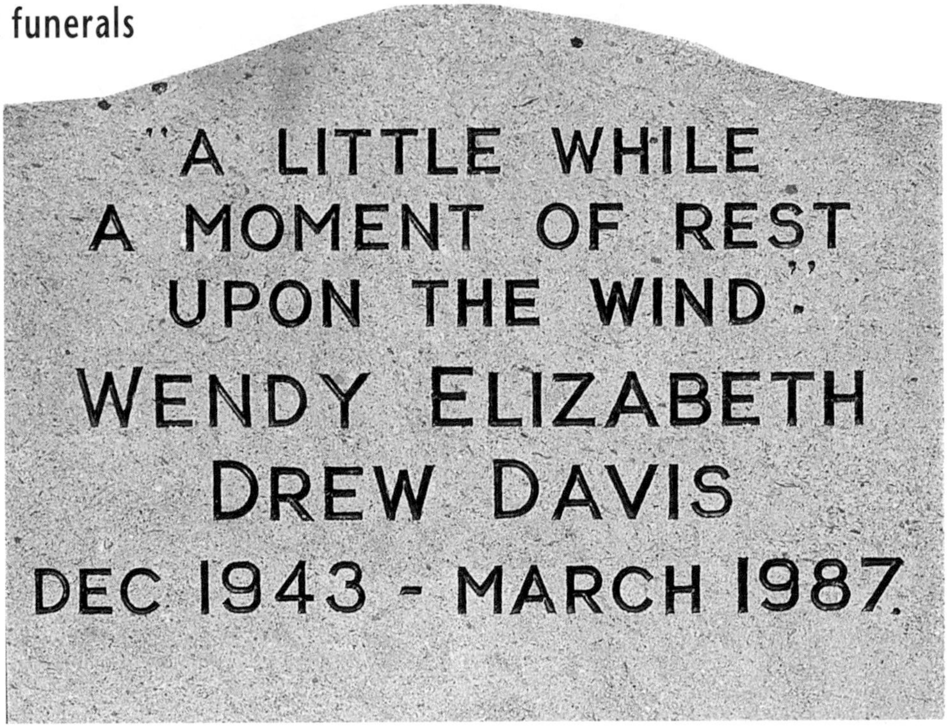

"A LITTLE WHILE
A MOMENT OF REST
UPON THE WIND"
WENDY ELIZABETH
DREW DAVIS
DEC 1943 - MARCH 1987.

In a Roman Catholic funeral the coffin is taken to the church the night before so that prayers can be said for the soul of the dead person. Catholics believe that each soul spends time in Purgatory after death – a place mid-way between Heaven and Hell – and the amount of time that it spends there can be directly affected by the prayers of people on Earth.

For the service itself the priest wears white robes – the colour traditionally associated with life after death and the resurrection of the body – and meets the coffin at the door of the church. As he sprinkles the coffin with holy water he recites words from John's Gospel: *'I am the resurrection and the life. Those who believe in me will live, even though they die; and all those who live and believe in me will never die'* (John 11.25). The service then takes the form of a Mass (the Requiem Mass), during which a prayer is offered: *'Eternal rest grant unto them, O Lord, and let light perpetual rest upon them'.*

B. Do you think that the inscription on this headstone reflects a Christian belief in life after death?

The brief funeral service in the Protestant Church includes hymns, prayers, Bible readings and usually a short eulogy (a sermon of praise) about the dead person. This is followed by the 'committal', a second service, which is held at the graveside, in which the person is committed to the earth and to God's safe keeping. As Christians allow cremation as well as burial this second service may take place at the crematorium.

DISCUSS

What beliefs do Christians hold about life after death, and how are these reflected in the funeral service?

FOR YOUR FOLDER

1 The Kontakion is an Orthodox funeral prayer:
'Give rest, O Christ, to all thy servants with thy saints. Where sorrow and pain are no more, neither sighing but life everlasting. Thou only art immortal, the creator and maker of man, And we are mortal born of earth, and unto earth will we return, all we go down to the dust.'

a) Orthodox Christians believe that the living and the dead are united in the one Christian family. How is this belief expressed in this prayer?
b) Who, alone, is untouched by death?
c) How does the promise that all return to dust after death reflect the words found in Genesis 3.19?

2 This prayer is often used at funeral services conducted in the United Reformed Church:
'For as much as it hath pleased Almighty God of His great mercy to take unto himself the soul of our dear brother/sister departed, we therefore commit his/her body to the ground: earth to earth, ashes to ashes, dust to dust; in sure and certain hope of resurrection to everlasting life through our Lord Jesus Christ.'

a) According to this extract who decides when a person must die?
b) What is the 'committal' and why is it so called?
c) Is it possible to have a *'sure and certain hope'*? Explain your answer.

In the glossary: Bible; Cremation; Heaven; Hell; Hymn; Incense; Mass; Orthodox; Priest; Protestant; Purgatory; Requiem Mass; Resurrection; Roman Catholic; Soul.

The Trinity

What *do Christians believe about the Trinity?*

FOCUSING QUESTIONS

What do Christians believe about God the Father?

What do Christians believe about Jesus Christ?

What do Christians believe about the Holy Spirit?

Christians start from the fundamental belief that there is just one God (monotheism) who has revealed Himself in three different forms – God the Father, God the Son and God the Holy Spirit. The relationship which links these three distinct yet perfectly united Persons together in the 'Godhead' is called the 'Trinity'. This belief is unique to Christianity and, throughout the ages, Christians have often been misunderstood as believing in three Gods. To Christians however, thritheism (believing in three gods) is heresy.

God the Father

From the opening words of The Bible *'...God created the universe...'* (Genesis 1.1) to the very last, The Bible insists on certain truths about God the Father. These are:

- That God is the creator of everything that exists including the universe, the world, nature and human beings. Nothing in the past or the present has been brought into existence by any other power than God.
- That God is the Father of everything that lives. Just as we expect a human father to look after his children with loving care so we expect God to do the same for everything He has created.

DISCUSS

Christians believe in three Persons in the Trinity, but not in three gods. How do they manage to do this?

A. What do you think Christians can learn about God from seeing this father play with his children?

B. This stained-glass window shows a representation of Jesus. What do Christians believe to be the link between Jesus and the other members of the Trinity?

- That God is a personal and not an abstract force. He takes a personal, everyday interest in the world that He has made. He is so deeply involved in the world that He even suffers when His children (humanity) suffer.

God the Son

Christians believe that God came to Earth as a baby who was born in a stable in Bethlehem. God taking on human form and flesh is called the 'Incarnation' and this idea is unique to Christianity amongst the monotheistic religions. In Christian belief Jesus lived on Earth as a human being before being crucified (hung up on a cross to die) by the Romans. After coming back to life – being 'resurrected' – he left the Earth and returned to Heaven. Christians believe that he will return to Earth, at some future time, to judge everyone and set up God's kingdom – a belief called the 'Second Coming'.

God the Holy Spirit

Before he left the Earth Jesus promised his disciples that he would always be with them. His physical presence would be removed but his spirit, the Holy Spirit, would guide them. The Holy Spirit was given to all Christians on the Day of Pentecost. The 'Trinity', then, is more a matter of revelation than anything else. God, the maker of Heaven and Earth, has revealed Himself to the human race as a Father who created the world and sent His Son to save it; as a man who has shown God to everyone, and as the Holy Spirit who is God active in the world today.

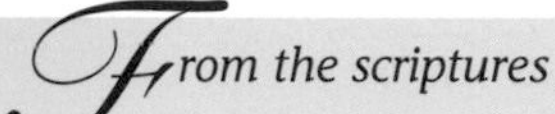

From the scriptures

Paul wrote this about Jesus:
'...of his own free will he gave up all he had [in Heaven with God], *and took the nature of a servant. He became like a human being and appeared in human likeness. He was humble and walked the path of obedience all the way to death – his death on the cross. For this reason God raised him to the highest place above and gave him the name that is greater than any other name.'*
(Philippians 2.7-9)

Make a list of the statements made in this extract about Jesus.

FOR YOUR FOLDER

Four very important ideas are contained in this unit: monotheism; the Incarnation; the Fatherhood of God; the Second Coming of Christ. Explain, in a paragraph each, what these ideas mean.

In the glossary: Bethlehem; Bible; Disciple; Heresy; Holy Spirit; Incarnation; Pentecost; Trinity.

The Creeds

What are Creeds and why are they important?

FOCUSING QUESTIONS

Where are the remnants of the earliest Christian Creeds to be found?

Why was the Apostles' Creed thought to be very special for a long time?

Which two needs do the Creeds still fulfil?

Several Creeds, official statements of Christian belief, have been drawn up during the long history of the Christian Church. However, only three of them – the Apostles' Creed, the Nicene Creed and the Athanasian Creed – have been used widely in Christian worship.

Why have Creeds?

Remnants of the earliest Creeds can be found in sections of the New Testament. These were set formulae of words that were taught to new converts. The converts would have to learn these 'statements of faith' off by heart and then, when they were baptised, would have to repeat a longer statement of faith, small pieces of which can also be found in parts of the letters of Paul in the New Testament. The shortest, and the earliest, of these statements is thought to be *'Jesus is Lord'* (1 Corinthians 12.3), but statements about God the Father and the Holy Spirit were soon added (1 Corinthians 8.6, 1 Timothy 2.5-6). For months before a Baptism the bishop would have 'handed out' these statements, commenting on them phrase by phrase. Then, during the Baptism itself, the converts were expected to 'give the Creeds back' as an indication of their own personal faith.

A. This carving shows a representation of Jesus and his disciples at the Last Supper.
Why was the 'Apostles' Creed' given its name?

B. What did the early Christians believe about Jesus?

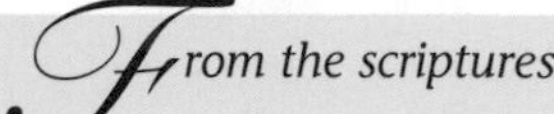
From the scriptures

In one of his statements that was probably repeating an early Creed Paul wrote:
'I passed on to you what I received, which is of the greatest importance: that Christ died for our sins, as is written in the Scriptures; that he was buried and that he was raised to life three days later, as written in the Scriptures....'
(1 Corinthians 15.3-4)

Look at the banner in Photograph B and the words of Paul above, and write down three things which Christians believe about Jesus – and which are contained in the Creeds.

The fight against heresy

There were three main Creeds used by the early Church. They were:

- The Apostles' Creed which was thought to be the oldest, since it was believed to have been drawn up by the disciples of Jesus soon after his death and resurrection. We now know that this story was invented to give the Creed, which did not exist in its present form until the eleventh century, as much authority as possible.
- The Nicene Creed which was drawn-up at a Church council held at Nicea in 325 CE. The Creed which is used today during Communion services comes from the fifth century. It was drawn up to outlaw heretics who taught things that the Church could not accept.
- The Athanasian Creed, which dates from the middle of the fourth century, but was too long to be used widely.

The Apostles' and the Nicene Creeds are still accepted and used by Christians throughout the world today. They still serve the same purpose as they always have – to preserve the traditional beliefs of the Church, and to protect the Church from false teaching.

FOR YOUR FOLDER

The Athanasian Creed begins with a statement which spells out the main reason for believing the Creeds:
'Whosoever will be saved: before all things it is necessary that he hold the Catholic faith. Which Faith except everyone do keep whole and undefiled; without doubt he shall perish everlastingly.'

a) What do you think the word '*Catholic*' means here?
b) What do you think it means when it says that the Catholic Faith must be kept *'whole and undefiled'*?
c) Can you think of one reason why those people who do not keep the Catholic Faith in its entirety are threatened with everlasting death?

In the glossary: Apostles' Creed; Athanasian Creed; Bishop; Creed; Disciples; Gospel; Holy Communion; Holy Spirit; New Testament; Nicene Creed; Paul.

The Death of Jesus

Which pictures are provided in the New Testament to help Christians to understand the death of Jesus?

FOCUSING QUESTIONS

What is the 'central truth' about the Christian faith?

What do Christians believe happened to the powers of evil and darkness when Jesus died?

Where do Christians turn for the most effective 'pictures' to explain the death of Jesus?

Christians believe in a God who intervenes and acts decisively in the world and this is why the New Testament and the Creeds deal with the death and resurrection of Jesus in such detail.

Death

The basic 'truth' about the Christian faith is that Jesus Christ was crucified while Pontius Pilate was Roman governor of Judea (26-36 CE) and brought back to life by God. These two themes take up much of the New Testament. These events are described, with many variations, in the four Gospels. Long before the Gospels were written, however, Paul wrote about the significance of the death and resurrection of Christ in his many letters. To underline their importance Paul used many 'pictures' to help his readers understand what had happened. He spoke of:

- Jesus being an innocent lamb who was sacrificed, just as the Jews sacrificed a lamb each year in the Temple in Jerusalem. Jews – and Paul was a Jew – believed that the blood of the lamb provided the means by which the sins of the people could be forgiven by God. Unlike the Jewish sacrifice which was offered each year, however, Jesus only needed to be sacrificed once to gain forgiveness from God for all of humankind's sins.

- The death of Jesus brought about the final defeat of the powers of evil and death which were opposed to Jesus. Earlier in his ministry we are told that Jesus fought against these powers when he cast out demons and healed the sick. His conquering of death, and return to life, was the final victory. Through this victory Paul believed that all human beings could be set free from the power of sin and death.

- Paul saw the death of Jesus as 'redeeming' the human race. By their sinful behaviour the human race has sold itself to Satan. Jesus, though, by his death paid the price needed to buy back humanity.

A. A popular image used in the New Testament to explain the death of Jesus is that of a lamb that was slaughtered. Use Isaiah 53.7-8 to help you explain why this was an effective picture of the death of Jesus.

B. A crucifix. The death of Jesus is often spoken of as an 'atonement' a 'bringing into harmony'. What do you think that this means?

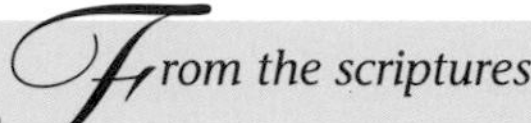

From the scriptures

In this extract Paul is writing about the death of Jesus:
'For when we were still helpless, Christ died for the wicked at the time that God chose...God has shown how much he loved us – it was while we were yet sinners that Christ died for us!...We were God's enemies, but he made us his friends through the death of his Son.'
(Romans 5.6-10)

According to this extract:
1 When did Christ die?
2 How has God shown his love for us?
3 What is one effect of the death of Jesus?

These are, of course, only 'pictures' which give Christians a way of understanding the death of Jesus. Paul drew his ideas from the imagery and thought of the religion out of which Christianity sprang and grew - Judaism. Brought together, these pictures present the death of Jesus as an 'atonement', an act that brought together God and human beings (see Photograph B).

FOR YOUR FOLDER

a) Which 'pictures' are used in the New Testament to speak of the death of Jesus?
b) Where are all of these 'pictures' taken from?
c) Why do you think that Christians need 'pictures' to help them to understand the death of Jesus?
d) Which of the pictures mentioned do you think are particularly useful – and why?

In the glossary: Creed; Gospels; Jerusalem; Judaism; New Testament; Paul; Pilate, Pontius; Satan.

The Holy Spirit

What do Christians mean when they speak of the Holy Spirit?

FOCUSING QUESTIONS

Who do Christians believe the Holy Spirit to be?

What relationship do Christians believe that the Holy Spirit has to the other members of the Trinity?

What do Christians mean when they speak of the 'Body of Christ'?

The Holy Spirit, or the Holy Ghost, is the third Person in the Trinity and is one with God the Father and God the Son. In the New Testament, the Holy Spirit is closely identified with Jesus, since it was promised by Jesus to his disciples and was given to them on the Day of Pentecost. Christians today still believe that the Holy Spirit is given to all those who believe in God.

Who is the Holy Spirit?

The word 'spirit' means 'power' and the Holy Spirit is the power of God active in the world. Luke's account in the Acts of the Apostles of the giving of the Holy Spirit on the Day of Pentecost stresses the powerful nature of the Spirit's arrival with *'...a sound like the blowing of a violent wind...'*. All those who were present were amazed at the power of God, yet this was not 'power' in the normal sense of that word. It was not the power to frighten, but a power that draws people to God's love. According to Luke the Christians in the New Testament were men and women who 'turned the world upside down' because they were filled with the love of God. To begin with, though, the disciples who were filled with God's Spirit acted rather strangely. Many people thought that the disciples on the Day of Pentecost were drunk (Acts 2.13) because of the way they were behaving!

DISCUSS

What do you think that Christians mean when they describe the Holy Spirit as 'God active in today's world'?

The Body of Christ

Refering to the time when Jesus received the Holy Spirit from Heaven at his Baptism, John the Baptist said:
'I saw the Spirit come down like a dove from heaven and stay on him. I still did not know that he was the one, but God, who sent me to baptise with water, had said to me, 'You will see the Spirit come down and stay on a man; he is the one who baptises with the Holy Spirit'' (John 1.32-33).

John knew from this that, while he baptised people with water, Jesus would baptise them in the Holy Spirit. This was a much more powerful Baptism since it marked each person's entry into a totally new life. A part of this 'new life' was to become a member of the Christian community – the Church. The early Christians described the Church as being the 'Body of Christ' and those who believed were baptised into the Church using the traditional formula of words: *'I baptise you in the name of the Father, and of the Son and of the Holy Spirit'* (Matthew 28.19).

FOR YOUR FOLDER

Answer each of these questions in your own words:

a) What was Paul referring to when he wrote about the *'Body of Christ'*?
b) Can you think of three ways in which the Christian Church resembles a body?
c) How did early Christians believe that the Holy Spirit strengthened the Church?

Within the early Church, 'gifts' given by the Holy Spirit were believed to strengthen the community. These gifts included performing miracles, healing, prophecy, speaking in tongues and teaching (1 Corinthians 12.27-30). The Church was seen as 'the body' into which all believers had been baptised by God's Spirit and in which everyone was equal. Modern Christians still believe this to be true.

A. What is the link between the Holy Spirit and Jesus in Christian belief?

B. The dove, as shown in this banner (left), is the favourite biblical symbol of the Holy Spirit. What qualities do you think are conveyed by using this symbol?

In the glossary: Acts of the Apostles; Baptism, Disciple; Holy Ghost; Holy Spirit; John the Baptist; Miracle; New Testament; Paul; Pentecost; Speaking in Tongues; Trinity.

The Bible

What is The Bible and what authority does it carry?

FOCUSING QUESTIONS

In what respect is The Bible unique among all the holy books?

What was the attitude of the earliest Christians was towards the Jewish Scriptures – and why?

What are the four kinds of writing that make up the New Testament?

Amongst holy books The Bible is unique since it contains texts which are considered sacred in two religions – Judaism and Christianity. The Bible is divided into two parts: the Old Testament and the New Testament. Some Bibles also contain an Apocrypha (meaning 'hidden'), containing books such as 1 and 2 Maccabees and Wisdom. Protestants do not include these books in their Bibles but Roman Catholic and Orthodox Christians do.

The Old Testament

The first part of The Bible is the Jewish Tenakh, which Christians call the Old Testament. Exactly the same books make up the Old Testament and the Jewish Tenakh. However, in the Tenakh there are twenty-four books. The Protestant Old Testament divides these into thirty-nine books and prints them in a slightly different order. In Roman Catholic Bibles, seven books, which Protestants consider to be part of the Apocrypha, are included in the Old Testament. The Orthodox Church follows the Catholic canon, but adds a further five books to this.

The books of the Old Testament were probably written over a period of 3,000 years and include laws, prophecies, history, poetry, myths, songs and stories. They tell the story of the Jewish people from Abraham, around 2,000 BCE, through to the years preceding the occupation of the Jewish homeland by the Romans in 63 BCE.

A. A Jewish scroll. What is the main theme running through the Jewish Scriptures?

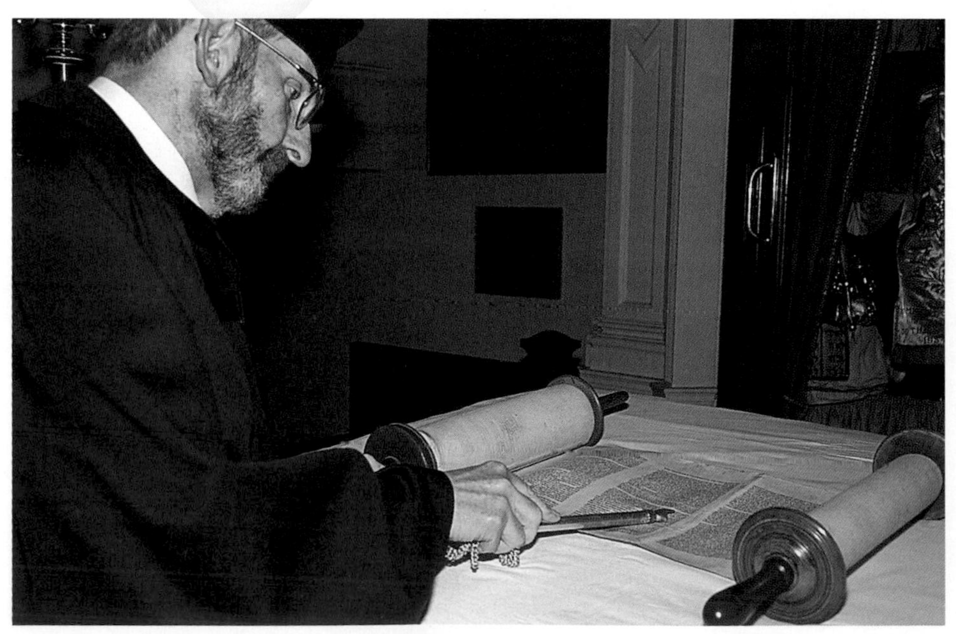

As most of the early followers of Jesus were Jews, they would have been taught to love and respect the Jewish Scriptures from childhood. The Gospels say that Jesus himself read from them in the synagogue, while writers like Peter and Paul used them to show that Jesus was indeed the Messiah that the Jewish people had long been expecting.

B. A Bible surrounded by Bible reading notes. What value do you think a Christian might find in reading The Bible systematically each day?

The New Testament

The twenty-seven books of the New Testament tell the story of Jesus and the early Christian Church – from the coming of Jesus to the deaths of Peter and Paul in 64 CE. The writings contained in the New Testament can be divided into four categories:

- The letters (or 'Epistles'), the oldest writings in the New Testament, which written by early Church leaders such as Peter, Paul, James and John. Most of them explain the importance of the death and resurrection of Jesus for those living the Christian life.
- The four Gospels – Matthew, Mark, Luke and John – which provide the only record of the birth, life, teaching, death and resurrection of Jesus. Three of the Gospels, Matthew, Mark and Luke (called the 'Synoptic Gospels'), share much of their material with each other and take a similar approach to the story they are telling. The first of them, Mark, was written about 65 CE with the other two following soon afterwards. The fourth Gospel, John's, takes a very different approach to Jesus.
- The history of the early Christian Church after Jesus left the Earth, which is contained in the Acts of the Apostles, and is believed to have been written by the same author that wrote Luke.
- Prophecy. The last book in the New Testament is Revelation which is a highly symbolic description of the end of the world.

The authority of the Bible

The 'canon' (the final list of books to be included) of the whole Bible was decided in 397 CE. Some Christians (Evangelicals) base their belief and lives simply on The Bible alone. Others believe that God has also spoken through inspired individuals and follow the traditions of the Church as well as The Bible. For almost all Christians, though, reading The Bible regularly is important. Some church services include as many as three Bible readings – from the Old Testament, the Gospels and the Epistles. To help in their personal devotions many Christians follow a pattern of daily reading with the help of specially prepared notes (see Photograph B).

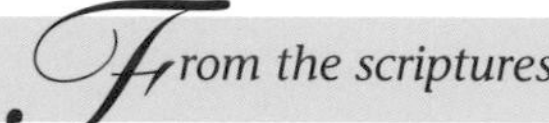
From the scriptures

This quote from The Bible is about The Bible:
'...continue in the truths that you were taught and firmly believe. You know who your teachers were, and you remember that ever since you were a child, you have known the Holy Scriptures, which are able to give you the wisdom that leads to salvation through faith in Christ Jesus. All Scripture is inspired by God and is useful for teaching the truth, rebuking error, correcting faults, and giving instruction for right living...'.
(2 Timothy 3.14-16)

1. Explain why this extract can only be referring to the Jewish Scriptures.
2. Make a list of the different claims that are made for the Scriptures in this extract.
3. What do you think is meant by the phrase *'All Scripture is inspired by God...'*?

FOR YOUR FOLDER

Answer each of these questions:
a) What is the Apocrypha?
b) What kinds of books make up the Old Testament and what stories do they tell?
c) What use did writers such as Paul and Peter make of the Jewsih Scriptures?

In the glossary: Acts of the Apostles; Apocrypha; Bible; Canon; Christianity; Epistle; Evangelical; Gospel; John's Gospel; Judaism; Luke; Mark's Gospel; Matthew's Gospel; Messiah; New Testament; Old Testament; Paul; Peter; Synoptic Gospels.

The Sacraments

What are the sacraments and why are they important to Christians?

FOCUSING QUESTIONS

What is the relationship between prayer and the sacraments?

How many sacraments are recognised by the Roman Catholic and Orthodox Churches?

How many sacraments are accepted by the Anglicans and Nonconformists?

The Roman Catholic Church teaches that believers receive God's 'grace' (God's favour or blessing) through prayer and the sacraments. To a Christian worshipper, prayer is viewed an activity by which a person 'approaches' God in worship and praise. The sacraments are given by God as divinely ordained channels by which His blessings can be received.

A. Which sacrament is being celebrated here and what physical elements are being used to represent a spiritual 'truth'?

What is a sacrament?

The most well-known definition of a sacrament came from St Augustine (354-430 CE): *'A sacrament is the visible sign of an invisible grace'*. This definition brings together the two most important elements of the sacraments. First, is the physical or material element – the part of the sacrament that can be felt, touched, tasted or smelled. For example, during Holy Communion, a worshipper drinks a small amount of wine and eats some bread. These physical elements are used to represent the worshipper 'sharing' in the death of Jesus. Similarly, in the sacrament of Infant Baptism water is poured over the baby to symbolise its cleansing from sin. Second is the spiritual or invisible element – the sacraments bring spiritual blessings within the reach of every worshipper.

FOR YOUR FOLDER

1
a) What is a sacrament?
b) Which two elements must be present in every sacrament?
c) How are the two elements brought together in the sacraments of Holy Communion and Infant Baptism?

2 The Orthodox Church prefers to call the sacraments 'mysteries'. To which aspect of the sacraments does this draw the attention of worshippers?

3 Find out why the Salvation Army and the Quakers do not celebrate any of the sacraments.

Roman Catholic and Orthodox Churches

In the Roman Catholic and Orthodox Churches seven sacraments are recognised:

- Holy Communion. In the Roman Catholic Church this is called the Mass whilst Orthodox churches call it the Divine Liturgy.
- Infant Baptism.
- Confirmation.
- Penance.
- Marriage.
- Ordination to the priesthood.
- Holy Unction.

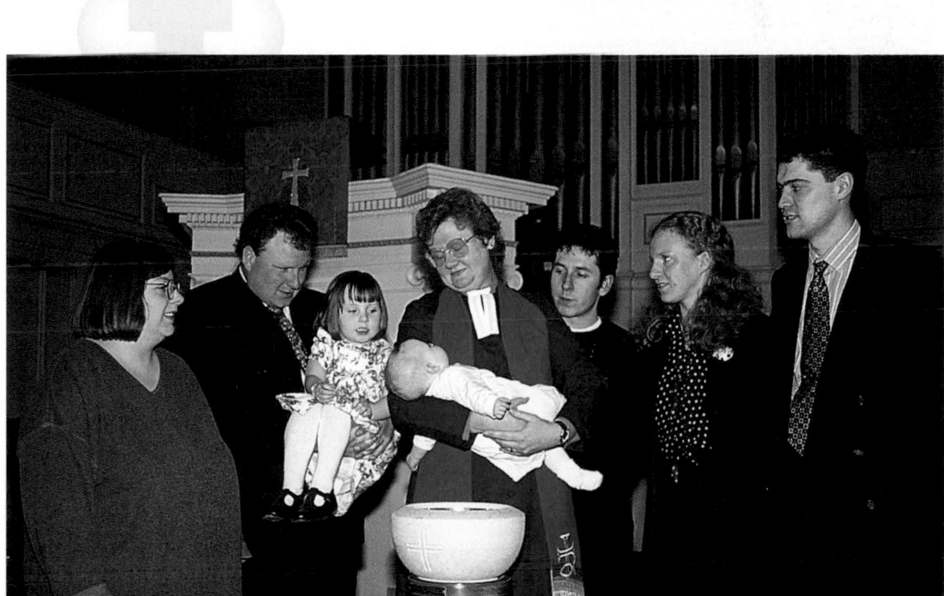

B. In which Churches would you find a service like this?

Protestant Churches

Protestant Churches only recognise two sacraments – Baptism and Holy Communion – since they are the only ones that can be traced back to Jesus himself. Most Anglican Churches agree with this, although some of the Nonconformist Churches call Holy Communion 'the Breaking of Bread' or the 'Lord's Supper'. Whilst most Churches baptise infants, the Baptist Church, and a few others, only baptise adults (the Believer's Baptism). The Salvation Army and the Quakers, alone amongst the major Christian Churches, do not celebrate any of the sacraments.

Most Christians do however believe that, when he was on Earth, Jesus showed the power of God in his life and that power now reaches them through the sacraments. This is particularly important to the Roman Catholic and Orthodox Churches which both see themselves as 'Sacramental Churches'. It is, they believe, through the sacraments that humankind gains some small understanding of the communion which exists between God the Father, God the Son and God the Holy Spirit.

In the glossary: Anglican; Baptist; Believer's Baptism; Breaking of Bread; Confirmation; Divine Liturgy; Holy Communion; Holy Spirit; Infant Baptism; Lord's Supper; Mass; Ordination; Orthodox; Penance; Protestant; Quaker; Roman Catholic; Sacrament; Salvation Army.

Suffering

What challenge does suffering present to the Christian faith and how is this challenge met?

FOCUSING QUESTIONS

Why does suffering present a particular problem for the man or woman who believes in the Christian God?

Which forms of suffering cause most anguish to the believer in God?

What 'answer' did Job put forward to the problem of suffering?

Suffering is a universal experience and everyone suffers at some time. To anyone who believes strongly in a God who loves and cares for His 'children' (humankind) this presents a very real challenge to faith. Amongst the many questions which must be asked, and answered, are:

Why is there so much suffering in the world?

Why do some people suffer much more than others?

Why do 'innocent' people often seem to suffer much more than those who 'deserve' it?

If God is all-powerful, as Christians say, why doesn't He do something to stop pain and suffering?

Who should be held to blame for most of the suffering in the world – God or the human race?

People have asked questions like these from the beginning of time and they remain largely unanswered today. Some, in the face of intolerable suffering, have found their faith in God destroyed. This happened to many people, Jews and Christians, during the Holocaust of the Second World War. Others, in the face of similar suffering, have managed to hold on to their faith – but only with difficulty.

A. This woman and her children are some of the many thousands of people affected by famine every year. Do you think that there can be any answers to suffering on this scale?

Christianity and suffering

The experience of suffering is as difficult for a Christian to understand as it is for anyone else. Here are some of the answers found in The Bible:

- God alone knows the reason for suffering. In the Book of Job, in the Old Testament, Job loses everything but reaches the conclusion that God alone knows the reason why he has suffered so much – and who is he, a mere human being, to question the wisdom of God?
- The Jewish Scriptures often linked suffering with a person's sin – or the sin of the person's parents or grandparents.

- In the New Testament suffering is the result of the activity of Satan in the world. Satan is totally opposed to God, and humans are caught up in the eternal battle between good (God) and evil (Satan).
- Sin and suffering is inevitable if all human beings are to be free to choose their own destinies. Some people bring suffering on themselves by making the wrong choices.

For a religious person, the answer to the problem of human suffering must lie with faith. Most Christians continue to trust that God is an active force for good in the world, although that does not always seem to be the case.

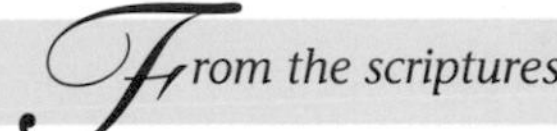

After hearing that he had lost everything Job said:
'..."I was born with nothing, and I will die with nothing. The Lord gave and now he has taken away. May his name be praised".'
(Job 1.21)

1 What point do you think this quotation is making about suffering?
2 Do you agree with it? Explain your answer.

B. A dead grey seal on an oil-polluted shore in the Shetlands, Scotland. Do you think that a Christian would blame disasters, such as the one shown in the photograph, on humankind, or do you think that they would see God's hand in every event, even disasters such as this?

FOR YOUR FOLDER

1 The Bible gives four answers to the problem of suffering. Draw up a table like the one below and write down, for each explanation, one argument in its favour and one against.

Explanation	In favour	Against

2 Do you find it convincing to fall back on faith when all other explanations of suffering fail? Give one reason why a person might be content to 'trust in God' for an explanation to human suffering, and one reason why a person might want a clearer reason.

In the glossary: Bible; Job; Old Testament; Satan.

A

Abbot The leader of a *monastery*.

Acts of the Apostles The fifth book in the *New Testament*, which contains the history of the early Church.

Advent The Church season which prepares people for the coming of *Jesus*.

Altar The stone or wooden platform at the front of a *church* behind which the *priest* stands for the *Holy Communion* or *Mass*.

Alternative Service Book The approved Prayer Book of the *Church of England*, which was introduced in 1980.

Angel A messenger from God.

Angel Gabriel God's main messenger in the Christian Scriptures.

Anglican Members of the worldwide Church based on the teachings of the *Church of England*.

Anglo-Catholic A member of the *Church of England* whose style of worship is similar to that of a *Roman Catholic*. Also called High *Anglican*.

Annunciation The announcement to *Mary* by the *Angel Gabriel* that she was going to carry God's Son, *Jesus*.

Anointing the Sick The practice in the *Roman Catholic Church* of anointing those who are seriously ill with oil.

Apocrypha Meaning 'hidden'. There are fifteen books in the Apocrypha, which can usually be found either at the end of The *Bible* or between the Old and *New Testaments*. Some Churches feel that the Apocrypha have no authority and accordingly some Bibles omit these texts entirely.

Apostle One of the twelve *disciples* of *Jesus*. The word apostle comes from the Greek word meaning 'to send'.

Apostles' Creed The oldest statement of Christian belief, dating to the second or third century.

Archbishop A senior *bishop* in the *Church of England* and *Roman Catholic Church*.

Ascension Day The day on which many churches celebrate the time when *Jesus* left the Earth.

Ash Wednesday The first day of *Lent*, traditionally a time of penitence.

Athanasian Creed A confession of faith used by some Western Christians.

Atonement The Christian belief that the death of *Jesus* brought together God and human beings.

Augustine A *monk* sent by Pope Gregory the Great as a missionary to England, who subsequently became first *Archbishop* of Canterbury in 597 CE.

B

Baptism Meaning 'to dip in water'. *See also* **Infant Baptism** and **Believer's Baptism**.

Baptist Church A *Nonconformist Church* which insists on the Baptism of adults, rather than children.

Beckett, Thomas à *Archbishop* of Canterbury in the eleventh century, who was murdered in Canterbury *Cathedral*.

Believer's Baptism The Baptism of adult believers.

Bernard of Clairvaux The founder of the Cistercian religious order.

Bethlehem The place where, according to the *Gospels, Jesus* was born.

Bible The name for the Christian Scriptures which contain the *Old and New Testaments*, and (in some versions) an *Apocrypha*.

Bishop A *priest* who carries the responsibility for all churches in a *diocese*.

Bishop of Rome The position in the *Roman Catholic Church* first held by St *Peter* and then by all later *popes*.

Book of Common Prayer The first Prayer Book of the *Church of England*, published in 1662.

Booth, William Founder of the *Salvation Army*.

Breaking of Bread A favourite term for *Holy Communion* in *Nonconformist* Churches.

C

Calvary A hill outside *Jerusalem* where, according to tradition, *Jesus* died.

Canon The list of books in The *Bible* authorised by the Church.

Canonisation A declaration by the *Pope* that a holy man or woman should be included among the *saints* of the Church.

Cathedaral The main church in *diocese*.

Chapel Small *Nonconformist* churches.

Chancel Part of a *church* building.

Chrism The consecrated oil used by *Roman Catholics* in their *sacraments*.

Chrismation The service in the *Orthodox Church* which unites *baptism* and *confirmation*.

Christianity The religion based on the teachings of *Jesus* of *Nazareth*.

Christmas The festival which celebrates the birth of *Jesus*.

Crucifix A cross containing an image of the body of *Jesus*.

Church A building dedicated to worship of the Christian God.

Church of England The *Established Church* in Britain, first formed by Henry VIII.

Citadel A *Salvation Army* place of worship.

Confirmation A service which admits a person into full membership of *Protestant* and *Roman Catholic* Churches.

Convent The building in which a community of *nuns* live.

Creed A statement of Christian belief.

Cremation The burning of the body of those who have died.

D

Day of Pentecost The day on which the *Holy Spirit* was given to the first *disciples*.

Deacon The lowest Order within the *Protestant* and *Roman Catholic* Churches.

Denomination A Christian Church.

Diocese An area for which a *bishop* carries responsibility.

Disciple One of the original followers of *Jesus*.

Divine Liturgy The service of *Holy Communion* in the *Orthodox Church*.

E

Easter The festival at which Christians remember the death and *resurrection of Jesus*.

Easter Saturday The day on which Christians remember the burial of *Jesus*.

Easter Sunday The day on which Christians celebrate the *resurrection* of *Jesus*.

Eastern Orthodox Church The section of the Christian Church which is dominant in Eastern Europe.

Epiphany The festival shortly after *Christmas* celebrating the visit of the Wise Men to the baby *Jesus,* as reported in the Christian *Gospels*.

Episcopacy Any Church which has *bishops*.

Epistle A letter. This term is used to describe many of the books in the *New Testament*.

Established Church The *Church of England* in Britain.

Eucharist The service of 'thanksgiving' which celebrates the death of Jesus. *See also* **Holy Communion**.

Evangelism The task of spreading the Christian message to those who do not believe.

Ex Cathedra Meaning 'from the throne'; a statement made by the *Pope* which is infallible.

F

Fasting The practice of going without food or water to devote oneself to God.

Font A receptacle in a *church* which is used to hold water for *Infant Baptism*.

Fox, George The founder of the *Quaker* movement.

Free Churches *See* **Nonconformist.**

G

Gentile A person who is not a Jew.

Gloria Patri A hymn sung by *Roman Catholics* as part of their *Mass*.

Golgotha Meaning the 'place of the skull'. Traditionally, this is the location of the execution of *Jesus*.

Good Friday The day on which Christians remember the death of *Jesus*.

Gospel The message of 'Good News'; the message of *Jesus*.

Gospels The four books in the *New Testament – Matthew, Mark, Luke* and *John* – which tell the story of *Jesus*.

Great Schism The split in 1054 which led to the breakaway of the *Orthodox Church* from the *Roman Catholic Church*.

H

Hail Mary An important *Roman Catholic* prayer addressed to the Virgin *Mary*.

Heaven The residence in the presence of God reserved for those who have lived righteous lives.

Hell The traditional place of fire and torment reserved for those who rejected God in this life.

Heresy A belief which goes against the official teaching of the Church.

Hermit A person who lives on their own in a lonely place in order to seek God.

Holy Communion The service held in most Christian Churches commemorating the death of *Jesus*. Also called the *Eucharist. See also* **Mass** and **Divine Liturgy**, **Breaking of Bread** and the **Lord's Supper.**

Holy Ghost An alternative name for the *Holy Spirit*.

Holy Land *Palestine;* the land in which *Jesus* lived.

Holy Week The week in the Christian calendar which starts with Palm Sunday and ends on *Easter Saturday.*

Holy Spirit The third Person of the Christian *Trinity* representing God. Also sometimes called *Holy Ghost.*

Homily The *sermon* delivered by a *priest* during the *Roman Catholic Mass*.

Host The wafer of bread used during the *Roman Catholic Mass*.

House Church A Church which meets in someone's house and does not belong to any of the recognised *denominations*.

Hymn A communal song that plays a very important role in Christian worship.

I

Icon A special painting of the Holy Family or a *saint* used as an aid to prayer by an *Orthodox* believer.

Iconostasis The screen which separates the *altar* from the people in an *Orthodox* church.

Incarnation The Christian belief that God became a human being with the birth of *Jesus*.

Incense A sweet-smelling odour used as part of worship in *Orthodox* and *Roman Catholic* churches.

Infant Baptism The practice of baptising children.

Intercessions Prayers in which the needs of other people are presented to God.

J

Jesus The Son of God whose teaching provided the inspiration for *Christianity.*

Jerusalem The city in modern-day Israel which is sacred to both Christians, Jews and Muslims.

Job A Book in the *Old Testament,* concerned with suffering.

John's Gospel The fourth *Gospel* in the *New Testament,* written towards the end of the first century.

John the Baptist The cousin of *Jesus,* his preaching prepared the people for the coming of *Jesus.*

Joseph The husband of *Mary,* the earthly father of *Jesus.*

Judaism The religion out of which Christianity and part of their Scriptures grew.

L

Last Supper The final meal that *Jesus* shared with his *disciples* before he was arrested.

Lectern The ledge at the front of a *church* which holds The *Bible.*

Lent A season of reflection and repentance before *Easter.*

Liturgy The services which are followed in the *Protestant, Roman Catholic* and *Orthodox* Churches.

Lord's Prayer The prayer taught by *Jesus* to his *disciples,* used in most acts of worship. The *Roman Catholic* term for the Lord's Prayer is the *Our Father.*

Lord's Supper The name used by *Nonconformists* for *Holy Communion.*

Low Anglican A practising *Protestant* whose religious worship is very different from that of a *Roman Catholic.*

Luke The name of one of the four *Gospels.* The same author is believed to have written the *Acts of the Apostles.*

M

Mark's Gospel The second book of the *New Testament.*

Mary The mother of *Jesus.*

Mass The central *Roman Catholic* service, similar to the *Protestant Holy Communion* service, which commemorates the death of *Jesus.*

Matthew's Gospel The first book of the *New Testament.*

Maundy Thursday The day before *Good Friday.*

Meeting House A *Quaker* place of worship.

Mercy-Seat A bench at the front of a *Salvation Army citadel* where people can kneel to seek God's forgiveness.

Messiah The person expected by the Jews to deliver them from their enemies, believed by Christians to be *Jesus.*

Methodist Church A *Nonconformist Church,* formed in the eighteenth century, and based on the teachings of *John Wesley.*

Midnight Mass The service held on *Christmas* Eve to celebrate the birth of *Jesus.*

Minister The leader of a *Nonconformist church.*

Miracle An event which appears to have no rational or normal explanation.

Missal The Prayer Book used by *Roman Catholics.*

Monastery The place in which *monks* live.

Monk A person who lives in a *monastery.*

Monotheism A belief in one God.

Mysteries The *Orthodox* name for the *sacraments.*

N

Nave The area of a *church* where the people sit. The nave runs from the western wall to the top of the *chancel.*

Nazareth The area in modern Israel where, according to the *Gospels, Jesus* grew up.

New Testament The second major division of The *Bible* which tells the story of Jesus and the early Church.

Nicene Creed One of the earliest and most important of the Christian *Creeds.*

Nonconformist Church A Church which does not 'conform' to the teachings of the *Church of England.* Nonconformist Churches are also called *Free Churches.*

Nun A woman who has given herself totally to God and follows the *Rule* of chastity, obedience and poverty.

O

Old Testament The Christian term for the Jewish Scriptures (the Tenkah), which form the first major division of the Christian *Bible.*

Ordination The ceremony by which a lay-person becomes a *priest.*

Orthodox Church Originally the Church of the Eastern region of the Roman Empire, which separated from the *Roman Catholic Church* in 1054.

Our Father The Catholic name for the *Lord's Prayer.*

P

Palestine The country in which *Jesus* is believed to have lived and died, now split into *Israel* and an Arab State.

Parable A story which has a moral or religious message, often used as a teaching device by *Jesus.*

Paschal Candle A candle lit in *Orthodox* and *Roman Catholic* churches on *Easter Sunday* to symbolise the hope of Jesus' *resurrection.*

Passover The Jewish festival of Pesach which celebrates the release of Jewish slaves from Egypt.

Patriarch The term for a *bishop* in the *Orthodox Church.*

Paul The leader of the early Church who wrote many of the books in the *New Testament. See also* **Saul.**

Peace Time in *Protestant* and *Roman Catholic* services when people offer each other 'The peace of God'.

Penance A penalty which a priest decides on after confession in the *Roman Catholic Church.*

Pentecost The Jewish Feast of Weeks (Shavuot) when the *Holy Spirit* was given to the first Christians. Also called *Whitsun.*

Peter A prominent *disciple* of *Jesus* and leader of early Church.

Pilate, Pontius The Roman procurator who condemned *Jesus* to death.

Pope The *Bishop of Rome* and the chief *bishop* in the *Roman Catholic Church.*

Presbyterian Church The Church which united with the Congregational Church to form the *United Reformed Church*.

Priest Someone ordained in the *Protestant* and *Roman Catholic* Churches and authorised to administer the *sacraments*.

Protestants Christians who do not belong to either the *Roman Catholic* or *Orthodox* Churches.

Pulpit A raised platform in a church from which the *sermon* is delivered.

Purgatory The state after death for those not ready for Heaven in *Roman Catholic* belief.

Q

Quaker The Church, also known as the *Society of Friends*, formed in the seventeenth century by *George Fox*.

Quiet Time Time set aside to pray and read The *Bible*.

R

Reformation The movement started in 1517 by Martin Luther which led to the formation of several *Protestant* Churches.

Relic The remains of a *saint* which have become venerated.

Requiem Mass *Mass* which is said after a person's death in the *Roman Catholic Church*.

Resurrection The belief that, at the end of time, the bodies of all those who have died will be brought back to life.

Roman Catholic Church The community of believers throughout the world who owe their allegiance to the *Pope*.

Rosary A string of 165 beads which encourages *Roman Catholics* to meditate on the fifteen 'mysteries' of Jesus' life and death.

Royal Doors Doors in the *iconostasis* in an *Orthodox church* through which the *priest* alone is allowed to pass.

Rule The Rule of St Benedict which relates to monastic life and demands chastity, poverty and obedience.

S

Sacrament An outward and visible sign of an inward and spiritual blessing.

Saint A person of outstanding religious commitment.

Salvation Army A *Protestant denomination* founded by *William* and *Catherine Booth*.

Satan A Hebrew word meaning 'the accuser'. Traditionally, Satan is the fallen angel who became the leader of the evil spirits opposed to God.

Saul of Tarsus The original name of *Paul*, a persecutor of the Christian Church who was converted on the road to Damascus, and who subsequently became a prominent leader of the early Church.

Sermon Part of the service in which someone, usually a *priest*, explains a passage from The *Bible*.

Sign of the Cross The tracing of the shape of a cross on the body by a *priest* or a member of the congregation.

Society of Friends Alternative name for *Quakers*.

Soul The spiritual part of a person.

Speaking in Tongues The practice of some Christians of speaking in an unknown language when praying.

Sunday The day set aside by Christians for prayer and worship.

Synoptic Gospels Meaning 'seeing together'. This term refers to the first three *Gospels* in the *New Testament*, since these have a similar approach to the life of *Jesus*.

T

Ten Commandaments The ten laws which are at the heart of the laws given by God to Moses on Mount Sinai. Jews usually call these the Ten Sayings.

Thirty-Nine Articles A statement of belief first accepted by the *Church of England* in 1574.

Tithe The practice of some Christians of giving $^1/_{10}$ of their income to the Church.

Transubstantiation The *Roman Catholic* belief that the bread and wine become the actual body and blood of *Jesus* during the *Mass*.

Trinity The Christian belief that there is one God in three Persons – God the Father, God the Son and God the *Holy Spirit*.

U

United Reformed Church The Church formed through the amalgamation of the Congregational and *Presbyterian* Churches.

V

Vigil A service which involves a time of 'waiting', held by some churches on *Good Friday*.

Virgin Birth The belief held by many Christians that *Mary*, the mother of *Jesus*, was a virgin after *Jesus* was conceived in her womb by the *Holy Spirit*.

W

Wesley, Charles Brother and partner of *John Wesley* who wrote hundreds of hymns.

Wesley, John The *Protestant* clergyman whose preaching led to the formation of the *Methodist Church*.

Whitsun 'White Sunday', referring to the ancient practice of baptismal candidates wearing white on *Pentecost*. *See* **Pentecost**.

Word of God Favourite description of many Christians for The *Bible*.

What is Islam?

What is Islam?

FOCUSING QUESTIONS

Why do Muslims believe that, whilst Islam is younger than Judaism and Christianity, it is really the religion which predates the other two?

What is the Shahadah is and what does it say?

What does the word 'din' mean?

Islam is one of three great religious faiths which have grown up, and flourished, in that part of the world called the Middle East – the others being Judaism and Christianity. Although Islam is the youngest of these religions Muslims (followers of Islam) argue that their religion actually forms the basis of the other two and predates them since the main prophets of the other religions were sent by Allah (God) to prepare the way for the coming of the Prophet Muhammad, the final prophet.

Being a Muslim

Although the word Islam is often translated as 'submission' it really means 'surrendering' and a Muslim is someone who 'surrenders themselves totally to Allah'. The Creed of Islam (called the Shahadah) simply says: '*There is no God except Allah, Muhammad is the Messenger of Allah*'. As the Shahadah tells us, a Muslim is someone who accepts two truths about God in his or her heart. First, that there is only one God, Allah, who is Supreme and Absolute. Secondly, the Prophet Muhammad was Allah's messenger, and Allah's revelations to Muhammad replace all others. Muslims believe that these revelations took place over many years and is faithfully and infallibly recorded in the Holy Scriptures, The Qur'an.

A. Which two beliefs do all of these Muslims have in common with each other?

The prophets and the Prophet
Muslims believe that Allah has sent many prophets including: Ibrahim (the Jewish Patriarch Abraham), Musa (Moses) and Isa (Jesus), who Christians believe to be the promised Messiah. According to Muslims, the last, and greatest, in this line of prophets was Muhammad. Muhammad, however, was not divine as Christians believe Jesus to have been, and Muslims are very clear on the point that Muhammad must not be worshipped – he is Allah's great Prophet but only a human being.

Din

Muslims emphasise that Islam is more than a set of beliefs ('iman') and acts of worship ('ibadah'), it is a complete way of life ('din'). Islam brings together belief and worship on the one hand, and manners and moral behaviour on the other to produce a whole way of life. This explains the Arabic greeting 'As-Salamu-Alaykum' (meaning 'Peace be upon you') which Muslims all over the world – no matter what language they speak – use when they meet a fellow-believer and when they part from them. This reinforces the basic message of Islam – peace between all people and peace within the human heart. In practice, for Muslims, this means a surrender of the heart and mind to Allah and the carrying out of acts of loving-kindness – in this way alone can they discover their true selves.

Where is Islam found?

Islam was born, in the sixth century CE, in the region where Africa and Asia meet – mid-way between the Mediterranean Sea and the Indian Ocean. This area is now called Saudi Arabia and the two most holy cities of Islam, Makkah and Madinah, are found there. Although Muslims can now be found in almost every country in the world, the majority of them are still in North Africa, the Middle East and South East Asia. It is something of a surprise to discover that, whilst the roots of Islam are firmly planted the Middle East, Arabs only make up seventeen per cent of the world's Muslim population. A surprisingly large number of Muslims live in Western countries including some 2,000,000 in Britain alone. These British Muslims belong to a worldwide Muslim community which now numbers around 1 billion people. Islam is the fastest-growing religion in the world, and only Christianity has more followers.

DISCUSS

Why do you think that Islam includes prophets from other religions as well as its own? What does this tell you about Islam?

B. This building bears the symbol of Islam – a crescent moon and a star.

FOR YOUR FOLDER

1
a) Look at Photograph **B.** Bearing in mind that the early followers of Muhammad lived in desert areas and had no compass to guide them from place to place why do you think these two symbols are appropriate for Islam?
b) What do you think is the spiritual significance of choosing the moon and the star as the two symbols of Islam?

2 Write two or three sentences to explain what each of the following mean: Islam; prophets; The Prophet; Allah; Muhammad; Shahadah.

In the glossary: Allah; Din; Ibadah; Ibrahim; Iman; Isa; Islam; Madinah; Makkah; Muhammad; Muslim; Musa; Prophet; Qur'an; Shahadah.

Muhammad – the Early Years

What *series of experiences changed the whole direction of Muhammad's life?*

FOCUSING QUESTIONS

How did Muhammad come to marry Khadijah?

What happened when Muhammad was meditating in the cave at Hira?

What is the 'Hijrah' and why is it important to Muslims?

From the scriptures

These words are taken from the Qur'an:
'In the name of God, the Compassionate, the Merciful, Recite in the name of your Lord who created – created man from clots of blood. Recite! Your Lord is the most Bountiful One, who by the pen taught man what he did not know. Indeed, man transgresses in thinking himself his own master: for to your Lord all things return.'
(Surah 96.1)

1 From this extract, which three names are applied to Allah, and what do you think they mean?
2 The extract tells us that Allah has done two things for humankind. What are they?

Makkah was a desert city in the sixth century, and its main feature was the Ka'bah, the house dedicated to the One True God and built under God's guidance by the Prophet Ibrahim. The majority of the people living in Makkah were idol worshippers who were fiercely loyal to their own tribes and gods. The city was a natural trading-centre with people bringing their goods to the town to be sold in the local market.

Muhammad's early life

Muhammad was born in Makkah in 570 CE but never knew his father, who died before he was born. His mother died when he was just six years old and the young Muhammad was brought up first by his grandfather and then by his uncle, Abu Talib. As a child he accompanied his uncle on business trips to Palestine and Syria. As he grew up, Muhammad became a camel-driver and then a trader. Because of his honesty in business he became known as 'Al-Amin' (meaning 'The trustworthy').

Before long, Muhammad was working for Khadijah, a rich widow, and although he was fifteen years younger than her, she became his first wife and bore him four daughters and two sons, although the two boys died in infancy.

The message of Allah

From his earliest years Muhammad was deeply religious, and by the time that he was forty he was spending much of his time praying and meditating in the desert. He was particularly worried by the idolatrous (idol worship) behaviour of the people of Makkah who worshipped the 360 idols – of clay, wood and stone – which were housed in the Ka'bah (see Photograph A). He was also concerned about the rich people who openly oppressed the poor in the city as well as the gambling, drunkenness, violence and the ill-treatment of women and children which were a feature of life in Makkah.

On 27 Ramadan 611 CE Muhammad was meditating in the cave at Hira, near Makkah – reflecting on the problems of life and death, and on the struggle between good and evil in the world. Whilst reflecting Muhammad had a vision in which he saw a superhuman being who ordered him to recite a text and called him 'the Messenger of God'. The text which Muhammad recited is now preserved in the 96th surah (division) of The Qur'an – the holy book of Islam.

A. This photograph shows the Ka'bah, which stands in the centre of the grand mosque in Makkah, Saudi Arabia. Why was Muhammad worried about what was happening in the Ka'bah, which was built to worship the One True God?

B. A Muslim praying

Muhammad returned home quickly and, after discussing his visions with Khadijah and a Christian cousin, became convinced that the vision came from Allah. For three years nothing more happened but then the visions started again. Some of Muhammad's closest friends, including Khadijah, began to commit the visions to memory and to write some of them down. Khadijah became Muhammad's first disciple, but she was soon followed by many others as Muhammad began to preach to the people of Makkah. The majority of people, however, rejected his message which denounced their ancestral gods and idols. The people launched a strong campaign to persecute the Prophet, as he had become known, and his small band of followers. Makkans forced the early Muslims to lie on the burning sand, placed great boulders on their chests and poured red-hot iron over them.

Many of the early converts to the faith died in this persecution – but none turned their back on their new beliefs. When the persecution became too great Muhammad advised his followers to leave the city and go to Abyssinia and many took his advice. Muhammad left Makkah in 622 CE to travel to Madinah on a journey known to all Muslims as the 'Hijrah' – or emigration. This was one of the most decisive events in Muslim history, and it is from this date that the Islamic calendar begins.

In the glossary: ALLAH; HIJRAH; IBRAHIM: KA'BAH; KHADIJAH; MADINAH; MAKKAH; MUHAMMAD; MUSLIM; QUR'AN; RAMADAN.

FOR YOUR FOLDER

a) Look at Photograph A which shows the Ka'bah as it is today. Millions of Muslim pilgrims visit Makkah every year to worship Allah at the Ka'bah. In this city, before Muhammad received his visions from Allah, people worshipped the Sun, the Moon, the stars and stone pillars. Why do you think that people worshipped these objects?

b) Can you suggest any reason why Judaism, Christianity and Islam all contain references to God speaking to individuals in the wilderness or desert? Why do you think that these places are suitable locations for people to hear the voice of God?

c) Why do you think that the time that Muhammad spent praying and meditating in the wilderness made an important contribution to him becoming Allah's messenger?

Muhammad – the Later Years

***How** did the people of Makkah and Madinah respond to the message preached by Muhammad?*

FOCUSING QUESTIONS

Which event in Muslim history marks the beginning of the Islamic calendar?

What did Muhammad do when he reached Madinah?

What does the mihrab in a mosque remind Muslims to do?

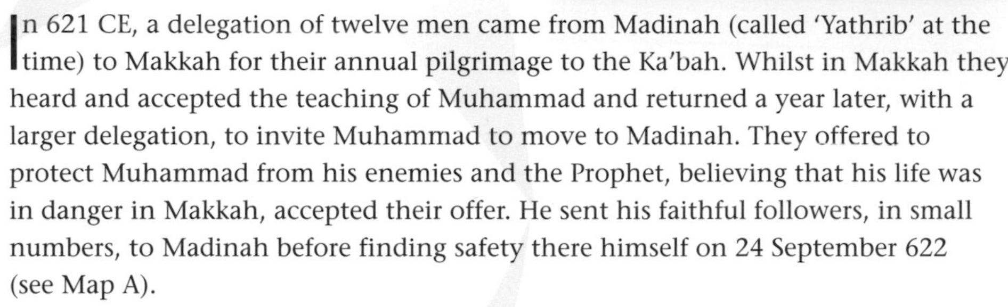

In 621 CE, a delegation of twelve men came from Madinah (called 'Yathrib' at the time) to Makkah for their annual pilgrimage to the Ka'bah. Whilst in Makkah they heard and accepted the teaching of Muhammad and returned a year later, with a larger delegation, to invite Muhammad to move to Madinah. They offered to protect Muhammad from his enemies and the Prophet, believing that his life was in danger in Makkah, accepted their offer. He sent his faithful followers, in small numbers, to Madinah before finding safety there himself on 24 September 622 (see Map A).

The Hijrah

The flight to Madinah is known in Arabic as the 'Hijrah' (meaning emigration) and all Muslim calendars are dated from the event (AH or Anno Hijrah). Muslims regard the Hijrah as not only one of the most important events in their history but as a turning-point in world history. Certainly, the success of Muhammad's later preaching depended on his decision to leave Makkah and move to Madinah when he did. He soon became recognised as the leader of the city and all disputes amongst the different tribes in the city were referred to him. More importantly, the religious rules of Islam were put in place in the city as more and more people were converted to the faith.

A. This map shows the locations of Makkah and Madinah. Why did Muhammad encourage his followers to leave Makkah and finally leave the city himself?

Back to Makkah

All the time that Muhammad was living in Madinah he intended to return to Makkah. In particular, he wanted to purge the Ka'bah of its idols and set it up as the most important shrine for the worship of the One God, Allah. To prepare his followers for the time when this would happen he taught them always to say their prayers facing the

B. The mihrab in a mosque. Why do you think that it is important for all Muslims prayers to be said facing Makkah – whether in a mosque or elsewhere?

city of Makkah – a custom which is still an important part of Islam today. In each mosque there is a niche in the wall, the mihrab, which indicates the direction of Makkah (see Photograph B) and worshippers face the mihrab whenever they pray.

Whilst he was waiting Muhammad taught his followers that it was their holy duty to attack caravans leaving Makkah as well as any people who stood in their way. A number of battles were fought against the Makkans and a notable victory was achieved at Badr where 300 men from Madinah defeated 1,000 fighters from Makkah. This convinced Muhammad that Allah was with him. Then, in March 629 CE, Muhammad entered Makkah at the head of a large army, walked around the Ka'bah seven times and touched the Black Stone set in the south-east corner of the structure with his staff. He then offered sacrifices to Allah and called the people to prayer. In November of the same year Makkah was totally conquered and Muhammad entered the city to be proclaimed the Prophet of Allah. Ever since, the city has remained at the heart of Islam and every Muslim believer is expected to make a pilgrimage, called a 'Hajj', to it at least once during their lifetime.

Muhammad's death

Muhammad went on his last pilgrimage to Makkah in 632 and it was on this occasion that he preached his famous Last Sermon. As soon as he returned home his health broke down and he died on 8 June 632. A day later he was buried in the house in which he had died, which was also recognised as the first mosque. Although he did not choose a successor, the task of leading the fledgling religion fell to Abu Bakr, Muhammad's trusted friend.

FOR YOUR FOLDER

1 Abu Bakr announced the death of Muhammad to the people with the words:
'Those of you who worship Muhammad, know that Muhammad is dead. As for those of you who worship God, God is living and will never die.'

a) What was Abu Bakr really trying to tell the people when he told them that, whilst Muhammad was dead, God was alive for evermore.
b) Abu Bakr quoted a verse from The Qur'an to the people: *'Muhammad is but a messenger; there have been prophets before him, and they all died. Will you now turn back?'* What do you think Abu Bakr meant by this?

2

a) What was the Hijrah?
b) Why did it take place?
c) What happened on the Hijrah?
d) Why do you think that Muslims consider the Hijrah to be such an important event?

In the glossary: Abu Bakr; Allah; Black Stone; Hajj; Hijrah; Ka'bah; Islam; Madinah; Makkah; Mihrab; Mosque; Yathrib.

The Spread of Islam

How did Islam grow after the death of Muhammad?

FOCUSING QUESTIONS

How extensive was the influence of Islam by the time that Muhammad died in 632?

Why did the invasion of Palestine upset the Christians and the Jews so much?

Why is the site on which the Dome of the Rock is built important to Jews as well as Muslims?

After the death of Muhammad in 632 CE Abu Bakr became the Khalifah ('custodian') and by that time most of Arabia had been converted to Islam. Muhammad's dream had been of winning the whole world for Islam and by his death a very large area had been brought under Allah's control. The followers of Muhammad had carried the message into Syria, Iraq, and had reached Jerusalem before going further west into Egypt and North Africa.

Rapid expansion

The spread of Islam was rapid, and by 711, Muslims had conquered Spain and Gibraltar – reaching the town of Poitiers, in southern France, in 732 (see Map A). There, however, they were defeated by the army of Charles Martel, who controlled northern France, and were forced to retreat. By the tenth century there were three great centres of Islam civilisation – Baghdad in Iraq, Cairo in Egypt and Cordoba in Spain.

A. This map shows the extent of the Muslim empire within 100 years of the death of the Prophet Muhammad. Why do you think that Islam was able to spread so rapidly in the early years of its history?

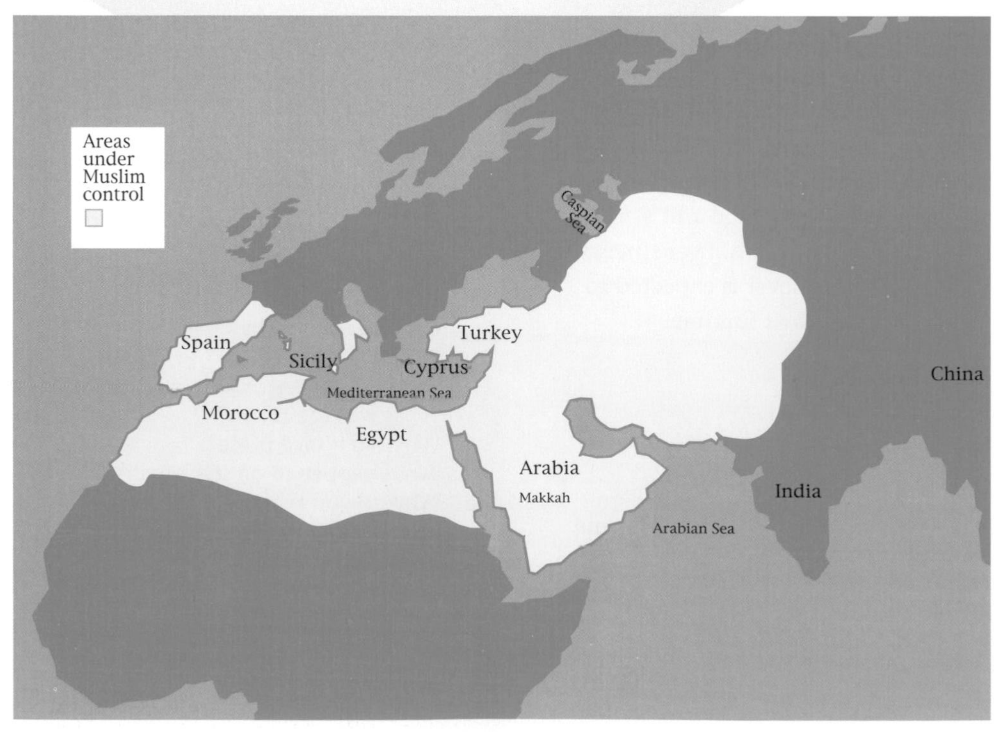

The Crusades

When the Muslims invaded Palestine they were attempting to conquer an area which was sacred to Jews and Christians as well as Muslims – particularly the city of Jerusalem. The Christian Church struck back and this led, in the Middle Ages, to a series of battles known as the Crusades. The fiercest of these battles were fought around Jerusalem, since most of the sites holiest to Jews, Christians and Muslims were found there. The most important Muslim shrine in the city is the Dome of the Rock. The Dome is built over the rock from which, according to Muslim tradition, Muhammad rose to Heaven with Jibril and spoke to Allah. It is built near to the Western Wall, which is all that remains of the ancient Jewish Temple

B. Jerusalem Old City, Israel. This photograph shows the Dome of the Rock, as seen from the Mount of Olives. Why is this site holy to both Muslims and Jews?

destroyed by the Romans in 70 CE. The same site is said to be the place where the Jewish Patriarch Abraham was willing to sacrifice his son at the command of God – a story which is, unusually, found in both the Jewish Scriptures and The Qur'an.

The great Muslim Empires

During the twelfth and thirteenth centuries the Muslim message spread into Africa (Nigeria and the Sudan) and Asia (China and South-East Asia). The message was often taken by Muslim travellers and merchants, but some notable cities also fell to the Muslim armies. Constantinople, for instance, was a great centre of Christianity before the Muslims captured it for their faith in 1453 and renamed it Istanbul. By the seventeenth century vast parts of the world were controlled by enormous Muslim Empires – the Safavids in Iran, the Moguls in India, and the Ottomans in Turkey. Although the other two empires were short-lived, the Ottoman Empire lasted from the sixteenth century until the First World War (1914-1918).

Jihad

There were many occasions when Islam expanded by force, and the Prophet Muhammad taught his followers that a 'Holy War' (jihad) in Allah's name was acceptable as long as two conditions were met:

- A holy war should never be an offensive action but only a defensive one when a country has already been attacked.
- A holy war could only be conducted in Allah's name and then only to extend the influence and authority of Islam.

Today many Muslims no longer use the term 'jihad' to indicate a physical battle but the struggle which all believers must fight against the enemies of the truth which lie within the human heart.

FOR YOUR FOLDER

1

a) Which countries were controlled by Islam by the time of Muhammad's death in 632?

b) Why do you think that Christians in Europe were largely unconcerned by the rapid expansion of Islam in the eighth century?

c) What is a jihad and why has it played a very important part in the history of Islam?

d) What conditions need to be fulfilled before a genuine jihad can take place?

2 Carry out some research of your own to discover the answers to these questions about the Crusades:

a) What and who started the Crusades and why?

b) What were the main motivations behind the Crusades?

c) How many Crusades were there and could anyone be said to have emerged victorious at the end?

In the glossary: Abu Bakr; Allah; Angel; Crusades; Dome of the Rock; Islam; Jerusalem; Jibril; Jihad; Khalifah; Muhammad; Muslim; Qur'an; Umar.

Sunni and Shi'ah Muslims

Who *are the Sunni and the Shi'ah Muslims and why did the two groups split from each other?*

FOCUSING QUESTIONS

What are the basic differences in beliefs between Sunni and Shi'ah Muslims?

Who is the Mahdi believed to be?

Between 632 and 661 four khalifahs led the worldwide Muslim community: Abu Bakr (632-634), Umar ibn-al-Khattab (634-644), Uthman (644-656) and Ali (656-661). Together these first four leaders of Islam are known as 'al-Khulafa-ur-Rashidun', which means the 'Rightly Guided' Khalifahs.

Abu Bakr

Believed to have been one of the first converts to Islam under Muhammad, Abu Bakr led the religion on the death of the Prophet. He spent the next two years trying to hold together the different Muslim tribes who had been converted. He also encouraged some of the friends of the Prophet to commit his teachings to memory – memories which were later written down to form The Qur'an.

Umar ibn-al-Khattab

Umar was responsible for leading many successful military campaigns, capturing Damascus, Jerusalem and Egypt. Umar also commissioned the building of the Mosque of Umar, also called the Dome of the Rock, in Jerusalem. This was the traditional spot where prophecies were made, and Umar set up many Qur'an study schools in the area.

Uthman

Uthman was Muhammad's son-in-law, and the third Khalifah of Islam. He was murdered by Egyptian Muslims.

A. An Egyptian Muslim and her family. What do the names Sunni and Shi'ah mean?

Ali

Cousin and son-in-law of the Prophet Muhammad, Ali established a tradition of scholarship although he, too, was assassinated. The speedy expansion of Islam was largely the result of the assurance that belief in Allah gave to the Khalifah. Ali, though, came to blows with Mu'awiya, the governor of Syria and cousin of Uthman, who demanded that the assassins of his cousin should be punished. When Ali himself was murdered, Ali's second son, Hussein, tried to take power but was killed in battle, and Mu'awiya declared himself to be Khalifah. Both he and Uthman were members of the Umayyad clan. Ali is the first successor accepted by the Shi'ah Muslims.

B. A group of Shi'ah Muslims in Iran. What do Shi'ah Muslim believe?

Sunni Muslims

Sunnis, who make up between eighty to ninety per cent of Muslims today, claim that no-one can succeed Muhammad since The Qur'an described him as the 'Seal of the Prophets'. His successors, then, can only be guardians of the faith that Allah revealed to Muhammad. Leadership of the Muslim community, Sunnis maintain, must pass to a member of Muhammad's own tribe – the Quraysh. Sunnis believe that, after the first four 'Rightly Guided Khalifahs', leadership passed to the Umayyad and Abbasid dynasties which were both members of the Quraysh tribe. It was then passed down through leaders of the Ottoman Empire until that Empire ceased during the First World War. Sunni Muslims believe that:

- All guidance can only come from Allah through The Qur'an and The Hadith. Together these holy books form the Shari'ah – Islamic law.
- The 'imam' (leader) is simply a teacher who tells the faithful about The Qur'an. The imam is not, in any sense, 'holy' or a channel for Allah's revelation.
- They alone, amongst Muslims, understand Allah's revelation in The Qur'an correctly. This is how the Sunni Muslims got their name; from the word 'sunnat' which means tradition. They believe that they alone hold to the true faith as it was received, and passed on, by Muhammad.

Shi'ah Muslims

The Shi'ah Muslims, who live mainly in Iraq, Iran, Lebanon and India, believe that the leadership of the Muslim community should have remained with the descendants of Ali (Shi'ah means 'the party of Ali'). They claim that Allah guided Muhammad to appoint Ali and that the first three Khalifah were usurpers. Some even curse them in their Friday prayers adding the words 'Ali is the friend of Allah' to the words of the Shahadah – the holy statement of faith. Shi'ah Muslims believe that the imams were Ali's true successors and that they should be regarded in the same way as the Khalifahs. They also believe that the last imam will appear at the end of the world as the 'Mahdi, al-Muntazar'. Shi'ahs believe that the Mahdi will lead the worldwide community of Muslims (the 'ummah') and restore justice to the Earth. The Mahdi will be the same person that is promised in both Christian and Jewish traditions.

FOR YOUR FOLDER

1 Make a list of three differences between the Sunni and the Shi'ah Muslims.

2
a) What is a Khalifah??
b) Who were the four 'Rightly Guided' Khalifahs and what contribution did they make to early Islam?
c) Who was Mu'awiya, and why did he fall out with the last of the 'Rightly Guided' Khalifahs?
d) Who is the Mahdi and who are expecting him?

3 Bearing in mind what you know about the Prophet Muhammad what do you think The Qur'an means when it calls him 'the Seal of the Prophets'?

In the glossary: ABU BAKR; ALI; ALLAH; KHALIFAH; DOME OF THE ROCK; HADITH; IMAM; ISLAM; MAHDI; MUHAMMAD; QUR'AN; SHAHADAH; SHARI'AH; SHI'AH; SUNNI; UMAR; UMMAH; UTHMAN.

Islam in Britain

What *do we know about the Muslim community in Britain?*

FOCUSING QUESTIONS

When did the first significant influx of Muslims into Great Britain take place – and why?

Why were so many mosques opened in Great Britain as the size of the Muslim population grew?

Some 2 million Muslims live in Great Britain. Muslim communities are found in most of the larger cities in this country. Generally speaking, immigrants from North Africa have tended to settle in London and south-east England (where there are 50,000 Muslims). Muslims from Pakistan have mostly settled in Birmingham (100,000), Bradford (80,000) and Manchester (45,000). Recently a number of Muslim refugees have also come to Britain from Eastern Europe (particularly former Yugoslavia). The number of British converts to Islam, whilst growing, is still very small.

Migration

Whilst British colonial rule was expanding in India in the early nineteenth century, so the first significant migration of Muslims to Britain took place, when sailors began to settle in British ports. Most of them came from West Africa and India and, after the Suez Canal was opened in 1869, from the Yemen. In the twentieth century the Muslim immigrants to western Europe were usually temporary workers who came to raise money to send back home before returning themselves. In the early years they were mainly students or, in larger numbers, those who had been demobbed from the armed forces. During the 1950s, however, the rate of immigration speeded up considerably as many Muslims came to Britain from India and the Turkish part of Cyprus. Like other immigrants they were attracted by the offer of work in a country which had lost so many men during the Second World War. These immigrants were soon followed by others from Pakistan, Bangladesh and the Middle East, together with Asians from East Africa. The Commonwealth Immigration Act (1962) virtually stopped any further immigration, but most of the temporary immigrants became permanent residents as their families joined them. The children of these first-generation immigrants are now making their way through the educational institutions, developing their own careers and starting families.

At the moment most Muslim parents send their children to ordinary schools, but the Muslim community has argued for a long time that it should be able to run its own schools supported by Government money – just as the Christians and Jews do. This would allow Muslim children to be taught The Qur'an and Arabic as part of their normal schooling, and for them to observe Muslim festivals and customs. At the start of 1997 there was some indication that this might be permitted in the very near future.

A. Why do you think that Muslims are anxious to maintain as many Islamic traditions as possible while they live in this country?

B. The mosque is called 'the house of prayer' but it fulfils a much wider role. What is that role?

Mosques

The first mosques in Great Britain to cater for the Muslim community were opened in Woking, Surrey and Liverpool as far back as the 1880s. An Islamic Cultural centre was opened in London between the two World Wars, and in 1940 it was given a large plot of land in London's Regent's Park in exchange for land in Cairo, Egypt, where a Protestant cathedral was built. During the 1970s a beautiful mosque was opened in Regent's Park, and Muslims from many different countries now travel to worship there.

The mosque in Regent's Park may be one of the most beautiful in the world but, during this century, some 400 mosques have opened in Britain to meet the spiritual and social needs of the Muslim community. This has been very important because, for a Muslim, a mosque is far more than simply a house of prayer – it is a social centre in which Muslims are taught The Qur'an and how to read the Arabic language. Whilst some of the mosques are purpose-built the majority are housed in converted churches, houses, factories or warehouses.

FOR YOUR FOLDER

1

a) What do you think are the main advantages of Jews and Christians having their own schools?
b) Why do you think that this privilege has always been refused to Muslims?
c) How do you think that the Muslim community might benefit by having its own schools?

2

a) Why did the Muslim community in Great Britain increase considerably during the 1950s?
b) Find out how the Muslim community in Britain acquired the land on which to build the mosque in Regent's Park.
c) Why do you think that the leaders of the Muslim community have stressed the important of their religion and culture to Muslims living here?

In the glossary: Arabic; Mosque; Muslim; Qur'an.

Islam Worldwide

***How** strong is Islam in today's world and where are most Muslims to be found?*

FOCUSING QUESTIONS

Which country has the two most important cities in Islam – Makkah and Madinah – within its borders?

Which country had a Muslim revolution in 1979 – and what was one outcome of it for the country's women?

Which natural resources has made the Gulf states very rich – and how do they regard their possession of this resource?

DISCUSS

1 Why do you think that some Muslim countries treat apostasy so seriously?

2 Why do you think that Indonesia restricts religion within its boarders to Islam, Christianity, Hinduism and Buddhism?

In the world today there are over 1 billion Muslims – making Islam is the fastest-spreading of the major religious faiths. Most of the followers of Islam are found in the countries to which Islam originally spread from Arabia. However, there are many other countries where Islam is the majority religion (see Map A).

Saudi Arabia, Egypt, and the Gulf states

Saudi Arabia is the heartland of Islam with its two most holy cities – Makkah and Madinah. Over 2 million Muslims visit Makkah each year on the holy pilgrimage called the Hajj. Islam is the official religion of the country and all of its permanent citizens must be Muslims. Non-Muslim places of worship are not allowed, and anyone who converts to another religion (a sin called 'apostasy') is put to death.

If Saudi Arabia is the spiritual centre of Islam, however, Egypt is its intellectual heart. Muslims from all over the world are sent to the Al-Azhar university in Cairo to be trained before returning to their own, and other, countries as missionaries.

The Gulf states – Kuwait, Qatar, the United Arab Emirates, Bahrain and the Sultanate of Oman are amongst the richest countries in the world because of their oil reserves. They consider such a rich natural resource to be a gift from Allah. Most of the leaders in these countries are Sunni Muslims whilst their subjects are mainly Shi'ahs, and this has caused many problems in the past.

Pakistan, the Sudan and Iran

Originally the two parts of Pakistan, East and West, were divided by Indian territory. Now East Pakistan is called Bangladesh and eighty-six per cent of its population are Muslims, whilst ninety-five per cent of people in Pakistan follow Islam – 80 million people in all.

Seventy-four per cent of Sudan's population are Muslim and the country has a Muslim government. The country follows Islamic (Shari'ah) law and the law on apostasy is still used. Similarly, Iran upholds strict Islamic law. The Revolution in 1979 brought Ayatollah Khomeini to power and all women in the country were ordered to return to wearing the veil. The Ayatollah has long since died, but there is still little political or religious freedom in Iran.

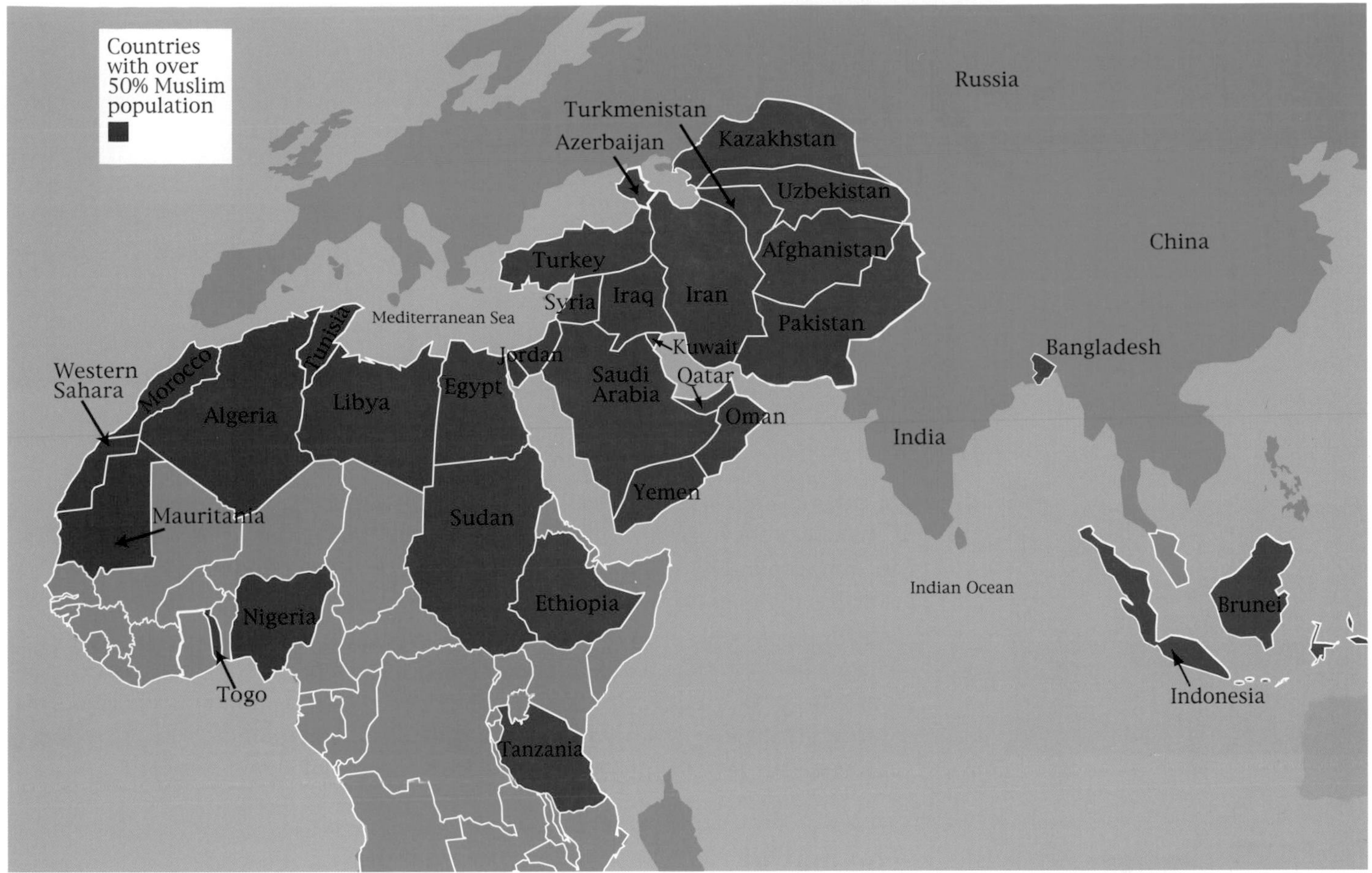

A. This map shows the main Muslim countries in the world – those where more than fifty per cent of the population are Muslims. In which countries is Islam the 'official' religion?

Indonesia

Although Islam is not the official religion of the country, Indonesia is the largest Muslim country in the world with over 100 million Muslims. Every member of the population is required by law to belong to one of five religious systems in Indonesia – Islam, the Roman Catholic Church, the Protestant Church, Hinduism or Buddhism.

There are now an estimated 1 billion Muslims in the world and they make up the majority of people in over thirty countries. In many more countries, such as Nigeria, India, the Philippines and north-west China, they make up a significant part of the population. The countries in which Islam is the major religion include some of the richest and poorest countries in the world – with Saudi Arabia at one end of the spectrum and the Sudan and Bangladesh at the other.

In the glossary: Allah; Apostasy; Hajj; Islam; Madinah; Makkah; Muslim; Roman Catholic; Shari'ah; Shi'ah; Sunni.

FOR YOUR FOLDER

1
a) How many Muslims are there in the world today?
b) Name ten countries in which the majority of the population are Muslims.
c) At which university are Muslims trained to be missionaries?
d) Which country has the largest majority Muslim population in the world?
f) What is every member of the population in Indonesia required to do?

2 The Penal Code introduced in Sudan in 1991 stipulates that:
'The death penalty is mandatory [compulsory] *for apostasy that is committed by any Muslim who advocates apostasy from Islam or openly declares his* [or her] *own apostasy openly or by their actions.'*
a) What is apostasy?
b) Name two countries in which people can be put to death for committing apostasy.
c) Why do you think that Islam treats apostasy so seriously?

The Mosque

Why *are mosques very important, and what are the main features of such buildings?*

FOCUSING QUESTIONS

What use have Muslims made of mosques over the centuries?

What is a mihrab, and why is it important?

What is the minbar, and to what use is it put?

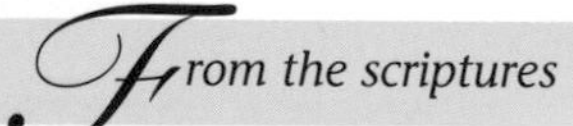

From the scriptures

The Adhan is the Call issued by the mu'adhin when he calls the faithful to prayer, and is an expanded form of the Shahadah: *'God is most great, God is most great, God is most great, God is most great. I bear witness that there is no God but Allah. I bear witness that there is no God but Allah. I bear witness that Muhammad is the Prophet of Allah. I bear witness that Muhammad is the Prophet of Allah. Come to prayer, Come to prayer, Come to success, Come to success, God is most great, God is most great. There is no God but Allah.'*

1 Where is a Muslim likely to hear this Call to Prayer, and why?
2 This Call makes reference to several aspects of Muslim belief. What are they?
3 Why do you think that several part of the Adhan is repeated more than once?

A mosque (or 'masjid') is literally a 'place of prostration', but throughout the whole of the history of Islam, it has been much more than that. It's value to the Muslim community worldwide has been immense. In addition to being places of worship, mosques are used as community centres, schools and law courts. In the early years, the mosque was also the place where pilgrims set out on a hajj, and where a holy war (jihad) was declared. Going to the mosque is the way that Muslims can express the idea of ummah – the worldwide community of Islam. For Muslims living in a new country, the mosque is also an important way of keeping in touch with their fellow Muslims, and with their religion and culture.

The masjid

Muhammad taught that prayer can be offered to Allah anywhere: '*Wherever the hour of prayer overtakes you, you shall perform it. The place is a mosque...*'. For a Muslim, anywhere that prayers can be made is a mosque, as long as the place is clean or is made clean by using a prayer mat. Yet Muhammad did not deny the importance of the building in which so much prayer takes place since he also said that anyone involved in building a mosque would pass straight into Heaven because their actions were so pleasing to Allah.

Muhammad built the very first mosque by his own hands, and the building in Madinah, Saudi Arabia, also doubled up as his own home. All subsequent mosques have been built as close to the pattern established by Muhammad as possible.

Outside the mosque

Although some of the world's most beautiful buildings are mosques, the majority of them are simple in design. Outside they have two distinguishing features:

- A dome. This is onion-shaped and represents the universe over which Allah has total control.
- Minarets. These are towers from which the mu'adhin issues the Call to Prayer (the 'Adhan') five times a day. There are usually four minarets, although the number is not fixed.

Each Muslim must wash thoroughly before entering a mosque. Generally running water is provided in the courtyard, although in Britain the washing facilities will almost certainly be indoors.

A. A prayer mat. There are two main reasons why Muslims use prayer mats when they pray. Can you work out what they are?

B. A minbar. To what use is the minbar put in a mosque?

Inside a mosque

When Muslims enter the mosque to pray they remove their shoes or sandals as a sign of respect to Allah – although, unlike other religions, the mosque is not considered to be the actual dwelling-place of God.

There are no seats in a mosque, so the worship-hall of the building is covered by carpet. Worshippers usually pray on their own prayer mats (see Photograph A), which often have a design on them which includes an arch. When laid out on the floor of the hall, the arch should point towards the mihrab, which is a niche in the wall of the mosque which indicates the direction of Makkah ('qiblah'). No pictures or statues are allowed in this building, although the walls and pillars are often ornately decorated with geometric patterns or verses from The Qur'an in Arabic.

The main time for assembling in the mosque is Friday Prayers at midday, when the imam leads the worshippers through their rak'ahs and delivers his sermon (the 'khutbah') from a raised platform called a minbar (see Photograph B). This usually has either three or five steps (one for Muhammad and four for the khalifahs.

The khutbah

The khutbah, or sermon is usually in two parts. The first generally deals with the problems that must be faced in the modern world. The second usually gives an explanation of a section of The Qur'an or of a specific religious practice. The khutbah is an important part of every Muslims visit to the mosque.

FOR YOUR FOLDER

a) What do you think that the mosque means to members of the Muslim community in Britain?
b) List some of the main uses for a mosque.

In the glossary: ADHAN; ALLAH; ARABIC; HAJJ; IMAM; JIHAD; MADINAH; MAKKAH; MIHRAB; MINARET; MOSQUE; MUHAMMAD; PROPHET; QUR'AN; RAK'AH; SHAHADAH; UMMAH.

The Five Pillars

What *are the Five Pillars and why are they so important to every Muslim?*

FOCUSING QUESTIONS

What are the five basic religious duties that were singled out as being particularly important to Muslims after the death of the Prophet Muhammad?

What does Islam teaches about enjoying the good things in life that Allah has provided?

What does Islam teach about the importance of love – and who must be loved first?

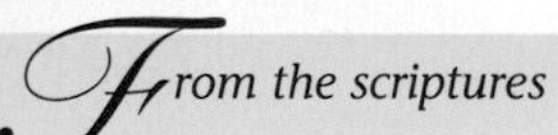

From the scriptures

The Qur'an reminds all Muslim believers of a very important principle regarding their behaviour:
'Your Lord best knows what is in your hearts; He knows if you are good. He will surely forgive those who turn to Him.'
(Surah 17.25)

1 In their moral behaviour what do Muslims think is most important – the motive behind an action or the outcome of that action itself?
2 What do you think The Qur'an means when it says *'Your Lord best knows what is in your hearts'*?

Soon after the Prophet Muhammad died, five basic religious duties were singled out as necessary acts of worship and obedience for every Muslim. These religious duties, known as the 'Five Pillars', are represented by the four minarets (prayer towers) and the dome of the mosque (the Muslim house of prayer). The Five Pillars consist of:

1 The Profession of Faith – the 'Shahadah'. This consists of the statement *'There is no god except Allah, Muhammad is the Messenger of Allah'*.

2 The worship of Allah. The form of worship taught by Muhammad, called the 'salah', is performed under certain conditions and in Arabic. Muslims believe that Allah fixed the five daily times that the salah should be performed.

3 The giving of alms – 'zakah'. This is an obligation of every Muslim adult and is a means of purifying their wealth. Zakah usually represents 2.5 per cent of the worshipper's income.

4 Fasting, called 'sawm'. This is the time, between sunrise and sunset, when every adult Muslim is expected to go without food and drink during the month of Ramadan.

5 Pilgrimage. Every Muslim is expected to undertake a pilgrimage to Makkah, called a 'Hajj', at least once during their lifetime.

Moral behaviour

Muslim tradition clearly states proper conduct and good works can improve the status even of those individuals who have been chosen by Allah to enter Paradise (Heaven). Because of this many Muslims go beyond a careful keeping of the Five Pillars, which they simply regard as the minimal standards that Allah expects of them. Many Muslims therefore will spend more time than prescribed fasting, will contribute more zakah, spend more time praying and reading The Qur'an and Hadith, and undertake pilgrimages to other sites significant in Muslim history than is simply considered 'necessary'.

Unlike some other religions, notably Christianity, Islam has never encouraged the monastic life. It teaches that Allah created everything in life to be enjoyed by humans and so any withdrawal from life is against the will and purpose of God. All human attributes, whether they are internal or external, are to be put to the appropriate use, since it is only in this way that Allah can be glorified. However, Muslims firmly believe that each individual must be disciplined. In Islam the value of all human conduct is determined by the motive behind it, rather than the outcome of it.

Love

Islam teaches that, to be really moral an action must be governed by love. This love, though, must be controlled and the most important form that it can take is the love of Allah. Muslims believe that loving Allah and Allah's Messenger, the Prophet Muhammad, is the most important activity of which human beings are capable. It is much more important than loving parents, children, family or anything else. Only when a person learns to love Allah, and express it in the keeping of the Five Pillars, can he or she truly love the other people in their life (see Photograph A).

FOR YOUR FOLDER

1
a) What do Muslims mean when they speak of the 'Five Pillars'?
b) Why do you think they are called the 'Five Pillars'?
c) Can you work out one way in which the first Pillar is different to all the others?

2 Give one sentence definitions of each of the following: the Shahadah; salah; zakah; sawm; Hajj.

In the glossary: Arabic; Five Pillars; Hadith; Hajj; Madinah; Makkah; Minaret; Mosque; Muhammad; Qur'an; Ramadan; Salah; Sawm; Shahadah; Zakah.

A. What do you think Islam means when it teaches that it is only when a person loves Allah properly that he or she can love their family?

The Shahadah

What is the Shahadah?

FOCUSING QUESTIONS

What does the Shahadah say?

How do Muslims demonstrate the importance of the Shahadah in their lives and in their worship?

What is apostasy, and how seriously it is treated in Islam?

No religion carries a shorter statement of faith than Islam – *'There is no god except Allah, Muhammad is the Messenger of Allah'* (La ilaha ill'Allah, Muhammad rasul Allah) This brief and simple statement of faith, called the Shahadah, is the only Creed in Islam. This statement is whispered in the ear of every new-born baby before he or she can hear anything else; it is one of the first sentences that a young child is taught to say; it is repeated several times each day by Muslim worshippers between getting up in the morning and going to bed at night and it is hoped that it will be the very last utterance of the dying.

Saying the Shahadah

It is often said that merely saying that you accept the Shahadah (see Photograph A) makes you a Muslim but that is not strictly true. Most Muslims insist that six conditions have to be met before repeating the Shahadah becomes a true sign of Muslim faith. It must be:

1 Said aloud.

2 Understood perfectly.

3 Believed in the heart.

4 Professed until the person dies.

5 Recited correctly.

6 Declared without any hesitation.

Five times each day a similar, but slightly longer, version of the Shahadah (called the 'Adhan') is said by the mu'adhin as he calls the faithful to prayer from the minaret in the mosque. He summons all Muslims within the sound of his voice to pray with the words:
'God is greater! God is greater! I bear witness that there is no god but Allah! I bear witness that Muhammad is the Prophet of God! Come to prayer! Come to prayer!'

Apostasy
The five beliefs of Islam are very closely associated with the Shahadah. Anyone who abandons Islam, whether voluntarily or under pressure, are seen as having committed the worst possible sin. This sin, called apostasy, is totally condemned. Both those who have been brought up as Muslims and those who convert to the faith are expected to be totally committed to it.

FOR YOUR FOLDER

a) Name three different occasions on which a Muslim is likely to repeat the Shahadah.
b) Why do you think that the Muslim belief in Allah comes before the other Pillars of faith?
c) What do you think Muslims really mean when they recite the Shahadah?
d) Which two other religions have very similar ideas about God to Islam?

Islamic law (called 'Shari'ah') stipulates that the punishment for apostasy amongst men is death. When the author Salman Rushdie wrote 'The Satanic Verses' in 1988 he was judged to have committed this sin because, as someone who was brought up as a Muslim, he had written material that was considered to show that he had turned his back on the faith. Shari'ah says that women who commit apostasy should be kept in confinement until they repent of their sin – or die. Any children who commit apostasy are watched carefully until they grow up – and then they are treated like adults. In practice, though, the law against apostasy is rarely used. In almost all Muslim countries it is forbidden for other religions to make converts.

A. This is what the Shahadah looks like in Arabic but what does it mean in English?

DISCUSS

Why do you think that Muslims try to ensure that the Shahadah is the first and last words that each Muslim hears?

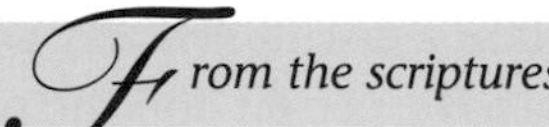

From the scriptures

This quotation from The Qur'an applies a very common symbol to Allah:
'God is the light of the heavens and earth. His light may be compared to a niche that enshrines a lamp, the lamp within a crystal of star-like brilliance. It is lit from a blessed olive tree neither eastern nor western. Its very oil would almost shine forth, though no fire touched it. Light upon light; God guides to His light whom He will. God speaks in parables to mankind. God has knowledge of all things.'
(Surah 24.35)

1 Why do you think that light is such a favourite symbol in all world religions – including Islam?
2 What qualities are there in light which a Muslim might want to apply to Allah – use the above quotation to help you to answer this question.

In the glossary: Adhan; Allah; Apostasy; Minaret; Mosque; Mu'adhin; Muhammad; Prophet; Shahadah; Shari'ah.

Salah (1)

How do Muslims prepare themselves for prayer and why are these preparations necessary?

FOCUSING QUESTIONS

How many times each day is a Muslim is expected to pray – and when?

Which two groups of people are allowed to have special praying arrangements – and what are they?

What is wudu?

After keeping the Shahadah the most important religious duty for every Muslim is prayer, which can be performed in any place at any time. Whilst the ritual prayers (the salah) are said in Arabic, private prayers (called 'du'a') can be said in the language of the worshipper. Private prayers are spontaneous and may include prayers of thanksgiving, a cry for help, or a prayer for success in a particular undertaking.

Ritual prayers

Ritual prayer forms the backbone of a Muslim's religious life. The Qur'an specifies three times each day that these prayers must be performed, but Muslim tradition prescribes five times – at dawn, noon, mid-afternoon, evening and night – and this is the custom followed by most Muslims. These prayers, called 'salah', may be said anywhere as long as it is a 'clean place', although many Muslims prefer to pray in a mosque under the guidance of the imam (leader of the mosque).

Every male Muslim is expected to be in the mosque for Friday noon prayers at which the imam delivers a sermon. Special allowances are made for two groups of people who cannot be in the mosque at this time – anyone who is sick, and travellers. The ill are allowed to pray in bed or lying down. Travellers can pray three times in the day instead of five – at dawn, combining noon with mid-afternoon prayers, and then bringing together evening prayers with those that follow nightfall.

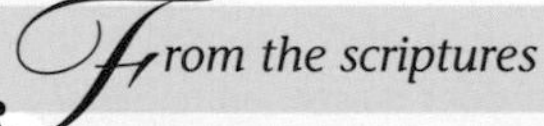

From the scriptures

This quotation comes from a Hadith:
'Abu Hurairah reports that he heard the Prophet say: 'If one of you has a river at his door in which he washes himself five times a day, what do you think? Would it leave any dirt on him? The Companions said, 'It would not leave any dirt on him [he would be perfectly clean]'. *The Prophet said, 'This is an example of the five prayers with which Allah blots out the evils of man.'*

On more than one occasion the Prophet likened prayer to washing in a stream. What do you think his listeners learned about prayer from this image?

Wudu

Ritual prayers are offered to Allah in a disciplined way and must be preceded by ritual cleansing (ablutions) of both the person and the place. This cleansing, called 'wudu', always follows the same, strict pattern and begins, as does the prayer sequence itself, with a declaration of intent by the worshipper that he or she will worship Allah with a pure heart. This declaration is called the 'niyyah'. Then the hands, the mouth, the face, the arms as far as the elbows, the top of the head, the ears, the back of the neck, and the feet as far as the ankles are all washed three times (see Photograph A).

Washing facilities are provided in or just outside the mosque for each worshipper to complete his ablutions. In areas where no running water is available for washing,

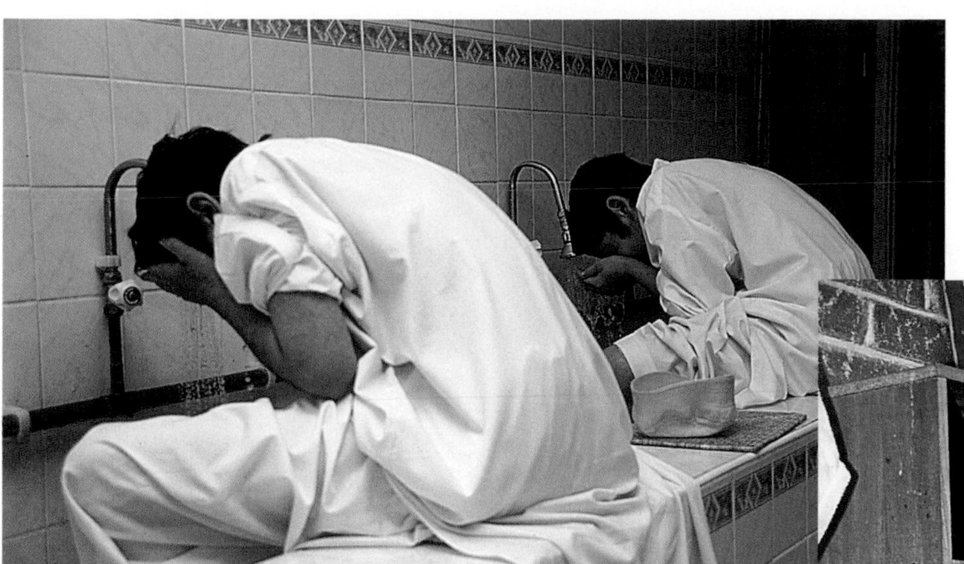

A. These people are washing in preparation for prayer. Many religions place a high degree of importance on physical as well as spiritual cleansing. Why do you think that they suggest that each person must be 'clean' before they enter God's presence?

The Qur'an permits the use of fine, clean sand. When they are not in a mosque, Muslims use a prayer mat on which to pray, since this guarantees that the place itself is 'clean'. Shoes or sandals are removed before a person enters the mosque and stored for collection afterwards (see Photograph B). Inside or outside the mosque each worshipper must face Makkah while praying, and Muslims who are travelling will usually carry a compass with them so that they can locate the holy city accurately. In the mosque the direction of Makkah (called 'qiblah') is indicated by a niche in the wall known as a mihrab.

B. Many religions expect worshippers to remove their shoes before they enter a religious building to pray and worship. Can you think of any reason why this is thought to be important?

FOR YOUR FOLDER

1 The Prophet Muhammad said this about prayer: *'Prayer said in a congregation is twenty-seven times more excellent than prayer said by a single person.'*

a) What do you think that Muhammad meant by '*Prayer said in a congregation*'?
b) What do Muslims call prayers which are said by a person on their own and how do they differ from prayers which Muslims offer together in the mosque?
c) Can you think of two reasons why Muhammad might have suggested that prayers said together in a congregation are much more (twenty-seven times more) effective than those which a person prays on their own?

2 Here are two quotations from The Hadith about prayer. Read them through carefully:
'He who abandons prayer demolishes the very pillar of religion.'
'Worship Allah as if you see Him; if you do not see Him know that He sees you.'

a) What do you think '*the very pillar of religion*' means and what does this tell you about the importance of prayer?
b) The second quotation makes a very important point about Allah and the nature of prayer. What is it?

In the glossary: Allah; Arabic; Du'a; Imam; Makkah; Mihrab; Mosque; Niyyah; Qur'an; Salah; Shahadah; Wudu.

Salah (2)

What *is Rak'ah and what are the first actions?*

FOCUSING QUESTIONS

How important is prayer to a faithful Muslim – and why?

What is rak'ah?

How does a Muslim expresses his or her belief in the greatness of Allah in each rak'ah sequence?

DISCUSS

Muslim prayer is not merely a means of submitting to Allah, but also bestows blessings on the person praying. What are these blessings and why do you think that they are important?

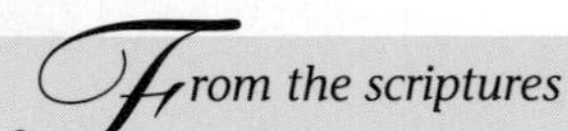

From the scriptures

This quotation from The Qur'an expresses a very important truth: *'Woe betide those who pray but are heedless in their prayer; who make a show of piety and forbid almsgiving* [giving to charity].' (Surah 10.77)

According to this extract, what link is made between prayer and working to help those who are in need?

Prayer is the heart and essence of Islam. Any Muslim who wilfully avoids prayer is considered to have forsaken the religion of Islam. So important is prayer to Muslims that it is considered to have been the first duty imposed by Allah on human beings after the belief in his Oneness. Muslims believe that prayer, submission to Allah, strengthens the very foundations of faith and helps the individual to gain peace and stability in their heart. The discipline of prayer leads to patience, courage, hope and sincerity. The obligation to pray is not just a command laid upon every Muslim as a duty – it is primarily an act of homage and submission offered to God.

Friday prayers

One day a week, Friday, is set aside for all male Muslims to gather in the mosque at noon to pray. Women are excused from this as they are considered as having family obligations, although some women do go to the mosque and pray separately from the men. This day is not a 'day of rest' like the Jewish Shabbat, but all trading activity is suspended for prayers: '*Believers, when you are summoned to Friday prayers hasten to the remembrance of God and cease your trading. That would be best for you, if you but knew it*' (Surah 62.9).

Rak'ahs

Prayer for Muslims involves sequences of inner and outer actions which include ablutions and the recitation of specific phrases accompanied by prescribed body movements. Each complete sequence of prayer is called a 'rak'ah' and the number of these sequences performed at any one time varies from two to four, depending on the time of the day. There are eight bodily movements in every rak'ah sequence, and each has a religious significance. Photographs 1 to 4, on the page opposite, show the first four actions in the sequence of prayer.

1. During the first stage of the rak'ah, the worshipper stands with their hands at their sides. This expresses the intent to begin devotions and an acknowledgement of Allah's lordship.

2. In the second stage, the worshiper stands with thumbs on the lobes of the ears and the fingers spread out whilst reciting the Shahadah.

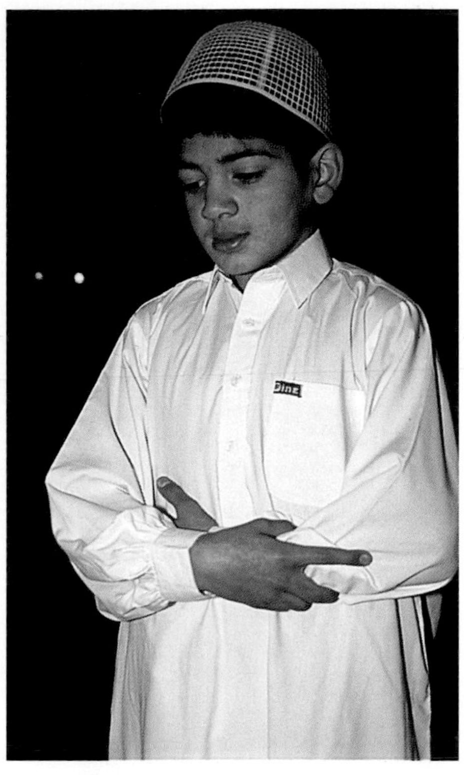

3. The worshipper then recites the al-Fatihah while standing with the palm of the right hand resting on the back of the left hand, which lies across the chest. The al-Fatihah, which means 'the opener', is the first surah (division) of The Qur'an. This includes the words *'You alone we worship, and to You alone we turn for help.'* Any other passage from The Qur'an may then be recited.

4. The worshipper then bends from the hips, keeping their back straight, and spreading their fingers on their knees. Three times the words are repeated: *'Glory be to my great Lord and praise be to Him'*. This is an expression of love for Allah whilst acknowledging His greatness and power.

FOR YOUR FOLDER

The Prophet Muhammad said:
'The prayer said in Madinah is worth thousands of others, except that in Makkah, which is worth a hundred thousand. But worth more than all this is the prayer said in the house where no-one sees but God, and which has no other object than to draw close to God.'

a) Why are Makkah and Madinah mentioned as the two places in which prayer is so valuable?
b) What do you think that the Prophet meant when he referred to *'prayer said in the house'*?
c) What is the sole object of the prayer which is worth so much more than all the others?

In the glossary: ALLAH; AL-FATIHAH; MADINAH; MAKKAH; MOSQUE; QUR'AN; RAK'AH; SHAHADAH.

Salah (3)

What are the final movements of the rak'ah?

FOCUSING QUESTIONS

Which emotions are being expressed by the worshipper as he or she works through the rak'ah sequence?

What is the worshipper expressing about Allah by adopting the prostrate position?

How do the arrangements for Muslim women to pray differ from those for men?

Both the words spoken and the actions performed in the final movements of the rak'ah sequence follow the example set by the Prophet Muhammad. They express the total submission to Allah which is the heart of true Islam. Photographs 5 to 8, on the opposite page, show the final movements of this sequence of prayer.

Blessing and the Shahadah

After the rak'ah sequence is completed blessings are asked in the name of the Prophet Muhammad. The index-finger of the right hand is raised during a declaration of the profession of faith (the Shahadah) and then a prayer of blessing follows for Muhammad and his family together with another prayer asking Allah to bless the worshipper in this world and the next – and to deliver him or her from the horrors of Hell. Next, the worshipper turns their head to the right and to the left while declaring: *'Peace be with you and the mercy of Allah.'* This is addressed to those who are on either side of him or her, the whole worshipping congregation, the angels in Heaven, and all departed spirits (the dead). Finally special prayers are made to God – with hands held open in front with palms facing upward.

Muslim women and prayer

In Muhammad's time women attended Friday prayers in the mosques, although they either stood behind the men or to one side of them. The Prophet believed, though, that it was preferable for women to pray at home and the majority of Muslim women still do so. In most mosques, however, a room is set aside for women to pray if they wish, since they are not allowed to pray alongside the men in public.

From the scriptures

This saying of the Prophet Muhammad comes from a Hadith:
'Make frequent prostrations before Allah, for you will not make one prostration without Him raising a degree because of it, and removing a sin because of it.'

1 What is a 'prostration'?
2 How many times does a worshipper adopt the prostrate position during a rak'ah, and what does adopting this position imply?
3 Why do you think that expressing praise and thankfulness for past blessings received from Allah is just as important as seeking forgiveness and peace?

FOR YOUR FOLDER

1 What influence do you think that praying five times a day is likely to have upon a Muslim worshipper and upon the 'health' of the Muslim community?

2
a) If a person believes it is their duty to humbly worship an Almighty God do you think a strict discipline of prayer is a valuable part of that worship?
b) What do you think might be gained from such a strict discipline?
c) Do you think there is anything to be gained from loosening the discipline and adopting a more spontaneous approach to prayer?
d) What do you think the lasting effect of disciplined prayer might be?

5. Going down on their knees the worshipper bends forward and touches the ground with their nose, forehead, and the palms of both hands. This humblest position is called 'sujud'. The worshipper repeats the words: '*Glory be to my Lord, the Most High, God is greater than all else*' three times. This assures the worshipper that Allah hears his or her prayers. The worshipper returns to the sujud position after movement 6.

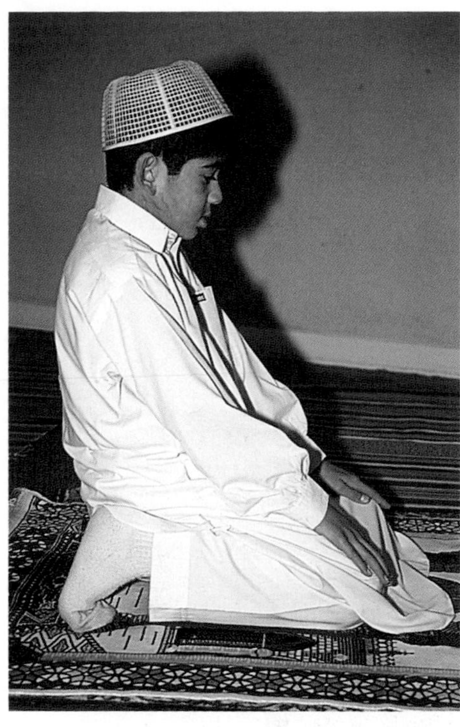

6. Following prostration the worshipper kneels again, resting the palms of both hands on the knees. Here he or she meditates for a moment before asking: '*O my Master, forgive me!*' At this point the rak'ah sequence is almost complete.

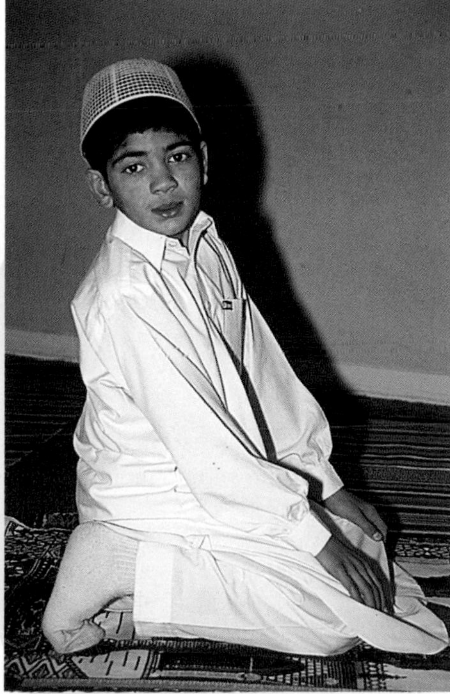

7 & 8. As the sequence ends the worshipper prays for the Prophet, for the faithful and for the congregation, and asks that his or her sins might be forgiven. The final action is to turn the head to the right and to the left to acknowledge the other worshippers and the guardian angels, before saying the words: '*Peace be upon you and the mercy of Allah*'. This final prayer is called the salam.

In the glossary: Allah; Angel; Mosque; Muhammad; Prostration; Rak'ah. Shahadah.

Zakah

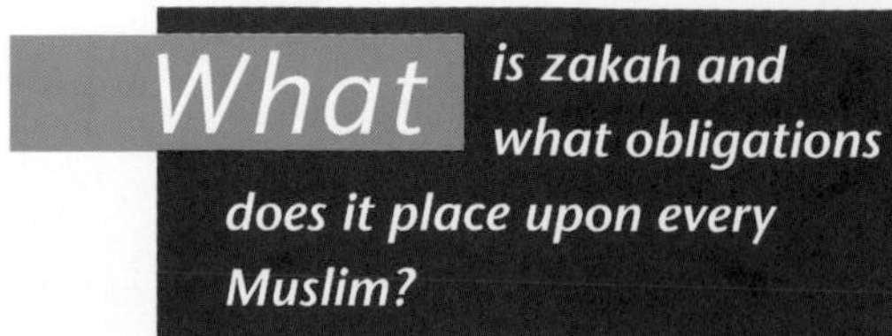

What is zakah and what obligations does it place upon every Muslim?

FOCUSING QUESTIONS

Which events in Muhammad's life gave him a great concern for widows and orphans?

What are the principles which should govern the giving of zakah to the poor?

Why is zakah such an important Muslim duty?

DISCUSS

Muslims believe that giving, and receiving, zakah is not charity. Why?

From his early experiences as an orphan who lost both of his parents by the age of six, Muhammad knew what it was like to be poor and he had a special concern for widows and those without parents throughout his life. This can be clearly seen by looking at the words of the Prophet, which are recorded in The Hadith: *'One who manages the affairs of the widow and the needy is like one who exerts himself very hard in the way of God.'* For modern Muslims, the concern for, and duty towards, the needy expressed by Muhammad, is still an important part of their faith.

The third Pillar

The third duty (Pillar) of every Muslim, is to give alms (money) to the poor as an outward sign of their devotion to Allah. There are two kinds of alms-giving which are encouraged:

1. The legal requirement – zakah – which stipulates that a Muslim must give 2.5 per cent of their wealth each year to charity. In Muslim countries this operates like a tax since the government collects it and distributes it to the poor in the community. In Britain, however, zakah is collected at the mosque (see Photograph A) and so the paying of it becomes a personal matter between the individual and Allah. Every Muslim is expected to make their own arrangements to pay it and to decide just how it is going to be used. Paying zakah is a test of a person's honesty – every Muslim knows that they will be accountable to Allah on the Day of Judgement if they do not pay what they owe.

2. The voluntary donation – sadaqah – which can be given to charity at any time. This donation should preferably be made in secret.

Spiritual duty

The donating of zakah is an important spiritual obligation which The Qur'an demands of every Muslim and which is the most important spiritual duty on every Muslim apart from praying. Although the minimum required by the holy book is $^{1}/_{40}$ of a person's wealth there is no upper limit on the amount given – as long as a person does not jeopardise the welfare of their family by their gift. Many Muslims show their devotion to Allah by giving a higher percentage than required. All giving to the poor should be generous since a person's wealth has been given to them in the first place by Allah. A Hadith reminds each Muslim that: *'He is not a believer who eats his fill while his neighbour remains hungry by his side.'*

The importance of zakah

Muslims consider zakah to be important for a number of reasons. First, it purifies the remainder of a person's money, whilst keeping their soul free from an excessive dependency on money and wealth. For those who give, zakah is a great spiritual blessing since they are only giving back to Allah what He has already given them. Secondly, zakah purifies the soul of the one who receives the gift. Zakah is not the giving of charity since Muslims believe that all members of the Muslim community have a right to share God's blessings.

A. This photograph shows zakah being collected in a mosque in London, but what is the basic difference between this collection and voluntary giving to the poor and those in need?

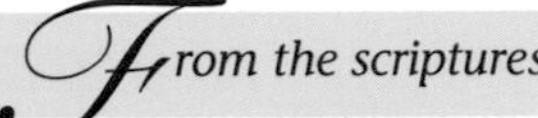

From the scriptures

1 The Qur'an explains the importance of giving zakah:
'Attend to your prayers, render the alms levy [zakah], *and give God a generous loan. Whatever good you do you shall surely find it with God, ennobled and richly rewarded by Him. Implore God to forgive you; God is forgiving and merciful.'*
(Surah 73.24)

a) What do you think The Qur'an means when it says *'...give God a generous loan'*?
b) What promise is implied in this extract for all those who do good to others?

2 This extract is from The Qur'an:
'Attend to your prayers and render the alms levy. Whatever good you do shall be rewarded by God. God is watching all your actions.'
(Surah 2.110)

a) Give one reason why you think that prayer and giving zakah go together?
b) What do you think The Qur'an means when it says: *'Whatever good you do shall be rewarded by God'*?

FOR YOUR FOLDER

1
a) What is zakah?
b) How does a Muslim seek to make sure that some of his or her wealth is used to meet the acute needs of others?
c) Why do you think that Islam encourages such generosity?
d) Why does it link this generosity with the receiving of spiritual blessings, including forgiveness, from Allah?

In the glossary: ALLAH; HADITH; MOSQUE; MUHAMMAD; QUR'AN; ZAKAH

Sawm

What happens during the month of Ramadan?

FOCUSING QUESTIONS

What is sawm?

What are Muslims remembering when they keep the fast of Ramadan?

How does the fast of Ramadan bring the Muslim community worldwide together?

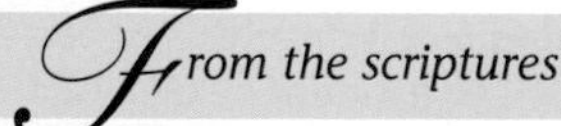

From the scriptures

The Qur'an gives this advice about fasting:
'Believers, fasting is decreed for you as it was decreed for those before you; perchance you will guard yourselves against evil. Fast a certain number of days, but if any one among you is ill or on a journey, let him fast a similar number of days later...He that does good of his own accord shall be well rewarded; but to fast is better for you, if you but knew it.'
(Sura 2.183-184)

1 What is fasting?
2 Why do many religious people fast?
3 Which month in the Muslim calendar is set aside specifically for fasting – and how does this fasting differ from that carried out at other times?
4 What does this extract from The Qur'an suggest might be a spiritual benefit from fasting?

Fasting, common in many religions, is the subjecting of the body to the absence of food and drink for lasting spiritual benefits. Many Muslims, like the followers of other world religions, fast for spiritual reasons throughout the year. The fourth duty (Pillar) of Islam, however, specifies that all Muslims must fast during the entire twenty-nine days of the ninth month of the Muslim calendar – the month of Ramadan. Fasting may take place at other times as well, but during Ramadan fasting (sawm) must be complete – abstaining totally from all food, drink and sexual intercourse during daylight hours.

Tradition states that it was during this month of Ramadan that Muhammad received the first revelation recorded in The Qur'an from the Angel Jibril. This took place on the 27 Ramadan, which is called the 'Night of Power'. As a consequence fasting, which takes place during this time, is thought to be thirty times more effective than any other fasting. Those who keep the fast faithfully during Ramadan, in a spirit of sincere repentance, are assured that all of their sins will be forgiven by Allah.

Fasting during Ramadan

The Islamic calendar is based on a lunar system which means that the month of Ramadan can fall at any time of the year. This makes a considerable difference to those fasting, since it is a major deprivation to go without food and drink during the very hot months. During the entire month of Ramadan all healthy Muslim adults are expected to fast each day from sunrise to sunset. The Qur'an lays down a simple rule for deciding exactly when the fast should start and end each day: *'Eat and drink until you can tell a white thread from a black one in the light of the coming dawn. Then resume the fast till nightfall.'* The only exceptions to the rule about fasting are children (who will be introduced to fasting gradually), the sick, the elderly, nursing or pregnant women and travellers.

Those whose inability to fast is only temporary are expected to make the full time up at a later date. No smoking is allowed during the fast and toothpaste cannot be used. A high level of behaviour is also expected to support the spiritual benefits derived from the fast. In addition, most Muslims observe 'the withdrawal to a mosque' during Ramadan – especially during the last ten days of the fast. This 'retreat' commemorates the time that the first revelation was received by the Prophet Muhammad.

A. This Muslim family are enjoying their last meal before the fast of Ramadan begins. What spiritual benefits do you think they are hoping to gain from the month ahead?

The spiritual benefits of Ramadan

The fast at Ramadan is an activity that links together Muslims throughout the world, and so is a very important way of strengthening the Muslim community. The fast is also a reminder to those Muslims who have never experienced hunger and poverty just what it is like to be poor. Hunger is a universal experience, and quite apart from making everyone equal for a time the fast also provides each Muslim with the opportunity of understanding why The Qur'an condemns poverty and need. The benefits of Ramadan for a Muslim, though, go much further. The month provides an opportunity to concentrate the heart and mind on Allah by praying more, giving to charity, contemplating on his or her relationship with God, and giving time to complete a full reading of The Qur'an. By increasing an individual's self-discipline, the fasting of Ramadan is also believed to draw worshippers a little closer to the angels who, Muslims believe, alone behave perfectly in God's presence.

DISCUSS

Do you think that it is a good idea for people to fast? What might people learn by experiencing – even for a short period of time – what it is like to be hungry?

FOR YOUR FOLDER

a) What is being celebrated during Ramadan?
b) Why is fasting carried out during Ramadan thought to be thirty times more effective than fasting at any other time?
c) Which groups of people are exempt from the Ramadan fast – and what are some of them expected to do later?
d) What are some of the spiritual benefits which come through fasting?

In the glossary: ANGEL; JIBRIL; MUHAMMAD; QUR'AN; RAMADAN; SAWM.

The Hajj (1)

What is a Hajj and how do Muslim pilgrims prepare for it?

FOCUSING QUESTIONS

What is a Hajj?

What conditions is a Muslim expected to meet before he or she undertakes a Hajj?

What is ihram?

The fifth, and final, duty (Pillar) for every Muslim is to make a pilgrimage to the holy shrine of the Ka'bah in Makkah, Saudi Arabia. It is an obligation which has to be fulfilled by every fit Muslim (those who are old, mentally ill, sick or disabled are exempt) at least once in his or her lifetime – as long as they can provide for their family when they are away and meet the cost of the journey. The pilgrimage can only be performed between the eighth and thirteenth days of the last month, Dhul-Hijjah, in the Islamic year.

The fifth Pillar

Hajj, meaning 'setting out on a definite purpose', is designed to purify all participants from their pride and prejudice and to make them realise that everyone, rich and poor, will be equal before Allah on the Day of Judgement. It is hoped that the spirit of companionship and oneness with other Muslims which are experienced on the Hajj will then be carried over into everyday life when they return. Moreover most Muslims find a visit to places closely associated with the Prophet Muhammad to be a deeply moving spiritual experience (see Photograph B).

A. A view the Ka'bah, covered by black cloth and surrounded by pilgrims. How was the Ka'bah first dedicated to the worship of Allah?

Makkah and the Ka'bah

Long before the time of Muhammad Makkah had been a holy centre to which Arabs came annually on a pilgrimage to the sacred, cube-shaped, shrine called the Ka'bah which was in the city. Set in the south-east corner of the Ka'bah is a black stone, over sixteen metres high, which tradition says was given to Ibrahim by the Angel Jibril. The stone was believed to be so holy that its pure white radiance drew pilgrims to Makkah like a shining light until human wickedness turned it black.

When Muhammad liberated the city of Makkah he cleansed the Ka'bah and dedicated it to the worship of the one God, Allah. The floor inside the shrine is made of marble and the walls are lined with marble slabs. Each year, for the Hajj, the Ka'bah is covered with a new black covering made of silk and

B. Muslim pilgrims outside the Dome of the Rock, Jerusalem, Israel. In addition to undertaking a Hajj to Makkah, many Muslims, also feel the need to undertake journeys to other places of religious significance. Why do you think this is?

wool and covered with texts from The Qur'an (see Photograph A). After Hajj this covering is cut up into small pieces and sold to the pilgrims. The one entrance in the Ka'bah is in the north-east side and rarely opened.

Ihram

Each year some two million pilgrims travel from all parts of the world and converge on the city of Makkah which is in Saudi Arabia. There are three stages to the Hajj. The first begins when the pilgrims discard their own clothing and remove their shoes or sandals. Men must put on two white, seamless, garments one of which is wrapped around the waist, reaching below the knees, and the other is draped around the left shoulder and tied at the right hand side. Women normally wear a long, plain dress and a head-covering – veils are not allowed during the Hajj. During this time, called 'ihram', pilgrims must also perform certain washing (ablution) rites, pray and make a declaration of an intention of completing the Hajj, and abstain from shaving any part of the body, cutting nails, using oil or perfumes, entering into any sexual relations, plucking grass or cutting down trees. When these measures have been taken the pilgrim is in the correct spiritual frame of mind to undertake the Hajj.

From the scriptures

This quotation is from The Qur'an:
'Make the pilgrimage in the appointed months. He that intends to perform it in those months must abstain from sexual intercourse, obscene language, and acrimonious disputes while on pilgrimage. God is aware of whatever good you do. Provide well for yourselves: the best provision is piety [holiness].'
(Surah 2.197)

1 When are the *'appointed months'* for making this pilgrimage?
2 What is the pilgrim to abstain from and what is he or she to do positively?
3 What do you think *'Provide well for yourselves: the best provision is piety'* means?

FOR YOUR FOLDER

1
a) What is ihram and what changes – outward and inward – are likely once the pilgrim has reached the holy city of Makkah?
b) Why do you think that all pilgrims, rich and poor, have to dress identically for the Hajj? What spiritual lesson might this teach them?
c) Why do you think that pilgrims are not allowed to take any steps to improve their appearance whilst they are on the Hajj?

2 A Muslim male who has successfully completed a Hajj is called a 'Hajji'. A Muslim woman is called a 'Hajjah'. Many Hajjis keep their pilgrimage clothes so that they can be buried in them. Why do you think that they associate the Hajj with their own death in this way?

3 See Photograph B. How do you think that religious people might benefit from undertaking a pilgrimage?

In the glossary: Allah; Day of Judgement; Dome of the Rock; Hajj; Hajjah; Hajji; Ibrahim; Jibril; Ka'bah; Makkah; Muhammad; Qur'an.

The Hajj (2)

What *does the Hajj mean for the Muslim pilgrim?*

FOCUSING QUESTIONS

What happens when the pilgrims enter Makkah?

What happens at Mina?

How does the Hajj end?

Once pilgrims have prepared themselves for the Hajj by entering a state of spiritual preparation called ihram, they finally enter the holy city of Makkah, Saudi Arabia. This marks the first part of the three stages to the Hajj that pilgrims must complete (see Map B).

The holy city

Just like the Prophet Muhammad on his final visit to Makkah, in 632, so pilgrims approach the Ka'bah in Makkah, and walk around the shrine seven times in an anti-clockwise direction in order to draw close to Allah. This action is called the 'tawaf'. Three of their circuits are completed quickly, but during the fourth, the pilgrims pause as they pass the Ka'bah to kiss or touch the Black Stone in the south-west corner. Sometimes, though, the crowd is so great that most pilgrims can only hope to touch the stone with a stick – if that! (See Photograph A.)

A. The Mosque complex at Makkah, Saudi Arabia. The Ka'bah, to the right of the photograph, is surrounded by thousands of pilgrims all hoping to touch the Black Stone. Why do you think that pilgrims hope to be able to kiss or touch the Black Stone in the Ka'bah?

Next, the pilgrims go to certain spots for prayer, after which they walk rapidly or run across the valley (now a covered walkway) between the two mounds of Safa and Marwah. These mounds are some 420 metres apart, and the journey between them reminds each pilgrim of Hajar's search for water. Desperate to help her son, Isma'il, she searched frantically with no luck, but on returning to her son found that he had dug his toes in the sand and discovered water (the well of Zamzam). This story is similar to that told in the Jewish Scriptures about Abraham's sending his concubine Hagar and her son Ishmael out into the desert. The running between Safa and Marwah is called 'sa'y'.

Mount Mercy

Following visit to the Ka'bah, pilgrims then travel from Makkah to Mount Mercy, in the plain of Arafat, about 24 kilometres from the holy city. A vast camp is erected on this site where Muhammad is believed to have preached his Last Sermon to the people on the last pilgrimage. Once there each pilgrim 'stands before God' from noon (as soon as the Sun has passed its meridian) to sunset in holy meditation. This act of 'standing before God' is the second of the three stages undertaken during the pilgrimage, and one of the most significant acts of the Hajj.

The Pillars of Mina

Stage three of the Hajj starts after sunset, when the pilgrims return to Muzdalifah, between Mina and Arafat, to spend the night camping out in the open. The following morning they return to Mina, a village east of Makkah, to throw seven stones at each of three pillars which represent Iblis (the devil). It was the devil who tempted Isma'il to run away three times when Abraham was about to sacrifice him at the command of God.

After this animals are sacrificed followed by four days of festivities which are celebrated by Muslims everywhere (in the festival of Id-ul-Adha). A final circuit of the Ka'bah back in Makkah, the discarding of the ihram garment and a haircut (for women just a symbolic clipping of a few hairs) mark the end of the Hajj. The pilgrim is now entitled to adopt the honoured title of 'Hajji' (for males) or 'Hajjah' (for females) meaning one who has made the pilgrimage to Makkah. Whilst most of the pilgrims return home, some travel on to Madinah to visit the tomb of the Prophet, Muhammad, or go on to visit other sites of religious significance.

There are millions of Muslims who cannot undertake the pilgrimage for reasons of health or poverty. The Qur'an excuses such people as long as they had the 'intention' of going if their circumstances had been different. The custom now, though, is for pilgrims who cannot go in person to contribute as much as they can to send a substitute. The pilgrimage by the substitute brings merit on all those who contributed to make the visit possible.

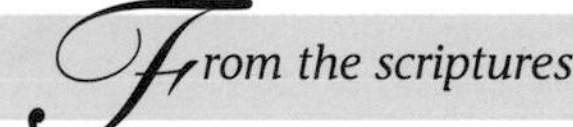

The words are found in The Qur'an about the Hajj:
'Exhort all men to make the pilgrimage. They will come to you on foot and on the backs of swift camels from every distant quarter; they will come to avail themselves of many a benefit, and to pronounce on the appointed days the name of God over the cattle which He has given them for food. Eat of their flesh, and feed the poor and the unfortunate. Then let the pilgrims tidy themselves, make their vows, and circle the Ancient House. Such is God's commandment.'

(Surah 22.28-29)

Explain how three of the directions in this quotation from The Qur'an are fulfilled in the way that the Hajj is carried out.

FOR YOUR FOLDER

1 Explain, in your own words, what happens at each of the following places on the Hajj: Makkah; Safa and Marwah; Mount Mercy; the Plain of Arafat; Mina.

2 Describe what is meant by: tawaf; sa'y; Hajji; Hajjah.

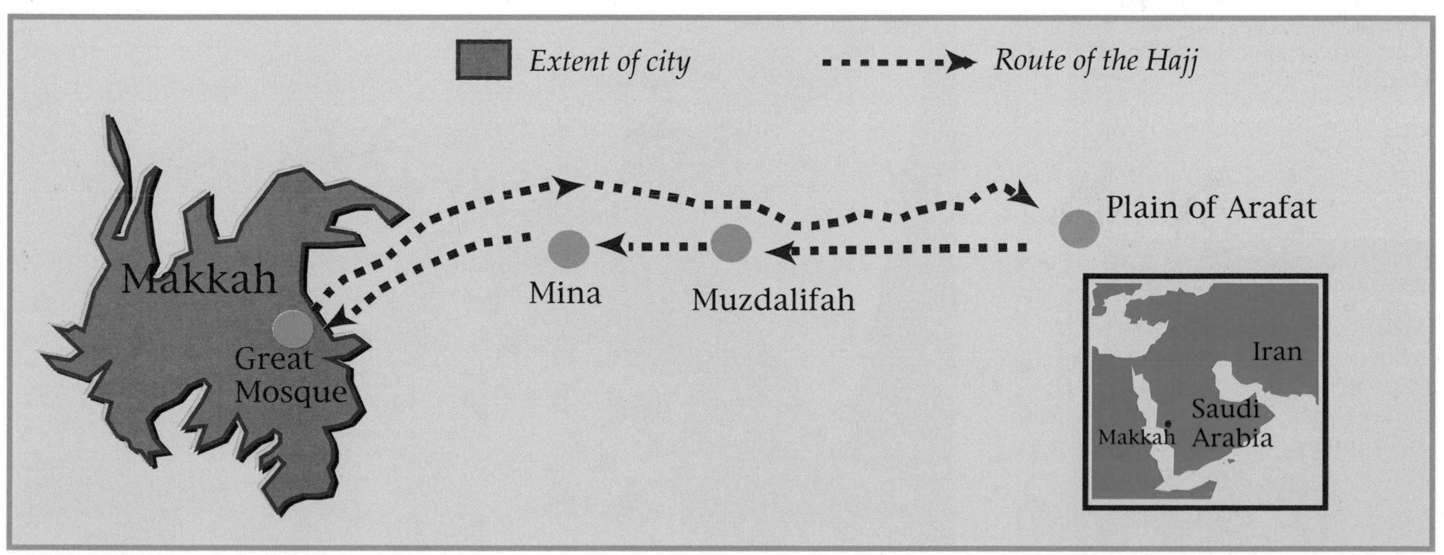

B. This map shows the route followed by the pilgrim on the Hajj.

In the glossary: Allah; Hajar; Hajj; Hajjah; Hajji; Iblis; Ibrahim; Id-ul-Adha; Isma'il; Ka'bah; Madinah; Makkah; Muhammad; Qur'an.

Id-ul-Fitr and Ramadan

***How** do Muslims celebrate the festival of Id-ul-Fitr and why is it an important festival?*

FOCUSING QUESTIONS

Why does Islam have fewer festivals and celebrations than almost any other religion?

What does the imam remind Muslims about in his sermon on Id-ul-Fitr?

How is Id-ul-Fitr celebrated?

Festivals and religious celebrations are not so important in Islam as they are in the other great world religions. In part, this may be due to the uncompromising belief in the one God held by Muhammad and his early companions as they tried to stamp out all pagan practices. It may also be due to the Muslim practice of praying five times a day and other religious activities which generate such a feeling of community amongst believers that festivals have been considered unnecessary and a distraction.

Two festivals, though, involve the Muslim community throughout the world. Id-ul-Adha, which comes at the end of the Hajj and Id-ul-Fitr. Id-ul-Fitr is also known as Id-ul-Saghir (meaning the 'lesser Id'), or (in Turkey) Sheker Bayram, meaning the 'sugar feast'. Id-ul-Fitr, marks the end of the fast of Ramadan. Both festivals act as a welcome reminder to Muslims that they are part of a worldwide Muslim 'family'.

A. Id-ul-Fitr cards, shown right, are sent as part of the celebrations for this festival. What is the link between Id-ul-Fitr and the fast of Ramadan?

DISCUSS

What do you think is the real value and purpose of religious festivals? Are they mainly a time of worship or do they have some other purpose?

B. This child's balloons carry the words 'Id mubarak', meaning 'Id blessings'. How do celebrations for Id-ul-Fitr traditionally start?

Attending the mosque

The three-day festival of Id-ul-Fitr begins on the first day of the tenth month of the Islamic year – Shawal. Before it begins, Muslims observe zakah when people give money to those in the Muslim community who are in need. The amount given should be enough for a poor family to buy a meal since no-one should feel hungry or deprived on Id-ul-Fitr.

Few people go to bed on the last night of Ramadan as they gather on the streets to watch the rising of the new Moon which marks the beginning of the festival. Sometimes the mosque is not large enough to hold the worshippers who wish to be there for this occasion and several services might need to be held or the crowd spills out into the open-air. The 'imam' (leader) leads the people in special prayers before delivering a sermon in which the people are reminded that they have a special responsibility towards the poor. The people are told that being generous to those in need is a way of expressing their thankfulness to Allah for all His blessings to them. The imam also reminds the people that they have only been able to successfully complete the fast of Ramadan through Allah's help. They are told that Muhammad himself promised his followers that two rewards would be theirs through fasting:

- The pleasure that is given to them by Allah when the fast has been successfully completed. 'Id' means 'reoccurring happiness', and Id-ul-Fitr is an occasion for celebration.
- A reward from Allah on the Day of Judgement – those who have successfully completed the fast of Ramadan can look forward to Allah's reward.

Celebrating Id-ul-Fitr

After the service has finished in the mosque everyone returns home – often to large family gatherings. The houses are decorated with Id cards and these carry the words 'Id Mubarak' (meaning 'Id blessings'). Potato pasties, called samosas, carrot pudding with salad mixed with yoghurt , and syrupy orange jalebi sweets are eaten. Presents are exchanged and opened by members of the family. Finally, a visit is paid to the cemetery since everyone is anxious to remember those who have been separated from them by death. At Id-ul-Fitr everyone – the living and the dead – are united.

So Ramadan ends. The fast and the festival of Id-ul-Fitr are reminders to everyone of the time when Muhammad was in the desert. For the whole month of Ramadan Muslims have passed through a spiritual 'desert' together but now, as they look towards the coming months, they can expect to enjoy Allah's blessings once again.

FOR YOUR FOLDER

a) Which two important events in the Muslim calendar provide the occasion for celebrating the festivals of: Id-ul-Fitr; Id-ul-Adha?
b) What are all Muslims expected to do before the festival of Id-ul-Fitr begins – and why?
c) How long does the festival of Id-ul-Fitr last for and when does it begin?
d) The imam, in his sermon, gives the people a reason why they should look after the needy. What is it?
e) Why does everyone visit the cemetery as part of their Id-ul-Fitr celebrations?
f) What are the people likely to have learned through the fast of Ramadan and the festival of Id-ul-Fitr?

In the glossary: Allah; Day of Judgement; Hajj; Id-ul-Adha; Id-ul-Fitr; Imam; Mosque; Muhammad; Ramadan; Zakah.

Id-ul-Adha

***What** is distinctive about the way that Muslims celebrate the festival of Id-ul-Adha?*

FOCUSING QUESTIONS

Why do Muslims celebrate the festival of Id-ul-Adha and what is the spiritual significance of the story of Ibrahim and Isma'il?

What conditions must be fulfilled for meat to be halal?

How does a visit to the cemetery play an important part of the Id-ul-Adha celebrations?

DISCUSS

Islam is the only religion which still slaughters animals as part of their worship. Why do you think that this is thought to be so important?

Id-ul-Adha, or Id-ul-Kabir, the 'greater Id' as it is sometimes called, begins on the tenth day of the month that pilgrimages to Mekkah occur and can last for two, three or four days – depending on the country in which it is being celebrated. Although the festival has particular significance for those on the hajj in Makkah it is celebrated by Muslims all over the world. The festival commemorates the story of Ibrahim's sacrifice of a sheep instead of killing his son, Isma'il (a story that is found in the Muslim, Jewish and Christian Scriptures), and pilgrims on the Hajj celebrate it in the valley of Mina where Muslims believe Ibrahim offered the sacrifice. In the story Ibrahim was willing to sacrifice his own son because he believed that Allah had ordered him to do so but Allah provided a ram at the last moment in Isma'il's place.

The Feast of Sacrifice

At the centre of the festival of Id-ul-Adha is the sacrifice of an animal (a sheep, goat, cow or camel) which has to be perfect in every way. In Muslim countries the responsibility for killing the animal falls on the man of the house since this forces the whole family to face up to the reality of sacrifice – an essential element in Muslim religious practice. In Western countries, however, Muslims are not allowed to carry out the slaughter of animals individually and they must be killed by a licensed slaughterer in an abattoir. Strict conditions are laid down in Islam for the slaughter of animals. They are:

- That the slaughter must be preceded by a short period of fasting and public prayer in the mosque. The sacrifice is a spiritual and not simply a practical act, although the animal will later be eaten.
- That the animal must not be frightened and that the death must take place in a humane way.
- That the animal must be turned towards Makkah and the slaughterer call on the name of Allah. He then recites verses from The Qur'an as he draws a very sharp knife across the animal's jugular vein in a single blow. All of the animal's blood is drained away since Muslims believe that eating any meat with blood in it is unclean. The life of the animal, it is believed, is found in its blood.

Meat which is killed in the correct ritual way is called 'halal' meat, whilst animals killed incorrectly, and so forbidden as food for Muslims, are called 'haram'. The animal killed at Id-ul-Adha is cooked and divided up into three parts: one for the family, one for neighbours and friends, and one for the poor. In poorer countries

A. What does halal mean?

In the glossary: ALLAH; HALAL; IBRAHIM; ID-UL-ADHA; ID-UL-FITR; HAJJ; ISLAM; MAKKAH; MUSLIM; QUR'AN.

B. Who slaughters the animals sold in this butchers in east London?

this festival is the only time that poorer members of the community have meat to eat.

At the end of the celebrations each Muslim visits the cemetery – as they do on Id-ul-Fitr. Palm branches are laid on the tombs of those members of the family who have died and food is given away to the poor at the cemetery. Professional mourners are hired to recite The Qur'an at the tombs before the men leave the cemetery. The women, however, keep up a vigil throughout the day and in many Muslim countries they remain watching throughout the night in tents specially erected for the occasion.

FOR YOUR FOLDER

1 Look at Photographs A and B.

a) What is the difference between halal and haram food?
b) What conditions have to be met if food is to be slaughtered in keeping with the halal regulations?
c) The slaughtering of animals for food in the Muslim community has been described as a 'spiritual exercise'. How is the process turned into a spiritual procedure and why do you think this is important?

2 The Islamic regulations about slaughtering animals often conflict with official regulations about slaughtering animals in other countries. As there are over two million Muslims in Britain do you think that all minority groups should be compelled to conform with the laws of the country – or should there be exceptions?

3 Why do you think that many religions teach that the life of an animal, or a human being, is in their blood?

4 Imagine that you are a Muslim celebrating the festival of Id-ul-Adha with your family.

a) How long will you spend celebrating the festival?
b) What reason will you be given for the celebration of the festival?
c) Why is it also called 'the Festival of Sacrifice'?
d) What spiritual benefits and blessings will you and your family hope to gain from the celebration?

Birth and Afterwards

How *is a baby welcomed into the community of Islam?*

FOCUSING QUESTIONS

Why is it important that a Muslim father whispers the Shahadah into the ear of a baby as soon as possible after birth?

Why is the head of a baby shaved soon after birth, and how does this help the poor in the community?

What is khitan?

All babies born into a Muslim family are considered to be gifts from Allah and so they must be welcomed into the ummah – the worldwide community of Islam – as soon as possible after birth. To do this the father takes the new baby into his arms and whispers the 'Shahadah' into the baby's right ear. This guarantees that the first word that the baby hears is the name of Allah. At the same time a small piece of sugar or a date is placed on the baby's tongue by an elderly relative to express the hope that the child will grow up to be generous and kind – a custom called tahnik.

Aqiqah

Seven days after birth the aqiqah ceremony is carried out at which time several important things take place:

- The child's head is shaved to symbolise the removal of all misfortune. Gold or silver equivalent to the same weight as the hair is distributed the poor before a sacrifice is carried out. Parents of children without any hair also make a suitable gift. If the child is a girl then one animal is sacrificed, and if it is a boy then two animals are killed. The meat is sweetened as it is cooked and one-third of the animal is eaten by members of the family and the remaining two-thirds distributed to the poor. These practices are all optional.

- The child is given a name. This happens after the father has read aloud several passages from The Qur'an. In Islam this carries a considerable significance and the child usually receives either one of Muhammad's many names, a name chosen from Muhammad's family, or one of Allah's ninety-nine names with the phrase 'abd', meaning servant added. The chosen name should be encouraging to the child but not encourage him or her to be conceited.

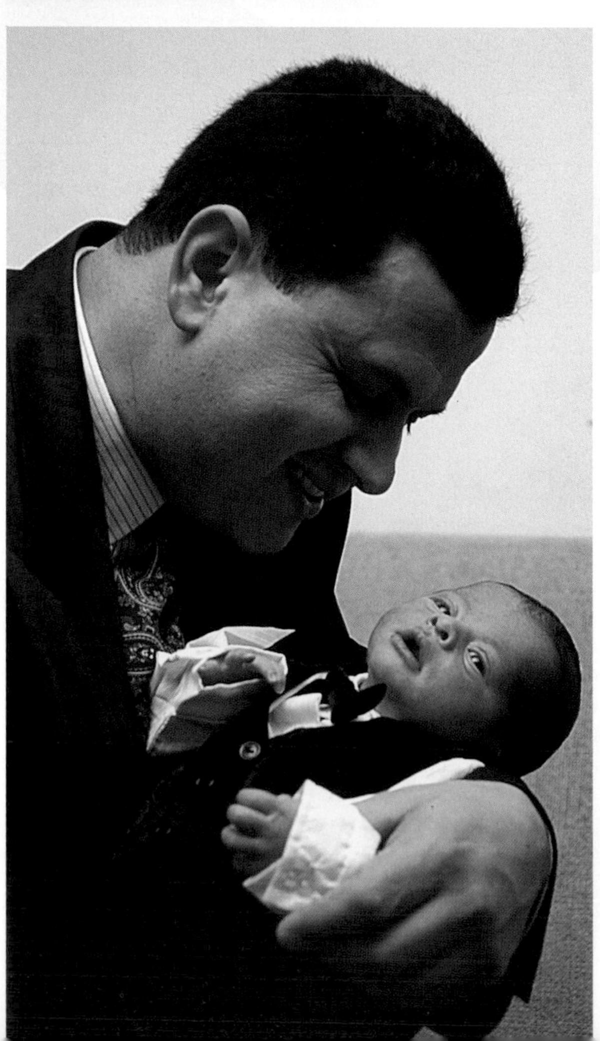

A. Why is it considered important that the child should hear the Shahadah within minutes of being born?

B. Girls studying in a madressah. Why do you think that Islam places such a high importance on the religious education of children?

Circumcision

Circumcision is an ancient religious practice in both Judaism and Islam. The early custom in Islam was to circumcise both boys and girls, but the circumcision of girls died out in almost all Muslim societies – although it still continues in a few places such as the Sudan in Africa. Due to the continual pain suffered by the girls however, it is strongly condemned by the vast majority of Muslims. There is no reference to circumcision (called 'khitan') in The Qur'an but it is mentioned in The Hadith – the sayings of the Prophet Muhammad. The operation is usually carried out when the child is a few days old but it can be delayed if there are medical reasons for doing so.

Bismillah

The bismillah ceremony usually takes place when the child is exactly four years, four months and four days old. The ceremony commemorates the first occasion when the Angel Jibril (Gabriel) appeared to Muhammad, and marks the beginning of the child's religious education – a very important event in the Muslim community. For the ceremony the child learns the first line of The Qur'an by heart.

Religious education

The religious education of a Muslim child is seen as a matter of great importance by parents and the community alike. The education which begins at bismillah is continued daily though the madressah (a school in the mosque) which the child attends after normal school. In the school every child learns to read and recite Arabic so that they can learn The Qur'an in its original language. Each child also learns how to perform the rak'ah in the madressah. (See Photograph B.)

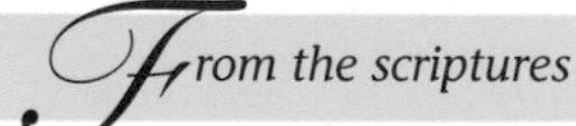

From the scriptures

This passage from The Qur'an speaks about the gift of children: *'To Allah belongs the kingdoms of the heaven and earth. He creates what He wills. He bestows sons and daughters according to His will. Or He bestows both sons and daughters, and leaves barren whom he chooses, for He is full of knowledge and power.'*

Describe, in your own words, the main point that this passage is making about the birth of children.

FOR YOUR FOLDER

1 Explain, in your own words:
a) The occasion on which the Shahadah is whispered into the baby's ear.
b) Tahnik.
c) Circumcision.
d) The bismillah ceremony.

2
a) Do you think that it is important for children of religious parents to be taught about their faith as soon as possible?
b) What do you think might be the main advantage of doing this?
c) What do you think might be the main disadvantage?

In the glossary: AQIQAH; ARABIC; BISMILLAH; JIBRIL; MOSQUE; MUHAMMAD; QUR'AN; RAK'AH; SHAHADAH; UMMAH.

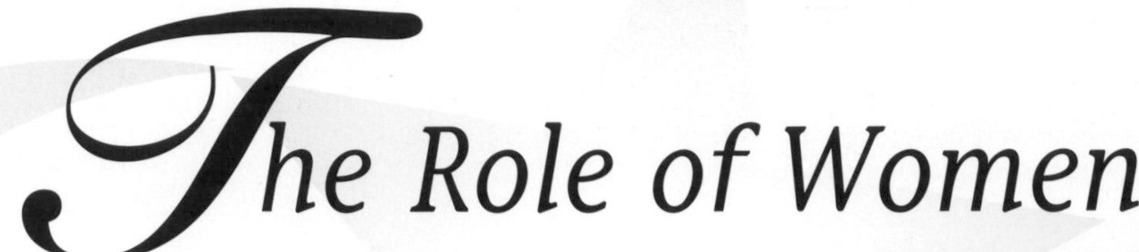

The Role of Women

What responsibilities and rights do women have in Islam?

FOCUSING QUESTIONS

What new teaching did Muhammad give his followers about women owning property?

What is 'hijab'?

What provision is made for women who want to pray in the mosque?

The Prophet Muhammad upheld the spiritual equality of all people – men and women. The Qur'an underlined that all people are the children of Adam and Eve and so are equal in God's sight. Muslims believe, however, that Allah has given men and women different, but complementary, roles to play in society and in the Muslim faith. Both The Qur'an and Muslim tradition have a great deal to say about the role that women should play in religious life, family life and, beyond that, in society generally.

Owning property

Before the time of Muhammad, women in Arabia had no rights and could not own any property in their own name. Muhammad changed that, and by so doing gave women a great deal of self-respect. He taught his followers that women could own property in their own name and dispose of it when they wished without needing the consent of a husband or male relative. They also were given the right to inherit property and wealth from a dead relative although they only receive fifty per cent of what a man in a similar position would inherit. This is not, though, because of any prejudice against women. The reason is that Muslim men are responsible for looking after and providing for their female relatives if they divorce. It is only fair, therefore, that a greater percentage of inherited money should go to them. Females carry no such responsibility for their male relatives.

A. Why was Muhammad's teaching that women could own property in their own right a very important step forward for women?

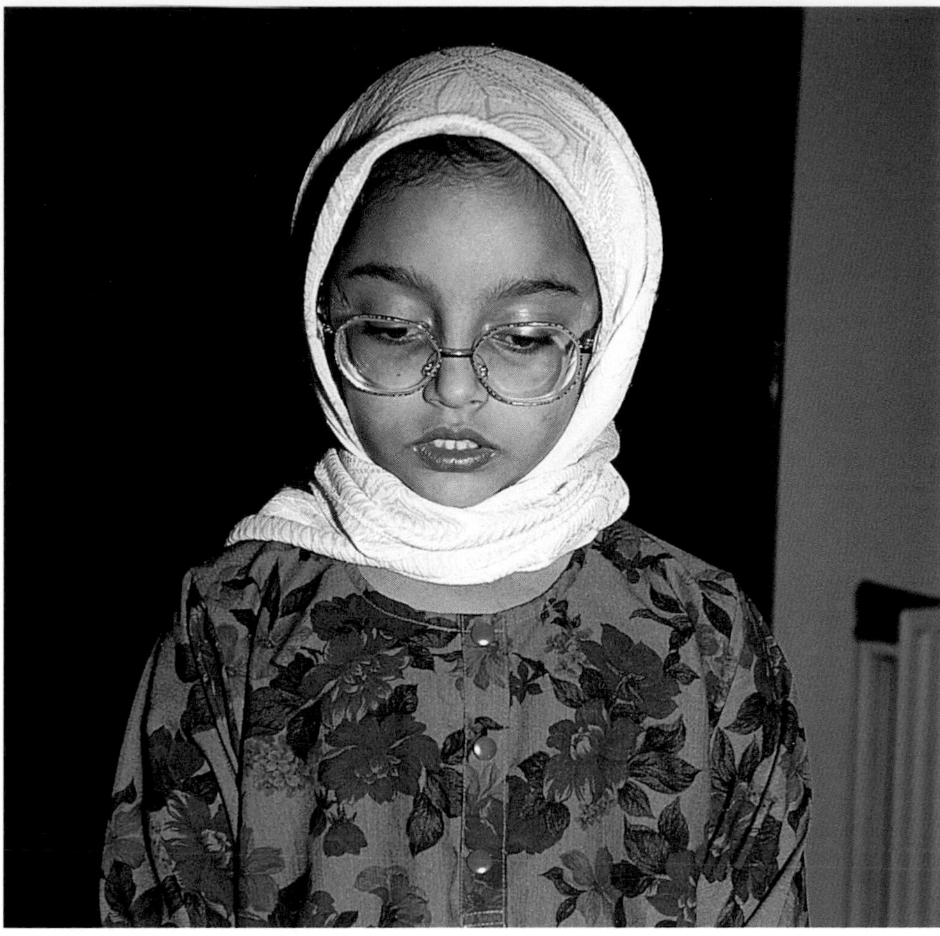

B. Bearing in mind the Muslim restrictions on female dress what problems do you think Muslim girls might face at school and how do you think those problems should be overcome?

From the scriptures

The Qur'an has this to say about the equality of men and women in God's sight:
'Be they men or women, to those that embrace the Faith and do what is right We will surely grant a happy life; We shall reward them according to their noblest deeds.'
(Surah 16.97)

This verse makes clear that anyone who does two things will be granted a happy life:

a) What do you think it means to *'embrace the Faith'*?
b) What do you think it means to *'do what is right'*?

Everyday life

In Muslim society the family is considered to be the main responsibility of a married woman and many Muslim women will only work outside the home if it does not interfere with their domestic responsibilities. Where women do work in large numbers in Muslim countries they tend to be employed mainly in the 'caring' professions – nursing, teaching, social work, etc. The Qur'an does insist that women should dress modestly in public, and in many Muslim countries they wear the traditional long dress and head veil. Dressing in this way is called the 'hijab'. For many centuries the practice of veiling has been common in many countries (most notably Saudi Arabia and the Gulf countries) although the practice is not mentioned in The Qur'an. Even in those Muslim societies where the veil is not encouraged, it is usual for Muslim women to have their hair covered. In this country many Muslim women and girls wear the shalwar (trousers) and kameez (tunic).

Women and religion

Whilst the main religious activities of a Muslim man revolve around the mosque, those of women centre around the home. It is assumed that women with young children will not be able to attend the mosque for Friday prayers or at other times. For women who wish to pray in the mosque, however, there is usually a separate area set aside with its own washing facilities. Women who are menstruating are excused from prayers and fasting, although the days missed from fasting must be made up later.

FOR YOUR FOLDER

1 The Prophet Muhammad said:
'A virtuous wife is a man's best treasure. The most perfect Muslims are those whose disposition is best; and the best of you are they who behave best with their wives. Paradise lies at the feet of mothers.'
What do you think that Muhammad meant when he said that *'Paradise lies at the feet of mothers'*?

2 According to The Hadith Muhammad told his followers:
'Modesty and faith are joined closely together; if either of them is lost, the other goes also.'
a) What do you think is meant here by *'modesty'*?
b) Why do you think that modesty and faith are so closely intertwined in Islam?
c) What did Muhammad teach about the main differences between men and women in the Muslim community?

In the glossary: Allah; Hijab; Mosque; Muhammad; Qur'an.

Marriage

What is distinctive about any marriage performed within the Muslim community?

FOCUSING QUESTIONS

Why is marriage considered to be so important within the Muslim community?

What are 'arranged marriages' and are they practised within the Muslim community?

What is the 'mahr' and why is it particularly important for a Muslim bride?

In Islam the family is the basic unit of society and marriage is the corner-stone of family life. Neither celibacy (living without sexual relations) nor monasticism (taking a deliberate religious vow not to marry) is encouraged in Islam. Marriage is seen as providing the God-given channel for physical, emotional and spiritual enjoyment. Muslim men may marry Jewish or Christian women as well as Muslims, but a Muslim woman can only marry a man from the same faith.

Sex outside marriage and polygamy

Celibacy (abstaining from sexual relations) outside marriage is considered to be a very important virtue. The Qur'an actually suggests that early marriage is desirable so that a person will not take part in any undesirable sexual activity. Those who reach marriageable age without finding a suitable partner are encouraged to abstain from all sexual relationships until someone comes along. Polygamy (taking more than one wife) is permitted in The Qur'an as long as a man does not have more than four wives – but it is rarely practised today. If it does happen then the husband must guarantee that all of his wives are treated fairly and equally. Polygamy is only usually allowed if:

- The first wife is unable to have children.
- The first wife is so ill that she is unable to run the home properly.

Polyandry (one wife and several husbands) is not allowed under any circumstances.

Arranged marriages

Muslims are encouraged by The Qur'an to see marriage as a life-long relationship based on friendship and trust, and so the Muslim community emphasises the importance of choosing the right partner. In most Muslim communities all members of the close family are involved in making a person's choice. If a man wishes to marry a Muslim girl he presents himself to her family and enquires about the conditions which they might demand for the marriage. Should they be able to reach an agreement then the engagement is announced and the wedding-day is fixed. Often, marriages will be 'arranged', although the wedding cannot go ahead unless the man and woman accept one another. The Qur'an makes it very clear that the only genuine marriage is one into which both the man and the woman have entered voluntarily.

From the scriptures

The Qur'an passes on this advice about marriage:
'...if you fear that you cannot maintain equality among them [more than one wife] *marry one only ...'*.

(Surah 4.3)

1 What is polygamy?
2 How many wives does The Qur'an allow a Muslim man to have?
3 How many husbands does The Qur'an allow a Muslim woman to have?
4 Why do you think that very few Muslim men practise polygamy today?

A. A Muslim bride in north London prepares for the wedding ceremony. What is a dowry, and how important is it to the bride?

B. The groom signs the wedding document. Why is it important that two male witnesses attend the ceremony?

An essential part of the wedding agreement is the 'mahr' or bridal dowry. This is something which still plays an important part in the marriage arrangements of many religions.

The dowry usually depends on the social standing of the bride and the customs of her local community. Money or goods are given by the bridegroom, or his father, in return for marital rights – as The Qur'an encourages them to do. This has always been a very important safeguard for a Muslim woman since many become housewives and do not earn money of their own. Usually only part of the 'price' is paid on marriage and this becomes the personal property of the woman. The remainder is paid over if and when the couple are divorced.

The wedding ceremony

A Muslim wedding is largely a civil affair with few religious overtones. The most important part of the ceremony is the signing of a formal contract between groom and bride in the presence of two male witnesses. Because the wedding is a civil matter it can take place anywhere although, in Britain, it is almost always performed by the imam in a mosque. He usually opens the ceremony by reading a passage from The Qur'an – usually from the 4th Surah which is entitled 'The Woman'. The imam tells the couple about the responsibilities that they have towards Allah and each other before they exchange rings. The ring that is placed on the man's finger must not be made of gold. Guests congratulate the couple saying to them: *'May God bless you and invoke his blessing on you'*.

FOR YOUR FOLDER

1 As part of the marriage ceremony the couple are asked three times if they agree to marry each other before exchanging rings.

a) Why do you think the couple are asked three times if they are assenting to the marriage?
b) Why do you think the couple exchange rings with each other?
c) Why do you think the couple are blessed by the imam in the name of Allah?

2 A tradition going back to Muhammad describes marriage as 'half religion'. What do you think this statement means?

In the glossary: Allah; Celibacy; Imam; Mosque; Polyandry; Polygamy; Qur'an.

ivorce

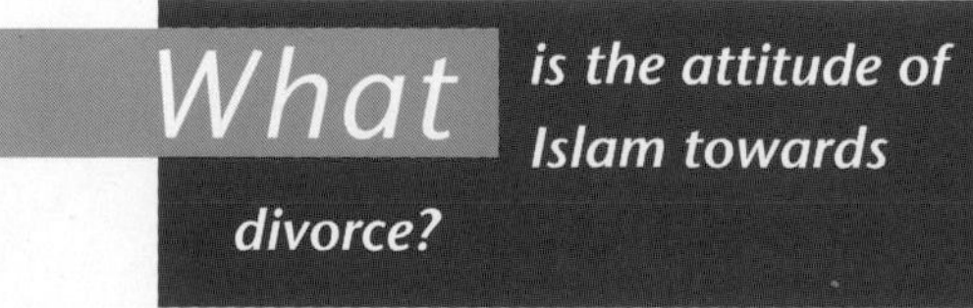

FOCUSING QUESTIONS

How did Muhammad change the status of women in Arabia?

How do Muslims try to prevent members of their community from divorcing too hastily?

Who takes on the responsibility for a divorced woman and her children?

Before the time of Muhammad, men in Arabia were able to discard their wives whenever they wished to marry someone else without the women having any rights or safeguards. By raising their status and granting them the right to own property in their own right the Prophet changed the position of women considerably. Yet, although Islam places a very high priority on marriage and family life it also takes a realistic attitude towards divorce. Muslim marriages are a civil agreement carrying certain responsibilities, and divorce is allowed if those responsibilities are not carried out properly. At the same time divorce is not a course of action that receives any encouragement from the Prophet: *'Among all things permitted, the most obnoxious in the sight of God is divorce.'*

Divorce

No Muslim can pursue a divorce without having a valid reason and, even then, every effort is made by the Muslim community to keep the marriage together. If, however, divorce becomes inevitable then certain conditions have to be met.

The waiting period

The divorce procedure of 'talaq' (repudiation) follows a set pattern allowing time (called 'iddah') for reconciliation. If a Muslim wife is to be divorced by her husband then she is entitled to demand a 'waiting period' at the end of which the couple are divorced and the woman is free to remarry after four months. This 'waiting period' is measured by three menstrual cycles at the end of which the woman is able to be certain that she is not pregnant. If the woman is pregnant then she is entitled to wait until her baby is born before the divorce goes through. During this time the husband and wife may become reconciled to each other, in which case the divorce is dropped. Should a couple wish to remarry after they have divorced then they can only do so if the woman has remarried and been divorced by her second husband.

The repudiation

Under Islamic law a husband can divorce his wife in person or by letter. Traditionally all that he needs to say is *'I divorce you'* three times in the presence of three witnesses. This is called the 'repudiation' and the husband can take back the first two of these. After the final repudiation, however, the divorce becomes final. All of the three repudiations can be given at the same time so making the divorce applicable immediately.

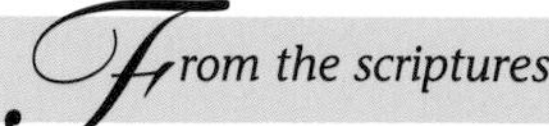

From the scriptures

The Qur'an says:
'If you fear a breach between a man and his wife, appoint an arbiter [mediator] *from his people and another from hers. If they wish to be reconciled, God will bring them together again. Surely God is all-knowing and wise.'*
(Surah 4.35)

Why do you think that this quotation suggests that Allah and the Muslim community are involved in a divorce as well as the husband and wife?

A. A Muslim couple. What must happen in a Muslim society if someone wishes to remarry a woman who they have already divorced?

B. If a Muslim family breaks up through divorce who has the right to have custody of the children?

A woman seeking a divorce, though, must persuade a court that she has legitimate grounds for a divorce – impotence, insanity, a debilitating disease, desertion, failure to pay the dowry, physical or emotional cruelty, a false accusation of adultery or apostasy. She does, though, have the right to insist on a separation followed by a divorce. It is possible for a woman to insist that she can divorce her husband on the same grounds as him if it is inserted in their marriage contract – although few women do this.

Custody of the children

The strong laws which apply to the custody of children must be followed. The custody of children up to a certain age (seven for boys and nine for girls) goes automatically to their mother unless there are strong reasons for considering her to be unsuitable. After this age, however, the children are considered to be old enough to decide whether they will live with their mother or father. The divorced woman receives back the dowry ('mahr') given to her when she married as well as the contents of her home but her male relatives, rather than her ex-husband, must take over the responsibility for her and her children.

FOR YOUR FOLDER

1 Explain the following and say why they are important: the waiting period (iddah); the repudiation (talaq); the custody of children.

2 Describe, in your own words, the Muslim attitude towards divorce.

3 Explain how the Muslim customs and traditions regarding divorce try to protect the Muslim community and the wife.

In the glossary: Apostasy; Islam; Muhammad; Muslim; Prophet.

Death

How do Muslims deal with death and how is their behaviour affected by their beliefs about life after death?

FOCUSING QUESTIONS

How does the example of the Prophet Muhammad help Muslims to cope with their impending death?

What does a Muslim hope to do as death approaches?

What happens to a Muslim once death has taken place?

When they realise that death is approaching Muslims try to follow the example of the Prophet Muhammad who prayed that Allah might help him through the hardship and agony of what lay ahead. He also asked God that his sins might be forgiven. Muslims believe strongly in the resurrection of the body and in a life after death so they approach their impending death in a spirit of hope. After death, they believe that their soul will enter into eternal life and that they will be reunited with their loved ones who have died before them.

Facing death

Each Muslim hopes that he or she will have the strength to recite the Shahadah before they depart from this life so that their sins might be forgiven by Allah. Relatives and friends gathered around the bed read passages from The Qur'an to comfort the person and pray that Allah might be merciful to the soul as death comes.

After death

Immediately after death, the body is washed three times (a man's by men and a woman's by women) in the mosque, wrapped in three white sheets (if possible, the same sheets that were worn by the person on their Hajj) and carried on a stretcher to the mosque or place of burial by male mourners whilst everyone recites the Shahadah. The imam leads the people in appropriate prayers including praise to Allah and the calling down of blessings on the Prophet Muhammad. The funeral prayers contain the words: '*O God, pardon this dead person; lo, Thou art the Most Forgiving, the Most Merciful.*' The mourners then spend some time in silent thought and meditation.

From the scriptures

This passage comes from The Qur'an:
'In the name of God,
We commit to the earth, according to the way of the Prophet God...
We created you from it, and return you into it,
and from it We will raise you again a second time.'

There is an immediate and a distant promise here for the Muslim believer. What is it?

Burial

The corpse is laid directly on the earth in the grave – resting on its right side and with the head facing Makkah. In some countries bodies cannot be laid directly on the earth but the authorities allow Muslims to invert a coffin over the body (see Photograph A). Males and females are never buried in the same grave unless this is unavoidable and then a partition is placed between them. After the grave is filled in the mourners recite the al-Fatihah – the first Surah (division) in The Qur'an before

DISCUSS

Why do you think that, in Muslim tradition, men and women are not buried in the same grave?

B. Male mourners, lead by the imam, recite the Shahadah over the body during a Muslim funeral in Spain. Why do they do this?

returning home. Muslim tradition teaches that two angels visit the grave and question the dead person about their fitness for the next life – and to prepare them for the forthcoming Day of Judgement. For this reason the al-Fatihah and the Shahadah are recited over the grave to help the dead person to answer the questions of the angels.

The Prophet Muhammad wept when his son died and Muslims do not feel ashamed at weeping when confronted with death either. They are, however, comforted with the thought that the soul has returned to Allah and will be raised on the Day of Judgement. For this reason the period of mourning is short – for a few nights friends and relatives visit the bereaved and say the same words that they said at the graveside. On the first Friday after the funeral members of the family might visit the grave and place a palm leaf on it – the symbol of peace – before giving food to the poor. The mourning continues until forty days after the funeral.

FOR YOUR FOLDER

1 In Muslim countries the body is laid in the grave in direct contact with the earth. In Britain an upturned coffin is placed over the body so that it is still in contact with the ground. What do you think is the symbolic importance of this to the Muslim?

2 Why do you think that Muslims hope to be buried in the cloak that they wore when they undertook the Hajj?

3 The strict Muslim teaching is that no monument or structure, including headstones, be erected to those who have died – although this ruling is ignored in some parts of the world. Why do you think that this prohibition was made?

In the glossary: Allah; Al-Fatihah; Angel; Day of Judgement; Hajj; Imam; Makkah; Mosque; Muhammad; Qur'an; Shahadah; Surah.

Allah

Who is Allah and what do Muslims believe about Him?

FOCUSING QUESTIONS

What are the basic Muslim beliefs about Allah?

What is one of the most unforgivable sins in Islam?

How many different names are given to Allah and what do they express about His character?

The first, and most important, element of belief in Islam is the doctrine of the Oneness of God, whom Muslims call Allah. This belief is called the tawhid. The Prophet Muhammad attacked all forms of belief in God which denied His Oneness and Unity. God, Muslims believe, is One and there is no other God except Him.

Shirk

The one unforgivable sin in Islam is that of 'association' – to talk in any way which denies God's absolute sovereignty over everything by associating Him with someone or something else. Anyone who does this commits the most awful sin. To emphasise this the Muslim name for God, Allah, in Arabic – the language of the Islamic Scriptures – has no plural form, and is neither male or female.

Muslims believe that Christians commit shirk when they worship Jesus, the Holy Spirit or the Virgin Mary. They also feel that the Christian belief in the Trinity, with three 'separate' gods is blasphemous since it 'associates' other beings with God. The Qur'an makes this clear: ...'*Praise be to God who has never begotten a son; who has no partner in His Kingdom...*' (Surah 17.111). Christians, however, strongly deny that they believe in three gods. They insist that they believe in the one God who reveals himself in three different forms.

From the scriptures

This quotation comes from The Qur'an:
'God forgives not the association of anything with Him; other than that, He forgives whomsoever He pleases. But whomsoever associates anything with God has conceived indeed a monstrous sin'

1. What does it mean when The Qur'an speaks of 'associating' something with God?
2. What do Christians mean by their belief in the Trinity and how is this belief condemned here in The Qur'an?
3. Why do you think that Muslims are told that *'association'* is such a *'monstrous'* sin?

The ninety-nine names of Allah

A Muslim is someone who has completely submitted himself or herself to the will of Allah, and by so doing has acknowledged the mystery that surrounds God. Since Allah is totally beyond all human understanding and human beings are only limited creatures they cannot understand or describe God in any real way. Allah is totally beyond all human thought and understanding. This does not mean, however, that Muslims cannot speak of Allah in a very close, and intimate, way. Islam provides worshippers with a list of ninety-nine of the 'most beautiful names' of God. Male Muslims recite all of these names by running their fingers through thirty-three beads on a rosary three times. These beads (see Photograph A) are called the misbeha and they allow the worshipper to choose a name from the list which is most in keeping with the prayer that they are saying.

A. How is this string of beads of particular help to the Muslim in his prayers?

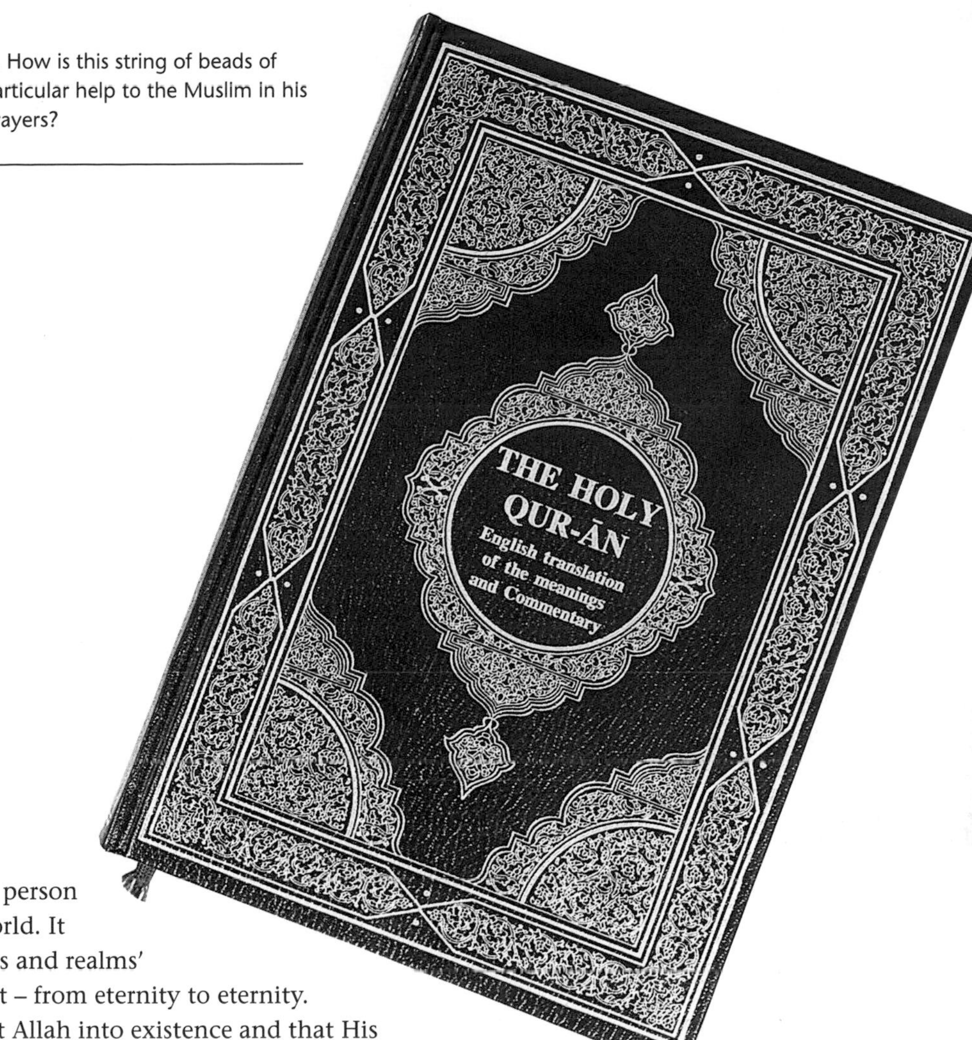

B. A copy of The Qur'an. What do Muslims believe would have happened if Allah had not given The Qur'an to the human race?

Reciting the ninety-nine names of Allah is an important devotional exercise since it makes the person constantly aware of Allah's greatness over the world. It reminds Muslims that Allah is 'Lord of all spheres and realms' who has always existed and will continue to exist – from eternity to eternity. Muslims believe that no-one or no thing brought Allah into existence and that His existence cannot be ended. He is the First, the Last, the Originator, the Producer and the Truth. Allah is the only one who exists by necessity. Everything else exists by the will of Allah. Both life and death are Allah's alone to give and to withdraw. He is the Giver and Restorer of life and yet He is also the Slayer who brings all things to pass.

What the names of Allah represent

All of Allah's many names underline the two sides to His character which are such an important part of Muslim belief and worship. They are:

- The frightening aspect. Allah is the Overpowering, the Abaser, the Humiliator, the Watcher, the Giver of Death, the Powerful, the Avenger, the Depriver and the Director.
- The welcoming aspect. Allah is Compassionate, Merciful, the Protector, the Provider, the Plentiful Giver, the Gracious, the Answerer and the Giver of Life.

The Qur'an emphasises these two aspects of the character of Allah time and time again. God is *'nearer to man than his neck-vein'* and yet never comes within reach of man's understanding. He is unknowable and can only be known in as much as He chooses to reveal himself. God, though, made himself known to Muhammad and, through the record of that revelation in The Qur'an, to the whole human race. Human beings are only called upon to believe and submit themselves to Allah.

FOR YOUR FOLDER

Explain in your own words:

a) The two aspects of Allah's character which are brought out in the ninety-nine different names.
b) What the tawhid expresses to Muslims about the kind of God that he or she worships.
c) What a misbeha is and how a Muslim might find one useful in his prayers.
d) How Muslims believe that Allah has made Himself known to the human race.

In the glossary: ALLAH; MISBEHA; MUHAMMAD; TAWHID.

Angels

Why *do angels play a very important role in Muslim belief and The Qur'an?*

FOCUSING QUESTIONS

What are the differences believed to be between angels and human beings?

Why do Muslims believe that angels carry out perfectly the will of Allah and human beings do not?

Who is Iblis and what does he do?

Angels are heavenly beings who live in Paradise. Angels play a very important role in Islam and figure prominently in The Qur'an. Like human beings they have been created by Allah but, unlike human beings, they are sexless and live for ever (are immortal). Created of light, unlike human beings who have been created from the earth, they inhabit the invisible world. They are Allah's and so have an important influence on the life of the universe and that of each human being.

Angels and Allah

Because of the nature that Allah has given to them angels perfectly obey the will of Allah at all times. They were created by Allah and are His servants – as are human beings. The only difference between angels and humans is that angels can be relied on to carry out the will of God. Human beings have free-will and so are able to act independently – angels do not have this gift. According to the Qur'an: '*They* [angels] *do not speak before He speaks, and they act by His command.*'

Iblis

In Muslim belief, angels guard the throne of Allah and determine who enters through the gates of Hell. According to Islamic tradition they rank higher than humankind but below the prophets. In the story of creation in The Qur'an they prostrate themselves before Adam, one of the prophets at Allah's command. There is, though, one exception. One angel refused to bow to Adam on the grounds that he was made of light while Adam was only made of clay. This act of disobedience to Allah, resulted in him losing Allah's favour. He was Iblis or 'Shaytan', who was reduced to the task of deceiving people and leading them astray from the true path – and this he has done ever since.

A. Angels praying, from a sixteenth-century Ottoman manuscript. How many archangels are there?

B. How does this Muslim believe that angels will affect his life?

Archangels

Four angels rank as archangels (chief angels) in Muslim belief, and each of them has been given a particular task to perform by Allah:

- Jibril (Gabriel), the angel who revealed Allah's will to Muhammad and is frequently referred to in The Qur'an as the Holy Spirit.
- Mikail, the angel who carries out Allah's will in the world, the protector of the holy places and the sustainer of life in times of trouble.
- Israfil, the angel who will blow the last trumpet sound before the Day of Judgement and call all souls to stand before Allah.
- Azrail, the angel that takes the souls at death.

Guardian and ministering angels

There are many, powerful angels – some of them surround the throne of Allah, some record the words and thoughts of all people on earth, and others receive the soul at the time of death. Other angels help people on Earth to pray – giving them a sense of peace and well-being. Each individual has two guardian angels and this is why, at the end of their prayers, Muslims they turn to the right and the left. They are acknowledging their guardian angels.

Jinns

Jinns are frequently mentioned in The Qur'an and, although they are not angels, they are frequently associated with them. Although they are normally invisible they can appear in human form, and are usually associated with desolate places. Muslims believe that Jinns were created by Allah from fire in the beginning and that they return to fire at the end, just as human beings return to dust.

From the scriptures

These quotations from The Qur'an describe part of the work of angels:

'You shall see the angels circling about the Throne, giving glory to their Lord. They shall be judged with fairness, and all shall say, 'Praise be to God, Lord of the Universe!'...The heavens above well-nigh split asunder as the angels give glory to their Lord and beg forgiveness for those on earth. Surely God is the Forgiving One, the Merciful.'

(Surah 39.75; 42.5)

These two verses from The Qur'an describe two of the most important functions of angels. What are they?

FOR YOUR FOLDER

a) What are angels?
b) Where do angels live and what were they created from?
c) What do human beings possess that Allah did not give to angels – and what is the consequence of this?
d) What are archangels and how many of them are there?
e) What are the particular roles given to the different archangels?
f) Which special tasks are carried out by the many guardian angels?

In the glossary: Allah; Angel; Day of Judgement; Iblis; Jibril; Jinn; Muhammad; Prophet; Qur'an.

The Prophets

***Who** were the prophets and why are they considered to be special by Muslims?*

FOCUSING QUESTIONS

What is a prophet?

What are the differences between a prophet and a messenger?

How many prophets have there been and what have they done?

Belief in the prophets of Allah is at the centre of Islam. These prophets were men who were chosen specially by Allah to be given insights about Him which they then passed on for the guidance of humanity. Muslims believe that Allah sent these messengers to proclaim His Oneness (the tawhid) to all people at all times. They were also sent to warn the human race about Allah's forthcoming judgement.

The special prophets

An Islamic tradition states that there have been 124,000 prophets and 315 of these were messengers. A messenger is sent by God to a special group of people or community with a holy book which contains the rules and laws which all human beings must follow. Prophets are not messengers since they merely preach the message that has been sent by Allah, but all messengers are prophets.

Twenty-five messengers, stretching from Adam (the first human being in Islamic, Jewish and Christian tradition) to Muhammad, are special prophets. The Qur'an identifies them by name and includes in the list prophets from other religious faiths including:

- Ibrahim. Ibrahim was born in the city of Ur, in the Chaldees, when many gods were worshipped by the people. He rejected the gods of the people and saw instead the hand of Allah in all things. Instead of worshipping many gods Ibrahim worshipped the one, true God – Allah.

- Musa. Musa was the only prophet that Allah spoke to directly rather than through the Angel Jibril. He was given the tablets of the law on Mount Sinai. These tablets are called the Tawrah, and Muslims regard them as the foundation for all later religion. The Tawrah included the Ten Commandments. Later, guided by the power of Allah, Musa led his people through the wilderness to the edge of the Promised Land.

- Isa. Allah sent Isa to the Jews when He saw that they had departed from the law of Musa. According to Muslim tradition, Isa preached to them for three years although he was not, as Christians believe, crucified. The Hadith says that one of his disciples was crucified in his place and Jesus was taken up directly by Allah into Heaven – from where he will return at the end of the world.

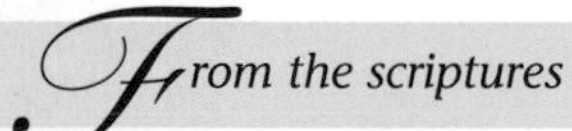

From the scriptures

The Qur'an has a very high regard for those people who are considered to be prophets in other religions:
'Say: 'We believe in God and that which was revealed to us; in what was revealed to Abraham, Ishmael, Isaac, Jacob, and the tribes; to Moses and Jesus and the other prophets by their Lord. We make no distinction among any of them, and to Him we submit.'
(Surah 2.136)

1 Which prophets are named in this extract and which religions hold them in the highest esteem?
2 This passage suggests that there is one distinguishing mark of a prophet. What is it?
3 What does The Qur'an say about the relationship between the prophets mentioned in the extract?
4 What does the extract mean by '*to Him we submit*'?

A. A geometric pattern in mosque. Why is there a strict prohibition in Islam against all representations of Muhammad and the prophets?

Muhammad

Muhammad was the last, and Muslims believe, the greatest, of Allah's prophets. Although all of the prophets were the vehicles of Allah's self-revelation, that revelation came most perfectly through Muhammad. Muhammad was the 'seal' of Allah. This uniqueness is recognised by calling Muhammad 'the Prophet' – the man who revealed Allah in a totally unique way.

Respecting the prophets

The Qur'an records that most, if not all, of the prophets were persecuted by their fellow-countrymen and their message rejected. Some, like Musa and Isa, were given special powers by Allah to carry out miracles. For these two reasons the prophets must be given the highest possible respect and this is why all drawings and pictures of the prophets in the mosque are forbidden. Muhammad preached very strongly against the worship of idols and this is why Muslim artists have also been forbidden to paint or sculpt any people or animals. Muslim homes and mosques are decorated with the most beautiful geometric patterns instead (see Photograph A).

DISCUSS

Why do you think that Muslims believe that Muhammad was unique amongst the many prophets that Allah sent to Earth?

FOR YOUR FOLDER

1 Ibrahim, one of the prophets, was confronted by Nimrod, a king who regarded himself as a god. Ibrahim himself had come to believe in the one God, Allah, although everyone around him believed in many gods. Ibrahim told Nimrod:

'"I acknowledge the Lord of the Universe exclusively as my Lord and God of worship, and I disown categorically the lordship and godhead of everyone else."'

a) How does Ibrahim the prophet underline the difference here between Allah and the other gods that people worshipped?

b) Why do you think that Ibrahim says that he '*disowns categorically*' the '*lordship and godhead*' of everyone else?

2 What do you think that Muslims mean when they refer to Muhammad as the 'seal' of the prophets?

In the glossary: Allah; Hadith; Ibrahim; Isa; Mosque; Muhammad; Musa; Prophet; Qur'an; Tawhid.

The Qur'an

What is The Qur'an and why is it such an important book for all Muslims?

FOCUSING QUESTIONS

Where do Muslims believe that The Qur'an came from and, in a phrase, what does it contain?

Which two things, in particular, are Muslims able to learn from The Qur'an?

How does The Qur'an help Muslims in their attempts to prepare themselves for the forthcoming Day of Judgement?

The sacred Scripture of Islam is The Qur'an (meaning 'that which is read or recited') and this holy book contains the revelations that Muslims believe Allah passed on to the Prophet Muhammad over a period of twenty-three years.

The Qur'an refers to itself as the '*Preserved Tablet*' and '*Mother of the Book*'. A single verse in The Qur'an is called an 'ayah', while a division is referred to as a 'surah'. There are 114 surahs in The Qur'an and all of these, save one, begin with the words '*In the name off Allah – All Gracious, All merciful*'. In Arabic this known as the 'bismillah' ('In the name of Allah') and is usually said by all Muslims before beginning any action.

Collecting the surahs together

The surahs are not included in the order that they were revealed to Muhammad but in the order in which they were collected together under the instructions of Khalifah Uthman (644-656). In practice, this means that the longer surahs were recorded first and the shorter surahs last. Within twenty years of the death of Muhammad The Qur'an was completed.

Each surah has been identified by a name which is taken from some word or subject in the division. The second surah, for instance, is called 'The Cow' since it contains the story of Musa trying to persuade the Israelites to sacrifice a cow. The most familiar of the surahs, the first, (called the al-Fatihah) is recited by Muslim worshippers each time they pray.

The contents of The Qur'an

The Qur'an is believed to be the actual 'word of God' which was revealed to the Prophet Muhammad by the Angel Jibril from an original that is preserved in Heaven. Because of this, the book carries a unique authority and gives guidance to Muslims on all aspects of their faith and behaviour. Muslims say that The Qur'an teaches them how to live a life in total submission to Allah and how to prepare themselves for the time when they will appear before Allah on the Day of Judgement.

From the scriptures

Here are three quotations from The Qur'an about itself:

'*We* [God] *have revealed the Qur'an in the Arabic tongue so that you may grow in understanding.*' (Surah 12.1)

'*This Qur'an could not have been devised by any but God. It confirms what was revealed before it and fully explains the Scriptures. It is beyond doubt from the Lord of the Universe.*' (Surah 10.37)

'*...a Qur'an in the Arabic tongue, free from any flaw, that they may guard themselves against evil.*' (Surah 39.28)

Describe, in your own words, all of the information about The Qur'an provided by these verses.

A. Why do you think that reading The Qur'an is thought to be so important – and especially during Ramadan?

B. The Qur'an. Where do Muslims believe that this book has come from?

To help them in the preparation for this great event Muslims are given in The Qur'an guidance about a very far-reaching range of everyday topics:

- The drinking of alcohol and gambling. Both of these are banned on the grounds that they are 'works of the devil'.
- Marriage and divorce.
- The treatment of widows and orphans, and the sharing of wealth with those who are needy. Zakah is a means of re-distributing wealth from the rich members of the Muslim community to those who are poor. Caring for the poor is a constant refrain in The Qur'an.
- The lending of money (usury). Muslims are forbidden from lending money to others except at very low rates of interest.

As The Qur'an is so highly revered passages from it are learned by heart and used in prayers every day. During the month of Ramadan male Muslims set aside time to read through the whole of The Qur'an since this is an essential part of their devotional life. At Friday Prayers in the mosque the imam (leader) uses a passage from The Qur'an as the basis for his sermon which often carries a political rather than a religious message.

FOR YOUR FOLDER

1 The Prophet Muhammad said this about The Qur'an:
'The best of you is he who has learnt The Qur'an and then taught it.'
Why do you think that Muhammad placed together the need to learn The Qur'an and to teach it?

2 An important part of respecting The Qur'an is for it to be reproduced beautifully, always read in Arabic, and to be learned by heart. Why do you think that such an emphasis is placed on respecting The Qur'an in this way?

In the glossary: Allah; Al-Fatihah; Day of Judgement; Imam; Jibril; Kalifah; Mosque; Muhammad; Musa; Qur'an; Ramadan; Surah; Uthman; Zakah.

The Hadith

What *is The Hadith and why is it important?*

FOCUSING QUESTIONS

What is the difference between the prophetic and the sacred Hadith?

How did the materials in The Hadith came into existence?

What are the names of the two most important collections found in The Hadith?

Next to The Qur'an the most important Muslim holy book is The Hadith – meaning 'narrative' or 'report'. The Hadith contains records of the actions ('sunnah') and words of the Prophet Muhammad and his closest friends. In many ways The Hadith has played as large a part in shaping the Muslim religion and culture as The Qur'an.

The Prophetic and Sacred Hadith

In The Hadith many sayings and stories of the Prophet are collection under two broad categories:

- The Prophetic Hadith. These are the words and sayings of Muhammad himself which show him to have been a wise, humorous and compassionate man.
- The Sacred Hadith. These Hadith are so called because their authority goes back through the Prophet to Allah Himself. Although these sayings were not included in The Qur'an they were revealed to Muhammad by Allah and, as such, demand the greatest possible respect.

FOR YOUR FOLDER

1
a) What is The Hadith?
b) How were the many sayings of the Prophet Muhammad kept in existence before they were finally written down?
c) What part did Muhammad ibn al-Bukhari and Muslim ibn al-Hajjaj play in the final composition of The Hadith?
d) What has to happen before a Hadith can finally be accepted as genuine? Why do you think this is very important?
e) What value do Muslims give to the sayings and events recorded in The Hadith?

2 The Hadith has been described as 'popular Islam' What do you think is meant by this phrase?

Sources of The Hadith

The distinguishing mark of an item in The Hadith is the chain of narrators presumed to have transmitted it from its source among the close companions of the Prophet or even the Prophet himself. In other words, an authentic item in The Hadith must include the name of every human link in the chain between the individual who finally transmitted it and the Prophet Muhammad. Here is an example:
al-Bukhari writes, *'Abdallah ibn al-Aswad told me: al-Fadl ibn al-Ata told us: Ismai'l ibn Ummayya told us on the authority of Yaha ibn Abdallah ibn Sayfi that he heard abu Mabad, the freedman of ibn Abbas say: When the Prophet, peace and blessings of God be upon him, sent Muadh to Yemen, he said to him...'.*

A large number of Hadith materials came into circulation within two or three generations after the death of the Prophet. At first the narratives were passed around by word of mouth. Later, they were written down, although we do not know exactly when. These narratives recorded facts and events, speeches and comments from Muhammad. So great was the number of these in circulation that two collections of those believed to be genuine were made. Of these, the Bukhari

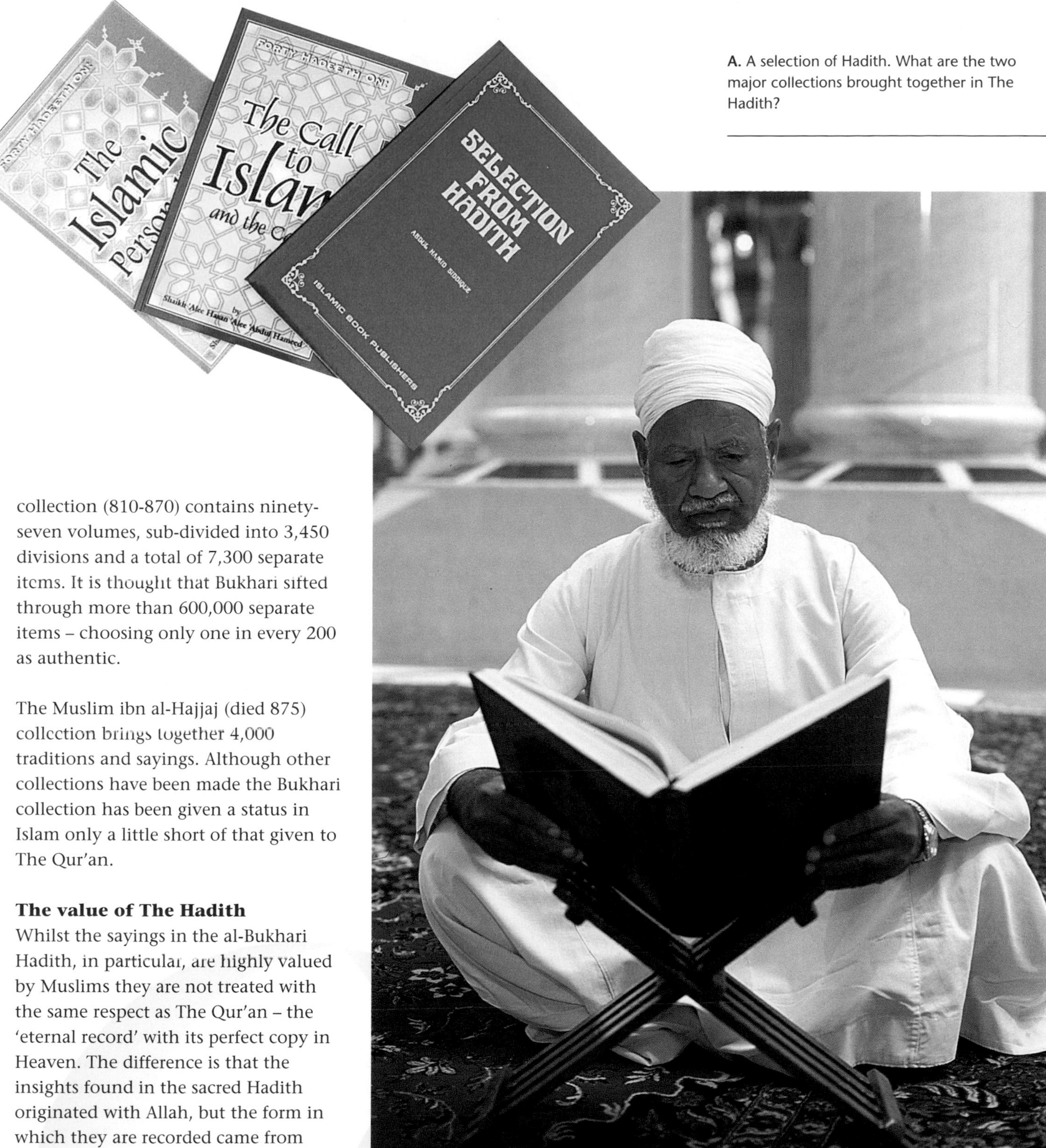

A. A selection of Hadith. What are the two major collections brought together in The Hadith?

B. Why do you think that this Muslim is reading The Hadith?

collection (810-870) contains ninety-seven volumes, sub-divided into 3,450 divisions and a total of 7,300 separate items. It is thought that Bukhari sifted through more than 600,000 separate items – choosing only one in every 200 as authentic.

The Muslim ibn al-Hajjaj (died 875) collection brings together 4,000 traditions and sayings. Although other collections have been made the Bukhari collection has been given a status in Islam only a little short of that given to The Qur'an.

The value of The Hadith

Whilst the sayings in the al-Bukhari Hadith, in particular, are highly valued by Muslims they are not treated with the same respect as The Qur'an – the 'eternal record' with its perfect copy in Heaven. The difference is that the insights found in the sacred Hadith originated with Allah, but the form in which they are recorded came from Muhammad. They are, therefore, open to discussion. The words of The Qur'an are believed to be beyond all debate. Yet the value of The Hadith to the Muslim community cannot be over-emphasised. The pages of The Hadith, sacred and prophetic, cover every issue that the Muslim community and individual believers are ever likely to face – the sacred dealing with religious issues, and the prophetic, with more everyday matters.

In the glossary: HADITH; MUHAMMAD; PROPHET; QUR'AN.

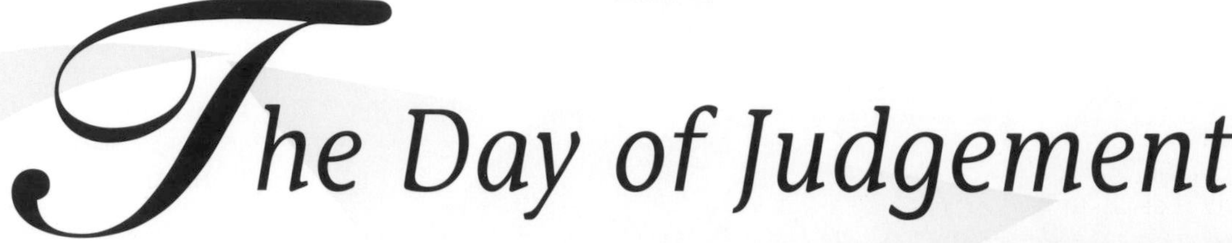

The Day of Judgement

What do Muslims believe about the Day of Judgement?

FOCUSING QUESTIONS

How do Muslims try to prepare those who have died for their interrogation by two angels on the Last Day?

What is the ultimate joy for those who enter Paradise after the Last Judgement?

What is the final act of Allah after the Last Judgement?

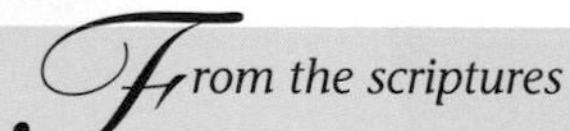

From the scriptures

On the Day of Judgement, according to The Qur'an: *'When the sun ceases to shine; when the stars fall down and the mountains are blown away; when camels big with young are left untended, and the wild beasts are brought together; when the seas are set alight and men's souls are reunited; when the infant girl, buried alive, is asked for what crime she was slain; when the records of men's deed are laid open, and heaven is stripped bare; when Hell burns fiercely and Paradise is brought near: then each soul shall know what it has done.'* (Surah 81.1-14)

1. What can you learn from these vivid descriptions about one side of the character of Allah?
2. What effect do you think warnings like this might have on the everyday lives of Muslims?

The Day of Judgement, on which all men and women will be called to account by Allah, is a central theme in The Qur'an. The shattering events of this Day will occur suddenly at a time known only to Allah and great changes will take place in the universe. Life will end and a new order of existence will begin which will last, under Allah's sovereignty, for ever.

A time of judgement

Quite apart from events in the universe on the Last Day, the graves will be opened, the dead will return to life, and all people will be sentenced by Allah according to their deeds on earth. Two terrible angels, Munkar and Nadir, will question each person and this event is viewed with so much dread by Muslims that they recite the Shahadah to all those dying – so that they can answer the questions of the angels. Only those who have died for Allah in the course of battle, martyrs, pass directly into Paradise. Others must stand before Allah, the Judge. Allah weighs the deeds of each person in the balance. His judgement is shown by the presentation of a book to each person. If the book is placed in their right hand then that person can be counted among the blessed and pass directly into Heaven. If the book is placed in the left hand, however, then they are counted among the damned and pass directly into Hell.

Heaven

Both Heaven and Hell, places of actual bliss and torment, are painted in very graphic terms in The Qur'an. Both the righteous and the damned, after the judgement of Allah, pass over the very narrow Assirat Bridge. Those who have lived charitable and faithful lives; those who have been persecuted for Allah's sake and those who have fought for Allah's sake will enjoy Heaven with its beautiful gardens, flowing rivers, lovely serving maidens, heavenly food and reclining couches. The imagery of Heaven with its rivers, plants and trees is much appreciated by those who have lived their entire lives in the desert: *'...His shall be a blissful state in a lofty garden, with clusters of fruit within his reach. We shall say to him: 'Eat and drink to your heart's content: your recompense for what you did in days gone by'.'* (Surah 69.19)
The ultimate joy, though, for those in Heaven is to experience the continual presence of Allah.

A. This book is an English translation of part of 'al-Bidayah wa'l-nihayah', which details the end of the world as described in Hadith literature, In that time, Muslims believe that Allah will claim '*the best people*'. What do you think will happen to '*the worst*'?

29. Signs of the Last Day

335. Anas reported that he heard the Messenger of Allah (peace and blessings of Allah be upon him) as saying : Verily, among the signs of the Last Day (the signs are) that knowledge would suffer complete extinction, ignorance, adultery and drinking of wine would be (alarmingly) on the increase. The number of male would decrease whereas that of female would increase till there will be only one male to look after fifty women. (Agreed upon)

170

336. Abu Hurairah reported that while the Holy Prophet (peace and blessings of Allah be upon him) was talking, a bedouin came and asked (the Holy Prophet) : When there would be the Last Day? He replied : When the integrity would be lost then wait for the coming of the Last Day. He asked : How would be it lost? He (the Holy Prophet) said : When the government will be entrusted to the undeserving (persons) then wait for the Last Day. (Bukhari)

337. Abu Hurairah reported that the Messenger of Allah (peace and blessings of Allah be upon him) said : When *fai* (booty acquired without fighting and reserved only for the poor and needy etc.) is considered as personal wealth, the trust as spoils of war and the Zakat as fine, and non-religious things are taught, and the husband obeys his wife and

171

B. Pages from a Hadith, dealing with the Day of Judgement. Why do you think that many religions look forward to a day when the 'bad' will be punished and the 'good' rewarded?

Hell

The wicked (those who are damned) will fall off the Assirat Bridge and go down to Hell. The damnation and suffering of those in Hell is eternal and without respite. The Qur'an describes what happens to them: '*...Garments of fire have been prepared for the unbelievers. Scalding water shall be poured upon their heads, melting their skins and that which is in their bellies. They shall be lashed with rods of iron*' (Surah 22.19).

According to tradition Heaven and Hell are both physical and spiritual places, although modern Muslim scholars have mostly understood them symbolically. Besides suffering physically in Hell those who are damned will suffer 'fire in their hearts'. Similarly those who are in Heaven experience the greatest possible spiritual as well as physical blessings. Allah's last act is to abolish death, so locking the damned into Hell for ever.

FOR YOUR FOLDER

Answer each of these questions in your own words:

a) What is Heaven and who goes there?
b) What is Hell and who goes there?
c) What part do the two angels of death play in deciding who goes to Heaven and Hell?
d) What qualifies a person for Heaven and how do they discover that they have been chosen to go there?
e) What kind of sight meets the righteous as they enter Heaven?
f) What kind of reception greets the damned as they arrive in Hell?
g) Do you find it surprising that Heaven and Hell are pictured in very human terms in The Qur'an? Why do you think that they are described in this way?

In the glossary: ALLAH; ANGEL; DAY OF JUDGEMENT; QUR'AN; SHAHADAH.

A

Abu Bakr The closest friend of *Muhammad*, the first convert to *Islam* and the leader of the followers of *Muhammad* after his death.

Adhan The Call to prayer made five times a day from the *minaret* by the *mu'adhin.*

Allah The *Muslim* name for God, the Almighty One.

Al-Fatihah The first *surah* of The *Qur'an*, recited during the *salah.*

Ali The fourth *khalifah* of *Islam.*

Angel Beings created by *Allah* from light. Angels have no free will and so completely obey Allah. In Muslim thought there are four archangels who rank as chief angels. These are *Jibril,* Mikail, Israfil, and Azrail.

Apostasy The sin committed by someone who was a *Muslim* but has given up the faith.

Aqiqah The ceremony when the hair of a baby is shaved and the equivalent in gold given to poor.

Arabic The sacred language of *Islam,* the language in which The *Qur'an* is written.

B

Bismillah A phrase meaning 'in the name of Allah'. The complete phrase 'Bismillah-ir-Rahman-ir-Rahim' ('In the name of Allah – All Gracious, All Merciful') is used at the beginning of every *surah* in The *Qur'an*, except the ninth. Many Muslims say this before beginning any action.

Black Stone A stone set in the south-east corner of the *Ka'bah*, thought to be part of a meteorite.

C

Celibacy A person's decision to live without sexual relationships. A married person can still choose this lifestyle.

Circumcision The removal of the foreskin of a boy's penis. Some Muslim countries circumcise girls, although this is not encouraged.

Crusades Military expeditions led by Christian armies to 'free' holy places in Palestine from Muslim control.

D

Day of Judgement The day on which *Allah* will judge every human being.

Din A *Muslim* term for religion in general and religious duties in particular.

Dome of the Rock A *mosque* in Jerusalem, Israel, built by the *khalifah Umar* over the rock from which *Muhammad* was believed to have ascended to *Heaven.* Also called the Mosque of Umar.

Du'a Voluntary prayers that are not part of the *rak'ah* routine.

F

Five Pillars The five beliefs on which the religion of *Islam* is based.

H

Hadith Stories and sayings of *Muhammad*, retold by his followers. Some Hadith are considered 'Hadith Qudsi' (sacred) – having been divinely communicated to *Muhammad.*

Hajar Wife of the *Prophet Ibrahim,* mother of *Isma'il.* In Jewish and Christian tradition, known as Hagar.

Hajj The pilgrimage to *Makkah* and other holy places undertaken by all Muslims.

Hajjah A woman who has completed a *Hajj.*

Hajji A man who has completed the *Hajj.*

Halal Any thing which is permitted.

Heaven Paradise, destination of those faithful to *Allah.*

Hijab Meaning veil – the modest clothing and head-dress worn by *Muslim* women.

Hijrah Meaning 'emigration'. The term applied to the journey of *Muhammad* and friends from *Makkah* to *Madinah* in 622 – the date from which the Islamic calendar begins.

I

Id Meaning 'reccurring happiness'; a religious holiday.

Ibadah Any act of worship.

Iblis Or Satan, the angel who disobeyed *Allah* by not bowing to Adam, and who became the tempter of humankind.

Ibrahim One of the earliest and most important *prophets.* In Jewish and Christian tradition known as Abraham.

Id-ul-Adha The feast commemorating the *Prophet Ibrahim's* willingness to sacrifice his son *Isma'il.* Also known as 'Qurban Bayram' (in Turkish, the 'Feast of Sacrifice') or 'Id-ul-Kabir, the 'Greater Id'.

Id-ul-Fitr Festival marking the end of *Ramadan.* Also called 'Id-ul-Saghor' (the 'Lesser Id'), or, in Turkish, 'Sheker Bayram meaning the sugar feast.

Imam The man who leads the prayers in the *mosque.*

Iman Faith.

Isa An early *prophet*. In Christian tradition Isa is the name for Jesus, the founder of the Christian religion.

Islam Peace through obedience to *Allah*.

Isma'il The eldest son of the *prophet, Ibrahim*. In Jewish and Christian tradition, Ishmael.

J

Jibril The main *angel* bringing messages and revelations to humanity.

Jihad A holy war.

Jinn A basic spirit, created by *Allah* out of fire.

K

Ka'bah The cube-shaped shrine in *Makkah*, Saudi Arabia.

Khadijah Employer and then first wife of *Muhammad*.

Khalifah A title meaning 'successor' and applied to the four 'Rightly Guided' khalifahs who led the *Muslim* faith after death of *Muhammad: Abu Bakr* (632-634), *Umar ibn-al-Khattab* (634-644), *Uthman* (644-656) and *Ali* (656-661).

M

Madinah The town of *Yathrib* whose inhabitants invited *Muhammad* and his friends to join them from *Makkah*.

Mahdi The one who will appear at the end of time to lead the *ummah*.

Makkah The birth-place in Saudi Arabia of *Muhammad* and the home of the *Ka'bah*.

Mihrab Niche in wall of *mosque* that indicates the direction of *Makkah* (*qiblah*).

Minaret Tall tower on a mosque from which the *Adhan* is delivered.

Minbar Platform of steps from which the *imam* delivers his sermon.

Misbeha Beads used by some Muslims to help them to remember the ninety-nine names of *Allah*.

Mosque The *Muslim* place of worship.

Mu'adhin Caller to prayer.

Muhammad The final *prophet*, and the only one chosen by *Allah* to receive the divine revelations.

Musa A prophet of *Allah* to whom the Tawrah was given. In Christian and Jewish tradition known as Moses.

Muslim Anyone who accepts the *Shahadah*.

N

Niyyah A statement of intent.

P

Polyandry The practice of a woman having more than one husband.

Polygamy The practice of a man having more than one wife.

Prophet A person chosen by *Allah* to receive an important message or revelation.

Prostration The repeated movement at the end of a *rak'ah* when the worshipper is on his or her knees with their face to the ground.

Q

Qiblah The direction of *Makkah*.

Qur'an Meaning 'that which is read or recited'. The holy book of *Islam*.

R

Rak'ah Part of the *salah;* a sequence of movements and recitations.

Ramadan The ninth month in the Islamic calendar, during which all Muslims must fast between dawn and sunset.

S

Salah The prescribed form of worship, as taught by the *Prophet Muhammad*.

Sawm Fasting from dawn to sunset. Sawm includes abstinence from smoking and sex, as well as food and drink.

Shahadah The *Muslim* declaration of faith: '*There is no God except Allah, Muhammad is the Messenger of Alllah*'.

Shari'ah Islamic law, based on The *Qur'an*.

Shi'ah Muslims who believe in *Ali* as the successor to *Muhammad*.

Sunni Muslims who believe in the sucessorship of *Abu Bakr, Umar, Uthman* and *Ali*.

Surah A division of The *Qur'an*.

T

Tawhid Belief in the Oneness of *Allah*.

U

Umar ibn-al-Khattab The second *khalifah* of *Islam*.

Ummah The worldwide community of *Islam*.

Uthman The third *khalifah* of *Islam*.

W

Wudu Ablutions carried out before *salah*.

Y

Yathrib The original name of *Madinah*.

Z

Zakah One of the five Pillars of *Islam*, giving money to the poor. A way of purifying wealth.

Index

Page references **in bold** indicate main entries. Page references *in italics* indicate definitions in the glossaries.

Acknowledgements

The publishers would like to thank the following for permission to reproduce photographs and illustrations (the page no. is followed, where necessary, by t-top, b-bottom, l-left, m-middle):

Page 8 Alex Keene & Jo MacLennan (The Walking Camera); Page 9 Ronald Sheridan/Ancient Art & Architecture Collection; Page 10 Robin Mills; Pages 11, 13, 14 Alex Keene & Jo MacLennan (The Walking Camera); Page 15 Anthea Sieveking/Collections; Pages 16, 17, 18, 19, 20, 21 Alex Keene & Jo MacLennan (The Walking Camera); Page 23 P.R. Gansham/DPA/Images of India; Page 24 Anthony Cassidy/Tony Stone Worldwide; Page 25 Ronald Sheridan/Ancient Art & Architecture Collection; Page 26 Orde Eliason/Link; Page 27 Liba Taylor/Collections; Page 28 Paul Harris/Tony Stone Worldwide; Page 29 R.S.3/DPA/Images of India; Page 30 Ronald Sheridan/Ancient Art & Architecture Collection; Page 31 Orde Eliason/Link; Page 32 Jan Knapik/Images of India; Page 33 Ann & Bury Peerless; Page 34 Anthea Sieveking/Collections; Page 35 Chandra Kishore Prasad/Link; Page 37 Anthea Sieveking/Collections; Page 38 Paul Sisul/Tony Stone Worldwide; Page 39 Ann & Bury Peerless; Page 40 Alex Keene & Jo MacLennan (The Walking Camera); Page 41 Ann & Bury Peerless; Page 43tr Chandra Kishore Prasad/Link; Page 43m Roderick Johnson/Images of India; Page 45 Anthony Cassidy/Tony Stone Worldwide; Pages 46, 48, 50 Ann & Bury Peerless; Page 51 John P. Stevens/Ancient Art & Architecture Collection; Page 53 Ronald Sheridan/Ancient Art & Architecture Collection; Page 55 Ann & Bury Peerless; Page 56 Ronald Sheridan/Ancient Art & Architecture Collection; Page 57, 58, 59 Alex Keene & Jo MacLennan (The Walking Camera); Page 60 Brian Shuel/Collections; Page 61 Ann & Bury Peerless; Page 62 Trevor Thompson/Images of India; Page 63 Peter Sanders Photography; Pages 64, 65 Ann & Bury Peerless; Page 66 Frank Herholdt/Tony Stone Worldwide; Page 67 Hulton Getty Collection Limited; Pages 70, 71 Alex Keene & Jo MacLennan (The Walking Camera); Page 72 Harper Collins Publishers; Page 73 Alex Keene & Jo MacLennan (The Walking Camera); Page 74; Ronald Sheridan/Ancient Art & Architecture Collection; Page 75 Robin Mills; Pages 76, 77 Alex Keene & Jo MacLennan (The Walking Camera); Page 79 Harper Collins Publishers; Page 79tr Paul Chesley/Tony Stone Worldwide; Page 80 Alex Keene & Jo MacLennan (The Walking Camera); Page 81 Hulton Getty Collection; Pages 82, 83 Alex Keene & Jo MacLennan (The Walking Camera); Page 84 Ronald Sheridan/Ancient Art & Architecture Collection; Page 87tr Derek Kartun/Tony Stone Worldwide; Page 87bl, 89, 90, 91, 92, 93, 94, 95, 96, 97 Alex Keene & Jo MacLennan (The Walking Camera); Page 99 Stephen Lillie; Page 101 Stephen Studd/Tony Stone Worldwide; Pages 102, 103, 104, 105, 107, 108, 109 Alex Keene & Jo MacLennan (The Walking Camera); Page 111 Penny Tweedie/Tony Stone Worldwide; Pages 113, 114, 115, 116 Alex Keene & Jo MacLennan (The Walking Camera); Page 117 Bill Aron/Tony Stone Worldwide; Page 119 Alex Keene & Jo MacLennan (The Walking Camera); Page 120 T. Stewart & R. Baxter/Tony Stone Worldwide; Page 121, 123 Alex Keene & Jo MacLennan (The Walking Camera); Page 124 Oliver Benn/Tony Stone Worldwide; Pages 126, 127, 128 Alex Keene & Jo MacLennan (The Walking Camera); Page 129 Peter Sanders Photography; Page 130 John Walmsley; Page 131 Hulton Getty Collection; Page 133 Robert Yager/Tony Stone Worldwide; Pages 134, 135, 138, 139, 140, 141, 142, 143, 144, 145 Alex Keene & Jo MacLennan (The Walking Camera); Page 146 Harper Collins Publishers; Pages 147, 148, 149, 150, 151, 153, 154, 155, 156, 157, 158, 159, 160, 161, 162, 163, 164, 165, 166, 167, 169, 170, 171, 173, 174, 175, 177, 178, 179, 180, 181, 182, 183, 184, 185, 186, 187 Alex Keene & Jo MacLennan (The Walking Camera); Pages 188, 189 Murray White; Page 190 Adrian Neal/Tony Stone Worldwide; Page 191 Richard Passmore/Tony Stone Worldwide; Page 192 Ronald Sheridan/Ancient Art & Architecture Collection; Page 193 Alan Smith/Tony Stone Worldwide; Page 194 Alex Keene & Jo MacLennan (The Walking Camera); Page 195 Geoff Howard/Collections; Pages 196, 197, 199 Alex Keene & Jo MacLennan (The Walking Camera); Page 201t Bob/Thomas/Tony Stone Worldwide; Page 201b Kaluzny/Thatcher/Tony Stone Worldwide; Pages 202, 203, 204, 205, 206, 207, 208, 209, 211, 212, 213, 214, 215 Alex Keene & Jo MacLennan (The Walking Camera); Page 216 Peter Sanders Photography; Page 217 David Woodfall/Tony Stone Worldwide; Pages 222, 223 Alex Keene & Jo MacLennan (The Walking Camera); Page 225 Nabeel Turner/Tony Stone Worldwide; Page 225l Alex Keene & Jo MacLennan (The Walking Camera); Page 226 Robin Mills; Page 227 Alex Keene & Jo MacLennan (The Walking Camera); Page 228 Robin Mills; Page 229 Richard Passmore/Tony Stone Worldwide; Pages 230, 231 Peter Sanders Photography; Page 232, 233 Alex Keene & Jo MacLennan (The Walking Camera); Page 235 Robin Mills; Pages 237, 239 Alex Keene & Jo MacLennan (The Walking Camera); Page 241 Stephen Lillie; Pages 243, 245, 247 Alex Keene & Jo MacLennan (The Walking Camera); Page 249 Liba Taylor/Collections; Page 251 Collections; Page 252 Nabeel Turner/Tony Stone Worldwide; Page 253 Rohan/Tony Stone Worldwide; Page 254 Nabeel Turner/Tony Stone Worldwide; Page 256 Alex Keene & Jo MacLennan (The Walking Camera); Page 257 Peter Sanders Photography; Page 259r Stephen Lillie; Page 259l, 260 Alex Keene & Jo MacLennan (The Walking Camera); Page 261 Liba Taylor/Collections; Page 262 Roger Scruton/Collections; Page 263 Alex Keene & Jo MacLennan (The Walking Camera); Page 265tl Geoff Howard/Collections; Page 265r Peter Sanders Photography; Page 267, 269 Peter Sanders Photography; Page 271 Alex Keene & Jo MacLennan (The Walking Camera); Page 272 Ronald Sheridan/Ancient Art & Architecture Collection; Page 273 Peter Sanders Photography; Page 275 Alex Keene & Jo MacLennan (The Walking Camera); Page 277 Alex Keene & Jo MacLennan (The Walking Camera); Page 279tl Stephen Lillie; Page 279tr Peter Sanders Photography; Page 281 Stephen Lillie.